W9-BQS-993

The Complete Works of Charles Dickens
(in 30 volumes, illustrated)

Martin Chuzzlewit, Vol. I

CHARLES DICKENS

COSIMOCLASSICS

NEW YORK

The Complete Works of Charles Dickens (in 30 volumes, illustrated):
Martin Chuzzlewit, Vol. I
Cover Copyright © 2009 by Cosimo, Inc.

*The Complete Works of Charles Dickens (in 30 volumes, illustrated):
Martin Chuzzlewit, Vol. I* was originally published in 1844.

For information, address:
P.O. Box 416, Old Chelsea Station
New York, NY 10011

or visit our website at:
www.cosimobooks.com

Ordering Information:
Cosimo publications are available at online bookstores. They may
also be purchased for educational, business or promotional use:
- *Bulk orders:* special discounts are available on bulk orders for reading
groups, organizations, businesses, and others. For details contact
Cosimo Special Sales at the address above or at info@cosimobooks.com.
- *Custom-label orders:* we can prepare selected books with your cover or
logo of choice. For more information, please contact Cosimo at
info@cosimobooks.com.

Cover Design by www.popshopstudio.com

ISBN: 978-1-61640-006-4

As no lady or gentleman with any claims to polite breeding, can possibly sympathize with the Chuzzlewit Family without being first assured of the extreme antiquity of the race, it is a great satisfaction to know that it undoubtedly descended in a direct line from Adam and Eve; and was, in the very earliest times, closely connected with the agricultural interest. If it should ever be urged by grudging and malicious persons, that a Chuzzlewit, in any period of the family history, displayed an overweening amount of family pride, surely the weakness will be considered not only pardonable but laudable, when the immense superiority of the house to the rest of mankind, in respect of this its ancient origin, is taken into account.

—from *The Life and Adventures of Martin Chuzzlewit*

Mr. Pecksniff and old Martin Chuzzlewit.
—*Martin Chuzzlewit*, ch. iii., p. 42.

TO

Miss Burdett Coutts

THIS TALE IS DEDICATED, WITH THE TRUE

AND EARNEST REGARD

OF

THE AUTHOR

PREFACE

My main object in this story was, to exhibit in a variety of aspects the commonest of all the vices; to show how Selfishness propagates itself; and to what a grim giant it may grow, from small beginnings.

All the Pecksniff family upon earth are quite agreed, I believe, that no such character as Mr. Pecksniff ever existed. I will not offer any plea on his behalf to so powerful and genteel a body, but I wish to make a remark here on the character of Jonas Chuzzlewit.

I conceive that the sordid coarseness and brutality of Jonas would be unnatural, if there had been nothing in his early education, and in the precept and example always before him, to engender and develop the vices that make him odious. But, so born and so bred; admired for that which made him hateful, and justified from his cradle in cunning, treachery, and avarice; I claim him as the legitimate issue of the father upon whom those vices are seen to recoil. And I submit that their recoil upon that old man, in his unhonoured age, is not a mere piece of poetical justice, but is the extreme exposition of a plain truth.

I make this comment on the character, and solicit the reader's attention to it in his or her consideration of this tale, because nothing is more common in real life than a want of profitable reflection on the causes of many vices and crimes that awaken the general horror. What is substantially true of families in this respect, is true of a whole commonwealth. As we sow, we reap. Let the reader go into the children's side of any prison in England, or, I grieve to add, of many workhouses, and judge whether those are monsters who disgrace our streets, people our hulks and penitentiaries, and overcrowd our penal colonies, or are creatures whom we have deliberately suffered to be bred for misery and ruin.

The American portion of this book is in no other respect a caricature than as it is an exhibition, for the most part, of the ludicrous side of the American character — of that side which is, from its very nature, the most obtrusive, and the most likely to be seen by such travellers as Young Martin and Mark Tapley. As I have never, in writing fictition, had any disposition to soften what is ridiculous or wrong at home, I hope (and believe) that the good-humoured people of the United States are not generally disposed to quarrel with me for carrying the same usage abroad. But I have been given to understand, by some authorities, that there are American scenes in these pages which are violent exaggerations; and that the Watertoast Association and eloquence, for example, are beyond all bounds of belief. Now, I wish to record the fact that all that portion of Martin Chuzzlewit's American experiences is a literal paraphrase of some reports of public proceedings in the United States (especially of the proceedings of a certain Brandywine Association), which were printed in the "Times" newspaper in June and July, 1843 — at about the time when I was engaged in writing those parts of the book. There were at that period, on the part of a frothy young American party, demonstrations making of "sympathy" towards Ireland and hostility towards England, in which such outrageous absurdities ran rampant, that, having the occasion ready to my hand, I ridiculed them. And this I did, not in any animosity towards America, but just as I should have done the same thing, if the same opportunity had arisen, in reference to London, or Dublin, or Paris, or Devonshire.

In all the tales comprised in this cheap series, and in all my writings, I hope I have taken every possible opportunity of showing the want of sanitary improvements in the neglected dwellings of the poor. Mrs. Sarah Gamp is a representation of the hired attendant on the poor in sickness. The hospitals of London are, in many respects, noble institutions; in others, very defective. I think it not the least among the instances of their mismanagement, that Mrs. Betsey Prig is a fair specimen of a Hospital Nurse; and that the hospitals, with their means and funds, should have left it to private humanity and enterprise, in the year Eighteen Hundred and Forty-nine, to enter on an attempt to improve that class of persons.

LONDON, *November*, 1849.

CONTENTS

CONTENTS

CONTENTS

INTRODUCTION.

BEFORE the conclusion of *Barnaby Rudge* was reached it became evident that the periodical *Master Humphrey's Clock*, in which it appeared, could not continue. The strain upon Dickens was too great, and help from others was inconsistent with the success of the venture. The *Clock* and *Barnaby* ended together, and in September, 1841, Dickens made an agreement with Chapman and Hall for a new novel (*Martin Chuzzlewit*), to be published on the old monthly plan. The publishers took all the risks, promising to pay the author two hundred pounds for each number, reckoning this payment as part of the expenses of the book's publication. Moreover, Dickens was to receive three-fourths of the profits until six months after the story's completion, after which the publishers were to have half ownership upon condition of paying him one-fourth of the value of all existing stock. The agreement also provided for an advance of one hundred and fifty pounds a month up to the time of the story's beginning, this payment to be deducted from Dickens's share of the profits.

The American trip came between the agreement for the story and its commencement, and after his return to England Dickens was, in the summer of 1842, chiefly occupied in the preparation of his *American Notes*. At this time, however, ideas for the new story were floating through his mind. A letter dated July 18th reveals an intention which was afterward abandoned: "I have never been in Cornwall, either. A mine certainly; and a letter for that purpose shall be got from Southwood Smith. I have some notion of opening the new book in the lantern of a lighthouse." In the autumn he made an excursion to Cornwall with Maclise, Stanfield, and Forster, and the desire to give his story a Cornish setting was still strong in him; but later, when he came seriously to consider the scheme, he gave up both the mine and the lighthouse.

The title gave him some trouble, and the various versions of it are interesting as showing that the names which in Dickens seem so characteristic and felicitous did not always come to him in a flash. "Martin," the hero was to be called from the first, but the surname was only decided upon after much debate. Some of the proposed forms were Sweezleden, Sweezleback, Sweezlewag, Chuzzletoe, Chuzzleboy, Chubblewig, and Chuzzlewig.

Dickens was in the best of good spirits during his Cornish trip, and he returned in a mood favorable for writing. *Chuzzlewit* was started somewhat hurriedly, but "perhaps no story was ever begun by him," says Forster, "with stronger heart or confidence." During its progress he had reason to believe that he was doing excellent work, and Sydney Smith soon wrote him to say that "Pecksniff and his daughters, and Pinch, are admirable—quite first-rate painting, such as no one but yourself can execute."

He himself had a high opinion of the book: "I think *Chuzzlewit* in a hundred points immeasurably the best of my stories." But although it subsequently rivaled *Pickwick* and *Copperfield* in popularity, its sale never exceeded twenty-three thousand. This relative unsuccess was disappointing to both author and publishers, and before the seventh number appeared Mr. Hall hinted that a clause in the agreement, by which the publishers were empowered to withhold a part of the monthly payment of two hundred pounds in case of the sales proving inadequate, might be enforced. "I am so irritated," wrote Dickens to Forster, "so rubbed in the tenderest part of my eyelids with bay salt—that a wrong kind of fire is burning in my head, and I don't think I *can* write." Discontent was increased by the smallness of the financial returns from *A Christmas Carol*, published in December, 1843, and Dickens was faced by the need of economizing. "What a wonderful thing it is," he wrote in December, 1844, "that such a great success should occasion me such intolerable anxiety and disappointment! My year's bills unpaid are so terrific that all the energy and determination I can possibly exert will be required to clear me before I go abroad." In June, before his departure for Italy, he made an arrangement with his printers, Bradbury and Evans, by which they advanced him twenty-eight hundred pounds in return for a fourth share in whatever he might write during the next eight years.

Martin Chuzzlewit belongs to Dickens's maturity as a writer, and his full power is put forth in it. The plot, indeed, is somewhat ill-constructed, not having been thoroughly thought out in the first place, but the story was elaborated with great care, as the numerous corrections in the MS. bear witness, and without any sacrifice of spontaneity an unusually finished effect was attained. The essential theme—selfishness—gave full play to Dickens's skill in delineating emphatic traits of character, and afforded a sound basis for his satire and real warmth of feeling. The character of Pecksniff was the fundamental conception of the book, and in him the vice of sanctimonious hypocrisy, which has given occasion to so much English satire, is immortally embodied. The story shows throughout an astonishing originality. Although the famous Mrs. Gamp is said to have had an original—a nurse employed by a friend of the author, a "most distinguished lady"—this character stands in the first rank of Dickens's creations. The original had the habit of "rubbing her nose against the tall fender," and other peculiarities of like nature; but whatever may have been the origin of her mannerisms, Mrs. Gamp in the story has a vitality and an individuality such as only Dickens could confer. The device, moreover, of Mrs. Gamp and Mrs. Harris is among the happiest of the author's humorous inventions. The elements of his genius had now become fused. He had learned to control his fancy. He had discovered his serious and pathetic vein, and was in little danger of becoming "gushy," as in some parts of *Oliver Twist.* He knew how to repress humorous extravagance and make the comic spirit join with serious intention. In short, he had matured and developed, and in *Martin Chuzzlewit* he produced a robust masterpiece.

LIFE AND ADVENTURES

OF

MARTIN CHUZZLEWIT.

CHAPTER I.

INTRODUCTORY, CONCERNING THE PEDIGREE OF THE CHUZZLEWIT FAMILY.

As no lady or gentleman with any claims to polite breeding, can possibly sympathise with the Chuzzlewit Family without being first assured of the extreme antiquity of the race, it is a great satisfaction to know that it undoubtedly descended in a direct line from Adam and Eve; and was, in the very earliest times, closely connected with the agricultural interest. If it should ever be urged by grudging and malicious persons, that a Chuzzlewit, in any period of the family history, displayed an overweening amount of family pride, surely the weakness will be considered not only pardonable but laudable, when the immense superiority of the house to the rest of mankind, in respect of this its ancient origin, is taken into account.

It is remarkable that as there was, in the oldest family of which we have any record, a murderer and a vagabond, so we never fail to meet, in the records of all old families, with innumerable repetitions of the same phase of character. Indeed, it may be laid down as a general principle, that the more extended the ancestry, the greater the amount of violence and vagabondism; for in ancient days, those two amusements, combining a wholesome excitement with a promising means of repairing shattered fortunes, were at once the ennobling pursuit and the healthful recreation of the Quality of this land.

1

Consequently, it is a source of inexpressible comfort and happiness to find, that in various periods of our history, the Chuzzlewits were actively connected with divers slaughterous conspiracies and bloody frays. It is further recorded of them, that being clad from head to heel in steel of proof, they did on many occasions lead their leather-jerkined soldiers to the death, with invincible courage, and afterwards return home gracefully to their relations and friends.

There can be no doubt that at least one Chuzzlewit came over with William the Conqueror. It does not appear that this illustrious ancestor "came over" that monarch, to employ the vulgar phrase, at any subsequent period: inasmuch as the Family do not seem to have been ever greatly distinguished by the possession of landed estate. And it is well known that for the bestowal of that kind of property upon his favourites, the liberality and gratitude of the Norman were as remarkable, as those virtues are usually found to be in great men when they give away what belongs to other people.

Perhaps in this place the history may pause to congratulate itself upon the enormous amount of bravery, wisdom, eloquence, virtue, gentle birth, and true nobility, that appears to have come into England with the Norman Invasion: an amount which the genealogy of every ancient family lends its aid to swell, and which would beyond all question have been found to be just as great, and to the full as prolific in giving birth to long lines of chivalrous descendants, boastful of their origin, even though William the Conqueror had been William the Conquered: a change of circumstances which, it is quite certain, would have made no manner of difference in this respect.

There was unquestionably a Chuzzlewit in the Gunpowder Plot, if indeed the arch-traitor, Fawkes himself, were not a scion of this remarkable stock; as he might easily have been, supposing another Chuzzlewit to have emigrated to Spain in the previous generation, and there intermarried with a Spanish lady, by whom he had issue, one olive-complexioned son. This probable conjecture is strengthened, if not absolutely confirmed, by a fact which cannot fail to be interesting to those who are curious in tracing the progress of hereditary tastes through the lives of their unconscious inheritors. It is a notable circumstance that, in these later times, many Chuzzlewits, being unsuccessful in other pursuits, have, without the smallest rational hope of enriching themselves, or any conceivable reason, set up as coal-merchants; and have, month after month, continued gloomily to watch a small stock of coals, without, in any one instance, negotiating with a purchaser. The remarkable similarity between this course of proceeding and that adopted by their Great Ancestor beneath the vaults of the Parliament House at Westminster, is too obvious and too full of interest, to stand in need of comment.

It is also clearly proved by the oral traditions of the Family, that there existed, at some one period of its history which is not distinctly stated, a matron of such destructive principles, and so familiarised to the use and composition of inflammatory and combustible engines, that she was called "The Match Maker:" by which nickname and byword she is recognised in the Family legends to this day. Surely there can be no reasonable doubt that this was the Spanish lady: the mother of Chuzzlewit Fawkes.

But there is one other piece of evidence, bearing immediate reference to their close connexion with this memorable event in English History, which must carry conviction, even to a mind (if such a mind there be) remaining unconvinced by these presumptive proofs.

There was, within a few years, in the possession of a highly respectable and in every way credible and unimpeachable member of the Chuzzlewit Family (for his bitterest enemy never dared to hint at his being otherwise than a wealthy man), a dark lantern of undoubted antiquity; rendered still more interesting by being, in shape and pattern, extremely like such as are in use at the present day. Now this gentleman, since deceased, was at all times ready to make oath, and did again and again set forth upon his solemn asseveration, that he had frequently heard his grandmother say, when contemplating this venerable relic, "Ay, ay! This was carried by my fourth son on the fifth of November, when he was a Guy Fawkes." These remarkable words wrought (as well they might) a strong impression on his mind, and he was in the habit of repeating them very often. The just interpretation which they bear, and the conclusion to which they lead, are triumphant and irresistible. The old lady, naturally strong-minded, was nevertheless frail and fading; she was notoriously subject to that confusion of ideas, or, to say the least, of speech, to which age and garrulity are liable. The slight, the very slight confusion, apparent in these expressions, is manifest and is ludicrously easy of correction. "Ay, ay," quoth she, and it will be observed that no emendation whatever is necessary to be made in these two initiative remarks, "Ay, ay. This lantern was carried by my forefather"— not fourth son, which is preposterous—"on the fifth of November. And *he* was Guy Fawkes." Here we have a remark at once consistent, clear, natural, and in strict accordance with the character of the speaker. Indeed the anecdote is so plainly susceptible of this meaning, and no other, that it would be hardly worth recording in its original state, were it no a proof of what may be (and very often is) effected not only in historical prose but in imaginative poetry, by the exercise of a little ingenious labour on the part of a commentator.

It has been said that there is no instance in modern times, of a Chuzzlewit having been found on terms of intimacy with the Great. But here again the sneering detractors who weave such miserable figments from their malicious brains, are stricken dumb by evidence. For letters are yet in the possession of various branches of the family, from which it distinctly appears, being stated in so many words, that one Diggory Chuzzlewit was in the habit of perpetually dining with Duke Humphrey. So constantly was he a guest at that nobleman's table, indeed; and so unceasingly were His Grace's hospitality and companionship forced, as it were, upon him; that we find him uneasy, and full of constraint and reluctance: writing his friends to the effect that if they fail to do so and so by bearer, he will have no choice but to dine again with Duke Humphrey: and expressing himself in a very marked and extraordinary manner as one surfeited of High Life and Gracious Company.

It has been rumoured, and it is needless to say the rumour originated in the same base quarters, that a certain male Chuzzlewit, whose birth must be admitted to be involved in some obscurity, was of very mean and low descent. How stands the proof? When the son of that Individual, to whom the secret of his father's birth was supposed to have been communicated by his father in his lifetime, lay upon his deathbed, this question was put to him in a distinct, solemn, and formal way: "Toby Chuzzlewit, who was your grandfather?" To which he, with his last breath, no less distinctly, solemnly, and formally replied: and his words were taken down at the time, and signed by six witnesses, each with his name and address in full: "The Lord No Zoo." It may be said—it *has* been said, for human wickedness has no limits—that there is no Lord of that name, and that among the titles which have become extinct, none at all resembling this, in sound even, is to be discovered. But what is the irresistible inference? Rejecting a theory broached by some well-meaning but mistaken persons, that this Mr. Toby Chuzzlewit's grandfather, to judge from his name, must surely have been a Mandarin (which is wholly insupportable, for there is no pretence of his grandmother ever having been out of this country, or of any Mandarin having been in it within some years of his father's birth: except those in the teashops, which cannot for a moment be regarded as having any bearing on the question, one way or other), rejecting this hypothesis, is it not manifest that Mr. Toby Chuzzlewit had either received the name imperfectly from his father, or that he had forgotten it, or that he had mispronounced it? and that even at the recent period in question, the Chuzzlewits were connected by a bend sinister, or kind of heraldic over-the-left, with some unknown noble and illustrious House?

From documentary evidence, yet preserved in the family, the fact is clearly established that in the comparatively modern days of the Diggory Chuzzlewit before mentioned, one of its members had attained to very great wealth and influence. Throughout such fragments of his correspondence as have escaped the ravages of the moths (who, in right of their extensive absorption of the contents of deeds and papers, may be called the general registers of the Insect World), we find him making constant reference to an uncle, in respect of whom he would seem to have entertained great expectations, as he was in the habit of seeking to propitiate his favour by presents of plate, jewels, books, watches, and other valuable articles. Thus, he writes on one occasion to his brother in reference to a gravy-spoon, the brother's property, which he (Diggory) would appear to have borrowed or otherwise possessed himself of: "Do not be angry, I have parted with it—to my uncle." On another occasion he expresses himself in a similar manner with regard to a child's mug which had been entrusted to him to get repaired. On another occasion he says, "I have bestowed upon that irresistible uncle of mine everything I ever possessed." And that he was in the habit of paying long and constant visits to this gentleman at his mansion, if, indeed, he did not wholly reside there, is manifest from the following sentence: "With the exception of the suit of clothes I carry about with me, the whole of my wearing apparel is at present at my uncle's." This gentleman's patronage and influence must have been very extensive, for his nephew writes, "His interest is too high"—"It is too much"—"It is tremendous"—and the like. Still it does not appear (which is strange) to have procured for him any lucrative post at court or elsewhere, or to have conferred upon him any other distinction than that which was necessarily included in the countenance of so great a man, and the being invited by him to certain entertainments, so splendid and costly in their nature that he emphatically calls them "Golden Balls."

It is needless to multiply instances of the high and lofty station, and the vast importance of the Chuzzlewits, at different periods. If it came within the scope of reasonable probability that further proofs were required, they might be heaped upon each other until they formed an Alps of testimony, beneath which the boldest scepticism should be crushed and beaten flat. As a goodly tumulus is already collected, and decently battened up above the Family grave, the present chapter is content to leave it as it is: merely adding, by way of a final spadeful, that many Chuzzlewits, both male and female, are proved to demonstration, on the faith of letters written by their own mothers, to have had chiselled noses, undeniable chins, forms that might have served the sculptor for a model, exquisitely-turned limbs, and polished foreheads of so transparent a texture that the blue veins might be seen branching off in various directions, like so many roads on an ethereal map. This fact in itself, though it had been a solitary one, would have utterly settled and clenched the business in hand; for it is well known, on the authority of all the books which treat of such matters, that every one of these phenomena, but especially that of the chiselling, are invariably peculiar to, and only make themselves apparent in, persons of the very best condition.

This history, having to its own perfect satisfaction (and,

consequently, to the full contentment of all its readers) proved the Chuzzlewits to have had an origin, and to have been at one time or other of an importance which cannot fail to render them highly improving and acceptable acquaintance to all right-minded individuals, may now proceed in earnest with its task. And having shown that they must have had, by reason of their ancient birth, a pretty large share in the foundation and increase of the human family, it will one day become its province to submit, that such of its members as shall be introduced in these pages, have still many counterparts and prototypes in the Great World about us. At present it contents itself with remarking, in a general way, on this head: Firstly, that it may be safely asserted, and yet without implying any direct participation in the Monboddo doctrine touching the probability of the human race having once been monkeys, that men do play very strange and extraordinary tricks. Secondly, and yet without trenching on the Blumenbach theory as to the descendants of Adam having a vast number of qualities which belong more particularly to swine than to any other class of animals in the creation, that some men certainly are remarkable for taking uncommon good care of themselves.

CHAPTER II.

WHEREIN CERTAIN PERSONS ARE PRESENTED TO
THE READER, WITH WHOM HE MAY, IF HE PLEASE,
BECOME BETTER ACQUAINTED.

IT was pretty late in the autumn of the year, when the declining sun, struggling through the mist which had obscured it all day, looked brightly down upon a little Wiltshire village, within an easy journey of the fair old town of Salisbury.

Like a sudden flash of memory or spirit kindling up the mind of an old man, it shed a glory upon the scene, in which its departed youth and freshness seemed to live again. The wet grass sparkled in the light; the scanty patches of verdure in the hedges—where a few green twigs

yet stood together bravely, resisting to the last the tyranny
of nipping winds and early frosts—took heart and brightened up; the stream which had been dull and sullen all
day long, broke out into a cheerful smile; the birds began
to chirp and twitter on the naked boughs, as though the
hopeful creatures half believed that winter had gone by,
and spring had come already. The vane upon the taper-
ing spire of the old church glistened from its lofty station
in sympathy with the general gladness; and from the ivy-
shaded windows such gleams of light shone back upon the
glowing sky, that it seemed as if the quiet building were
the hoarding-place of twenty summers, and all their ruddi-
ness and warmth were stored within.

Even those tokens of the season which emphatically
whispered of the coming winter, graced the landscape, and,
for the moment, tinged its livelier features with no oppres-
sive air of sadness. The fallen leaves, with which the
ground was strewn, gave forth a pleasant fragrance, and
subduing all harsh sounds of distant feet and wheels, created a repose in gentle unison with the light scattering of
seed hither and thither by the distant husbandman, and
with the noiseless passage of the plough as it turned up the
rich brown earth, and wrought a graceful pattern in the
stubbled fields. On the motionless branches of some trees,
autumn berries hung like clusters of coral beads, as in those
fabled orchards where the fruits were jewels; others,
stripped of all their garniture, stood, each the centre of its
little heap of bright red leaves, watching their slow decay;
others again, still wearing theirs, had them all crunched
and crackled up, as though they had been burnt; about the
stems of some were piled, in ruddy mounds, the apples
they had borne that year; while others (hardy evergreens
this class) showed somewhat stern and gloomy in their
vigour, as charged by nature with the admonition that it is
not to her more sensitive and joyous favourites she grants
the longest term of life. Still athwart their darker boughs,
the sunbeams struck out paths of deeper gold; and the red
light, mantling in among their swarthy branches, used
them as foils to set its brightness off, and aid the lustre of
the dying day.

A moment, and its glory was no more. The sun went
down beneath the long dark lines of hill and cloud which
piled up in the west an airy city, wall heaped on wall,

and battlement on battlement; the light was all withdrawn ; the shining church turned cold and dark; the stream forgot to smile; the birds were silent; and the gloom of winter dwelt on everything.

An evening wind uprose too, and the slighter branches cracked and rattled as they moved, in skeleton dances, to its moaning music. The withering leaves, no longer quiet, hurried to and fro in search of shelter from its chill pursuit; the labourer unyoked his horses, and with head bent down, trudged briskly home beside them; and from the cottage windows lights began to glance and wink upon the darkening fields.

Then the village forge came out in all its bright importance. The lusty bellows roared Ha ha! to the clear fire, which roared in turn, and bade the shining sparks dance gaily to the merry clinking of the hammers on the anvil. The gleaming iron, in its emulation, sparkled too, and shed its red-hot gems around profusely. The strong smith and his men dealt such strokes upon their work, as made even the melancholy night rejoice ; and brought a glow into its dark face as it hovered about the door and windows, peeping curiously in above the shoulders of a dozen loungers. As to this idle company, there they stood, spellbound by the place, and, casting now and then a glance upon the darkness in their rear, settled their lazy elbows more at ease upon the sill, and leaned a little further in: no more disposed to tear themselves away, than if they had been born to cluster around the blazing hearth like so many crickets.

Out upon the angry wind! how from sighing, it began to bluster round the merry forge, banging at the wicket, and grumbling in the chimney, as if it bullied the jolly bellows for doing anything to order. And what an impotent swaggerer it was too, for all its noise: for if it had any influence on that hoarse companion, it was but to make him roar his cheerful song the louder, and by consequence to make the fire burn the brighter, and the sparks to dance more gaily yet: at length, they whizzed so madly round and round, that it was too much for such a surly wind to bear: so off it flew with a howl: giving the old sign before the alehouse door such a cuff as it went, that the Blue Dragon was more rampant than usual ever afterwards, and indeed, before Christmas, reared clean out of his crazy frame.

It was small tyranny for a respectable wind to go wreaking its vengeance on such poor creatures as the fallen leaves, but this wind happening to come up with a great heap of them just after venting his humour on the insulted Dragon, did so disperse and scatter them that they fled away, pell-mell, some here, some there, rolling over each other, whirling round and round upon their thin edges, taking frantic flights into the air, and playing all manner of extraordinary gambols in the extremity of their distress. Nor was this enough for its malicious fury: for not content with driving them abroad, it charged small parties of them and hunted them into the wheelwright's saw-pit, and below the planks and timbers in the yard, and, scattering the sawdust in the air, it looked for them underneath, and when it did meet with any, whew! how it drove them on and followed at their heels!

The scared leaves only flew the faster for all this, and a giddy chase it was: for they got into unfrequented places, where there was no outlet, and where their pursuer kept them eddying round and round at his pleasure; and they crept under the eaves of houses, and clung tightly to the sides of hay-ricks, like bats; and tore in at open chamber-windows, and cowered close to hedges; and in short went anywhere for safety. But the oddest feat they achieved was, to take advantage of the sudden opening of Mr. Pecksniff's front-door, to dash wildly into his passage; whither the wind following close upon them, and finding the back-door open, incontinently blew out the lighted candle held by Miss Pecksniff, and slammed the front-door against Mr. Pecksniff who was at that moment entering, with such violence, that in the twinkling of an eye he lay on his back at the bottom of the steps. Being by this time weary of such trifling performances, the boisterous rover hurried away rejoicing, roaring over moor and meadow, hill and flat, until it got out to sea, where it met with other winds similarly disposed, and made a night of it.

In the meantime Mr. Pecksniff, having received, from a sharp angle in the bottom step but one, that sort of knock on the head which lights up, for the patient's entertainment, an imaginary general illumination of very bright short-sixes, lay placidly staring at his own street-door. And it would seem to have been more suggestive in its aspect than street-doors usually are; for he continued to lie there, rather a lengthy and unreasonable time, without so much as wondering whether he was hurt or no: neither, when Miss Pecksniff inquired through the key-hole in a shrill voice, which might have belonged to a wind in its teens, "Who's there?" did he make any reply: nor, when Miss Pecksniff opened the door again, and shading the candle with her hand, peered out, and looked provokingly round him, and about him, and over, and everywhere but at him, did he offer any remark, or indicate in any manner the least hint of a desire to be picked up.

"*I* see you," cried Miss Pecksniff, to the ideal inflictor of a runaway knock. "You'll catch it, Sir!"

Still Mr. Pecksniff, perhaps from having caught it already, said nothing.

"You're round the corner now," cried Miss Pecksniff. She said it at a venture, but there was appropriate matter in it too; for Mr. Pecksniff, being in the act of extinguishing the candles before mentioned pretty rapidly, and of reducing the number of brass knobs on his street-door from four or five hundred (which had previously been juggling of their own accord before his eyes in a very novel manner) to a dozen or so, might in one sense have been said to be coming round the corner, and just turning it.

With a sharply-delivered warning relative to the cage and the constable, and the stocks and the gallows, Miss Pecksniff was about to close the door again, when Mr. Pecksniff (being still at the bottom of the steps) raised himself on one elbow, and sneezed.

"That voice!" cried Miss Pecksniff, "my parent!"

At this exclamation, another Miss Pecksniff bounced out of the parlour: and the two Miss Pecksniffs, with many incoherent expressions, dragged Mr. Pecksniff into an upright posture.

"Pa!" they cried in concert. "Pa! Speak, Pa! Do not look so wild, my dearest Pa!"

But as a gentleman's looks, in such a case of all others, are by no means under his own control, Mr. Pecksniff continued to keep his mouth and his eyes very wide open, and to drop his lower jaw, somewhat after the manner of a toy nut-cracker: and as his hat had fallen off, and his face was pale, and his hair erect, and his coat muddy, the spectacle he presented was so very doleful, that neither of the Miss Pecksniffs could repress an involuntary screech.

"That'll do," said Mr. Pecksniff. "I'm better."
"He's come to himself!" cried the youngest Miss Pecksniff.
"He speaks again!" exclaimed the eldest.
With which joyful words they kissed Mr. Pecksniff on
either cheek; and bore him into the house. Presently,
the youngest Miss Pecksniff ran out again to pick up his
hat, his brown-paper parcel, his umbrella, his gloves, and
other small articles: and that done, and the door closed,
both young ladies applied themselves to tending Mr. Pecksniff's wounds in the back parlour.

They were not very serious in their nature: being limited
to abrasions on what the eldest Miss Pecksniff called "the
knobby parts" of her parent's anatomy, such as his knees
and elbows, and to the development of an entirely new organ, unknown to phrenologists, on the back of his head.
These injuries having been comforted externally, with
patches of pickled brown paper, and Mr. Pecksniff having
been comforted internally, with some stiff brandy-and-
water, the eldest Miss Pecksniff sat down to make the tea,
which was all ready. In the meantime the youngest Miss
Pecksniff brought from the kitchen a smoking dish of ham
and eggs, and, setting the same before her father, took up
her station on a low stool at his feet: thereby bringing her
eyes on a level with the teaboard.

It must not be inferred from this position of humility,
that the youngest Miss Pecksniff was so young as to be, as
one may say, forced to sit upon a stool, by reason of the
shortness of her legs. Miss Pecksniff sat upon a stool,
because of her simplicity and innocence, which were very
great: very great. Miss Pecksniff sat upon a stool, because she was all girlishness, and playfulness, and wildness, and kittenish buoyancy. She was the most arch and
at the same time the most artless creature, was the youngest
Miss Pecksniff, that you can possibly imagine. It was her
great charm. She was too fresh and guileless, and too
full of child-like vivacity, was the youngest Miss Pecksniff, to wear combs in her hair, or to turn it up, or to
frizzle it, or braid it. She wore it in a crop, a loosely
flowing crop, which had so many rows of curls in it, that
the top row was only one curl. Moderately buxom was her
shape, and quite womanly too; but sometimes—yes, sometimes—she even wore a pinafore; and how charming *that*

was! Oh! she was indeed "a gushing thing" (as a young
gentleman had observed in verse, in the Poet's-corner of a
provincial newspaper), was the youngest Miss Pecksniff!

Mr. Pecksniff was a moral man: a grave man, a man of
noble sentiments, and speech: and he had had her chris-
tened Mercy. Mercy! oh, what a charming name for such
a pure-souled being as the youngest Miss Pecksniff! Her
sister's name was Charity. There was a good thing!
Mercy and Charity! And Charity, with her fine strong
sense, and her mild, yet not reproachful gravity, was so
well named, and did so well set off and illustrate her sister! What a pleasant sight was that, the contrast they
presented: to see each loved and loving one sympathising
with, and devoted to, and leaning on, and yet correcting
and counter-checking, and, as it were, antidoting, the
other! To behold each damsel, in her very admiration of
her sister, setting up in business for herself on an entirely
different principle, and announcing no connexion with over-
the-way, and if the quality of goods at that establishment
don't please you, you are respectfully invited to favour ME
with a call! And the crowning circumstance of the whole
delightful catalogue was, that both the fair creatures were
so utterly unconscious of all this! They had no idea of it.
They no more thought or dreamed of it, than Mr. Pecksniff did. Nature played them off against each other:
they had no hand in it, the two Miss Pecksniffs.

It has been remarked that Mr. Pecksniff was a moral
man. So he was. Perhaps there never was a more moral
man than Mr. Pecksniff: especially in his conversation and
correspondence. It was once said of him by a homely
admirer, that he had a Fortunatus's purse of good sentiments in his inside. In this particular he was like the girl
in the fairy tale, except that if they were not actual diamonds which fell from his lips, they were the very brightest paste, and shone prodigiously. He was a most exem-
plary man: fuller of virtuous precept than a copy-book.
Some people likened him to a direction-post, which is always telling the way to a place, and never goes there: but
these were his enemies; the shadows cast by his brightness;
that was all. His very throat was moral. You saw a
good deal of it. You looked over a very low fence of white
cravat (whereof no man had ever beheld the tie, for he
fastened it behind), and there it lay, a valley between two

7—2

jutting heights of collar, serene and whiskerless before you.
It seemed to say, on the part of Mr. Pecksniff, "There is
no deception, ladies and gentlemen, all is peace: a holy
calm pervades me." So did his hair, just grizzled with an
iron-gray, which was all brushed off his forehead, and
stood bolt upright, or slightly drooped in kindred action
with his heavy eyelids. So did his person, which was
sleek though free from corpulency. So did his manner,
which was soft and oily. In a word, even his plain black
suit, and state of widower, and dangling double eyeglass,
all tended to the same purpose, and cried aloud, "Behold
the moral Pecksniff!"

The brazen plate upon the door (which being Mr. Pecksniff's, could not lie) bore this inscription, "PECKSNIFF,
ARCHITECT," to which Mr. Pecksniff, on his cards of business, added, "AND LAND SURVEYOR." In one sense, and
only one, he may be said to have been a Land Surveyor on
a pretty large scale, as an extensive prospect lay stretched
out before the windows of his house. Of his architectural
doings, nothing was clearly known, except that he had
never designed or built anything; but it was generally
understood that his knowledge of the science was almost
awful in its profundity.

Mr. Pecksniff's professional engagements, indeed, were
almost, if not entirely, confined to the reception of pupils;
for the collection of rents, with which pursuit he occasionally varied and relieved his graver toils, can hardly be said
to be a strictly architectural employment. His genius lay
in ensnaring parents and guardians, and pocketing pre-
miums. A young gentleman's premium being paid, and the
young gentleman come to Mr. Pecksniff's house, Mr. Pecksniff borrowed his case of mathematical instruments (if
silver-mounted or otherwise valuable); entreated him,
from that moment, to consider himself one of the family;
complimented him highly on his parents or guardians, as
the case might be; and turned him loose in a spacious room
on the two-pair front; where, in the company of certain
drawing-boards, parallel rulers, very stiff-legged compasses,
and two, or perhaps three, other young gentlemen, he improved himself, for three or five years, according to his
articles, in making elevations of Salisbury Cathedral from
every possible point of sight; and in constructing in the air
a vast quantity of Castles, Houses of Parliament, and other

Mr. Pecksniff.
—*Martin Chuzzlewit*, ch. ii., p. 14.

Public Buildings. Perhaps in no place in the world were so many gorgeous edifices of this class erected as under Mr. Pecksniff's auspices; and if but one-twentieth part of the churches which were built in that front room, with one or other of the Miss Pecksniffs at the altar in the act of marrying the architect, could only be made available by the parliamentary commissioners, no more churches would be wanted for at least five centuries.

"Even the worldly goods of which we have just disposed," said Mr. Pecksniff, glancing round the table when he had finished, "even cream, sugar, tea, toast, ham,—"

"And eggs," suggested Charity in a low voice.

"And eggs," said Mr. Pecksniff, "even they have their moral. See how they come and go! Every pleasure is transitory. We can't even eat, long. If we indulge in harmless fluids, we get the dropsy; if in exciting liquids, we get drunk. What a soothing reflection is that!"

"Don't say we get drunk, Pa," urged the eldest Miss Pecksniff.

"When I say, we, my dear," returned her father, "I mean mankind in general; the human race, considered as a body, and not as individuals. There is nothing personal in morality, my love. Even such a thing as this," said Mr. Pecksniff, laying the forefinger of his left hand upon the brown-paper patch on the top of his head, "slight casualty, baldness though it be, reminds us that we are but"—he was going to say "worms," but recollecting that worms were not remarkable for heads of hair, he substituted "flesh and blood."

"Which," cried Mr. Pecksniff after a pause, during which he seemed to have been casting about for a new moral, and not quite successfully, "which is also very soothing. Mercy, my dear, stir the fire and throw up the cinders."

The young lady obeyed, and having done so, resumed her stool, reposed one arm upon her father's knee, and laid her blooming cheek upon it. Miss Charity drew her chair nearer the fire, as one prepared for conversation, and looked towards her father.

"Yes," said Mr. Pecksniff, after a short pause, during which he had been silently smiling, and shaking his head at the fire, "I have again been fortunate in the attainment of my object. A new inmate will very shortly come among us."

"A youth, papa?" asked Charity.

"Ye-es, a youth," said Mr. Pecksniff. "He will avail himself of the eligible opportunity which now offers, for uniting the advantages of the best practical architectural education, with the comforts of a home, and the constant association with some who (however humble their sphere, and limited their capacity) are not unmindful of their moral responsibilities."

"Oh Pa!" cried Mercy, holding up her finger archly. "See advertisement!"

"Playful—playful warbler," said Mr. Pecksniff. It may be observed in connexion with his calling his daughter "a warbler," that she was not at all vocal, but that Mr. Pecksniff was in the frequent habit of using any word that occurred to him as having a good sound, and rounding a sentence well, without much care for its meaning. And he did this so boldly, and in such an imposing manner, that he would sometimes stagger the wisest people with his eloquence, and make them gasp again.

His enemies asserted, by the way, that a strong trustfulness in sounds and forms, was the master-key to Mr. Pecksniff's character.

"Is he handsome, Pa?" inquired the younger daughter.

"Silly Merry!" said the eldest: Merry being fond for Mercy. "What is the premium, Pa? tell us that."

"Oh good gracious, Cherry!" cried Miss Mercy, holding up her hands with the most winning giggle in the world, "what a mercenary girl you are! oh you naughty, thoughtful, prudent thing!"

It was perfectly charming, and worthy of the Pastoral age, to see how the two Miss Pecksniffs slapped each other after this, and then subsided into an embrace expressive of their different dispositions.

"He is well looking," said Mr. Pecksniff, slowly and distinctly: "well looking enough. I do not positively expect any immediate premium with him."

Notwithstanding their different natures, both Charity and Mercy concurred in opening their eyes uncommonly wide at this announcement, and in looking for the moment as blank as if their thoughts had actually had a direct bearing on the main-chance.

"But what of that?" said Mr. Pecksniff, still smiling at the fire. "There is disinterestedness in the world, I hope?

We are not all arrayed in two opposite ranks: the *off*ensive
and the *de*fensive. Some few there are who walk between;
who help the needy as they go; and take no part with
either side: umph?"

There was something in these morsels of philanthropy
which reassured the sisters. They exchanged glances, and
brightened very much.

"Oh! let us not be for ever calculating, devising, and
plotting for the future," said Mr. Pecksniff, smiling more
and more, and looking at the fire as a man might who was
cracking a joke with it: "I am weary of such arts. If our
inclinations are but good and open-hearted, let us gratify
them boldly, though they bring upon us Loss instead of
Profit. Eh, Charity?"

Glancing towards his daughters for the first time since
he had begun these reflections, and seeing that they both
smiled, Mr. Pecksniff eyed them for an instant so jocosely
(though still with a kind of saintly waggishness) that the
younger one was moved to sit upon his knee forthwith,
put her fair arms round his neck, and kissed him twenty
times. During the whole of this affectionate display she
laughed to a most immoderate extent: in which hilarious
indulgence even the prudent Cherry joined.

"Tut, tut," said Mr. Pecksniff, pushing his latest-born
away, and running his fingers through his hair, as he resumed his tranquil face. "What folly is this! Let us
take heed how we laugh without reason, lest we cry with
it. What is the domestic news since yesterday? John
Westlock is gone, I hope?"

"Indeed no," said Charity.

"And why not?" returned her father. "His term ex-
pired yesterday. And his box was packed, I know; for I
saw it, in the morning, standing in the hall."

"He slept last night at the Dragon," returned the
young lady, "and had Mr. Pinch to dine with him. They
spent the evening together, and Mr. Pinch was not home
till very late."

"And when I saw him on the stairs this morning, Pa,"
said Mercy with her usual sprightliness, "he looked, oh
goodness, *such* a monster with his face all manner of colours,
and his eyes as dull as if they had been boiled, and his
head aching dreadfully, I am sure from the look of it, and
his clothes smelling, oh it's impossible to say how strong,

2

of "—here the young lady shuddered—"of smoke and punch."

"Now I think," said Mr. Pecksniff with his accustomed gentleness, though still with the air of one who suffered under injury without complaint, " I think Mr. Pinch might have done better than choose for his companion one who, at the close of a long intercourse, had endeavoured, as he knew, to wound my feelings. I am not quite sure that this was delicate in Mr. Pinch. I am not quite sure that this was kind in Mr. Pinch. I will go further and say, I am not quite sure that this was even ordinarily grateful in Mr. Pinch."

"But what can anyone expect from Mr. Pinch!" cried Charity, with as strong and scornful an emphasis on the name as if it would have given her unspeakable pleasure to express it, in an acted charade, on the calf of that gentleman's leg.

" Ay, ay," returned her father, raising his hand mildly: "it is very well to say what can we expect from Mr. Pinch, but Mr. Pinch is a fellow-creature, my dear; Mr. Pinch is an item in the vast total of humanity, my love; and we have a right, it is our duty, to expect in Mr. Pinch some development of those better qualities, the possession of which in our own persons inspires our humble self-respect. No," continued Mr. Pecksniff. "No! Heaven forbid that I should say, nothing can be expected from Mr. Pinch; or that I should say, nothing can be expected from any man alive (even the most degraded, which Mr. Pinch is not, no really); but Mr. Pinch has disappointed me: he has hurt me: I think a little the worse of him on this account, but not of human nature. Oh no, no!"

"Hark!" said Miss Charity, holding up her finger, as a gentle rap was heard at the street-door. "There is the creature! Now mark my words, he has come back with John Westlock for his box, and is going to help him to take it to the mail. Only mark my words, if that isn't his intention!"

Even as she spoke, the box appeared to be in progress of conveyance from the house, but after a brief murmuring of question and answer, it was put down again, and somebody knocked at the parlour door.

"Come in!" cried Mr. Pecksniff—not severely; only virtuously. "Come in!"

An ungainly, awkward-looking man, extremely short-sighted, and prematurely bald, availed himself of this permission; and seeing that Mr. Pecksniff sat with his back towards him, gazing at the fire, stood hesitating, with the door in his hand. He was far from handsome certainly; and was drest in a snuff-coloured suit, of an uncouth make at the best, which, being shrunken with long wear, was twisted and tortured into all kinds of odd shapes; but notwithstanding his attire, and his clumsy figure, which a great stoop in his shoulders, and a ludicrous habit he had of thrusting his head forward, by no means redeemed, one would not have been disposed (unless Mr. Pecksniff said so) to consider him a bad fellow by any means. He was perhaps about thirty, but he might have been almost any age between sixteen and sixty: being one of those strange creatures who never decline into an ancient appearance, but look their oldest when they are very young, and get it over at once.

Keeping his hand upon the lock of the door, he glanced from Mr. Pecksniff to Mercy, from Mercy to Charity, and from Charity to Mr. Pecksniff again, several times; but the young ladies being as intent upon the fire as their father was, and neither of the three taking any notice of him, he was fain to say, at last,

"Oh! I beg your pardon, Mr. Pecksniff: I beg your pardon for intruding; but—"

"No intrusion, Mr. Pinch," said that gentleman very sweetly, but without looking round. "Pray be seated, Mr. Pinch. Have the goodness to shut the door, Mr. Pinch, if you please."

"Certainly, Sir," said Pinch: not doing so, however, but holding it rather wider open than before, and beckoning nervously to somebody without: "Mr. Westlock, Sir, hearing that you were come home—"

"Mr. Pinch, Mr. Pinch!" said Pecksniff, wheeling his chair about, and looking at him with an aspect of the deepest melancholy, "I did not expect this from you. I have not deserved this from you!"

"No, but upon my word, Sir"—urged Pinch.

"The less you say, Mr. Pinch," interposed the other, "the better. I utter no complaint. Make no defence."

"No, but do have the goodness, Sir," cried Pinch, with great earnestness, "if you please. Mr. Westlock, Sir, going away for good and all, wishes to leave none but friends behind him. Mr. Westlock and you, Sir, had a little difference the other day; you have had many little differences."

"Little differences!" cried Charity.

"Little differences!" echoed Mercy.

"My loves!" said Mr. Pecksniff, with the same serene upraising of his hand; "My dears!" After a solemn pause he meekly bowed to Mr. Pinch, as who should say, "Proceed;" but Mr. Pinch was so very much at a loss how to resume, and looked so helplessly at the two Miss Pecksniffs, that the conversation would most probably have terminated there, if a good-looking youth, newly arrived at man's estate, had not stepped forward from the doorway and taken up the thread of the discourse.

"Come, Mr. Pecksniff," he said, with a smile, "don't let there be any ill-blood between us, pray. I am sorry we have ever differed, and extremely sorry I have ever given you offence. Bear me no ill-will at parting, Sir."

"I bear," answered Mr. Pecksniff, mildly, "no ill-will to any man on earth."

"I told you he didn't," said Pinch in an under tone; "I knew he didn't! He always says he don't."

"Then you will shake hands, Sir?" cried Westlock, advancing a step or two, and bespeaking Mr. Pinch's close attention by a glance.

"Umph!" said Mr. Pecksniff, in his most winning tone.

"You will shake hands, Sir."

"No, John," said Mr. Pecksniff, with a calmness quite ethereal; "no, I will not shake hands, John. I have forgiven you. I had already forgiven you, even before you ceased to reproach and taunt me. I have embraced you in the spirit, John, which is better than shaking hands."

"Pinch," said the youth, turning towards him, with a hearty disgust of his late master, "what did I tell you?"

Poor Pinch looked down uneasily at Mr. Pecksniff, whose eye was fixed upon him as it had been from the first: and looking up at the ceiling again, made no reply.

"As to your forgiveness, Mr. Pecksniff," said the youth, "I'll not have it upon such terms. I won't be forgiven."

"Won't you, John?" retorted Mr. Pecksniff, with a smile. "You must. You can't help it. Forgiveness is a high quality; an exalted virtue; far above *your* control or

influence, John. I *will* forgive you. You cannot move
me to remember any wrong you have ever done me, John."
"Wrong!" cried the other, with all the heat and impetuosity of his age. "Here's a pretty fellow! Wrong!
Wrong I have done him! He'll not even remember the
five hundred pounds he had with me under false pretences;
or the seventy pounds a-year for board and lodging that
would have been dear at seventeen! Here's a martyr!"
"Money, John," said Mr. Pecksniff, "is the root of all
evil. I grieve to see that it is already bearing evil fruit
in you. But I will not remember its existence. I will not
even remember the conduct of that misguided person"—
and here, although he spoke like one at peace with all the
world, he used an emphasis that plainly said 'I have my
eye upon the rascal now'—"that misguided person who
has brought you here to-night, seeking to disturb (it is a
happiness to say, in vain) the heart's repose and peace of
one who would have shed his dearest blood to serve him."
The voice of Mr. Pecksniff trembled as he spoke, and
sobs were heard from his daughters. Sounds floated on the
air, moreover, as if two spirit voices had exclaimed: one,
"Beast!" the other, "Savage!"
"Forgiveness," said Mr. Pecksniff, "entire and pure forgiveness is not incompatible with a wounded heart; perchance when the heart *is* wounded, it becomes a greater
virtue. With my breast still wrung and grieved to its in-
most core by the ingratitude of that person, I am proud
and glad to say, that I forgive him. Nay! I beg," cried
Mr. Pecksniff, raising his voice, as Pinch appeared about
to speak, "I beg that individual not to offer a remark: he
will truly oblige me by not uttering one word, just now. I
am not sure that I am equal to the trial. In a very short
space of time, I shall have sufficient fortitude, I trust, to
converse with him as if these events had never happened.
But not," said Mr. Pecksniff, turning round again towards
the fire, and waving his hand in the direction of the door,
"not now."
"Bah!" cried John Westlock, with the utmost disgust
and disdain the monosyllable is capable of expressing.
"Ladies, good evening. Come, Pinch, it's not worth
thinking of. I was right and you were wrong. That's a
small matter; you'll be wiser another time."
So saying, he clapped that dejected companion on the

shoulder, turned upon his heel, and walked out into the passage, whither poor Mr. Pinch, after lingering irresolutely in the parlour for a few seconds, expressing in his countenance the deepest mental misery and gloom, followed him. Then they took up the box between them, and sallied out to meet the mail.

That fleet conveyance passed, every night, the corner of a lane at some distance; towards which point they bent their steps. For some minutes they walked along in silence, until at length young Westlock burst into a loud laugh, and at intervals into another, and another. Still there was no response from his companion.

"I'll tell you what, Pinch!" he said abruptly, after another lengthened silence—"You haven't half enough of the devil in you   Half enough!   You haven't any."

"Well!" said Pinch with a sigh, "I don't know, I'm sure. It's a compliment to say so. If I haven't, I suppose I'm all the better for it."

"All the better!" repeated his companion tartly: "All the worse, you mean to say."

"And yet," said Pinch, pursuing his own thoughts and not this last remark on the part of his friend, "I must have a good deal of what you call the devil in me, too, or how could I make Pecksniff so uncomfortable? I wouldn't have occasioned him so much distress—don't laugh, please —for a mine of money: and Heaven knows I could find good use for it too, John. How grieved he was!"

"*He* grieved!" returned the other.

"Why didn't you observe that the tears were almost starting out of his eyes!" cried Pinch. "Bless my soul, John, is it nothing to see a man moved to that extent and know one's self to be the cause! And did you hear him say that he could have shed his blood for me?"

"Do you *want* any blood shed for you?" returned his friend, with considerable irritation. "Does he shed anything for you that you *do* want? Does he shed employment for you, instruction for you, pocket-money for you? Does he shed even legs of mutton for you in any decent proportion to potatoes and garden stuff?"

"I am afraid," said Pinch, sighing again, "that I am a great eater: I can't disguise from myself that I'm a great eater. Now you know that, John."

"*You* a great eater!" retorted his companion, with no

less indignation than before. "How do you know you are?"

There appeared to be forcible matter in this inquiry, for Mr. Pinch only repeated in an under-tone that he had a strong misgiving on the subject, and that he greatly feared he was:

"Besides, whether I am or no," he added, "that has little or nothing to do with his thinking me ungrateful. John, there is scarcely a sin in the world that is in my eyes such a crying one as ingratitude; and when he taxes me with that, and believes me to be guilty of it, he makes me miserable and wretched."

"Do you think he don't know that?" returned the other scornfully. "But come, Pinch, before I say anything more to you, just turn over the reasons you have for being grateful to him at all, will you? change hands first, for the box is heavy. That'll do. Now, go on."

"In the first place," said Pinch, "he took me as his pupil for much less than he asked."

"Well," rejoined his friend, perfectly unmoved by this instance of generosity. "What in the second place?"

"What in the second place!" cried Pinch, in a sort of desperation, "why, everything in the second place. My poor old grandmother died happy to think that she had put me with such an excellent man. I have grown up in his house, I am in his confidence, I am his assistant, he allows me a salary: when his business improves, my prospects are to improve too. All this, and a great deal more, is in the second place. And in the very prologue and preface to the first place, John, you must consider this, which nobody knows better than I: that I was born for much plainer and poorer things, that I am not a good hand at his kind of business, and have no talent for it, or indeed for anything else but odds and ends that are of no use or service to anybody."

He said this with so much earnestness, and in a tone so full of feeling, that his companion instinctively changed his manner as he sat down on the box (they had by this time reached the finger-post at the end of the lane); motioned him to sit down beside him; and laid his hand upon his shoulder.

"I believe you are one of the best fellows in the world," he said, "Tom Pinch."

"Not at all," rejoined Tom. "If you only knew Pecksniff as well as I do, you might say it of him, indeed, and say it truly."

"I'll say anything of him, you like," returned the other, "and not another word to his disparagement."

"It's for my sake, then; not his, I am afraid," said Pinch, shaking his head gravely.

"For whose you please, Tom, so that it does please you. Oh! He's a famous fellow! *He* never scraped and clawed into his pouch all your poor grandmother's hard savings— she was a housekeeper, wasn't she, Tom?"

"Yes," said Mr. Pinch, nursing one of his large knees, and nodding his head: "a gentleman's housekeeper."

"*He* never scraped and clawed into his pouch all her hard savings; dazzling her with prospects of your happiness and advancement, which he knew (and no man better) never would be realized! *He* never speculated and traded on her pride in you, and her having educated you, and on her desire that you at least should live to be a gentleman. Not he, Tom!"

"No," said Tom, looking into his friend's face, as if he were a little doubtful of his meaning; "of course not."

"So I say," returned the youth, "of course he never did. *He* didn't take less than he had asked, because that less was all she had, and more than he expected: not he, Tom! He doesn't keep you as his assistant because you are of any use to him; because your wonderful faith in his pretensions is of inestimable service in all his mean dis- • putes; because your honesty reflects honesty on him; because your wandering about this place all your spare hours, reading in ancient books and foreign tongues, gets noised abroad, even as far as Salisbury, making of him, Pecksniff the master, a man of learning and of vast importance. *He* gets no credit from you, Tom, not he."

"Why, of course he don't," said Pinch, gazing at his friend with a more troubled aspect than before. "Pecksniff get credit from *me!* Well!"

"Don't I say that it's ridiculous," rejoined the other, "even to think of such a thing?"

"Why, it's madness," said Tom.

"Madness!" returned young Westlock. "Certainly, it's madness. Who but a madman would suppose he cares to hear it said on Sundays, that the volunteer who plays the organ in the church, and practises on summer evenings in the dark, is Mr. Pecksniff's young man, eh, Tom? Who but a madman would suppose it is the game of such a man as he, to have his name in everybody's mouth, connected with the thousand useless odds and ends you do (and which, of course, he taught you), eh, Tom? Who but a madman would suppose you advertise him hereabouts, much cheaper and much better than a chalker on the walls could, eh, Tom? As well might one suppose that he doesn't on all occasions pour out his whole heart and soul to you; that he doesn't make you a very liberal and indeed rather an extravagant allowance; or, to be more wild and monstrous still, if that be possible, as well might one suppose," and here, at every word, he struck him lightly on the breast, "that Pecksniff traded in your nature, and that your nature was, to be timid and distrustful of yourself, and trustful of all other men, but most of all, of him who least deserves it. There would be madness, Tom!"

Mr. Pinch had listened to all this with looks of bewilderment, which seemed to be in part occasioned by the matter of his companion's speech, and in part by his rapid and vehement manner. Now that he had come to a close, he drew a very long breath; and gazing wistfully in his face as if he were unable to settle in his own mind what expression it wore, and were desirous to draw from it as good a clue to his real meaning as it was possible to obtain in the dark, was about to answer, when the sound of the mail guard's horn came cheerily upon their ears, putting an immediate end to the conference: greatly as it seemed to the satisfaction of the younger man, who jumped up briskly, and gave his hand to his companion.

"Both hands, Tom. I shall write to you from London, mind!"

"Yes," said Pinch. "Yes. Do, please. Good bye. Good bye. I can hardly believe you're going. It seems now but yesterday that you came. Good bye! my dear old fellow!"

John Westlock returned his parting words with no less heartiness of manner, and sprang up to his seat upon the roof. Off went the mail at a canter down the dark road: the lamps gleaming brightly and the horn awakening all the echoes far and wide.

"Go your ways," said Pinch, apostrophising the coach:
"I can hardly persuade myself but you're alive, and are
some great monster who visits this place at certain intervals, to bear my friends away into the world. You're more
exulting and rampant than usual to-night, I think: and
you may well crow over your prize; for he is a fine lad, an
ingenuous lad, and has but one fault that I know of: he
don't mean it, but he is most cruelly unjust to Pecksniff!"

CHAPTER III.

IN WHICH CERTAIN OTHER PERSONS ARE INTRO-
DUCED; ON THE SAME TERMS AS IN THE LAST
CHAPTER.

MENTION has been already made more than once, of a
certain Dragon who swung and creaked complainingly before
the village ale-house door. A faded, and an ancient dragon he was; and many a wintry storm of rain, snow, sleet,
and hail, had changed his colour from a gaudy blue to a
faint lack-lustre shade of gray. But there he hung;
rearing, in a state of monstrous imbecility, on his hind legs;
waxing, with every month that passed, so much more dim
and shapeless, that as you gazed at him on one side of the
sign-board it seemed as if he must be gradually melting
through it, and coming out upon the other.
He was a courteous and considerate dragon too, or had
been in his distincter days; for in the midst of his rampant
feebleness, he kept one of his fore paws near his nose, as
though he would say, "Don't mind me—it's only my fun;"
while he held out the other, in polite and hospitable entreaty. Indeed it must be conceded to the whole brood of
dragons of modern times, that they have made a great advance in civilization and refinement. They no longer
demand a beautiful virgin for breakfast every morning,
with as much regularity as any tame single gentleman expects his hot roll, but rest content with the society of idle
bachelors and roving married men: and they are now
remarkable rather for holding aloof from the softer sex and
discouraging their visits (especially on Saturday nights),

than for rudely insisting on their company without any reference to their inclinations, as they are known to have done in days of yore.

Nor is this tribute to the reclaimed animals in question, so wide a digression into the realms of Natural History, as it may, at first sight, appear to be: for the present business of these pages is with the dragon who had his retreat in Mr. Pecksniff's neighbourhood, and that courteous animal being already on the carpet, there is nothing in the way of its immediate transaction.

For many years, then, he had swung and creaked, and flapped himself about, before the two windows of the best bedroom in that house of entertainment to which he lent his name: but never in all his swinging, creaking, and flapping, had there been such a stir within its dingy precincts, as on the evening next after that upon which the incidents, detailed in the last chapter, occurred; when there was such a hurrying up and down stairs of feet, such a glancing of lights, such a whispering of voices, such a smoking and sputtering of wood newly lighted in a damp chimney, such an airing of linen, such a scorching smell of hot warming-pans, such a domestic bustle and to-do, in short, as never dragon, griffin, unicorn, or other animal of that species presided over, since they first began to interest themselves in household affairs.

An old gentleman and a young lady, travelling, unattended, in a rusty old chariot with post-horses; coming nobody knew whence, and going nobody knew whither; had turned out of the high road, and driven unexpectedly to the Blue Dragon: and here was the old gentleman, who had taken this step by reason of his sudden illness in the carriage, suffering the most horrible cramps and spasms, yet protesting and vowing in the very midst of his pain, that he wouldn't have a doctor sent for, and wouldn't take any remedies but those which the young lady administered from a small medicine-chest, and wouldn't, in a word, do anything but terrify the landlady out of her five wits, and obstinately refuse compliance with every suggestion that was made to him.

Of all the five hundred proposals for his relief which the good woman poured out in less than half-an-hour, he would entertain but one. That was, that he should go to bed. And it was in the preparation of his bed, and the arrangement of his chamber, that all the stir was made in the room behind the Dragon.

He was, beyond all question, very ill, and suffered exceedingly: not the less, perhaps, because he was a strong and vigorous old man, with a will of iron, and a voice of brass. But neither the apprehensions which he plainly entertained, at times, for his life, nor the great pain he underwent, influenced his resolution in the least degree. He would have no person sent for. The worse he grew, the more rigid and inflexible he became in this determination. If they sent for any person to attend him, man, woman, or child, he would leave the house directly (so he told them), though he quitted it on foot, and died upon the threshold of the door.

Now there being no medical practitioner actually resident in the village, but a poor apothecary who was also a grocer and general dealer, the landlady had upon her own responsibility sent for him, in the very first burst and outset of the disaster. Of course it followed, as a necessary result of his being wanted, that he was not at home. He had gone some miles away, and was not expected home until late at night; so the landlady, being by this time pretty well beside herself, dispatched the same messenger in all haste for Mr. Pecksniff, as a learned man who could bear a deal of responsibility, and a moral man who could administer a word of comfort to a troubled mind. That her guest had need of some efficient services under the latter head was obvious enough from the restless expressions, importing, however, rather a worldly than a spiritual anxiety, to which he gave frequent utterance.

From this last-mentioned secret errand, the messenger returned with no better news than from the first; Mr. Pecksniff was not at home. However, they got the patient into bed, without him; and in the course of two hours, he gradually became so far better that there were much longer intervals than at first between his terms of suffering. By degrees, he ceased to suffer at all: though his exhaustion was occasionally so great, that it suggested hardly less alarm than his actual endurance had done.

It was in one of his intervals of repose, when, looking round with great caution, and reaching uneasily out of his nest of pillows, he endeavoured, with a strange air of secrecy and distrust, to make use of the writing-materials which he had ordered to be placed on a table beside him, that the young lady and the mistress of the Blue Dragon found themselves sitting side by side before the fire in the sick-chamber.

The mistress of the Blue Dragon was in outward appearance just what a landlady should be: broad, buxom, comfortable, and good-looking, with a face of clear red and white, which, by its jovial aspect, at once bore testimony to her hearty participation in the good things of the larder and the cellar, and to their thriving and healthful influences. She was a widow, but years ago had passed through her state of weeds, and burst into flower again; and in full bloom she had continued ever since; and in full bloom she was now; with roses on her ample skirts, and roses on her bodice, roses in her cap, roses in her cheeks,—ay, and roses, worth the gathering too, on her lips, for that matter. She had still a bright black eye, and jet black hair; was comely, dimpled, plump, and tight as a gooseberry; and though she was not exactly what the world calls young, you may make an affidavit, on trust, before any mayor or magistrate in Christendom, that there are a great many young ladies in the world (blessings on them, one and all!) whom you wouldn't like half as well, or admire half as much, as the beaming hostess of the Blue Dragon.

As this fair matron sat beside the fire, she glanced occasionally, with all the pride of ownership, about the room, which was a large apartment, such as one may see in country places, with a low roof and a sunken flooring, all downhill from the door, and a descent of two steps on the inside so exquisitely unexpected, that strangers, despite the most elaborate cautioning, usually dived in head-first, as into a plunging-bath. It was none of your frivolous and preposterously bright bedrooms, where nobody can close an eye with any kind of propriety or decent regard to the association of ideas; but it was a good, dull, leaden, drowsy place, where every article of furniture reminded you that you came there to sleep, and that you were expected to go to sleep. There was no wakeful reflection of the fire there, as in your modern chambers, which upon the darkest nights have a watchful consciousness of French polish; the old Spanish mahogany winked at it now and then, as a dozing cat or dog might, nothing more. The very size and shape, and hopeless immovability, of the bedstead, and wardrobe, and in a minor degree of even the chairs and tables, provoked sleep; they were plainly apoplectic and disposed to snore. There were no staring portraits to remonstrate with you for being lazy; no round-eyed birds upon the curtains, disgustingly wide awake, and insufferably prying. The thick neutral hangings, and the dark blinds, and the heavy heap of bed-clothes, were all designed to hold in sleep, and act as non-conductors to the day and getting up. Even the old stuffed fox upon the top of the wardrobe was devoid of any spark of vigilance, for his glass eye had fallen out, and he slumbered as he stood.

The wandering attention of the mistress of the Blue Dragon roved to these things but twice or thrice, and then for but an instant at a time. It soon deserted them, and even the distant bed with its strange burden, for the young creature immediately before her, who, with her downcast eyes intently fixed upon the fire, sat wrapped in silent meditation.

She was very young; apparently not more than seventeen; timid and shrinking in her manner, and yet with a greater share of self-possession and control over her emotions than usually belongs to a far more advanced period of female life. This she had abundantly shown, but now, in her tending of the sick gentleman. She was short in stature; and her figure was slight, as became her years; but all the charms of youth and maidenhood set it off, and clustered on her gentle brow. Her face was very pale, in part no doubt from recent agitation. Her dark brown hair, disordered from the same cause, had fallen negligently from its bonds, and hung upon her neck: for which instance of its waywardness, no male observer would have had the heart to blame it.

Her attire was that of a lady, but extremely plain; and in her manner, even when she sat as still as she did then, there was an indefinable something which appeared to be in kindred with her scrupulously unpretending dress. She had sat, at first, looking anxiously towards the bed; but seeing that the patient remained quiet, and was busy with his writing, she had softly moved her chair into its present place: partly, as it seemed, from an instinctive consciousness that he desired to avoid observation; and partly that she might, unseen by him, give some vent to the natural feelings she had hitherto suppressed.

Of all this, and much more, the rosy landlady of the
Blue Dragon took as accurate note and observation as only
woman can take of woman. And at length she said, in a
voice too low, she knew, to reach the bed:
"You have seen the gentleman in this way before, Miss?
Is he used to these attacks?"

"I have seen him very ill before, but not so ill as he has
been to-night."

"What a Providence!" said the landlady of the Dragon,
"that you had the prescriptions and the medicines with
you, Miss!"

"They are intended for such an emergency. We never
travel without them."

"Oh!" thought the hostess, "then *we* are in the habit
of travelling, and of travelling together."

She was so conscious of expressing this in her face, that
meeting the young lady's eyes immediately afterwards,
and being a very honest hostess, she was rather confused.

"The gentleman—your grandpapa"—she resumed, after
a short pause, "being so bent on having no assistance,
must terrify you very much, Miss?"

"I have been very much alarmed to-night. He—he is
not my grandfather."

"Father, I should have said," returned the hostess, sensible of having made an awkward mistake.

"Nor my father," said the young lady. "Nor," she
added, slightly smiling with a quick perception of what the
landlady was going to add, "Nor my uncle. We are not
related."

"Oh dear me!" returned the landlady, still more embarrassed than before: "how could I be so very much mistaken; knowing, as anybody in their proper senses might,
that when a gentleman is ill, he looks so much older than
he really is! That I should have called you 'Miss,' too,
Ma'am!" But when she had proceeded thus far, she
glanced involuntarily at the third finger of the young
lady's left hand, and faltered again: for there was no ring
upon it.

"When I told you we were not related," said the other
mildly, but not without confusion on her own part, "I
meant not in any way. Not even by marriage. Did you
call me, Martin?"

"Call you?" cried the old man, looking quickly up, and

hurriedly drawing beneath the coverlet, the paper on which he had been writing. "No."

She had moved a pace or two towards the bed, but stopped immediately, and went no farther.

"No," he repeated, with a petulant emphasis. "Why do you ask me? If I had called you, what need for such a question?"

"It was the creaking of the sign outside, Sir, I dare say," observed the landlady: a suggestion by the way (as she felt a moment after she had made it), not at all complimentary to the voice of the old gentleman.

"No matter what, Ma'am," he rejoined: "it wasn't I. Why how you stand there, Mary, as if I had the plague! But they're all afraid of me," he added, leaning helplessly backward on his pillow, "even she! There is a curse upon me. What else have I to look for!"

"Oh dear, no. Oh no, I'm sure," said the good-tempered landlady, rising, and going towards him. "Be of better cheer, Sir. These are only sick fancies."

"What are only sick fancies?" he retorted. "What do you know about fancies? Who told *you* about fancies? The old story! Fancies!"

"Only see again there, how you take one up!" said the mistress of the Blue Dragon, with unimpaired good humour. "Dear heart alive, there is no harm in the word, Sir, if it is an old one. Folks in good health have their fancies too, and strange ones, every day."

Harmless as this speech appeared to be, it acted on the traveller's distrust, like oil on fire. He raised his head up in the bed, and, fixing on her two dark eyes whose brightness was exaggerated by the paleness of his hollow cheeks, as they in turn together with his straggling locks of long gray hair, were rendered whiter by the tight black velvet skull-cap which he wore, he searched her face intently.

"Ah! you begin too soon," he said, in so low a voice that he seemed to be thinking it, rather than addressing her. "But you lose no time. You do your errand, and you earn your fee. Now, who may be *your* client?"

The landlady looked in great astonishment at her whom he called Mary, and finding no rejoinder in the drooping face, looked back again at him. At first she had recoiled involuntarily, supposing him disordered in his mind; but the slow composure of his manner, and the settled purpose announced in his strong features, and gathering, most of all, about his puckered mouth, forbade the supposition.

"Come," he said, "tell me who is it? Being here, it is not very hard for me to guess, you may suppose."

"Martin," interposed the young lady, laying her hand upon his arm; "reflect how short a time we have been in this house, and that even your name is unknown here."

"Unless," he said, "you—" He was evidently tempted to express a suspicion of her having broken his confidence in favour of the landlady, but either remembering her tender nursing, or being moved in some sort, by her face, he checked himself, and changing his uneasy posture in the bed, was silent.

"There!" said Mrs. Lupin: for in that name the Blue Dragon was licensed to furnished entertainment, both to man and beast. "Now, you will be well again, Sir. You forgot, for the moment, that there were none but friends here."

"Oh!" cried the old man moaning impatiently, as he tossed one restless arm upon the coverlet, "why do you talk to me of friends! Can you or anybody teach me to know who are my friends, and who my enemies?"

"At least," urged Mrs. Lupin, gently, "this young lady is your friend, I am sure."

"She has no temptation to be otherwise," cried the old man, like one whose hope and confidence were utterly exhausted. "I suppose she is. Heaven knows. There: let me try to sleep. Leave the candle where it is."

As they retired from the bed, he drew forth the writing which had occupied him so long, and holding it in the flame of the taper burnt it to ashes. That done, he extinguished the light, and turning his face away with a heavy sigh, drew the coverlet about his head, and lay quite still.

This destruction of the paper, both as being strangely inconsistent with the labour he had devoted to it and as involving considerable danger of fire to the Dragon, occasioned Mrs. Lupin not a little consternation. But the young lady evincing no surprise, curiosity, or alarm, whispered her, with many thanks for her solicitude and company, that she would remain there some time longer; and that she begged her not to share her watch, as she was well used to being alone, and would pass the time in reading.

3

Mrs. Lupin had her full share and dividend of that large capital of curiosity which is inherited by her sex, and at another time it might have been difficult so to impress this hint upon her as to induce her to take it. But now, in sheer wonder and amazement at these mysteries, she withdrew at once, and repairing straightway to her own little parlour below-stairs, sat down in her easy-chair with unnat-ural composure. At this very crisis, a step was heard in the entry, and Mr. Pecksniff, looking sweetly over the half-door of the bar, and into the vista of snug privacy beyond, murmured:

"Good evening, Mrs. Lupin!"

"Oh dear me, Sir!" she cried, advancing to receive him, "I am so very glad you have come."

"And *I* am very glad I have come." said Mr. Pecksniff, "if I can be of service. I am very glad I have come. What is the matter, Mrs. Lupin?"

"A gentleman taken ill upon the road, has been so very bad up-stairs, Sir," said the tearful hostess.

"A gentleman taken ill upon the road, has been so very bad up-stairs, has he?" repeated Mr. Pecksniff. "Well, well!"

Now there was nothing that one may call decidedly original in this remark, nor can it be exactly said to have contained any wise precept theretofore unknown to mankind, or to have opened any hidden source of consolation: but Mr. Pecksniff's manner was so bland, and he nodded his head so soothingly, and showed in everything such an affable sense of his own excellence, that anybody would have been, as Mrs. Lupin was, comforted by the mere voice and presence of such a man; and, though he had merely said "a verb must agree with its nominative case in number and person, my good friend," or "eight times eight are sixty-four, my worthy soul," must have felt deeply grateful to him for his humanity and wisdom.

"And how," asked Mr. Pecksniff, drawing off his gloves and warming his hands before the fire, as benevolently as if they were somebody else's, not his: "and how is he now?"

"He is better, and quite tranquil," answered Mrs. Lupin.

"He is better, and quite tranquil," said Mr. Pecksniff. "Very well! ve-ry well!"

Here again, though the statement was Mrs. Lupin's and

not Mr. Pecksniff's, Mr. Pecksniff made it his own and consoled her with it. It was not much when Mrs. Lupin said it, but it was a whole book when Mr. Pecksniff said it. "*I* observe," he seemed to say, "and, through me, morality in general remarks, that he is better and quite tranquil."

"There must be weighty matters on his mind though," said the hostess, shaking her head, "for he talks, Sir, in the strangest way you ever heard. He is far from easy in his thoughts, and wants some proper advice from those whose goodness makes it worth his having."

"Then," said Mr. Pecksniff, "he is the sort of customer for me." But though he said this in the plainest language, he didn't speak a word. He only shook his head: disparagingly of himself too.

"I am afraid, Sir," continued the landlady, first looking round to assure herself that there was nobody within hearing, and then looking down upon the floor. "I am very much afraid, Sir, that his conscience is troubled by his not being related—or—or even married to—a very young lady—"

"Mrs. Lupin!" said Mr. Pecksniff, holding up his hand with something in his manner as nearly approaching to severity, as any expression of his, mild being that he was, could ever do. "Person! young person?"

"A very young person," said Mrs. Lupin, courtesying and blushing: "I beg your pardon, Sir, but I have been so hurried to-night that I don't know what I say: who is with him now."

"Who is with him now," ruminated Mr. Pecksniff, warming his back (as he had warmed his hands) as if it were a widow's back, or an orphan's back, or an enemy's back, or a back that any less excellent man would have suffered to be cold: "Oh dear me, dear me!"

"At the same time I am bound to say, and I do say with all my heart," observed the hostess, earnestly, "that her looks and manner almost disarm suspicion."

"Your suspicion, Mrs. Lupin," said Mr. Pecksniff gravely, "is very natural."

Touching which remark, let it be written down to their confusion, that the enemies of this worthy man unblushingly maintained that he always said of what was very bad, that it was very natural; and that he unconsciously betrayed his own nature in doing so.

"Your suspicion, Mrs. Lupin," he repeated, "is **very** natural, and I have no doubt correct. I will wait upon these travellers."

With that he took off his great-coat, and having run his fingers through his hair, thrust one hand gently in the bosom of his waistcoat and meekly signed to her to lead the way.

"Shall I knock?" asked Mrs. Lupin, when they reached the chamber door.

"No," said Mr. Pecksniff, "enter if you please."

They went in on tiptoe: or rather the hostess took that precaution, for Mr. Pecksniff always walked softly. The old gentleman was still asleep, and his young companion still sat reading by the fire.

"I am afraid," said Mr. Pecksniff, pausing at the door, and giving his head a melancholy roll, "I am afraid that this looks artful. I am afraid, Mrs. Lupin, do you know, that this looks very artful!"

As he finished this whisper, he advanced, before the hostess; and at the same time the young lady, hearing footsteps, rose. Mr. Pecksniff glanced at the volume she held and whispered Mrs. Lupin again: if possible with increased despondency.

"Yes, Ma'am," he said, "it is a good book. I was fearful of that beforehand. I am apprehensive that this is a very deep thing indeed!"

"What gentleman is this?" inquired the object of his virtuous doubts.

"Hush! don't trouble yourself, Ma'am," said Mr. Pecksniff, as the landlady was about to answer. "This young" —in spite of himself he hesitated when 'person' rose to his lips, and substituted another word: "this young stranger, Mrs. Lupin, will excuse me for replying briefly, that I reside in this village; it may be in an influential manner, however undeserved; and that I have been summoned here, by you. I am here, as I am everywhere, I hope, in sympathy for the sick and sorry."

With these impressive words, Mr. Pecksniff passed over to the bedside, where, after patting the counterpane once or twice in a very solemn manner, as if by that means he gained a clear insight into the patient's disorder, he took his seat in a large arm-chair, and in an attitude of some thoughtfulness and much comfort, waited for his waking.

Whatever objection the young lady urged to Mrs. Lupin went no further, for nothing more was said to Mr. Pecksniff, and Mr. Pecksniff said nothing more to anybody else.

Full half-an-hour elapsed before the old man stirred, but at length he turned himself in bed, and, though not yet awake, gave tokens that his sleep was drawing to an end. By little and little he removed the bed-clothes from about his head, and turned still more towards the side where Mr. Pecksniff sat. In course of time his eyes opened; and he lay for a few moments as people newly roused sometimes will, gazing indolently at his visitor, without any distinct consciousness of his presence.

There was nothing remarkable in these proceedings, except the influence they worked on. Mr. Pecksniff, which could hardly have been surpassed by the most marvellous of natural phenomena. Gradually his hands became tightly clasped upon the elbows of the chair, his eyes dilated with surprise, his mouth opened, his hair stood more erect upon his forehead than its custom was, until at length, when the old man rose in bed, and stared at him with scarcely less emotion than he showed himself, the Pecksniff doubts were all resolved, and he exclaimed aloud:

" You *are* Martin Chuzzlewit! "

His consternation of surprise was so genuine, that the old man, with all the disposition that he clearly entertained to believe it assumed, was convinced of its reality.

" I *am* Martin Chuzzlewit," he said, bitterly: " and Martin Chuzzlewit wishes you had been hanged, before you had come here to disturb him in his sleep. Why, I dreamed of this fellow! " he said, lying down again, and turning away his face, " before I knew that he was near me! "

" My good cousin— " said Mr. Pecksniff.

" There! His very first words! " cried the old man, shaking his gray head to and fro upon the pillow, and throwing up his hands. " In his very first words he asserts his relationship! I knew he would: they all do it! Near or distant, blood or water, it's all one. Ugh! What a calendar of deceit, and lying, and false-witnessing, the sound of any word of kindred opens before me! "

" Pray do not be hasty, Mr. Chuzzlewit," said Pecksniff, in a tone that was at once in the sublimest degree compassionate and dispassionate; for he had by this time recov-

ered from his surprise, and was in full possession of his
virtuous self. "You will regret being hasty, I know you
will."

"*You* know!" said Martin, contemptuously.

"Yes," retorted Mr. Pecksniff. "Ay, ay, Mr. Chuzzlewit: and don't imagine that I mean to court or flatter you:
for nothing is further from my intention. Neither, Sir,
need you entertain the least misgiving that I shall repeat
that obnoxious word which has given you so much offence
already. Why should I? What do I expect or want from
you? There is nothing in your possession that *I* know of,
Mr. Chuzzlewit, which is much to be coveted for the happiness it brings you."

"That's true enough," muttered the old man.

"Apart from that consideration," said Mr. Pecksniff,
watchful of the effect he made, "it must be plain to you (I
am sure) by this time, that if I had wished to insinuate
myself into your good opinion, I should have been, of all
things, careful not to address you as a relative: knowing
your humour, and being quite certain beforehand that I
could not have a worse letter of recommendation."

Martin made not any verbal answer; but he as clearly
implied, though only by a motion of his legs beneath the
bedclothes, that there was reason in this and he could not
dispute it, as if he had said as much in good set terms.

"No," said Mr. Pecksniff, keeping his hand in his waistcoat as though he were ready, on the shortest notice, to
produce his heart for Martin Chuzzlewit's inspection, "I
came here to offer my services to a stranger. I make no
offer of them to you, because I know you would distrust
me if I did. But lying on that bed, Sir, I regard you as a
stranger, and I have just that amount of interest in you
which I hope I should feel in any stranger, circumstanced
as you are. Beyond that, I am quite as indifferent to you,
Mr. Chuzzlewit, as you are to me."

Having said which, Mr. Pecksniff threw himself back in
the easy-chair: so radiant with ingenuous honesty, that
Mrs. Lupin almost wondered not to see a stained-glass
Glory, such as the Saint wore in the church, shining about
his head.

A long pause succeeded. The old man, with increased
restlessness, changed his posture several times. Mrs.
Lupin and the young lady gazed in silence at the counter-

pane. Mr. Pecksniff toyed abstractedly with his eye-glass, and kept his eyes shut, that he might ruminate the better. "Eh?" he said at last: opening them suddenly, and looking towards the bed. "I beg your pardon. I thought you spoke. Mrs. Lupin," he continued, slowly rising, "I am not aware that I can be of any service to you here. The gentleman is better, and you are as good a nurse as he can have. Eh?"

This last note of interrogation bore reference to another change of posture on the old man's part, which brought his face towards Mr. Pecksniff for the first time since he had turned away from him.

"If you desire to speak to me before I go, Sir," continued that gentleman, after another pause, "you may command my leisure; but I must stipulate, in justice to myself, that you do so as to a stranger: strictly as to a stranger."

Now if Mr. Pecksniff knew, from anything Martin Chuzzlewit had expressed in gestures, that he wanted to speak to him, he could only have found it out on some such principle as prevails in melodramas, and in virtue of which the elderly farmer with the comic son always knows what the dumb girl means when she takes refuge in his garden, and relates her personal memoirs in incomprehensible pantomime. But without stopping to make any inquiry on this point, Martin Chuzzlewit signed to his young companion to withdraw, which she immediately did, along with the landlady: leaving him and Mr. Pecksniff alone together. For some time they looked at each other in silence; or rather the old man looked at Mr. Pecksniff, and Mr. Pecksniff, again closing his eyes on all outward objects, took an inward survey of his own breast. That it amply repaid him for his trouble, and afforded a delicious and enchanting prospect, was clear from the expression of his face.

"You wish me to speak to you as to a total stranger," said the old man, "do you?"

Mr. Pecksniff replied, by a shrug of his shoulders and an apparent turning-round of his eyes in their sockets before he opened them, that he was still reduced to the necessity of entertaining that desire.

"You shall be gratified," said Martin. "Sir, I am a rich man. Not so rich as some suppose, perhaps, but yet wealthy. I am not a miser, Sir, though even that charge is made against me, as I hear, and currently believed. I have no pleasure in hoarding. I have no pleasure in the possession of money. The devil that we call by that name can give me nothing but unhappiness."

It would be no description of Mr. Pecksniff's gentleness of manner to adopt the common parlance, and say, that he looked at this moment as if butter wouldn't melt in his mouth. He rather looked as if any quantity of butter might have been made out of him, by churning the milk of human kindness, as it spouted upwards from his heart.

"For the same reason that I am not a hoarder of money," said the old man, "I am not lavish of it. Some people find their gratification in storing it up; and others theirs in parting with it; but I have no gratification connected with the thing. Pain and bitterness are the only goods it ever could procure for me. I hate it. It is a spectre walking before me through the world, and making every social pleasure hideous."

A thought arose in Mr. Pecksniff's mind, which must have instantly mounted to his face, or Martin Chuzzlewit would not have resumed as quickly and as sternly as he did:

"You would advise me for my peace of mind, to get rid of this source of misery, and transfer it to some one who could bear it better. Even you, perhaps, would rid me of a burden under which I suffer so grievously. But, kind stranger," said the old man, whose every feature darkened as he spoke, "good Christian stranger, that is a main part of my trouble. In other hands, I have known money do good; in other hands I have known it triumphed in, and boasted of with reason, as the master-key to all the brazen gates that close upon the paths to worldly honour, fortune, and enjoyment. To what man or woman; to what worthy, honest, incorruptible creature; shall I confide such a talisman either now or when I die? Do you know any such person? Your virtues are of course inestimable, but can you tell me of any other living creature who will bear the test of contact with myself?"

"Of contact with yourself, Sir?" echoed Mr. Pecksniff.

"Ay," returned the old man, "the test of contact with me—with me. You have heard of him whose misery (the gratification of his own foolish wish) was, that he turned every thing he touched to gold. The curse of my exist-

ence, and the realization of my own mad desire, is that by
the golden standard which I bear about me, I am doomed
to try the metal of all other men, and find it false and
hollow."

Mr. Pecksniff shook his head, and said, "You think so."

"Oh yes," cried the old man, "I think so! and in your
telling me 'I think so,' I recognise the true unworldly ring
of *your* metal. I tell you, man," he added, with increasing bitterness, "that I have gone, a rich man, among people
of all grades and kinds; relatives, friends, and strangers;
among people in whom, when I was poor, I had confidence,
and justly, for they never once deceived me then, or, to
me, wronged each other. But I have never found one
nature, no, not one, in which, being wealthy and alone, I
was not forced to detect the latent corruption that lay hid
within it, waiting for such as I to bring it forth. Treachery, deceit, and low design; hatred of competitors, real or
fancied, for my favour; meanness, falsehood, baseness,
and servility; or," and here he looked closely in his cousin's
eyes, "or an assumption of honest independence, almost
worse than all; these are the beauties which my wealth has
brought to light. Brother against brother, child against
parent, friends treading on the faces of friends, this is the
social company by which my way has been attended.
There are stories told—they may be true or false—of rich
men, who, in the garb of poverty, have found out virtue
and rewarded it. They were dolts and idiots for their
pains. They should have made the search in their own
characters. They should have shown themselves fit objects
to be robbed and preyed upon and plotted against and adu-
lated by any knaves, who, but for joy, would have spat
upon their coffins when they died their dupes; and then
their search would have ended as mine has done, and they
would be what I am."

Mr. Pecksniff, not at all knowing what it might be best
to say in the momentary pause which ensued upon these
remarks, made an elaborate demonstration of intending to
deliver something very oracular indeed: trusting to the certainty of the old man interrupting him, before he should
utter a word. Nor was he mistaken, for Martin Chuzzlewit having taken breath, went on to say:

"Hear me to an end; judge what profit you are like to
gain from any repetition of this visit; and leave me. I

have so corrupted and changed the nature of all those who have ever attended on me, by breeding avaricious plots and hopes within them; I have engendered such domestic strife and discord, by tarrying even with members of my own family; I have been such a lighted torch in peaceful homes, kindling up all the bad gases and vapours in their moral atmosphere, which, but for me, might have proved harmless to the end; that I have, I may say, fled from all who knew me, and taking refuge in secret places have lived, of late, the life of one who is hunted. The young girl whom you just now saw—what! your eye lightens when I talk of her! You hate her already, do you?"

"Upon my word, Sir!" said Mr. Pecksniff, laying his hand upon his breast, and dropping his eyelids.

"I forgot," cried the old man, looking at him with a keenness which the other seemed to feel, although he did not raise his eyes so as to see: "I ask your pardon. I forgot you were a stranger. For the moment you reminded me of one Pecksniff, a cousin of mine. As I was saying— the young girl whom you just now saw, is an orphan child, whom, with one steady purpose, I have bred and educated, or, if you prefer the word, adopted. For a year or more she has been my constant companion, and she is my only one. I have taken, as she knows, a solemn oath never to leave her sixpence when I die, but while I live, I make her an annual allowance: not extravagant in its amount, and yet not stinted. There is a compact between us that no term of affectionate cajolery shall ever be addressed by either to the other, but that she call me always by my Christian name, I her, by hers. She is bound to me in life by ties of interest, and losing by my death, and having no expectation disappointed, will mourn it, perhaps: though for that I care little. This is the only kind of friend I have or will have. Judge from such premises what a profitable hour you have spent in coming here, and leave me; to return no more."

With these words, the old man fell slowly back upon his pillow. Mr. Pecksniff as slowly rose, and, with a prefatory hem, began as follows:

"Mr. Chuzzlewit."

"There. Go!" interposed the other. "Enough of this. I am weary of you."

"I am sorry for that, Sir," rejoined Mr. Pecksniff, "because I have a duty to discharge, from which, depend upon it, I shall not shrink. No, Sir, I shall not shrink."

It is a lamentable fact, that as Mr. Pecksniff stood erect beside the bed, in all the dignity of Goodness, and addressed him thus, the old man cast an angry glance towards the candlestick, as if he were possessed by a strong inclination to launch it at his cousin's head. But he constrained himself, and pointing with his finger to the door, informed him that his road lay there.

"Thank you," said Mr. Pecksniff, "I am aware of that; I am going. But before I go I crave your leave to speak, and more than that, Mr. Chuzzlewit, I must and will—yes indeed, I repeat it, must and will—be heard. I am not surprised, Sir, at anything you have told me to-night. It is natural, very natural, and the great part of it was known to me before. I will not say," continued Mr. Pecksniff, drawing out his pocket-handkerchief, and winking with both eyes at once, as it were, against his will, "I will not say that you are mistaken in me. While you are in your present mood I would not say so for the world. I almost wish, indeed, that I had a different nature, that I might repress even this slight confession of weakness, which I cannot disguise from you: which I feel is humiliating: but which you will have the goodness to excuse. We will say, if you please," added Mr. Pecksniff, with great tenderness of manner, "that it arises from a cold in the head, or is attributable to snuff, or smelling-salts, or onions, or anything but the real cause."

Here he paused for an instant, and concealed his face behind his pocket-handkerchief. Then, smiling faintly, and holding the bed-furniture with one hand, he resumed:

"But, Mr. Chuzzlewit, while I am forgetful of myself, I owe it to myself, and to my character—ay, Sir, and I *have* a character which is very dear to me, and will be the best inheritance of my two daughters—to tell you, on behalf of another, that your conduct is wrong, unnatural, indefensible, monstrous. And I tell you, Sir," said Mr. Pecksniff, towering on tiptoe among the curtains, as if he were literally rising above all worldly considerations, and were fain to hold on tight, to keep himself from darting skywards like a rocket, "I tell you without fear or favour, that it will not do for you to be unmindful of your grandson, young Martin, who has the strongest natural claim upon you. It will not do, Sir," repeated Mr. Pecksniff, shaking his head. "You may think it will do, but it won't. You must provide for that young man; you shall provide for him; you *will* provide for him. I believe," said Mr. Pecksniff, glancing at the pen and ink, "that in secret you have already done so. Bless you for doing so. Bless you for doing right, Sir. Bless you for hating me. And good night!"

So saying, Mr. Pecksniff waved his right hand with much solemnity; and once more inserting it in his waistcoat, departed. There was emotion in his manner, but his step was firm. Subject to human weaknesses, he was upheld by conscience.

Martin lay for some time, with an expression on his face of silent wonder, not unmixed with rage : at length he muttered in a whisper :

"What does this mean? Can the false-hearted boy have chosen such a tool as yonder fellow who has just gone out? Why not! He has conspired against me, like the rest, and they but birds of one feather. A new plot; a new plot! Oh self, self, self! At every turn nothing but self!"

He fell to trifling, as he ceased to speak, with the ashes of the burnt paper in the candlestick. He did so, at first in pure abstraction, but they presently became the subject of his thoughts.

"Another will made and destroyed," he said, "nothing determined on, nothing done, and I might have died to-night! I plainly see to what foul uses all this money will be put at last," he cried, almost writhing in the bed : "after filling me with cares and miseries all my life, it will perpetuate discord and bad passions when I am dead. So it always is. What lawsuits grow out of the graves of rich men, every day : sowing perjury, hatred, and lies among near kindred, where there should be nothing but love! Heaven help us, we have much to answer for! Oh self, self, self! Every man for himself, and no creature for me!"

Universal self! Was there nothing of its shadow in these reflections, and in the history of Martin Chuzzlewit, on his own showing?

CHAPTER IV.

FROM WHICH IT WILL APPEAR THAT IF UNION BE STRENGTH, AND FAMILY AFFECTION BE PLEASANT TO CONTEMPLATE, THE CHUZZLEWITS WERE THE STRONGEST AND MOST AGREEABLE FAMILY IN THE WORLD.

THAT worthy man Mr. Pecksniff having taken leave of his cousin in the solemn terms recited in the last chapter, withdrew to his own home, and remained there three whole days: not so much as going out for a walk beyond the boundaries of his own garden, lest he should be hastily summoned to the bedside of his penitent and remorseful relative, whom, in his ample benevolence, he had made up his mind to forgive unconditionally, and to love on any terms. But such was the obstinacy and such the bitter nature of that stern old man, that no repentant summons came; and the fourth day found Mr. Pecksniff apparently much farther from his Christian object than the first.

During the whole of this interval, he haunted the Dragon at all times and seasons in the day and night, and, returning good for evil, evinced the deepest solicitude in the progress of the obdurate invalid; insomuch that Mrs. Lupin was fairly melted by his disinterested anxiety (for he often particularly required her to take notice that he would do the same by any stranger or pauper in the like condition), and shed many tears of admiration and delight.

Meantime, old Martin Chuzzlewit remained shut up in his own chamber, and saw no person but his young companion, saving the hostess of the Blue Dragon, who was, at certain times, admitted to his presence. So surely as she came into the room, however, Martin feigned to fall asleep. It was only when he and the young lady were alone, that he would utter a word, even in answer to the simplest inquiry; though Mr. Pecksniff could make out, by hard listening at the door, that they two being left together, he was talkative enough.

It happened on the fourth evening, that Mr. Pecksniff

7—3

walking, as usual, into the bar of the Dragon and finding
no Mrs. Lupin there, went straight upstairs: purposing, in
the fervour of his affectionate zeal, to apply his ear once
more to the keyhole, and quiet his mind by assuring himself that the hard-hearted patient was going on well.   It
happened that Mr. Pecksniff, coming softly upon the dark
passage into which a spiral ray of light usually darted
through this same keyhole, was astonished to find no such
ray visible; and it happened that Mr. Pecksniff, when he
had felt his way to the chamber-door, stooping hurriedly
down to ascertain by personal inspection whether the
jealousy of the old man had caused this keyhole to be
stopped on the inside, brought his head into such violent
contact with another head, that he could not help uttering
in an audible voice the monosyllable "Oh!" which was, as
it were, sharply unscrewed and jerked out of him by very
anguish.   It happened then, and lastly, that Mr. Pecksniff
found himself immediately collared by something which
smelt like several damp umbrellas, a barrel of beer, a cask
of warm brandy-and-water, and a small parlour-full of
stale tobacco smoke, mixed; and was straightway led down
stairs into the bar from which he had lately come, where
he found himself standing opposite to, and in the grasp of
a perfectly strange gentleman of still stranger appearance,
who, with his disengaged hand, rubbed his own head very
hard, and looked at him, Pecksniff, with an evil countenance.

The gentleman was of that order of appearance, which is
currently termed shabby-genteel, though in respect of his
dress he can hardly be said to have been in any extremi-
ties, as his fingers were a long way out of his gloves, and
the soles of his feet were at an inconvenient distance from
the upper leather of his boots.   His nether garments were
of a bluish gray—violent in its colours once, but sobered
now by age and dinginess—and were so stretched and
strained in a tough conflict between his braces and his
straps, that they appeared every moment in danger of flying asunder at the knees.   His coat, in colour blue and of
a military cut, was buttoned and frogged, up to his chin.
His cravat was, in hue and pattern, like one of those man-
tles which hair-dressers are accustomed to wrap about their
clients, during the progress of the professional mysteries.
His hat had arrived at such a pass that it would have

been hard to determine whether it was originally white or black. But he wore a moustache—a shaggy moustache too: nothing in the meek and merciful way, but quite in the fierce and scornful style: the regular Satanic sort of thing —and he wore, besides, a vast quantity of unbrushed hair. He was very dirty and very jaunty; very bold and very mean; very swaggering and very slinking; very much like a man who might have been something better, and unspeakably like a man who deserved to be something worse.

"You were eaves-dropping at that door, you vagabond!" said this gentleman.

Mr. Pecksniff cast him off, as Saint George might have repudiated the Dragon in that animal's last moments, and said:

"Where is Mrs. Lupin, I wonder! can the good woman possibly be aware that there is a person here who—"

"Stay!" said the gentleman. "Wait a bit. She *does* know. What then?"

"What then, Sir?" cried Mr. Pecksniff. "What then? Do you know, Sir, that I am the friend and relative of that sick gentleman? That I am his protector, his guardian, his—"

"Not his niece's husband," interposed the stranger, "I'll be sworn; for he was there before you."

"What do you mean?" said Mr. Pecksniff, with indignant surprise. "What do you tell me, Sir?"

"Wait a bit!" cried the other. "Perhaps you are a cousin—the cousin who lives in this place?"

"I am the cousin who lives in this place," replied the man of worth.

"Your name is Pecksniff?" said the gentleman.

"It is."

"I am proud to know you, and I ask your pardon," said the gentleman touching his hat, and subsequently diving behind his cravat for a shirt-collar, which however he did not succeed in bringing to the surface. "You behold in me, Sir, one who has also an interest in that gentleman upstairs. Wait a bit."

As he said this, he touched the tip of his high nose, by way of intimation that he would·let Mr. Pecksniff into a secret presently; and pulling off his hat, began to search inside the crown among a mass of crumpled documents and small pieces of what may be called the bark of broken

cigars: whence he presently selected the cover of an old
letter, begrimed with dirt and redolent of tobacco.

"Read that," he cried, giving it to Mr. Pecksniff.

"This is addressed to Chevy Slyme, Esquire," said that
gentleman.

"You know Chevy Slyme, Esquire, I believe?" returned
the stranger.

Mr. Pecksniff shrugged his shoulders as though he would
say, "I know there is such a person, and I am sorry
for it."

"Very good," remarked the gentleman. "That is my
interest and business here." With that he made another
dive for his shirt-collar, and brought up a string.

"Now this is very distressing, my friend," said Mr.
Pecksniff, shaking his head and smiling composedly. "It
is very distressing to me, to be compelled to say that you
are not the person you claim to be. I know Mr. Slyme,
my friend: this will not do: honesty is the best policy:
you had better not; you had indeed "

"Stop!" cried the gentleman, stretching forth his right
arm, which was so tightly wedged into his threadbare
sleeve that it looked like a cloth sausage. "Wait a bit!"

He paused to establish himself immediately in front of
the fire, with his back towards it. Then gathering the
skirts of his coat under his left arm, and smoothing his
moustache with his right thumb and forefinger, he resumed:

"I understand your mistake, and I am not offended.
Why? Because it's complimentary. You suppose I would
set myself up for Chevy Slyme. Sir, if there is a man on
earth whom a gentleman would feel proud and honoured to
be mistaken for, that man is my friend Slyme. For he is,
without an exception, the highest-minded, the most inde-
pendent-spirited, most original, spiritual, classical, talented, the most thoroughly Shakspearian, if not Miltonic,
and at the same time the most disgustingly-unappreciated
dog I know. But, Sir, I have not the vanity to attempt to
pass for Slyme. Any other man in the wide world, I am
equal to; but Slyme is, I frankly confess, a great many
cuts above me. Therefore you are wrong."

"I judged from this," said Mr. Pecksniff, holding out
the cover of the letter.

"No doubt you did," returned the gentleman. "But,
Mr. Pecksniff, the whole thing resolves itself into an in-

stance of the peculiarities of genius. Every man of true genius has his peculiarity. Sir, the peculiarity of my friend Slyme is, that he is always waiting round the corner. He is perpetually round the corner, Sir. He is round the corner at this instant. Now," said the gentleman, shaking his forefinger before his nose, and planting his legs wider apart as he looked attentively in Mr. Pecksniff's face, "that is a remarkably curious and interesting trait in Slyme's character; and whenever Slyme's life comes to be written, that trait must be thoroughly worked out by his biographer, or society will not be satisfied. Observe me, society will not be satisfied."

Mr. Pecksniff coughed.

"Slyme's biographer, Sir, whoever he may be," resumed the gentleman, "must apply to me; or if I am gone to that what's-his-name from which no thingumbob comes back, he must apply to my executors for leave to search among my papers. I have taken a few notes in my poor way, of some of that man's proceedings—my adopted brother, Sir —which would amaze you. He made use of an expression, Sir, only on the fifteenth of last month when he couldn't meet a little bill and the other party wouldn't renew, which would have done honour to Napoleon Bonaparte in addressing the French army."

"And pray," asked Mr. Pecksniff, obviously not quite at his ease, "what may be Mr. Slyme's business here, if I may be permitted to inquire, who am compelled by a regard for my own character to disavow all interest in his proceedings?"

"In the first place," returned the gentleman, "you will permit me to say, that I object to that remark, and that I strongly and indignantly protest against it on behalf of my friend Slyme. In the next place, you will give me leave to introduce myself. My name, Sir, is Tigg. The name of Montague Tigg will perhaps be familiar to you, in connexion with the most remarkable events of the Peninsular War?"

Mr. Pecksniff gently shook his head.

"No matter," said the gentleman. "That man was my father, and I bear his name. I am consequently proud— proud as Lucifer. Excuse me one moment: I desire my friend Slyme to be present at the remainder of this conference."

4

With this announcement he hurried away to the outer
door of the Blue Dragon, and almost immediately returned
with a companion shorter than himself, who was wrapped
in an old blue camlet cloak with a lining of faded scarlet.
His sharp features being much pinched and nipped by long
waiting in the cold, and his straggling red whiskers and
frowzy hair being more than usually dishevelled from the
same cause, he certainly looked rather unwholesome and
uncomfortable than Shakspearian or Miltonic.

"Now," said Mr. Tigg, clapping one hand on the shoulder of his prepossessing friend, and calling Mr. Pecksniff's
attention to him with the other, "you two are related; and
relations never did agree, and never will; which is a wise
dispensation and an inevitable thing, or there would be
none but family parties, and everybody in the world would
bore everybody else to death. If you were on good terms,
I should consider you a most confoundedly unnatural pair;
but standing towards each other as you do, I look upon you
as a couple of devilish deep-thoughted fellows, who may be
reasoned with to any extent."

Here Mr. Chevy Slyme, whose great abilities seemed one
and all to point towards the sneaking quarter of the moral
compass, nudged his friend stealthily with his elbow, and
whispered in his ear.

"Chiv," said Mr. Tigg aloud, in the high tone of one
who was not to be tampered with. 'I shall come to that,
presently. I act upon my own responsibility, or not at all.
To the extent of such a trifling loan as a crownpiece to a
man of your talents, I look upon Mr. Pecksniff as certain : "
and seeing at this juncture that the expression of Mr. Pecksniff's face by no means betokened that he shared this certainty, Mr. Tigg laid his finger on his nose again for that
gentleman's private and especial behoof : calling upon him
thereby to take notice, that the requisition of small loans
was another instance of the peculiarities of genius as developed in his friend Slyme; that he, Tigg, winked at the
same, because of the strong metaphysical interest which
these weaknesses possessed; and that in reference to his
own personal advocacy of such small advances, he merely
consulted the humour of his friend, without the least regard
to his own advantage or necessities.

"Oh, Chiv, Chiv," added Mr. Tigg, surveying his
adopted brother with an air of profound contemplation

after dismissing this piece of pantomime. "You are, upon my life, a strange instance of the little frailties that beset a mighty mind. If there had never been a telescope in the world, I should have been quite certain from my observation of you, Chiv, that there were spots on the sun! I wish I may die, if this isn't the queerest state of existence that we find ourselves forced into, without knowing why or wherefore, Mr. Pecksniff! Well, never mind. Moralise as we will, the world goes on. As Hamlet says, Hercules may lay about him with his club in every possible direction, but he can't prevent the cats from making a most intolerable row on the roofs of the houses, or the dogs from being shot in the hot weather if they run about the streets unmuzzled. Life's a riddle: a most infernally hard riddle to guess, Mr. Pecksniff. My own opinion is, that like that celebrated conundrum, 'Why's a man in jail like a man out of jail?' there's no answer to it. Upon my soul and body, it's the queerest sort of thing altogether—but there's no use in talking about it. Ha! ha!"

With which consolatory deduction from the gloomy premises recited, Mr. Tigg roused himself by a great effort, and proceeded in his former strain.

"Now I'll tell you what it is. I'm a most confoundedly soft-hearted kind of fellow in my way, and I cannot stand by, and see you two blades cutting each other's throats when there's nothing to be got by it. Mr. Pecksniff, you're the cousin of the testator up-stairs and we're the nephew—I say we, meaning Chiv. Perhaps in all essential points, you are more nearly related to him than we are. Very good. If so, so be it. But you can't get at him, neither can we. I give you my brightest honour, Sir, that I've been looking through that keyhole, with short intervals of rest, ever since nine o'clock this morning, in expectation of receiving an answer to one of the most moderate and gentlemanly applications for a little temporary assistance—only fifteen pound, and *my* security—that the mind of man can conceive. In the mean time, Sir, he is perpetually closeted with, and pouring his whole confidence into the bosom of, a stranger. Now I say decisively, with regard to this state of circumstances, that it won't do; that it won't act; that it can't be; and that it must not be suffered to continue."

"Every man," said Mr Pecksniff, "has a right, an un-

doubted right (which I, for one, would not call in question
for any earthly consideration: oh no!) to regulate his own
proceedings by his own likings and dislikings, supposing
they are not immoral and not irreligious. I may feel in
my own breast, that Mr. Chuzzlewit does not regard—me,
for instance: say me—with exactly that amount of Christian love which should subsist between us; I may feel
grieved and hurt at the circumstance; still, I may not rush
to the conclusion that Mr. Chuzzlewit is wholly without a
justification in all his coldness: Heaven forbid! Besides;
how, Mr. Tigg," continued Pecksniff even more gravely
and impressively than he had spoken yet, "how could Mr.
Chuzzlewit be prevented from having these peculiar and
most extraordinary confidences of which you speak; the
existence of which I must admit; and which I cannot but
deplore—for his sake? Consider, my good Sir—" and
here Mr. Pecksniff eyed him wistfully—"how very much
at random you are talking."

"Why as to that," rejoined Tigg, "it certainly is a difficult question."

"Undoubtedly it is a difficult question," Mr. Pecksniff
answered: and as he spoke he drew himself aloof, and
seemed to grow more mindful, suddenly, of the moral gulf
between himself and the creature he addressed. "Undoubtedly it is a very difficult question. And I am far
from feeling sure that it is a question any one is authorised
to discuss. Good evening to you."

"You don't know that the Spottletoes are here, I suppose?" said Mr. Tigg.

"What do you mean, Sir? what Spottletoes?" asked
Pecksniff, stopping abruptly on his way to the door.

"Mr. and Mrs. Spottletoe," said Chevy Slyme, Esquire,
speaking aloud for the first time, and speaking very sulkily:
shambling with his legs the while. "Spottletoe married
my father's brother's child, didn't he? And Mrs. Spottletoe is Chuzzlewit's own niece, isn't she? She was his
favourite once. You may well ask what Spottletoes."

"Now, upon my sacred word," cried Mr. Pecksniff, looking upwards. "This is dreadful. The rapacity of these
people is absolutely frightful!"

"It's not only the Spottletoes either, Tigg," said Slyme,
looking at that gentleman and speaking at Mr. Pecksniff.
"Anthony Chuzzlewit and his son have got wind of it, and

have come down this afternoon. I saw 'em not five minutes ago, when I was waiting round the corner."

"Oh, Mammon, Mammon!" cried Mr. Pecksniff, smiting his forehead.

"So there," said Slyme, regardless of the interruption, "are his brother and another nephew for you, already."

"This is the whole thing, Sir," said Mr. Tigg; "this is the point and purpose at which I was gradually arriving when my friend Slyme here, with six words, hit it full. Mr. Pecksniff, now that your cousin (and Chiv's uncle) has turned up, some steps must be taken to prevent his disappearing again; and, if possible, to counteract the influence which is exercised over him now, by this designing favourite. Everybody who is interested feels it, Sir. The whole family is pouring down to this place. The time has come when individual jealousies and interests must be forgotten for a time, Sir, and union must be made against the common enemy. When the common enemy is routed, you will all set up for yourselves again; every lady and gentleman who has a part in the game, will go in on their own account and bowl away, to the best of their ability, at the testator's wicket; and nobody will be in a worse position than before. Think of it. Don't commit yourself now. You'll find us at the Half Moon and Seven Stars in this village, at any time, and open to any reasonable proposition. Hem! Chiv, my dear fellow, go out and see what sort of a night it is."

Mr. Slyme lost no time in disappearing, and, it is to be presumed, in going round the corner. Mr. Tigg, planting his legs as wide apart as he could be reasonably expected by the most sanguine man to keep them, shook his head at Mr. Pecksniff and smiled.

"We must not be too hard," he said, "upon the little eccentricities of our friend Slyme. You saw him whisper me?"

Mr. Pecksniff had seen him.

"You heard my answer, I think?"

Mr. Pecksniff had heard it.

"Five shillings, eh?" said Mr. Tigg, thoughtfully. "Ah! what an extraordinary fellow! Very moderate too!"

Mr. Pecksniff made no answer.

"Five shillings!" pursued Mr. Tigg, musing: "and to be punctually repaid next week; that's the best of it. You heard that?"

Mr. Pecksniff had not heard that.

"No! You surprise me!" cried Tigg. "That's the cream of the thing, Sir. I never knew that man fail to redeem a promise, in my life. You're not in want of change, are you?"

"No," said Mr. Pecksniff, "thank you. Not at all."

"Just so," returned Mr. Tigg. "If you had been, I'd have got it for you." With that he began to whistle; but a dozen seconds had not elapsed when he stopped short, and, looking earnestly at Mr. Pecksniff, said:

"Perhaps you'd rather not lend Slyme five shillings?"

"I would much rather not," Mr. Pecksniff rejoined.

"Egad!" cried Tigg, gravely nodding his head as if some ground of objection occurred to him at that moment for the first time, "it's very possible you may be right. Would you entertain the same sort of objection to lending *me* five shillings, now?"

"Yes, I couldn't do it, indeed," said Mr. Pecksniff.

"Not even half-a-crown, perhaps?" urged Mr. Tigg.

"Not even half-a-crown."

"Why, then we come," said Mr. Tigg, "to the ridiculously small amount of eighteenpence. Ha! ha!"

"And that," said Mr. Pecksniff, "would be equally objectionable."

On receipt of this assurance, Mr. Tigg shook him heartily by both hands, protesting with much earnestness, that he was one of the most consistent and remarkable men he had ever met, and that he desired the honour of his better acquaintance. He further observed that there were many little characteristics about his friend Slyme, of which he could by no means, as a man of strict honour, approve; but that he was prepared to forgive him all these slight drawbacks, and much more, in consideration of the great pleasure he himself had that day enjoyed in his social intercourse with Mr. Pecksniff, which had given him a far higher and more enduring delight than the successful negotiation of any small loan on the part of his friend could possibly have imparted. With which remarks he would beg leave, he said, to wish Mr. Pecksniff a very good evening. And so he took himself off: as little abashed by his recent failure as any gentleman would desire to be.

The meditations of Mr. Pecksniff that evening at the bar of the Dragon, and that night in his own house, were very serious and grave indeed; the more especially as the intelligence he had received from Messrs. Tigg and Slyme touching the arrival of other members of the family, was fully confirmed on more particular inquiry. For the Spottletoes had actually gone straight to the Dragon, where they were at that moment housed and mounting guard, and where their appearance had occasioned such a vast sensation, that Mrs. Lupin, scenting their errand before they had been under her roof half-an-hour, carried the news herself with all possible secrecy straight to Mr. Pecksniff's house: indeed it was her great caution in doing so which occasioned her to miss that gentleman, who entered at the front door of the Dragon, just as she emerged from the back one. Moreover, Mr. Anthony Chuzzlewit and his son Jonas were economically quartered at the Half Moon and Seven Stars, which was an obscure alehouse; and by the very next coach there came posting to the scene of action, so many other affectionate members of the family (who quarrelled with each other, inside and out, all the way down, to the utter distraction of the coachman) that in less than four-and-twenty hours the scanty tavern accommodation was at a premium, and all the private lodgings in the place, amounting to full four beds and a sofa, rose cent. per cent. in the market.

In a word, things came to that pass that nearly the whole family sat down before the Blue Dragon, and formally invested it; and Martin Chuzzlewit was in a state of siege. But he resisted bravely; refusing to receive all letters, messages, and parcels; obstinately declining to treat with anybody; and holding out no hope or promise of capitulation. Meantime the family forces were perpetually encountering each other in divers parts of the neighbourhood: and, as no one branch of the Chuzzlewit tree had ever been known to agree with another within the memory of man, there was such a skirmishing, and flouting, and snapping off of heads, in the metaphorical sense of that expression; such a bandying of words and calling of names; such an upturning of noses and wrinkling of brows; such a formal interment of good feelings and violent resurrection of ancient grievances; as had never been known in those quiet parts since the earliest record of their civilized existence.

At length, in utter despair and hopelessness, some few

of the belligerents began to speak to each other in only
moderate terms of mutual aggravation; and nearly all addressed themselves with a show of tolerable decency to Mr.
Pecksniff, in recognition of his high character and influential position. Thus, by little and little they made common
cause of Martin Chuzzlewit's obduracy, until it was agreed
—if such a word can be used in connexion with the Chuzzlewits—that there should be a general council and conference held at Mr. Pecksniff's house upon a certain day at
noon: which all members of the family who had brought
themselves within reach of the summons, were forthwith
bidden and invited, solemnly, to attend.

If ever Mr. Pecksniff wore an apostolic look, he wore it
on this memorable day. If ever his unruffled smile proclaimed the words, "I am a messenger of peace!" that
was its mission now. If ever man combined within himself all the mild qualities of the lamb with a considerable
touch of the dove, and not a dash of the crocodile, or the
least possible suggestion of the very mildest seasoning of
the serpent, that man was he. And, Oh, the two Miss
Pecksniffs! Oh, the serene expression on the face of
Charity, which seemed to say, "I know that all my family
have injured me beyond the possibility of reparation, but I
forgive them, for it is my duty so to do!" And, Oh, the
gay simplicity of Mercy: so charming, innocent, and in-
fant-like, that if she had gone out walking by herself, and
it had been a little earlier in the season, the robin-red-
breasts might have covered her with leaves against her will,
believing her to be one of the sweet children in the wood,
come out of it, and issuing forth once more to look for
blackberries in the young freshness of her heart! What
words can paint the Pecksniffs in that trying hour? Oh,
none: for words have naughty company among them, and
the Pecksniffs were all goodness.

But when the company arrived! That was the time.
When Mr. Pecksniff, rising from his seat at the table's
head, with a daughter on either hand, received his guests
in the best parlour and motioned them to chairs, with eyes
so overflowing and countenance so damp with gracious perspiration, that he may be said to have been in a kind of
moist meekness! And the company: the jealous, stony-
hearted, distrustful company, who were all shut up in themselves, and had no faith in anybody, and wouldn't believe

anything, and would no more allow themselves to be softened or lulled asleep by the Pecksniffs than if they had
been so many hedgehogs or porcupines!

First, there was Mr. Spottletoe, who was so bald and
had such big whiskers, that he seemed to have stopped his
hair, by the sudden application of some powerful remedy,
in the very act of falling off his head, and to have fastened
it irrevocably on his face. Then there was Mrs. Spottletoe,
who being much too slim for her years, and of a poetical
constitution, was accustomed to inform her more intimate
friends that the said whiskers were "the lode-star of
her existence;" and who could now, by reason of her
strong affection for her uncle Chuzzlewit, and the shock
it gave her to be suspected of testamentary designs upon
him, do nothing but cry—except moan. Then there were
Anthony Chuzzlewit, and his son Jonas: the face of the
old man so sharpened by the wariness and cunning of
his life, that it seemed to cut him a passage through the
crowded room, as he edged away behind the remotest
chairs; while the son had so well profited by the precept
and example of the father that he looked a year or two the
elder of the twain, as they stood winking their red eyes,
side by side, and whispering to each other, softly. Then
there was the widow of a deceased brother of Mr. Martin
Chuzzlewit, who being almost supernaturally disagreeable,
and having a dreary face and a bony figure and a masculine
voice, was, in right of these qualities, what is commonly
called a strong-minded woman; and who, if she could,
would have established her claim to the title, and have
shown herself, mentally speaking, a perfect Sampson, by
shutting up her brother-in-law in a private madhouse, until
he proved his complete sanity by loving her very much.
Beside her sat her spinster daughters, three in number, and
of gentlemanly deportment, who had so mortified themselves with tight stays, that their tempers were reduced to
something less than their waists, and sharp lacing was expressed in their very noses. Then there was a young gentleman, grand-nephew of Mr. Martin Chuzzlewit, very
dark and very hairy, and apparently born for no particular
purpose but to save looking-glasses the trouble of reflecting
more than just the first idea and sketchy notion of a face,
which had never been carried out. Then there was a solitary female cousin who was remarkable for nothing but

being very deaf, and living by herself, and always having the toothache. Then there was George Chuzzlewit, a gay bachelor cousin, who claimed to be young but had been younger, and was inclined to corpulency, and rather over-fed himself: to that extent, indeed, that his eyes were strained in their sockets, as if with constant surprise; and he had such an obvious disposition to pimples, that the bright spots on his cravat, the rich pattern on his waist-coat, and even his glittering trinkets, seemed to have broken out upon him, and not to have come into existence com-fortably. Last of all, there were present Mr. Chevy Slyme and his friend Tigg. And it is worthy of remark, that although each person present disliked the other mainly be-cause he or she *did* belong to the family, they one and all concurred in hating Mr. Tigg because he didn't.

Such was the pleasant little family circle now assembled in Mr. Pecksniff's best parlour, agreeably prepared to fall foul of Mr. Pecksniff or anybody else who might venture to say anything whatever upon any subject.

"This," said Mr. Pecksniff rising, and looking round upon them, with folded hands, "does me good. It does my daughters good. We thank you for assembling here. We are grateful to you with our whole hearts. It is a blessed distinction that you have conferred upon us, and believe me"—it is impossible to conceive how he smiled here—"we shall not easily forget it."

"I am sorry to interrupt you, Pecksniff," remarked Mr. Spottletoe, with his whiskers in a very portentous state; "but you are assuming too much to yourself, Sir. Who do you imagine has it in contemplation to confer a distinc-tion upon *you*, Sir?"

A general murmur echoed this inquiry, and applauded it.

"If you are about to pursue the course with which you have begun, Sir," pursued Mr. Spottletoe in a great heat, and giving a violent rap on the table with his knuckles, "the sooner you desist, and this assembly separates, the better. I am no stranger, Sir, to your preposterous desire to be regarded as the head of this family, but I can tell *you*, Sir—"

Oh yes, indeed! *He* tell. *He!* What? He was the head, was he? From the strong-minded woman down-wards everybody fell, that instant, upon Mr. Spottletoe, who after vainly attempting to be heard in silence was fain to sit down again, folding his arms and shaking his head, most wrathfully, and giving Mrs. Spottletoe to understand in dumb show that that scoundrel Pecksniff might go on for the present, but he would cut in presently, and annihilate him.

"I am not sorry," said Mr. Pecksniff in resumption of his address, "I am really not sorry that this little incident has happened. It is good to feel that we are met here without disguise. It is good to know that we have no reserve before each other, but are appearing freely in our own characters."

Here, the eldest daughter of the strong-minded woman rose a little way from her seat, and trembling violently from head to foot, more as it seemed with passion than timidity, expressed a general hope that some people *would* appear in their own characters, if it were only for such a proceeding having the attraction of novelty to recommend it; and that when they (meaning the some people before mentioned) talked about their relations, they would be careful to observe who was present in company at the time; otherwise it might come round to those relations ears, in a way they little expected; and as to red noses (she observed) she had yet to learn that a red nose was any disgrace, inasmuch as people neither made nor coloured their own noses, but had that feature provided for them without being first consulted; though even upon that branch of the subject she had great doubts whether certain noses were redder than other noses, or indeed half as red as some. This remark being received with a shrill titter by the two sisters of the speaker, Miss Charity Pecksniff begged with much politeness to be informed whether any of those very low observations were levelled at her; and receiving no more explanatory answer than was conveyed in the adage, "Those the cap fits, let them wear it," immediately commenced a somewhat acrimonious and personal retort, wherein she was much comforted and abetted by her sister Mercy, who laughed at the same with great heartiness: indeed far more naturally than life. And it being quite impossible that any difference of opinion can take place among women without every woman who is within hearing taking active part in it, the strong-minded lady and her two daughters, and Mrs. Spottletoe, and the deaf cousin (who was not at all disqualified from joining in the dispute by reason of

being perfectly unacquainted with its merits), one and all
plunged into the quarrel directly.

The two Miss Pecksniffs being a pretty good match for
the three Miss Chuzzlewits, and all five young ladies having, in the figurative language of the day, a great amount
of steam to dispose of, the altercation would no doubt have
been a long one but for the high valour and prowess of the
strong-minded woman, who, in right of her reputation for
powers of sarcasm, did so belabour and pummel Mrs. Spottletoe with taunting words that that poor lady, before the
engagement was two minutes old, had no refuge but in
tears.   These she shed so plentifully, and so much to the
agitation and grief of Mr. Spottletoe, that that gentleman,
after holding his clenched fist close to Mr. Pecksniff's eyes,
as if it were some natural curiosity from the near inspection whereof he was likely to derive high gratification and
improvement, and after offering (for no particular reason
that anybody could discover) to kick Mr. George Chuzzlewit for, and in consideration of, the trifling sum of sixpence,
took his wife under his arm, and indignantly withdrew.
This diversion, by distracting the attention of the comba-
tants, put an end to the strife, which, after breaking out
afresh some twice or thrice in certain inconsiderable spirts
and dashes, died away in silence.

It was then that Mr. Pecksniff once more rose from his
chair.   It was then that the two Miss Pecksniffs composed
themselves to look as if there were no such beings—not to
say present, but in the whole compass of the world—as the
three Miss Chuzzlewits: while the three Miss Chuzzlewits
became equally unconscious of the existence of the two
Miss Pecksniffs.

"It is to be lamented," said Mr. Pecksniff, with a forgiving recollection of Mr. Spottletoe's fist, "that our friend
should have withdrawn himself so very hastily, though we
have cause for mutual congratulation even in that, since
we are assured that he is not distrustful of us in regard to
anything we may say or do, while he is absent.   Now, that
is very soothing, is it not?"

"Pecksniff," said Anthony, who had been watching the
whole party with peculiar keenness from the first—"don't
you be a hypocrite."

"A what, my good Sir?" demanded Mr. Pecksniff.

"A hypocrite."

"Charity, my dear," said Mr. Pecksniff, "when I take my chamber candlestick to-night, remind me to be more than usually particular in praying for Mr. Anthony Chuzzlewit; who has done me an injustice."

This was said in a very bland voice, and aside, as being addressed to his daughter's private ear. With a cheerfulness of conscience, prompting almost a sprightly demeanour, he then resumed:

"All our thoughts centring in our very dear, but unkind relative, and he being as it were beyond our reach, we are met to-day, really as if we were a funeral party, except—a blessed exception—that there is no body in the house."

The strong-minded lady was not at all sure that this was a blessed exception. Quite the contrary.

"Well, my dear madam!" said Mr. Pecksniff. "Be that as it may, here we are; and being here, we are to consider whether it is possible by any justifiable means—"

"Why, you know as well as I," said the strong-minded lady, "that any means are justifiable in such a case, don't you?"

"Very good, my dear madam, very good—whether it is possible by *any* means, we will say by *any* means, to open the eyes of our valued relative to his present infatuation. Whether it is possible to make him acquainted by any means with the real character and purpose of that young female whose strange, whose very strange position, in reference to himself"—here Mr. Pecksniff sank his voice to an impressive whisper—"really casts a shadow of disgrace and shame upon this family; and who, we know"—here he raised his voice again—"else why is she his companion? harbours the very basest designs upon his weakness and his property."

In their strong feeling on this point, they, who agreed in nothing else, all concurred as one mind. Good Heaven, that she should harbour designs upon his property! The strong-minded lady was for poison, her three daughters were for Bridewell and bread-and-water, and the cousin with the toothache advocated Botany Bay, and the two Miss Pecksniffs suggested flogging. Nobody but Mr. Tigg, who, notwithstanding his extreme shabbiness, was still understood to be in some sort a lady's man, in right of his upper-lip and his frogs, indicated a doubt of the justifiable nature of these measures; and he only ogled the three Miss Chuz-

zlewits with the least admixture of banter in his admiration, as though he would observe, "You are positively
down upon her to too great an extent, my sweet creatures,
upon my soul you are!"

"Now," said Mr. Pecksniff, crossing his two forefingers
in a manner which was at once conciliatory and argumenta-
tive: "I will not upon the one hand, go so far as to say
that she deserves all the inflictions which have been so very
forcibly and hilariously suggested;" one of his ornamental
sentences; "nor will I, upon the other, on any account
compromise my common understanding as a man by making
the assertion that she does not. What I would observe is,
that I think some practical means might be devised of in-
ducing our respected—shall I say our revered—?"

"No!" interposed the strong-minded woman in a loud
voice.

"Then I will not," said Mr. Pecksniff. "You are quite
right, my dear madam, and I appreciate and thank you for
your discriminating objection—our respected relative, to
dispose himself to listen to the promptings of nature, and
not to the—"

"Go on, pa!" cried Mercy.

"Why, the truth is, my dear," said Mr. Pecksniff, smiling upon his assembled kindred, "that I am at a loss for
a word. The name of those fabulous animals (pagan, I
regret to say) who used to sing in the water, has quite
escaped me."

Mr. George Chuzzlewit suggested "Swans."

"No," said Mr. Pecksniff. "Not swans. Very like
swans, too   Thank you."

The nephew with the outline of a countenance, speaking
for the first and last time on that occasion, propounded
"Oysters."

"No," said Mr. Pecksniff, with his own peculiar urbanity,
"nor oysters. But by no means unlike oysters; a very excellent idea; thank you, my dear Sir, very much. Wait!
Sirens. Dear me! sirens, of course. I think, I say, that
means might be devised of disposing our respected relative
to listen to the promptings of nature, and not to the siren-
like delusions of art. Now we must not lose sight of the
fact that our esteemed friend has a grandson, to whom he
was, until lately, very much attached, and whom I could
have wished to see here to-day, for I have a real and deep

regard for him. A fine young man: a very fine young man! I would submit to you, whether we might not remove Mr. Chuzzlewit's distrust of us, and vindicate our own disinterestedness by—"

"If Mr. George Chuzzlewit has anything to say to *me*," interposed the strong-minded woman, sternly, "I beg him to speak out, like a man; and not to look at me and my daughters as if he could eat us."

"As to looking, I have heard it said, Mrs. Ned," returned Mr. George, angrily, "that a cat is free to contemplate a monarch; and therefore I hope I have some right, having been born a member of this family, to look at a person who only came into it by marriage. As to eating, I beg to say, whatever bitterness your jealousies and disappointed expectations may suggest to you, that I am not a cannibal, ma'am."

"I don't know that!" cried the strong-minded woman.

"At all events, if I was a cannibal," said Mr. George Chuzzlewit, greatly stimulated by this retort, "I think it would occur to me that a lady who had outlived three husbands and suffered so very little from their loss, must be most uncommonly tough."

The strong-minded woman immediately rose.

"And I will further add," said Mr. George, nodding his head violently at every second syllable; "naming no names, and therefore hurting nobody but those whose consciences tell them they are alluded to, that I think it would be much more decent and becoming, if those who hooked and crooked themselves into this family by getting on the blind side of some of its members before marriage, and manslaughtering them afterwards by crowing over them to that strong pitch that they were glad to die, would refrain from acting the part of vultures in regard to other members of his family who are living. I think it would be full as well, if not better, if those individuals would keep at home, contenting themselves with what they have got (luckily for them) already; instead of hovering about, and thrusting their fingers into, a family pie; which they flavour much more than enough, I can tell them, when they are fifty miles away."

"I might have been prepared for this!" cried the strong-minded woman, looking about her with a disdainful smile as she moved towards the door, followed by her three daughters: "indeed I was fully prepared for it, from the first. What else could I expect in such an atmosphere as this!"

"Don't direct your half-pay-officer's gaze at me, ma'am, if you please," interposed Miss Charity; "for I won't bear it."

This was a smart stab at a pension enjoyed by the strong-minded woman, during her second widowhood and before her last coverture. It told immensely.

"I passed from the memory of a grateful country, you very miserable minx," said Mrs. Ned, "when I entered this family; and I feel now, though I did not feel then, that it served me right, and that I lost my claim upon the United Kingdom of Great Britain and Ireland when I so degraded myself. Now my dears, if you're quite ready, and have sufficiently improved yourselves by taking to heart the genteel example of these two young ladies, I think we'll go. Mr. Pecksniff, we are very much obliged to you, really. We came to be entertained, and you have far surpassed our utmost expectations, in the amusement you have provided for us. Thank you. Good bye."

With such departing words, did this strong-minded female paralyse the Pecksniffian energies; and so she swept out of the room, and out of the house, attended by her daughters, who, as with one accord, elevated their three noses in the air, and joined in a contemptuous titter. As they passed the parlour window on the outside, they were seen to counterfeit a perfect transport of delight among themselves; and with this final blow and great discouragement for those within, they vanished.

Before Mr. Pecksniff or any of his remaining visitors could offer a remark, another figure passed this window, coming, at a great rate, in the opposite direction: and immediately afterwards, Mr. Spottletoe burst into the chamber. Compared with his present state of heat, he had gone out a man of snow or ice. His head distilled such oil upon his whiskers, that they were rich and clogged with unctuous drops; his face was violently inflamed, his limbs trembled; and he gasped and strove for breath.

"My good Sir!" cried Mr. Pecksniff.

"Oh yes!" returned the other: "Oh yes, certainly! Oh to be sure! Oh of course! You hear him? You hear him? all of you!"

"What's the matter!" cried several voices.

"Oh nothing!" cried Spottletoe, still gasping. "Nothing at all! It's of no consequence! Ask him! *He*'ll tell you!"

"I do not understand our friend," said Mr. Pecksniff, looking about him in utter amazement. "I assure you that he is quite unintelligible to me."

"Unintelligible, Sir!" cried the other. "Unintelligible! Do you mean to say, Sir, that you don't know what has happened! That you haven't decoyed us here, and laid a plot and a plan against us! Will you venture to say that you didn't know Mr. Chuzzlewit was going, Sir, and that you don't know he's gone, Sir?"

"Gone!" was the general cry.

"Gone," echoed Mr. Spottletoe. "Gone while we were sitting here. Gone. Nobody knows where he's gone. Oh of course not! Nobody knew he was going. Oh of course not! The landlady thought up to the very last moment that they were merely going for a ride; she had no other suspicion. Oh of course not! She's not this fellow's creature. Oh of course not!"

Adding to these exclamations a kind of ironical howl, and gazing upon the company for one brief instant afterwards, in a sudden silence, the irritated gentleman started off again at the same tremendous pace, and was seen no more.

It was in vain for Mr. Pecksniff to assure them that this new and opportune evasion of the family was at least as great a shock and surprise to him, as to anybody else. Of all the bullyings and denunciations that were ever heaped on one unlucky head, none can ever have exceeded in energy and heartiness those with which he was complimented by each of his remaining relatives, singly, upon bidding him farewell.

The moral position taken by Mr. Tigg was something quite tremendous; and the deaf cousin, who had had the complicated aggravation of seeing all the proceedings and hearing nothing but the catastrophe, actually scraped her shoes upon the scraper, and afterwards distributed impressions of them all over the top step, in token that she shook the dust from her feet before quitting that dissembling and perfidious mansion.

Mr. Pecksniff had, in short, but one comfort, and that

5

was the knowledge that all these his relations and friends had hated him to the very utmost extent before; and that he, for his part, had not distributed among them any more love, than, with his ample capital in that respect, he could comfortably afford to part with. This view of his affairs yielded him great consolation; and the fact deserves to be noted, as showing with what ease a good man may be consoled under circumstances of failure and disappointment.

CHAPTER V.

CONTAINING A FULL ACCOUNT OF THE INSTALLATION OF MR. PECKSNIFF'S NEW PUPIL INTO THE BOSOM OF MR. PECKSNIFF'S FAMILY. WITH ALL THE FESTIVITIES HELD ON THAT OCCASION, AND THE GREAT ENJOYMENT OF MR. PINCH.

THE best of architects and land surveyors kept a horse, in whom the enemies already mentioned more than once in these pages, pretended to detect a fanciful resemblance to his master. Not in his outward person, for he was a rawboned, haggard horse, always on a much shorter allowance of corn than Mr. Pecksniff; but in his moral character, wherein, said they, he was full of promise, but of no performance. He was always, in a manner, going to go, and never going. When at his slowest rate of travelling, he would sometimes lift up his legs so high, and display such mighty action, that it was difficult to believe he was doing less than fourteen miles an hour; and he was for ever so perfectly satisfied with his own speed, and so little disconcerted by opportunities of comparing himself with the fastest trotters, that the illusion was the more difficult of resistance. He was a kind of animal who infused into the breasts of strangers a lively sense of hope, and possessed all those who knew him better with a grim despair. In what respect, having these points of character, he might be fairly likened to his master, that good man's slanderers only can explain. But it is a melancholy truth, and a deplorable instance of the uncharitableness of the world, that they made the comparison.

In this horse, and the hooded vehicle, whatever its proper name might be, to which he was usually harnessed —it was more like a gig with a tumor, than anything else —all Mr. Pinch's thoughts and wishes centred, one bright frosty morning: for with this gallant equipage he was about to drive to Salisbury alone, there to meet with the new pupil, and thence to bring him home in triumph.

Blessings on thy simple heart, Tom Pinch, how proudly dost thou button up thy scanty coat, called by a sad misnomer, for these many years, a "great" one; and how thoroughly as with thy cheerful voice thou pleasantly adjurest Sam the hostler "not to let him go yet," dost thou believe that quadruped desires to go, and would go if he might! Who could repress a smile—of love for thee, Tom Pinch, and not in jest at thy expense, for thou art poor enough already, Heaven knows—to think that such a holiday as lies before thee, should awaken that quick flow and hurry of the spirits, in which thou settest down again, almost untasted, on the kitchen window-sill, that great white mug (put by, by thy own hands, last night, that breakfast might not hold thee late), and layest yonder crust upon the seat beside thee, to be eaten on the road, when thou art calmer in thy high rejoicing! Who, as thou drivest off, a happy man, and noddest with a grateful lovingness to Pecksniff in his nightcap at his chamber-window, would not cry: "Heaven speed thee, Tom, and send that thou wert going off for ever to some quiet home where thou mightst live at peace, and sorrow should not touch thee!"

What better time for driving, riding, walking, moving through the air by any means, than a fresh, frosty morning, when hope runs cheerily through the veins with the brisk blood, and tingles in the frame from head to foot! This was the glad commencement of a bracing day in early winter, such as may put the languid summer season (speaking of it when it can be had) to the blush, and shame the spring for being sometimes cold by halves. The sheep-bells rang as clearly in the vigorous air, as if they felt its wholesome influence like living creatures; the trees, in lieu of leaves or blossoms, shed upon the ground a frosty rime that sparkled as it fell, and might have been the dust of diamonds—so it was, to Tom. From cottage chimneys, smoke went streaming up high, high, as if the earth had lost its grossness, being so fair, and must not be oppressed by heavy vapour. The crust of ice on the else rippling brook, was so transparent and so thin in texture, that the lively water might, of its own free will, have stopped—in Tom's glad mind it had—to look upon the lovely morning. And lest the sun should break this charm too eagerly, there moved between him and the ground a mist like that which waits upon the moon on summer nights—the very same to Tom—and wooed him to dissolve it gently.

Tom Pinch went on; not fast, but with a sense of rapid motion, which did just as well; and as he went, all kinds of things occurred to keep him happy. Thus when he came within sight of the turnpike, and was—Oh a long way off!—he saw the tollman's wife, who had that moment checked a waggon, run back into the little house again like mad, to say (he knew) that Mr. Pinch was coming up. And he was right, for when he drew within hail of the gate, forth rushed the tollman's children, shrieking in tiny chorus, "Mr. Pinch!"—to Tom's intense delight. The very tollman, though an ugly chap in general, and one whom folks were rather shy of handling, came out himself to take the toll, and give him rough good morning: and what with all this, and a glimpse of the family breakfast on a little round table before the fire, the crust Tom Pinch had brought away with him acquired as rich a flavour as though it had been cut from a fairy loaf.

But there was more than this. It was not only the married people and the children who gave Tom Pinch a welcome as he passed. No, no. Sparkling eyes and snowy breasts came hurriedly to many an upper casement as he clattered by, and gave him back his greeting: not stinted either, but sevenfold, good measure. They were all merry. They all laughed. And some of the wickedest among them even kissed their hands as Tom looked back. For who minded poor Mr. Pinch? There was no harm in *him*.

And now the morning grew so fair, and all things were so wide awake and gay, that the sun seeming to say—Tom had no doubt he said—"I can't stand it any longer: I must have a look"—streamed out in radiant majesty. The mist, too shy and gentle for such lusty company, fled off, quite scared, before it; and as it swept away, the hills and mounds and distant pasture lands, teeming with placid sheep and noisy crows, came out as bright as though they were unrolled brand new for the occasion. In compliment

to which discovery, the brook stood still no longer, but ran
briskly off to bear the tidings to the water-mill, three miles
away.

Mr. Pinch was jogging along, full of pleasant thoughts
and cheerful influences, when he saw, upon the path before
him, going in the same direction with himself, a traveller
on foot, who walked with a light, quick step, and sang as
he went—for certain in a very loud voice, but not unmusi-
cally. He was a young fellow, of some five or six-and-
twenty perhaps, and was drest in such a free and fly-away
fashion, that the long ends of his loose red neckcloth were
streaming out behind him quite as often as before; and the
bunch of bright winter berries in the buttonhole of his vel-
veteen coat, was as visible to Mr. Pinch's rearward observation, as if he had worn that garment wrong side foremost.
He continued to sing with so much energy, that he did not
hear the sound of wheels until it was close behind him;
when he turned a whimsical face and very merry pair of
blue eyes on Mr. Pinch, and checked himself directly.

"Why, Mark!" said Tom Pinch, stopping. "Who'd
have thought of seeing you here? Well! this is surprising!"

Mark touched his hat, and said, with a very sudden de-
crease of vivacity, that he was going to Salisbury.

"And how spruce you are, too!" said Mr. Pinch, surveying him with great pleasure. "Really I didn't think
you were half such a tight-made fellow, Mark!"

"Thankee, Mr. Pinch. Pretty well for that, I believe.
It's not my fault, you know. With regard to being spruce,
Sir, that's where it is, you see." And here he looked par-
ticularly gloomy.

"Where what is?" Mr. Pinch demanded.

"Where the aggravation of it is. Any man may be in
good spirits and good temper when he's well drest. There
ain't much credit in that. If I was very ragged and very
jolly, then I should begin to feel I had gained a point, Mr.
Pinch."

"So you were singing just now, to bear up, as it were,
against being well dressed, eh, Mark?" said Pinch.

"Your conversation's always equal to print, Sir," rejoined Mark, with a broad grin. "That was it."

"Well!" cried Pinch, "you are the strangest young
man, Mark, I ever knew in my life. I always thought so;

but now I am quite certain of it. I am going to Salisbury,
too. Will you get in? I shall be very glad of your company."

The young fellow made his acknowledgments and accepted the offer; stepping into the carriage directly, and
seating himself on the very edge of the seat with his body
half out of it, to express his being there on sufferance, and
by the politeness of Mr. Pinch. As they went along, the
conversation proceeded after this manner.

"I more than half believed, just now, seeing you so very
smart," said Pinch, "that you must be going to be married,
Mark."

"Well, Sir, I've thought of that, too," he replied.
"There might be some credit in being jolly with a wife,
'specially if the children had the measles and that, and
was very fractious indeed. But I'm a'most afraid to try
it. I don't see my way clear."

"You're not very fond of anybody, perhaps?" said
Pinch.

"Not particular, Sir, I think."

"But the way would be, you know, Mark, according to
your views of things," said Mr. Pinch, "to marry somebody you didn't like, and who was very disagreeable."

"So it would, Sir; but that might be carrying out a principle a little too far, mightn't it?"

"Perhaps it might," said Mr. Pinch. At which they
both laughed gaily.

"Lord bless you, Sir," said Mark, "you don't half know
me, though. I don't believe there ever was a man as could
come out so strong under circumstances that would make
other men miserable, as I could, if I could only get a
chance. But I can't get a chance. It's my opinion, that
nobody never will know half of what's in me, unless
something very unexpected turns up. And I don't see
any prospect of that. I'm a going to leave the Dragon,
Sir."

"Going to leave the Dragon!" cried Mr. Pinch, looking
at him with great astonishment. "Why, Mark, you take
my breath away!"

"Yes, Sir," he rejoined, looking straight before him and
a long way off, as men do sometimes when they cogitate
profoundly. "What's the use of my stopping at the
Dragon? It an't at all the sort of place for *me*. When I

left London (I'm a Kentish man by birth, though), and took that sitivation here, I quite made up my mind that it was the dullest little out-of-the-way corner in England, and that there would be some credit in being jolly under such circumstances. But, Lord, there's no dulness at the Dragon! Skittles, cricket, quoits, nine-pins, comic songs, choruses, company round the chimney corner every winter's evening—any man could be jolly at the Dragon. There's no credit in *that*."

"But if common report be true for once, Mark, as I think it is, being able to confirm it by what I know myself," said Mr. Pinch, "you are the cause of half this merriment, and set it going."

"There may be something in that, too, Sir," answered Mark. "But that's no consolation."

"Well!" said Mr. Pinch, after a short silence, his usually subdued tone being even more subdued than ever. "I can hardly think enough of what you tell me. Why, what will become of Mrs. Lupin, Mark?"

Mark looked more fixedly before him, and further off still, as he answered that he didn't suppose it would be much of an object to her. There were plenty of smart young fellows as would be glad of the place. He knew a dozen himself.

"That's probable enough," said Mr. Pinch, "but I am not at all sure that Mrs. Lupin would be glad of them. Why, I always supposed that Mrs. Lupin and you would make a match of it, Mark: and so did every one, as far as I know."

"I never," Mark replied, in some confusion, "said nothing as was in a direct way courting-like to her, nor she to me, but I don't know what I mightn't do one of these odd times, and what she mightn't say in answer. Well, Sir, *that* wouldn't suit."

"Not to be landlord of the Dragon, Mark?" cried Mr. Pinch.

"No Sir, certainly not," returned the other, withdrawing his gaze from the horizon, and looking at his fellow-traveller. "Why, that would be the ruin of a man like me. I go and sit down comfortably for life, and no man never finds me out. What would be the credit of the landlord of the Dragon's being jolly? Why, he couldn't help it, if he tried."

"Does Mrs. Lupin know you are going to leave her?"
Mr. Pinch enquired.

"I haven't broke it to her yet, Sir, but I must. I'm
looking out this morning for something new and suitable,"
he said, nodding towards the city.

"What kind of thing now?" Mr. Pinch demanded.

"I was thinking," Mark replied, "of something in the
grave-digging way."

"Good Gracious, Mark!" cried Mr. Pinch.

"It's a good damp, wormy sort of business, Sir," said
Mark, shaking his head, argumentatively, "and there
might be some credit in being jolly, with one's mind in
that pursuit, unless grave-diggers is usually given that
way; which would be a drawback. You don't happen to
know how that is, in general, do you, Sir?"

"No," said Mr. Pinch, "I don't indeed. I never
thought upon the subject."

"In case of that not turning out as well as one could
wish, you know," said Mark, musing again, "there's other
businesses. Undertaking now. That's gloomy. There
might be credit to be gained there. A broker's man in a
poor neighbourhood wouldn't be bad perhaps. A jailor
sees a deal of misery. A doctor's man is in the very midst
of murder. A bailiff's an't a lively office nat'rally. Even
a tax-gatherer must find his feelings rather worked upon,
at times. There's lots of trades, in which I should have
an opportunity, I think?"

Mr. Pinch was so perfectly overwhelmed by these remarks that he could do nothing but occasionally exchange
a word or two on some indifferent subject, and cast sidelong
glances at the bright face of his odd friend (who seemed
quite unconscious of his observation), until they reached a
certain corner of the road, close upon the outskirts of the
city, when Mark said he would jump down there, if he
pleased.

"But bless my soul, Mark," said Mr. Pinch, who in the
progress of his observation just then made the discovery
that the bosom of his companion's shirt was as much exposed as if it were Midsummer, and was ruffled by every
breath of air, "why don't you wear a waistcoat?"

"What's the good of one, Sir?" asked Mark.

"Good of one?" said Mr. Pinch. "Why, to keep your
chest warm."

"Lord love you, Sir!" cried Mark, "you don't know me. *My* chest don't want no warming. Even if it did, what would no waistcoat bring it to? Inflammation of the lungs, perhaps? Well, there'd be some credit in being jolly, with an inflammation of the lungs."

As Mr. Pinch returned no other answer than such as was conveyed in his drawing his breath very hard, and opening his eyes very wide, and nodding his head very much, Mark thanked him for his ride, and without troubling him to stop, jumped lightly down. And away he fluttered, with his red neckerchief, and his open coat, down a cross-lane: turning back from time to time to nod to Mr. Pinch, and looking one of the most careless, good-humoured, comical fellows in life. His late companion, with a thoughtful face, pursued his way to Salisbury.

Mr. Pinch had a shrewd notion that Salisbury was a very desperate sort of place; an exceeding wild and dissipated city; and when he had put up the horse, and given the hostler to understand that he would look in again in the course of an hour or two to see him take his corn, he set forth on a stroll about the streets with a vague and not unpleasant idea that they teemed with all kinds of mystery and bedevilment. To one of his quiet habits this little delusion was greatly assisted by the circumstance of its being market-day, and the thoroughfares about the market-place being filled with carts, horses, donkeys, baskets, waggons, garden-stuff, meat, tripe, pies, poultry, and hucksters' wares of every opposite description and possible variety of character. Then there were young farmers and old farmers, with smock-frocks, brown great-coats, drab great-coats, red worsted comforters, leather-leggings, wonderful shaped hats, hunting-whips, and rough sticks, standing about in groups, or talking noisily together on the tavern steps, or paying and receiving huge amounts of greasy wealth, with the assistance of such bulky pocket-books that when they were in their pockets it was apoplexy to get them out, and when they were out, it was spasms to get them in again. Also there were farmers' wives in beaver bonnets and red cloaks, riding shaggy horses purged of all earthly passions, who went soberly into all manner of places without desiring to know why, and who, if required, would have stood stock still in a china-shop, with a complete dinner-service at each hoof. Also a great many dogs, who were strongly

interested in the state of the market and the bargains of
their masters; and a great confusion of tongues, both brute
and human.

Mr. Pinch regarded everything exposed for sale with
great delight, and was particularly struck by the itinerant
cutlery, which he considered of the very keenest kind, insomuch that he purchased a pocket knife with seven blades
in it, and not a cut (as he afterwards found out) among
them. When he had exhausted the market-place, and
watched the farmers safe into the market dinner, he went
back to look after the horse. Having seen him eat unto
his heart's content, he issued forth again, to wander round
the town and regale himself with the shop windows: previously taking a long stare at the bank, and wondering in
what direction underground, the caverns might be, where
they kept the money; and turning to look back at one or
two young men who passed him, whom he knew to be arti-
cled to solicitors in the town; and who had a sort of fearful interest in his eyes, as jolly dogs who knew a thing or
two, and kept it up tremendously.

But the shops. First of all, there were the jewellers'
shops, with all the treasures of the earth displayed therein,
and such large silver watches hanging up in every pane of
glass, that if they were anything but first-rate goers it certainly was not because the works could decently complain
of want of room. In good sooth they were big enough,
and perhaps, as the saying is, ugly enough, to be the most
correct of all mechanical performers; in Mr. Pinch's eyes,
however, they were smaller than Geneva ware; and when
he saw one very bloated watch announced as a repeater
gifted with the uncommon power of striking every quarter
of an hour inside the pocket of its happy owner, he almost
wished that he were rich enough to buy it.

But what were even gold and silver, precious stones and
clockwork, to the bookshops, whence a pleasant smell of
paper freshly pressed came issuing forth, awakening instant recollections of some new grammar had at school,
long time ago, with "Master Pinch, Grove House Acade-
my," inscribed in faultless writing on the fly-leaf! That
whiff of Russia leather, too, and all those rows on rows of
volumes, neatly ranged within—what happiness did they
suggest! And in the window were the spick-and-span new
works from London, with the title-pages, and sometimes

even the first page of the first chapter, laid wide open:
tempting unwary men to begin to read the book, and then,
in the impossibility of turning over, to rush blindly in, and
buy it. Here too were the dainty frontispiece and trim
vignette, pointing like hand-posts on the outskirts of great
cities to the rich stock of incident beyond; and store of
books, with many a grave portrait and time-honoured name,
whose matter he knew well, and would have given mines
to have, in any form, upon the narrow shelf beside his bed
at Mr. Pecksniff's. What a heart-breaking shop it was!

There was another; not quite so bad at first, but still a trying shop; where children's books were sold, and where
poor Robinson Crusoe stood alone in his might, with dog
and hatchet, goat-skin cap and fowling-pieces: calmly surveying Philip Quarll and the host of imitators round him,
and calling Mr. Pinch to witness that he, of all the crowd,
impressed one solitary foot-print on the shore of boyish
memory, whereof the tread of generations should not stir
the lightest grain of sand. And there too were the Per-
sian tales, with flying chests, and students of enchanted
books shut up for years in caverns: and there too was Abu-
dah, the merchant, with the terrible little old woman hob-
bling out of the box in his bedroom: and there the mighty
talisman—the rare Arabian Nights—with Cassim Baba,
divided by four, like the ghost of a dreadful sum, hanging
up, all gory, in the robbers' cave   Which matchless won-
ders, coming fast on Mr. Pinch's mind, did so rub up and
chafe that wonderful lamp within him, that when he
turned his face towards the busy street, a crowd of phan-
toms waited on his pleasure, and he lived again, with new
delight, the happy days before the Pecksniff era.

He had less interest now in the chemists' shops, with
their great glowing bottles (with smaller repositories of
brightness in their very stoppers); and in their agreeable
compromises between medicine and perfumery, in the shape
of toothsome lozenges and virgin honey. Neither had he
the least regard (but he never had much) for the tailors',
where the newest metropolitan waistcoat patterns were
hanging up, which by some strange transformation always
looked amazing there, and never appeared at all like the
same thing anywhere else. But he stopped to read the
playbill at the theatre, and surveyed the doorway with a
kind of awe, which was not diminished when a sallow gen-

tleman with long dark hair came out, and told a boy to
run home to his lodgings and bring down his broadsword.
Mr. Pinch stood rooted to the spot on hearing this, and
might have stood there until dark, but that the old cathedral bell began to ring for vesper service, on which he tore
himself away.

Now, the organist's assistant was a friend of Mr. Pinch's,
which was a good thing, for he too was a very quiet, gentle
soul, and had been, like Tom, a kind of old-fashioned boy
at school, though well-liked by the noisy fellows too. As
good luck would have it (Tom always said he had great
good luck) the assistant chanced that very afternoon to be
on duty by himself, with no one in the dusty organ-loft but
Tom: so while he played, Tom helped him with the stops;
and finally, the service being just over, Tom took the organ
himself. It was then turning dark, and the yellow light
that streamed in through the ancient windows in the choir
was mingled with a murky red. As the grand tones resounded through the church, they seemed, to Tom, to find
an echo in the depth of every ancient tomb, no less than in
the deep mystery of his own heart. Great thoughts and
hopes came crowding on his mind as the rich music rolled
upon the air, and yet among them—something more grave
and solemn in their purpose, but the same—were all the
images of that day, down to its very lightest recollection of
childhood. The feeling that the sounds awakened, in the
moment of their existence, seemed to include his whole life
and being; and as the surrounding realities of stone and
wood and glass grew dimmer in the darkness, these visions
grew so much the brighter that Tom might have forgotten
the new pupil and the expectant master, and have sat
there pouring out his grateful heart till midnight, but for
a very earthy old verger insisting on locking up the cathedral forthwith. So he took leave of his friend, with many
thanks, groped his way out, as well as he could, into the
now lamp-lighted streets, and hurried off to get his dinner.

All the farmers being by this time jogging homewards,
there was nobody in the sanded parlour of the tavern where
he had left the horse; so he had his little table drawn out
close before the fire, and fell to work upon a well-cooked
steak and smoking hot potatoes, with a strong appreciation
of their excellence, and a very keen sense of enjoyment.
Beside him, too, there stood a jug of most stupendous

Wiltshire beer; and the effect of the whole was so transcendent, that he was obliged every now and then to lay down his knife and fork, rub his hands, and think about it. By the time the cheese and celery came, Mr. Pinch had taken a book out of his pocket, and could afford to trifle with the viands; now eating a little, now drinking a little, now reading a little, and now stopping to wonder what sort of a young man the new pupil would turn out to be. He had passed from this latter theme and was deep in his book again, when the door opened, and another guest came in, bringing with him such a quantity of cold air, that he positively seemed at first to put the fire out.

"Very hard frost to-night, Sir," said the new-comer, couteously acknowledging Mr. Pinch's withdrawal of the little table, that he might have place. "Don't disturb yourself, I beg."

Though he said this with a vast amount of consideration for Mr. Pinch's comfort, he dragged one of the great leather-bottomed chairs to the very centre of the hearth, notwithstanding; and sat down in front of the fire, with a foot on each hob.

"My feet are quite numbed. Ah! Bitter cold to be sure."

"You have been in the air some considerable time, I dare say?" said Mr. Pinch.

"All day. Outside a coach, too."

"That accounts for his making the room so cool," thought Mr. Pinch. "Poor fellow! How thoroughly chilled he must be!"

The stranger became thoughtful, likewise, and sat for five or ten minutes looking at the fire in silence. At length he rose and divested himself of his shawl and great-coat, which (far different from Mr. Pinch's) was a very warm and thick one; but he was not a whit more conversational out of his great-coat than in it, for he sat down again in the same place and attitude, and leaning back in his chair, began to bite his nails. He was young—one-and-twenty, perhaps—and handsome; with a keen dark eye, and a quickness of look and manner which made Tom sensible of a great contrast in his own bearing, and caused him to feel even more shy than usual.

There was a clock in the room, which the stranger often turned to look at. Tom made frequent reference to it also: partly from a nervous sympathy with its taciturn companion; and partly because the new pupil was to inquire for him at half after six, and the hands were getting on towards that hour. Whenever the stranger caught him looking at this clock, a kind of confusion came upon Tom as if he had been found out in something; and it was a perception of his uneasiness which caused the younger man to say, perhaps, with a smile:

"We both appear to be rather particular about the time. The fact is, I have an engagement to meet a gentleman here."

"So have I," said Mr. Pinch.

"At half-past six," said the stranger.

"At half-past six," said Tom in the very same breath; whereupon the other looked at him with some surprise.

"The young gentleman, I expect," remarked Tom, timidly, "was to inquire at that time for a person of the name of Pinch."

"Dear me!" cried the other, jumping up. "And I have been keeping the fire from you all this while! I had no idea you were Mr. Pinch. I am the Mr. Martin for whom you were to inquire. Pray excuse me. How do you do? Oh, do draw nearer, pray!"

"Thank you," said Tom, "thank you. I am not at all cold; and you are; and we have a cold ride before us. Well, if you wish it, I will. I—I am very glad," said Tom, smiling with an embarrassed frankness peculiarly his, and which was as plainly a confession of his own imperfections, and an appeal to the kindness of the person he addressed, as if he had drawn one up in simple language and committed it to paper: "I am very glad indeed that you turn out to be the party I expected. I was thinking, but a minute ago, that I could wish him to be like you."

"I am very glad to hear it," returned Martin, shaking hands with him again; "for I assure you, I was thinking there could be no such luck as Mr. Pinch's turning out like you."

"No, really!" said Tom, with great pleasure. "Are you serious?"

"Upon my word I am," replied his new acquaintance. "You and I will get on excellently well, I know: which it's no small relief to me to feel, for to tell you the truth, I am not at all the sort of fellow who could get on with everybody, and that's the point on which I had the greatest doubts. But they're quite relieved now.—Do me the favour to ring the bell, will you?"

Mr. Pinch rose, and complied with great alacrity—the handle hung just over Martin's head, as he warmed himself—and listened with a smiling face to what his friend went on to say. It was:

"If you like punch, you'll allow me to order a glass a-piece, as hot as it can be made, that we may usher in our friendship in a becoming manner. To let you into a secret, Mr. Pinch, I never was so much in want of something warm and cheering in my life; but I didn't like to run the chance of being found drinking it, without knowing what kind of person you were; for first impressions, you know, often go a long ways and last a long time."

Mr. Pinch assented, and the punch was ordered. In due course it came: hot and strong. After drinking to each other in the steaming mixture, they became quite confidential.

"I'm a sort of relation of Pecksniff's, you know," said the young man.

"Indeed!" cried Mr. Pinch.

"Yes. My grandfather is his cousin, so he's kith and kin to me, somehow, if you can make that out. *I* can't."

"Then Martin is your Christian name?" said Mr. Pinch, thoughtfully. "Oh!"

"Of course it is," returned his friend: "I wish it was my surname, for my own is not a very pretty one, and it takes a long time to sign. Chuzzlewit is my name."

"Dear me!" cried Mr. Pinch, with an involuntary start.

"You're not surprised at my having two names, I suppose?" returned the other, setting his glass to his lips. "Most people have."

"Oh, no," said Mr. Pinch, "not at all. Oh dear no! Well!" And then remembering that Mr. Pecksniff had privately cautioned him to say nothing in reference to the old gentleman of the same name who had lodged at the Dragon, but to reserve all mention of that person for him, he had no better means of hiding his confusion, than by raising his own glass to his mouth. They looked at each other out of their respective tumblers, for a few seconds, and then put them down empty.

"I told them in the stable to be ready for us ten minutes

ago," said Mr. Pinch, glancing at the clock. "Shall we
go?"

"If you please," returned the other.

"Would you like to drive?" said Mr. Pinch; his whole
face beaming with a consciousness of the splendour of his
offer. "You shall, if you wish."

"Why, that depends, Mr. Pinch," said Martin, laughing, "upon what sort of horse you have. Because if he's
a bad one, I would rather keep my hands warm by holding
them comfortably in my great-coat pockets."

He appeared to think this such a good joke, that Mr.
Pinch was quite sure it must be a capital one. Accordingly, he laughed too, and was fully persuaded that he
enjoyed it very much. Then he settled his bill, and Mr.
Chuzzlewit paid for the punch; and having wrapped themselves up, to the extent of their respective means, they
went out together to the front door, where Mr. Pecksniff's
property stopped the way.

"I won't drive, thank you, Mr. Pinch," said Martin, getting into the sitter's place. "By-the-bye, there's a box of
mine. Can we manage to take it?"

"Oh, certainly," said Tom. "Put it in, Dick, anywhere!"

It was not precisely of that convenient size which would
admit of its being squeezed into any odd corner, but Dick
the hostler got it in somehow, and Mr. Chuzzlewit helped
him. It was all on Mr. Pinch's side, and Mr. Chuzzlewit
said he was very much afraid it would encumber him; to
which Tom said, "Not at all;" though it forced him into
such an awkward position that he had much ado to see
anything but his own knees. But it is an ill wind that
blows nobody any good; and the wisdom of the saying was
verified in this instance; for the cold air came from Mr.
Pinch's side of the carriage, and by interposing a perfect
wall of box and man between it and the new pupil, he
shielded that young gentleman effectually: which was a
great comfort.

It was a clear evening, with a bright moon. The whole
landscape was silvered by its light and by the hoar-frost;
and everything looked exquisitely beautiful. At first, the
great serenity and peace through which they travelled, disposed them both to silence; but in a very short time the
punch within them and the healthful air without, made

them loquacious, and they talked incessantly. When they were half-way home, and stopped to give the horse some water, Martin (who was very generous with his money) ordered another glass of punch, which they drank between them, and which had not the effect of making them less conversational than before. Their principal topic of discourse was naturally Mr. Pecksniff and his family; of whom, and of the great obligations they had heaped upon him, Tom Pinch, with the tears standing in his eyes, drew such a picture, as would have inclined any one of common feeling almost to revere them: and of which Mr. Pecksniff had not the slightest foresight or preconceived idea, or he certainly (being very humble) would not have sent Tom Pinch to bring the pupil home.

In this way they went on, and on, and on—in the language of the story-books—until at last the village lights appeared before them, and the church spire cast a long reflection on the grave-yard grass: as if it were a dial (alas, the truest in the world!) marking, whatever light shone out of Heaven, the flight of days and weeks and years, by some new shadow on that solemn ground.

"A pretty church!" said Martin, observing that his companion slackened the slack pace of the horse, as they approached.

"Is it not?" cried Tom, with great pride. "There's the sweetest little organ there you ever heard. I play it for them."

"Indeed?" said Martin. "It is hardly worth the trouble, I should think. What do you get for that, now?"

"Nothing," answered Tom.

"Well," returned his friend, "you *are* a very strange fellow!"

To which remark there succeeded a brief silence.

"When I say nothing," observed Mr. Pinch, cheerfully, "I am wrong, and don't say what I mean, because I get a great deal of pleasure from it, and the means of passing some of the happiest hours I know. It led to something else the other day—but you will not care to hear about that I dare say?"

"Oh, yes, I shall. What?"

"It led to my seeing," said Tom, in a lower voice, "one of the loveliest and most beautiful faces you can possibly picture to yourself."

6

"And yet I am able to picture a beautiful one," said his friend, thoughtfully, "or should be, if I have any memory."

"She came," said Tom, laying his hand upon the other's arm, "for the first time, very early in the morning, when it was hardly light; and when I saw her, over my shoulder, standing just within the porch, I turned quite cold, almost believing her to be a spirit. A moment's reflection got the better of that of course, and fortunately it came to my relief so soon, that I didn't leave off playing."

"Why fortunately?"

"Why? Because she stood there, listening. I had my spectacles on, and saw her through the chinks in the curtains as plainly as I see you; and she was beautiful. After a while she glided off, and I continued to play until she was out of hearing."

"Why did you do that?"

"Don't you see?" responded Tom. "Because she might suppose I hadn't seen her; and might return."

"And did she?"

"Certainly she did. Next morning, and next evening too: but always when there were no people about, and always alone. I rose earlier and sat there later, that when she came, she might find the church door open, and the organ playing, and might not be disappointed. She strolled that way for some days, and always staid to listen. But she is gone now, and of all unlikely things in this wide world, it is perhaps the most improbable that I shall ever look upon her face again."

"You don't know anything more about her?"

"No."

"And you never followed her, when she went away?"

"Why should I distress her by doing that?" said Tom Pinch. "Is it likely that she wanted my company? She came to hear the organ, not to see me; and would you have had me scare her from a place she seemed to grow quite fond of? Now, Heaven bless her!" cried Tom, "to have given her but a minute's pleasure every day, I would have gone on playing the organ at those times until I was an old man: quite contented if she sometimes thought of a poor fellow like me, as a part of the music; and more than recompensed if she ever mixed me up with anything she liked as well as she liked that!"

The new pupil was clearly very much amazed by Mr.

Pinch's weakness, and would probably have told him so, and given him some good advice, but for their opportune arrival at Mr. Pecksniff's door: the front door this time, on account of the occasion being one of ceremony and rejoicing. The same man was in waiting for the horse who had been adjured by Mr. Pinch in the morning not to yield to his rabid desire to start; and after delivering the animal into his charge, and beseeching Mr. Chuzzlewit in a whisper never to reveal a syllable of what he had just told him in the fulness of his heart, Tom led the pupil in, for instant presentation.

Mr. Pecksniff had clearly not expected them for hours to come: for he was surrounded by open books, and was glancing from volume to volume, with a black-lead pencil in his mouth, and a pair of compasses in his hand, at a vast number of mathematical diagrams, of such extraordinary shapes that they looked like designs for fireworks. Neither had Miss Charity expected them, for she was busied, with a capacious wicker basket before her, in making impracticable nightcaps for the poor. Neither had Miss Mercy expected them, for she was sitting upon her stool, tying on the—oh good gracious—the petticoat of a large doll that she was dressing for a neighbour's child: really, quite a grown-up doll, which made it more confusing: and had its little bonnet dangling by the ribbon from one of her fair curls, to which she had fastened it, lest it should be lost, or sat upon. It would be difficult, if not impossible, to conceive a family so thoroughly taken by surprise as the Pecksniffs were, on this occasion.

"Bless my life!" said Mr. Pecksniff, looking up, and gradually exchanging his abstracted face for one of joyful recognition. "Here already! Martin, my dear boy, I am delighted to welcome you to my poor house!"

With this kind greeting, Mr. Pecksniff fairly took him to his arms, and patted him several times upon the back with his right hand the while, as if to express that his feelings during the embrace were too much for utterance.

"But here," he said, recovering, "are my daughters, Martin: my two only children, whom (if you ever saw them) you have not beheld—ah, these sad family divisions! —since you were infants together. Nay, my dears, why blush at being detected in your every-day pursuits? We had prepared to give you the reception of a visitor, Martin,

in our little room of state," said Mr. Pecksniff, smiling,
but I like this better—I like this better!"

Oh blessed star of Innocence, wherever you may be, how
did you glitter in your home of ether, when the two Miss
Pecksniffs put forth, each her lily hand, and gave the
same, with mantling cheeks, to Martin! How did you
twinkle, as if fluttering with sympathy, when Mercy, reminded of the bonnet in her hair, hid her fair face and
turned her head aside: the while her gentle sister plucked
it out, and smote her, with a sister's soft reproof, upon her
buxom shoulder!

"And how," said Mr. Pecksniff, turning round after the
contemplation of these passages, and taking Mr. Pinch in
a friendly manner by the elbow, "how has our friend here
used you, Martin?"

"Very well indeed, Sir. We are on the best terms, I
assure you."

"Old Tom Pinch!" said Mr. Pecksniff, looking on him
with affectionate sadness. "Ah! It seems but yesterday
that Thomas was a boy, fresh from a scholastic course.
Yet years have passed, I think, since Thomas Pinch and
I first walked the world together!"

Mr. Pinch could say nothing. He was too much moved.
But he pressed his master's hand, and tried to thank him.

"And Thomas Pinch and I," said Mr. Pecksniff, in a
deeper voice, "will walk it yet, in mutual faithfulness and
friendship! And if it comes to pass that either of us be
run over, in any of those busy crossings which divide the
streets of life, the other will convey him to the hospital in
Hope, and sit beside his bed in Bounty!"

"Well, well, well!" he added in a happier tone, as he
shook Mr. Pinch's elbow, hard. "No more of this! Martin, my dear friend, that you may be at home within these
walls, let me show you how we live, and where. Come!"

With that he took up a lighted candle, and, attended by
his young relative, prepared to leave the room. At the
door, he stopped.

"You'll bear us company, Tom Pinch?"

Ay, cheerfully, though it had been to death, would Tom
have followed him: glad to lay down his life for such a
man!

"This," said Mr. Pecksniff, opening the door of an opposite parlour, "is the little room of state, I mentioned to

you. My girls have pride in it, Martin! This," opening another door, "is the little chamber in which my works (slight things at best) have been concocted. Portrait of myself by Spiller. Bust by Spoker. The latter is considered a good likeness. I seem to recognise something about the left-hand corner of the nose, myself."

Martin thought it was very like, but scarcely intellectual enough. Mr. Pecksniff observed that the same fault had been found with it before. It was remarkable it should have struck his young relation too. He was glad to see he had an eye for art.

"Various books you observe," said Mr. Pecksniff, waving his hand towards the wall, "connected with our pursuit. I have scribbled myself, but have not yet published. Be careful how you come up stairs. This," opening another door, "is my chamber. I read here when the family suppose I have retired to rest. Sometimes I injure my health, rather more than I can quite justify to myself, by doing so; but art is long and time is short. Every facility you see for jotting down crude notions, even here."

These latter words were explained by his pointing to a small round table on which were a lamp, divers sheets of paper, a piece of India rubber, and a case of instruments: all put ready, in case an architectural idea should come into Mr. Pecksniff's head in the night; in which event he would instantly leap out of bed, and fix it for ever.

Mr. Pecksniff opened another door on the same floor, and shut it again, all at once, as if it were a Blue Chamber. But before he had well done so, he looked smilingly round, and said "Why not?"

Martin couldn't say why not, because he didn't know anything at all about it. So Mr. Pecksniff answered himself, by throwing open the door, and saying:

"My daughters' room. A poor first-floor to us, but a bower to them. Very neat. Very airy. Plants you observe; hyacinths; books again; birds." These birds, by-the-bye, comprised in all one staggering old sparrow without a tail, which had been borrowed expressly from the kitchen. "Such trifles as girls love are here. Nothing more. Those who seek heartless splendour, would seek here in vain."

With that he led them to the floor above.

"This," said Mr. Pecksniff, throwing wide the door of

the memorable two-pair front; "is a room where some
talent has been developed, I believe. This is a room in
which an idea for a steeple occurred to me, that I may one
day give to the world. We work here, my dear Martin.
Some architects have been bred in this room: a few, I
think, Mr. Pinch?"

Tom fully assented; and, what is more, fully believed
it.

"You see," said Mr Pecksniff, passing the candle rapidly
from roll to roll of paper, "some trace of our doings here.
Salisbury Cathedral from the north. From the south.
From the east. From the west. From the south-east.
From the nor'-west. A bridge. An almshouse. A jail.
A church. A powder-magazine. A wine-cellar. A portico. A summer-house. An ice-house. Plans, elevations,
sections, every kind of thing. And this," he added, having by this time reached another large chamber on the
same story, with four little beds in it, "this is your room,
of which Mr. Pinch here, is the quiet sharer. A southern
aspect; a charming prospect; Mr. Pinch's little library,
you perceive; everything agreeable and appropriate. If
there is any additional comfort you would desire to have
here at any time, pray mention it. Even to strangers—
far less to you, my dear Martin—there is no restriction on
that point."

It was undoubtedly true, and may be stated in corrobora-
tion of Mr. Pecksniff, that any pupil had the most liberal
permission to mention anything in this way that suggested
itself to his fancy. Some young gentlemen had gone on
mentioning the very same thing for five years without
ever being stopped.

"The domestic assistants," said Mr. Pecksniff, "sleep
above; and that is all." After which, and listening complacently as he went, to the encomiums passed by his
young friend on the arrangements generally, he led the
way to the parlour again.

Here a great change had taken place; for festive preparations on a rather extensive scale were already completed,
and the two Miss Pecksniffs were awaiting their return
with hospitable looks. There were two bottles of currant
wine, white and red; a dish of sandwiches (very long and
very slim); another of apples; another of captain's biscuits (which are always a moist and jovial sort of viand);

a plate of oranges cut up small and gritty; with powdered
sugar, and a highly geological home-made cake. The magnitude of these preparations quite took away Tom Pinch's
breath: for though the new pupils were usually let down
softly, as one may say, particularly in the wine department, which had so many stages of declension, that sometimes a young gentleman was a whole fortnight in getting
to the pump; still this was a banquet: a sort of Lord
Mayor's feast in private life: a something to think of, and
hold on by, afterwards.

To this entertainment, which, apart from its own intrin-
sic merits, had the additional choice quality that it was in
strict keeping with the night, being both light and cool,
Mr. Pecksniff besought the company to do full justice.

"Martin," he said, "will seat himself between you two,
my dears, and Mr. Pinch will come by me. Let us drink
to our new inmate, and may we be happy together! Martin, my dear friend, my love to you! Mr. Pinch, if you
spare the bottle we shall quarrel."

And trying (in his regard for the feelings of the rest) to
look as if the wine were not acid and didn't make him
wink, Mr. Pecksniff did honour to his own toast.

"This," he said, in allusion to the party, not the wine,
"is a mingling that repays one for much disappointment
and vexation. Let us be merry." Here he took a captain's biscuit. "It is a poor heart that never rejoices; and
our hearts are not poor. No!"

With such stimulants to merriment did he beguile the
time, and do the honours of the table; while Mr. Pinch,
perhaps to assure himself that what he saw and heard was
holiday reality, and not a charming dream, ate of everything, and in particular disposed of the slim sandwiches
to a surprising extent. Nor was he stinted in his draughts
of wine; but on the contrary, remembering Mr. Pecksniff's speech, attacked the bottle with such vigour, that
every time he filled his glass anew, Miss Charity, despite
her amiable resolves, could not repress a fixed and stony
glare, as if her eyes had rested on a ghost. Mr. Pecksniff
also became thoughtful at those moments, not to say dejected: but, as he knew the vintage, it is very likely he
may have been speculating on the probable condition of
Mr. Pinch upon the morrow, and discussing within himself
the best remedies for colic.

Martin and the young ladies were excellent friends already, and compared recollections of their childish days, to their mutual liveliness and entertainment. Miss Mercy laughed immensely at everything that was said; and sometimes, after glancing at the happy face of Mr. Pinch, was seized with such fits of mirth as brought her to the very confines of hysterics. But, for these bursts of gaiety, her sister, in her better sense, reproved her; observing, in an angry whisper, that it was far from being a theme for jest; and that she had no patience with the creature; though it generally ended in her laughing too—but much more moderately—and saying, that indeed it was a little too ridiculous and intolerable to be serious about.

At length it became high time to remember the first clause of that great discovery made by the ancient philosopher, for securing health, riches, and wisdom; the infallibility of which has been for generations verified by the enormous fortunes, constantly amassed by chimney-sweepers and other persons who get up early and go to bed betimes. The young ladies accordingly rose, and having taken leave of Mr. Chuzzlewit with much sweetness, and of their father with much duty, and of Mr. Pinch with much condescension, retired to their bower. Mr. Pecksniff insisted on accompanying his young friend up-stairs, for personal superintendence of his comforts; and taking him by the arm, conducted him once more to his bedroom, followed by Mr. Pinch, who bore the light.

"Mr. Pinch," said Pecksniff, seating himself with folded arms on one of the spare beds. "I don't see any snuffers in that candlestick. Will you oblige me by going down, and asking for a pair?"

Mr. Pinch, only too happy to be useful, went off directly.

"You will excuse Thomas Pinch's want of polish, Martin," said Mr. Pecksniff, with a smile of patronage and pity, as soon as he had left the room. "He means well."

"He is a very good fellow, Sir."

"Oh, yes," said Mr. Pecksniff. "Yes. Thomas Pinch means well. He is very grateful. I have never regretted having befriended Thomas Pinch."

"I should think you never would, Sir."

"No," said Mr. Pecksniff. "No. I hope not. Poor fellow, he is always disposed to do his best; but he is not gifted. You will make him useful to you, Martin, if you please. If Thomas has a fault, it is that he is sometimes a little apt to forget his position. But that is soon checked. Worthy soul! You will find him easy to manage. Good night!"

"Good night, Sir."

By this time Mr. Pinch had returned with the snuffers.

"And good night to *you*, Mr. Pinch," said Pecksniff. "And sound sleep to you both. Bless you! Bless you!"

Invoking this benediction on the heads of his young friends with great fervour, he withdrew to his own room; while they, being tired, soon fell asleep. If Martin dreamed at all, some clew to the matter of his visions may possibly be gathered from the after-pages of this history. Those of Thomas Pinch were all of holidays, church organs, and seraphic Pecksniffs. It was some time before Mr. Pecksniff dreamed at all, or even sought his pillow, as he sat for full two hours before the fire in his own chamber, looking at the coals and thinking deeply. But he, too, slept and dreamed at last. Thus in the quiet hours of the night, one house shuts in as many incoherent and incongruous fancies as a madman's head.

CHAPTER VI.

COMPRISES, AMONG OTHER IMPORTANT MATTERS, PECKSNIFFIAN AND ARCHITECTURAL, AN EXACT RELATION OF THE PROGRESS MADE BY MR. PINCH IN THE CONFIDENCE AND FRIENDSHIP OF THE NEW PUPIL.

IT was morning; and the beautiful Aurora, of whom so much hath been written, said, and sung, did, with her rosy fingers, nip and tweak Miss Pecksniff's nose. It was the frolicsome custom of the Goddess, in her intercourse with the fair Cherry, so to do; or in more prosaic phrase, the tip of that feature in the sweet girl's countenance, was always very red at breakfast-time. For the most part, indeed, it wore, at that season of the day, a scraped and frosty look, as if it had been rasped; while a similar phenomenon developed itself in her humour, which was then observed to be of a sharp and acid quality, as though an extra lemon (figuratively speaking) had been squeezed into the nectar of her disposition, and had rather damaged its flavour.

This additional pungency on the part of the fair young creature led, on ordinary occasions, to such slight consequences as the copious dilution of Mr. Pinch's tea, or to his coming off uncommonly short in respect of butter, or to other the like results. But on the morning after the Installation Banquet, she suffered him to wander to and fro among the eatables and drinkables, a perfectly free and unchecked man; so utterly to Mr. Pinch's wonder and confusion, that like the wretched captive who recovered his liberty in his old age, he could make but little use of his enlargement, and fell into a strange kind of flutter for want of some kind hand to scrape his bread, and cut him off in the article of sugar with a lump, and pay him those other little attentions to which he was accustomed. There was something almost awful, too, about the self-possession of the new pupil; who "troubled" Mr. Pecksniff for the loaf, and helped himself to a rasher of that gentleman's own particular and private bacon, with all the coolness in life. He even seemed to think that he was doing quite a regular thing, and to expect that Mr. Pinch would follow his example, since he took occasion to observe of that young man "that he didn't get on:" a speech of so tremendous a character, that Tom cast down his eyes involuntarily, and felt as if he himself had committed some horrible deed and heinous breach of Mr. Pecksniff's confidence. Indeed, the agony of having such an indiscreet remark addressed to him before the assembled family, was breakfast enough in itself, and would without any other matter of reflection have settled Mr. Pinch's business and quenched his appetite for one meal, though he had been never so hungry.

The young ladies, however, and Mr. Pecksniff likewise, remained in the very best of spirits in spite of these severe trials, though with something of a mysterious understanding among themselves. When the meal was nearly over, Mr. Pecksniff smilingly explained the cause of their common satisfaction.

"It is not often," he said, "Martin, that my daughters and I desert our quiet home to pursue the giddy round of pleasures that revolves abroad. But we think of doing so to-day."

"Indeed, Sir!" cried the new pupil.

"Yes," said Mr. Pecksniff, tapping his left hand with a letter which he held in his right. "I have a summons here to repair to London; on professional business, my dear Martin; strictly on professional business; and I promised my girls, long ago, that whenever that happened again, they should accompany me. We shall go forth to-night by the heavy coach—like the dove of old, my dear Martin—and it will be a week before we again deposit our olive-branches in the passage. When I say olive-branches," observed Mr. Pecksniff, in explanation, "I mean, our unpretending luggage."

"I hope the young ladies will enjoy their trip," said Martin.

"Oh! that I'm sure we shall!" cried Mercy, clapping her hands. "Good gracious, Cherry, my darling, the idea of London!"

"Ardent child!" said Mr. Pecksniff, gazing on her in a dreamy way. "And yet there is a melancholy sweetness in these youthful hopes! It is pleasant to know that they never can be realised. I remember thinking once myself, in the days of my childhood, that pickled onions grew on trees, and that every elephant was born with an impregnable castle on his back. I have not found the fact to be so; far from it; and yet those visions have comforted me under circumstances of trial. Even when I have had the anguish of discovering that I have nourished in my breast an ostrich, and not a human pupil—even in that hour of agony, they have soothed me."

At this dread allusion to John Westlock, Mr. Pinch precipitately choked in his tea; for he had that very morning received a letter from him, as Mr. Pecksniff very well knew.

"You will take care, my dear Martin," said Mr. Pecksniff, resuming his former cheerfulness, "that the house does not run away in our absence. We leave you in charge of everything. There is no mystery; all is free and open. Unlike the young man in the Eastern tale—who is described as a one-eyed almanack, if I am not mistaken, Mr. Pinch?"

"A one-eyed calender, I think, Sir," faltered Tom.

"They are pretty nearly the same thing, I believe," said
Mr. Pecksniff, smiling compassionately; "or they used to
be in my time. Unlike that young man, my dear Martin,
you are forbidden to enter no corner of this house; but are
requested to make yourself perfectly at home in every part
of it. You will be jovial, my dear Martin, and will kill
the fatted calf if you please!"

There was not the least objection, doubtless, to the
young man's slaughtering and appropriating to his own use
any calf, fat or lean, that he might happen to find upon
the premises; but as no such animal chanced at that time
to be grazing on Mr. Pecksniff's estate, this request must
be considered rather as a polite compliment than a substantial hospitality. It was the finishing ornament of the conversation; for when he had delivered it, Mr. Pecksniff
rose, and led the way to that hotbed of architectural genius,
the two-pair front.

"Let me see," he said, searching among the papers,
"how you can best employ yourself, Martin, while I am
absent. Suppose you were to give me your idea of a monument to a Lord Mayor of London; or a tomb for a sheriff;
or your notion of a cowhouse to be erected in a nobleman's
park. Do you know, now," said Mr. Pecksniff, folding
his hands, and looking at his young relation with an air of
pensive interest, "that I should very much like to see your
notion of a cow-house?"

But Martin by no means appeared to relish this suggestion.

"A pump," said Mr. Pecksniff, "is very chaste practice.
I have found that a lamp-post is calculated to refine the
mind and give it a classical tendency. An ornamental
turnpike has a remarkable effect upon the imagination.
What do you say to beginning with an ornamental turnpike?"

"Whatever Mr. Pecksniff pleased," said Martin, doubt-
fully.

"Stay," said that gentleman. "Come! as you're ambi-
tious, and are a very neat draughtsman, you shall—ha ha!
—you shall try your hand on these proposals for a grammar-school: regulating your plan, of course, by the printed
particulars. Upon my word, now," said Mr. Pecksniff,
merrily, "I shall be very curious to see what you make of
the grammar-school. Who knows but a young man of

your taste might hit upon something, impracticable and unlikely in itself, but which I could put into shape? For it really is, my dear Martin, it really is in the finishing touches alone, that great experience and long study in these matters tell. Ha, ha, ha! Now it really will be," continued Mr. Pecksniff, clapping his young friend on the back in his droll humour, "an amusement to me, to see what you make of the grammar-school."

Martin readily undertook this task, and Mr. Pecksniff forthwith proceeded to entrust him with the materials necessary for its execution: dwelling meanwhile on the magical effect of a few finishing touches from the hand of a master; which, indeed, as some people said (and these were the old enemies again!) was unquestionably very surprising, and almost miraculous; as there were cases on record in which the masterly introduction of an additional back window, or a kitchen door, or half-a-dozen steps, or even a water spout, had made the design of a pupil Mr. Pecksniff's own work, and had brought substantial rewards into that gentleman's pocket. But such is the magic of genius, which changes all it handles into gold!

"When your mind requires to be refreshed, by change of occupation," said Mr. Pecksniff, "Thomas Pinch will instruct you in the art of surveying the back garden, or in ascertaining the dead level of the road between this house and the finger-post, or in any other practical and pleasing pursuit. There are a cart-load of loose bricks, and a score or two of old flower-pots, in the back yard. If you could pile them up, my dear Martin, into any form which would remind me on my return—say of St. Peter's at Rome, or the Mosque of St. Sophia at Constantinople—it would be at once improving to you and agreeable to my feelings. And now," said Mr. Pecksniff, in conclusion, "to drop, for the present, our professional relations and advert to private matters, I shall be glad to talk with you in my own room, while I pack up my portmanteau."

Martin attended him; and they remained in secret conference together for an hour or more; leaving Tom Pinch alone. When the young man returned, he was very taciturn and dull, in which state he remained all day; so that Tom, after trying him once or twice with indifferent conversation, felt a delicacy in obtruding himself upon his thoughts, and said no more.

He would not have had leisure to say much, had his new friend been ever so loquacious: for first of all Mr. Pecksniff called him down to stand upon the top of his portmanteau and represent ancient statues there, until such time as it would consent to be locked; and then Miss Charity called him to come and cord her trunk; and then Miss Mercy sent for him to come and mend her box; and then he wrote the fullest possible cards for all the luggage; and then he volunteered to carry it all down stairs; and after that to see it safely carried on a couple of barrows to the old finger-post at the end of the lane; and then to mind it till the coach came up. In short, his day's work would have been a pretty heavy one for a porter, but his thorough good-will made nothing of it; and as he sat upon the luggage at last, waiting for the Pecksniffs, escorted by the new pupil, to come down the lane, his heart was light with the hope of having pleased his benefactor.

"I was almost afraid," said Tom, taking a letter from his pocket, and wiping his face, for he was hot with bustling about though it was a cold day, "that I shouldn't have had time to write it, and that would have been a thousand pities: postage from such a distance being a serious consideration, when one's not rich. She will be glad to see my hand, poor girl, and to hear that Pecksniff is as kind as ever. I would have asked John Westlock to call and see her, and tell her all about me by word of mouth, but I was afraid he might speak against Pecksniff to her, and make her uneasy. Besides, they are particular people where she is, and it might have rendered her situation uncomfortable if she had had a visit from a young man like John. Poor Ruth!"

Tom Pinch seemed a little disposed to be melancholy for half a minute or so, but he found comfort very soon, and pursued his ruminations thus:

"I'm a nice man, I don't think, as John used to say (John was a kind, merry-hearted fellow: I wish he had liked Pecksniff better), to be feeling low, on account of the distance between us, when I ought to be thinking, instead, of my extraordinary good-luck in having ever got here. I must have been born with a silver spoon in my mouth, I am sure, to have ever come across Pecksniff. And here have I fallen again into my usual good-luck with the new pupil! Such an affable, generous, free fellow, as he is, I never saw. Why, we were companions directly! and he a relation of Pecksniff's too, and a clever, dashing youth who might cut his way through the world as if it were a cheese! Here he comes while the words are on my lips," said Tom: "walking down the lane as if the lane belonged to him."

In truth, the new pupil, not at all disconcerted by the honour of having Miss Mercy Pecksniff on his arm, or by the affectionate adieux of that young lady, approached as Mr. Pinch spoke, followed by Miss Charity and Mr. Pecksniff. As the coach appeared at the same moment, Tom lost no time in entreating the gentleman last mentioned, to undertake the delivery of his letter.

"Oh!" said Mr. Pecksniff, glancing at the superscription. "For your sister, Thomas. Yes, oh yes, it shall be delivered, Mr. Pinch. Make your mind easy upon that score. She shall certainly have it, Mr. Pinch."

He made the promise with so much condescension and patronage, that Tom felt he had asked a great deal (this had not occurred to his mind before), and thanked him earnestly. The Miss Pecksniffs, according to a custom they had, were amused beyond description, at the mention of Mr. Pinch's sister. Oh the fright! The bare idea of a Miss Pinch! Good heavens!

Tom was greatly pleased to see them so merry, for he took it as a token of their favour, and good-humoured regard. Therefore he laughed too and rubbed his hands, and wished them a pleasant journey and safe return, and was quite brisk. Even when the coach had rolled away with the olive-branches in the boot and the family of doves inside, he stood waving his hand and bowing: so much gratified by the unusually courteous demeanour of the young ladies, that he was quite regardless, for the moment, of Martin Chuzzlewit, who stood leaning thoughtfully against the finger-post, and who after disposing of his fair charge had hardly lifted his eyes from the ground.

The perfect silence which ensued upon the bustle and departure of the coach, together with the sharp air of the wintry afternoon, roused them both at the same time. They turned, as by mutual consent, and moved off, arm-in-arm.

"How melancholy you are!" said Tom; "what is the matter?"

"Nothing worth speaking of," said Martin. "Very little more than was the matter yesterday, and much more, 1 hope, than will be the matter to-morrow. I'm out of spirits, Pinch."

"Well," cried Tom, "now do you know I am in capital spirits to-day, and scarcely ever felt more disposed to be good company. It was a very kind thing in your predecessor, John, to write to me, was it not?"

"Why, yes," said Martin carelessly: "I should have thought he would have had enough to do to enjoy himself, without thinking of you, Pinch."

"Just what I felt to be so very likely," Tom rejoined: "but no, he keeps his word, and says, 'My dear Pinch, I often think of you,' and all sorts of kind and considerate things of that description."

"He must be a devilish good-natured fellow," said Martin, somewhat peevishly: "because he can't mean that, you know."

"I don't suppose he can, eh?" said Tom, looking wistfully in his companion's face. "He says so to please me, you think?"

"Why, is it likely," rejoined Martin, with greater earnestness, "that a young man newly escaped from this kennel of a place, and fresh to all the delights of being his own master in London, can have much leisure or inclination to think favourably of anything or anybody he has left behind him here? I put it to you, Pinch, is it natural?"

After a short reflection, Mr. Pinch replied, in a more subdued tone, that to be sure it was unreasonable to expect any such thing, and that he had no doubt Martin knew best.

"Of course I know best," Martin observed.

"Yes, I feel that," said Mr. Pinch, mildly. "I said so." And when he had made this rejoinder, they fell into a blank silence again, which lasted until they reached home: by which time it was dark.

Now, Miss Charity Pecksniff, in consideration of the inconvenience of carrying them with her in the coach, and the impossibility of preserving them by artificial means until the family's return, had set forth, in a couple of plates, the fragments of yesterday's feast. In virtue of which liberal arrangement, they had the happiness to find awaiting them in the parlour two chaotic heaps of the remains of last night's pleasure, consisting of certain filmy bits of oranges, some mummied sandwiches, various disrupted masses of the geological cake, and several entire captain's biscuits. That choice liquor in which to steep these dainties might not be wanting, the remains of the two bottles of currant wine had been poured together and corked with a curl-paper; so that every material was at hand for making quite a heavy night of it.

Martin Chuzzlewit beheld these roystering preparations with infinite contempt, and stirring the fire into a blaze (to the great destruction of Mr. Pecksniff's coals), sat moodily down before it, in the most comfortable chair he could find. That he might the better squeeze himself into the small corner that was left for him, Mr. Pinch took up his position on Miss Mercy Pecksniff's stool, and setting his glass down upon the hearth-rug and putting his plate upon his knees, began to enjoy himself.

If Diogenes coming to life again could have rolled himself, tub and all, into Mr. Pecksniff's parlour, and could have seen Tom Pinch as he sat on Mercy Pecksniff's stool, with his plate and glass before him, he could not have faced it out, though in his surliest mood, but must have smiled good-temperedly. The perfect and entire satisfaction of Tom; his surpassing appreciation of the husky sandwiches, which crumbled in his mouth like sawdust; the unspeakable relish with which he swallowed the thin wine by drops, and smacked his lips, as though it were so rich and generous that to lose an atom of its fruity flavour were a sin; the look with which he paused sometimes, with his glass in his hand, proposing silent toasts to himself; and the anxious shade that came upon his contented face when after wandering round the room, exulting in its uninvaded snugness, his glance encountered the dull brow of his companion; no cynic in the world, though in his hatred of its men a very griffin, could have withstood these things in Thomas Pinch.

Some men would have slapped him on the back, and pledged him in a bumper of the currant wine, though it had been the sharpest vinegar—ay, and liked its flavour too; some would have seized him by his honest hand, and thanked him for the lesson that his simple nature taught them. Some would have laughed with, and others would have laughed at him; of which last class was Martin Chuzzlewit, who, unable to restrain himself at last, laughed loud and long.

7

"That's right," said Tom, nodding approvingly. "Cheer up! That's capital!"

At which encouragement, young Martin laughed again; and said, as soon as he had breath and gravity enough:

"I never saw such a fellow as you are, Pinch."

"Didn't you though?" said Tom. "Well, it's very likely you do find me strange, because I have hardly seen anything of the world, and you have seen a good deal I dare say?"

"Pretty well for my time of life," rejoined Martin, drawing his chair still nearer to the fire, and spreading his feet out on the fender. "Deuce take it, I must talk openly to somebody. I'll talk openly to you, Pinch."

"Do!" said Tom. "I shall take it as being very friendly of you."

"I'm not in your way, am I?" inquired Martin, glancing down at Mr. Pinch, who was by this time looking at the fire over his leg.

"Not at all!" cried Tom.

"You must know then, to make short of a long story," said Martin, beginning with a kind of effort, as if the revelation were not agreeable to him: "that I have been bred up from childhood with great expectations, and have always been taught to believe that I should be, one day, very rich. So I should have been, but for certain brief reasons which I am going to tell you, and which have led to my being disinherited."

"By your father?" inquired Mr. Pinch, with open eyes.

"By my grandfather. I have had no parents these many years. Scarcely within my remembrance."

"Neither have I," said Tom, touching the young man's hand with his own and timidly withdrawing it again. "Dear me!"

"Why as to that you know, Pinch," pursued the other, stirring the fire again, and speaking in his rapid, off-hand way: "it's all very right and proper to be fond of parents when we have them, and to bear them in remembrance after they're dead, if you have ever known anything of them. But as I never did know anything about mine personally, you know, why I can't be expected to be very sentimental about 'em. And I am not: that's the truth."

Mr. Pinch was just then looking thoughtfully at the bars. But on his companion pausing in this place, he started, and said "Oh! of course "—and composed himself to listen again.

"In a word," said Martin, "I have been bred and reared all my life by this grandfather of whom I have just spoken. Now, he has a great many good points; there is no doubt about that; I'll not disguise the fact from you; but he has two very great faults, which are the staple of his bad side. In the first place, he has the most confirmed obstinacy of character you ever met with in any human creature. In the second, he is most abominably selfish."

"Is he indeed?" cried Tom.

"In these two respects," returned the other, "there never was such a man. I have often heard from those who know, that they have been, time out of mind, the failings of our family; and I believe there's some truth in it. But I can't say of my own knowledge. All I have to do, you know, is to be very thankful that they haven't descended to me, and to be very careful that I don't contract 'em."

"To be sure," said Mr. Pinch. "Very proper."

"Well, Sir," resumed Martin, stirring the fire once more, and drawing his chair still closer to it, "his selfishness makes him exacting, you see; and his obstinacy makes him resolute in his exactions. The consequence is that he has always exacted a great deal from me in the way of respect, and submission, and self-denial when his wishes were in question, and so forth. I have borne a great deal from him, because I have been under obligations to him (if one can ever be said to be under obligations to one's own grandfather), and because I have been really attached to him; but we have had a great many quarrels for all that, for I could not accommodate myself to his ways very often—not out of the least reference to myself you understand, but because——" he stammered here, and was rather at a loss.

Mr. Pinch being about the worst man in the world to help anybody out of a difficulty of this sort, said nothing.

"Well! as you understand me," resumed Martin quickly, "I needn't hunt for the precise expression I want. Now, I come to the cream of my story, and the occasion of my being here. I am in love, Pinch."

Mr. Pinch looked up into his face with increased interest.

"I say I am in love. I am in love with one of the most beautiful girls the sun ever shone upon. But she is wholly and entirely dependent upon the pleasure of my grandfather;

and if he were to know that she favoured my passion, she would lose her home and every thing she possesses in the world. There is nothing very selfish in *that* love, I think?"

"Selfish!" cried Tom. "You have acted nobly. To love her as I am sure you do, and yet in consideration for her state of dependence, not even to disclose——"

"What are you talking about, Pinch?" said Martin pettishly: "don't make yourself ridiculous, my good fellow! What do you mean by not disclosing?"

"I beg your pardon," answered Tom. "I thought you meant that, or I wouldn't have said it."

"If I didn't tell her I loved her, where would be the use of my being in love?" said Martin: "unless to keep myself in a perpetual state of worry and vexation?"

"That's true," Tom answered. "Well! I can guess what *she* said when you told her," he added, glancing at Martin's handsome face.

"Why, not exactly, Pinch," he rejoined, with a slight frown: "because she has some girlish notions about duty and gratitude, and all the rest of it, which are rather hard to fathom; but in the main you are right. Her heart was mine, I found."

"Just what I supposed," said Tom. "Quite natural!" and, in his great satisfaction, he took a long sip out of his wine-glass.

"Although I had conducted myself from the first with the utmost circumspection," pursued Martin, "I had not managed matters so well but that my grandfather, who is full of jealousy and distrust, suspected me of loving her. He said nothing to her, but straightway attacked me in private, and charged me with designing to corrupt the fidelity to himself (there you observe his selfishness), of a young creature whom he had trained and educated to be his only disinterested and faithful companion when he should have disposed of me in marriage to his heart's content. Upon that, I took fire immediately, and told him that with his good leave I would dispose of myself in marriage, and would rather not be knocked down by him or any other auctioneer to any bidder whomsoever."

Mr. Pinch opened his eyes wider and looked at the fire harder than he had done yet.

"You may be sure," said Martin, "that this nettled him,

MARTIN CHUZZLEWIT. 101

and that he began to be the very reverse of complimentary to myself. Interview succeeded interview; words engendered words, as they always do; and the upshot of it was, that I was to renounce her, or be renounced by him. Now you must bear in mind, Pinch, that I am not only desperately fond of her (for though she is poor, her beauty and intellect would reflect great credit on anybody, I don't care of what pretensions, who might become her husband), but that a chief ingredient in my composition is a most determined—"

"Obstinacy," suggested Tom in perfect good faith. But the suggestion was not so well received as he had expected; for the young man immediately rejoined, with some irritation,

"What a fellow you are, Pinch!"

"I beg your pardon," said Tom, "I thought you wanted a word."

"I didn't want that word," he rejoined. "I told you obstinacy was no part of my character, did I not? I was going to say, if you had given me leave, that a chief ingredient in my composition is a most determined firmness."

"Oh!" cried Tom, screwing up his mouth, and nodding. "Yes, yes; I see!"

"And being firm," pursued Martin, "of course I was not going to yield to him, or give way by so much as the thousandth part of an inch."

"No, no," said Tom.

"On the contrary; the more he urged, the more I was determined to oppose him."

"To be sure!" said Tom.

"Very well," rejoined Martin, throwing himself back in his chair, with a careless wave of both hands, as if the subject were quite settled, and nothing more could be said about it—"There is an end of the matter, and here am I!"

Mr. Pinch sat staring at the fire for some minutes with a puzzled look, such as he might have assumed if some uncommonly difficult conundrum had been proposed, which he found it impossible to guess. At length he said:

"Pecksniff, of course, you had known before?"

"Only by name. No, I had never seen him, for my grandfather kept not only himself but me, aloof from all his relations. But our separation took place in a town in the adjoining county. From that place I came to Salisbury, and there I saw Pecksniff's advertisement, which I answered, having always had some natural taste, I believe, in the matters to which it referred, and thinking it might suit me. As soon as I found it to be his, I was doubly bent on coming to him if possible, on account of his being—"

"Such an excellent man," interposed Tom, rubbing his hands: "so he is. You were quite right."

" Why not so much on that account, if the truth must be spoken," returned Martin, "as because my grandfather has an inveterate dislike to him, and after the old man's arbitrary treatment of me I had a natural desire to run as directly counter to all his opinions as I could. Well! as I said before, here I am. My engagement with the young lady I have been telling you about, is likely to be a tolerably long one; for neither her prospects, nor mine, are very bright; and of course I shall not think of marrying until I am well able to do so. It would never do, you know, for me to be plunging myself into poverty and shabbiness and love in one room up three pair of stairs, and all that sort of thing."

"To say nothing of her," remarked Tom Pinch, in a low voice.

"Exactly so," rejoined Martin, rising to warm his back, and leaning against the chimney-piece. "To say nothing of her. At the same time, of course it's not very hard upon her to be obliged to yield to the necessity of the case: first, because she loves me very much; and secondly, because I have sacrificed a great deal on her account, and might have done much better, you know."

It was a very long time before Tom said "Certainly;" so long, that he might have taken a nap in the interval, but he did say it at last.

"Now, there is one odd coincidence connected with this love-story," said Martin, "which brings it to an end. You remember what you told me last night as we were coming here, about your pretty visitor in the church?"

"Surely I do," said Tom, rising from his stool, and seating himself in the chair from which the other had lately risen, that he might see his face. "Undoubtedly."

"That was she."

"I knew what you were going to say," cried Tom, looking fixedly at him, and speaking very softly. "You don't tell me so?"

"That was she," repeated the young man. "After what I have heard from Pecksniff, I have no doubt that she came and went with my grandfather.—Don't you drink too much of that sour wine, or you'll have a fit of some sort, Pinch, I see."

"It is not very wholesome, I am afraid," said Tom, setting down the empty glass he had for some time held. "So that was she, was it?"

Martin nodded assent: and adding, with a restless impatience, that if he had been a few days earlier he would have seen her; and that now she might be, for anything he knew, hundreds of miles away; threw himself, after a few turns across the room, into a chair, and chafed like a spoilt child.

Tom Pinch's heart was very tender, and he could not bear to see the most indifferent person in distress; still less one who had awakened an interest in him, and who regarded him (either in fact, or as he supposed) with kindness, and in a spirit of lenient construction. Whatever his own thoughts had been a few moments before—and to judge from his face they must have been pretty serious—he dismissed them instantly, and gave his young friend the best counsel and comfort that occurred to him.

"All will be well in time," said Tom, "I have no doubt; and some trial and adve:sity just now will only serve to make you more attached to each other in better days. I have always read that the truth is so, and I have a feeling within me, which tells me how natural and right it is that it should be. What never ran smooth yet," said Tom, with a smile, which despite the homeliness of his face, was pleasanter to see than many a proud beauty's brightest glance: "what never ran smooth yet, can hardly be expected to change its character for us; so we must take it as we find it, and fashion it into the very best shape we can, by patience and good-humour. I have no power at all; I needn't tell you that; but I have an excellent will; and if I could ever be of use to you, in any way whatever, how very glad I should be!"

"Thank you," said Martin, shaking his hand. "You're a good fellow, upon my word, and speak very kindly. Of course, you know," he added, after a moment's pause, as he drew his chair towards the fire again, "I should not hesitate to avail myself of your services if you could help me at all; but mercy on us!"—Here he rumpled his hair impatiently with his hand, and looked at Tom as if he took it rather ill that he was not somebody else—"you might as well be a toasting-fork or a frying-pan, Pinch, for any help you can render me."

"Except in the inclination," said Tom, gently.

"Oh! to be sure. I meant that, of course. If inclination went for anything, I shouldn't want help. I tell you what you may do, though, if you will—at the present moment too."

"What is that?" demanded Tom.

"Read to me."

"I shall be delighted," cried Tom, catching up the candle, with enthusiasm. "Excuse my leaving you in the dark a moment, and I'll fetch a book directly. What will you like? Shakspeare?"

"Ay!" replied his friend, yawning and stretching himself. "He'll do. I am tired with the bustle of to-day, and the novelty of everything about me; and in such a case, there's no greater luxury in the world, I think, than being read to sleep. You won't mind my going to sleep, if I can?"

"Not at all!" cried Tom.

"Then begin as soon as you like. You needn't leave off when you see me getting drowsy (unless you feel tired), for it's pleasant to wake gradually to the sounds again. Did you ever try that?"

"No, I never tried that," said Tom.

"Well! You can, you know, one of these days when we're both in the right humour. Don't mind leaving me in the dark. Look sharp!"

Mr. Pinch lost no time in moving away; and in a minute or two returned with one of the precious volumes from the shelf beside his bed. Martin had in the meantime made himself as comfortable as circumstances would permit, by constructing before the fire a temporary sofa of three chairs with Mercy's stool for a pillow, and lying down at full length upon it.

"Don't be too loud, please," he said to Pinch.

"No, no," said Tom.

"You're sure you're not cold?"

"Not at all!" cried Tom.

"I am quite ready then."

Mr. Pinch accordingly, after turning over the leaves of his book with as much care as if they were living and highly cherished creatures, made his own selection, and began to read. Before he had completed fifty lines, his friend was snoring.

"Poor fellow!" said Tom, softly, as he stretched out his head to peep at him over the backs of the chairs. "He is very young to have so much trouble. How trustful and generous in him to bestow all this confidence in me. And that was she, was it?"

But suddenly remembering their compact, he took up the poem at the place where he had left off, and went on reading; always forgetting to snuff the candle, until its wick looked like a mushroom. He gradually became so much interested, that he quite forgot to replenish the fire; and was only reminded of his neglect by Martin Chuzzlewit starting up after the lapse of an hour or so, and crying with a shiver:

"Why, it's nearly out, I declare! No wonder I dreamed of being frozen. Do call for some coals. What a fellow you are, Pinch!"

CHAPTER VII.

IN WHICH MR. CHEVY SLYME ASSERTS THE INDE-
PENDENCE OF HIS SPIRIT; AND THE BLUE DRAG-
ON LOSES A LIMB.

MARTIN began to work at the grammar-school next morning, with so much vigour and expedition, that Mr. Pinch had new reason to do homage to the natural endowments of that young gentleman, and to acknowledge his infinite superiority to himself. The new pupil received Tom's compliments very graciously; and having by this time conceived a real regard for him, in his own peculiar way, predicted that they would always be the very best of friends, and that neither of them, he was certain (but particularly Tom), would ever have reason to regret the day on which they became acquainted. Mr. Pinch was delighted to hear him say this, and felt so much flattered by his kind assurances of friendship and protection, that he was at a loss how to express the pleasure they afforded him. And indeed it may be observed of this friendship, such as it was, that it had within it more likely materials of endurance than many a sworn brotherhood that has been rich in promise; for so long as the one party found a pleasure in patronising, and the other in being patronised (which was in the very essence of their respective characters), it was of all possible events among the least probable, that the twin demons, Envy and Pride, would ever arise between them. So in very many cases of friendship, or what passes for it, the old axiom is reversed, and like clings to unlike more than to like.

They were both very busy on the afternoon succeeding the family's departure—Martin with the grammar-school, and Tom in balancing certain receipts of rents, and deducting Mr. Pecksniff's commission from the same; in which abstruse employment he was much distracted by a habit his new friend had of whistling aloud, while he was drawing —when they were not a little startled by the unexpected obtrusion into that sanctuary of genius, of a human head, which although a shaggy and somewhat alarming head, in appearance, smiled affably upon them from the doorway, in a manner that was at once waggish, conciliatory, and expressive of approbation.

"I am not industrious myself, gents both," said the head, "but I know how to appreciate that quality in others. I wish I may turn gray and ugly, if it isn't, in my opinion, next to genius, one of the very charmingest qualities of the human mind. Upon my soul, I am grateful to my friend Pecksniff for helping me to the contemplation of such a delicious picture as you present. You remind me of Whittington, afterwards thrice Lord Mayor of London. I give you my unsullied word of honour, that you very strongly remind me of that historical character. You are a pair of Whittingtons, gents, without the cat; which is a most agreeable and blessed exception to me, for I am not attached to the feline species. My name is Tigg; how do you do?"

Martin looked to Mr. Pinch for an explanation; and Tom, who had never in his life set eyes on Mr. Tigg before, looked to that gentleman himself.

"Chevy Slyme?" said Mr. Tigg, interrogatively, and

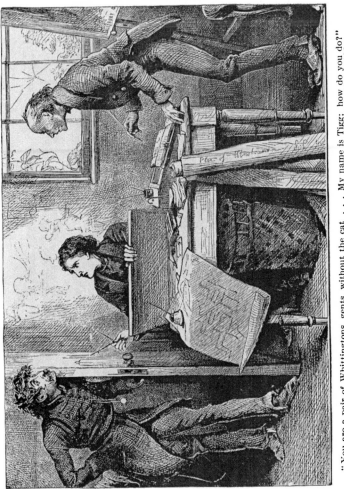

"You are a pair of Whittingtons, gents, without the cat . . . My name is Tigg; how do you do?"
—*Martin Chuzzlewit*, ch. vii., p. 106.

kissing his left hand in token of friendship. "You will understand me when I say that I am the accredited agent of Chevy Slyme—that I am the ambassador from the court of Chiv? Ha ha!"

"Heyday!" asked Martin, starting at the mention of a name he knew. "Pray, what does he want with me?"

"If your name is Pinch—" Mr. Tigg began.

"It is not," said Martin, checking himself. "That is Mr. Pinch."

"If that is Mr. Pinch," cried Tigg, kissing his hand again, and beginning to follow his head into the room, "he will permit me to say that I greatly esteem and respect his character, which has been most highly commended to me by my friend Pecksniff; and that I deeply appreciate his talent for the organ, notwithstanding that I do not, if I may use the expression, grind, myself. If that is Mr. Pinch, I will venture to express a hope that I see him well, and that he is suffering no inconvenience from the easterly wind?"

"Thank you," said Tom, "I am very well."

"That is a comfort," Mr. Tigg rejoined. "Then," he added, shielding his lips with the palm of his hand, and applying them close to Mr. Pinch's ear, "I have come for the letter."

"For the letter?" said Tom, aloud. "What letter?"

"The letter," whispered Tigg, in the same cautious manner as before, "which my friend Pecksniff addressed to Chevy Slyme, Esquire, and left with you."

"He didn't leave any letter with me," said Tom.

"Hush!" cried the other. "It's all the same thing, though not so delicately done by my friend Pecksniff as I could have wished—the money."

"The money!" cried Tom, quite scared.

"Exactly so," said Mr. Tigg. With which he rapped Tom twice or thrice upon the breast and nodded several times, as though he would say, that he saw they understood each other; that it was unnecessary to mention the circumstance before a third person; and that he would take it as a particular favour if Tom would slip the amount into his hand, as quietly as possible.

Mr. Pinch, however, was so very much astounded by this (to him) inexplicable deportment, that he at once openly declared there must be some mistake, and that he had been entrusted with no commission whatever having any reference to Mr. Tigg or to his friend either.—Mr. Tigg received this declaration with a grave request that Mr. Pinch would have the goodness to make it again; and on Tom's repeating it in a still more emphatic and unmistakable manner, checked it off, sentence for sentence, by nodding his head solemnly at the end of each. When it had come to a close for the second time, Mr. Tigg sat himself down in a chair and addressed the young men as follows:

"Then I tell you what it is, gents both. There is at this present moment in this very place, a perfect constellation of talent and genius, who is involved, through what I cannot but designate as the culpable negligence of my friend Pecksniff, in a situation as tremendous, perhaps, as the social intercourse of the nineteenth century will readily admit of. There is actually at this instant, at the Blue Dragon in this village—an alehouse observe; a common, paltry, low-minded, clodhopping, pipe-smoking alehouse—an individual, of whom it may be said, in the language of the Poet, that nobody but himself can in any way come up to him; who is detained there for his bill. Ha! ha! For his bill. I repeat it—for his bill. Now," said Mr. Tigg, " we have heard of Fox's Book of Martyrs, I believe, and we have heard of the Court of Requests, and the Star Chamber; but I fear the contradiction of no man alive or dead, when I assert that my friend Chevy Slyme being held in pawn for a bill, beats any amount of cock-fighting with which I am acquainted."

Martin and Mr. Pinch looked, first at each other, and afterwards at Mr. Tigg, who with his arms folded on his breast surveyed them, half in despondency and half in bitterness.

" Don't mistake me, gents both," he said, stretching forth his right hand. " If it had been for anything but a bill, I could have borne it, and could still have looked upon mankind with some feeling of respect: but when such a man as my friend Slyme is detained for a score—a thing in itself essentially mean; a low performance on a slate, or possibly chalked upon the back of a door—I do feel that there is a screw of such magnitude loose somewhere, that the whole framework of society is shaken, and the very first principles of things can no longer be trusted. In short, gents both," said Mr. Tigg with a passionate flourish of his

nands and head, "when a man like Slyme is detained for
such a thing as a bill, I reject the superstitions of ages,
and believe nothing. I don't even believe that I *don't* believe, curse me if I do!"

"I am very sorry, I am sure," said Tom after a pause,
"but Mr. Pecksniff said nothing to me about it, and I
couldn't act without his instructions. Wouldn't it be better, Sir, if you were to go to—to wherever you came from
—yourself, and remit the money to your friend?"

"How can that be done, when I am detained also?" said
Mr. Tigg; "and when moreover, owing to the astounding,
and I must add, guilty negligence of my friend Pecksniff,
I have no money for coach-hire?"

Tom thought of reminding the gentleman (who, no
doubt, in his agitation had forgotten it) that there was a
post-office in the land; and that possibly if he wrote to
some friend or agent for a remittance it might not be lost
upon the road; or at all events that the chance, however
desperate, was worth trusting to. But, as his good-nature
presently suggested to him certain reasons for abstaining
from this hint, he paused again, and then asked:

"Did you say, Sir, that you were detained also?"

"Come here," said Mr. Tigg, rising. "You have no objection to my opening this window for a moment?"

"Certainly not," said Tom.

"Very good," said Mr. Tigg, lifting the sash. "You
see a fellow down there in a red neckcloth and no waistcoat?"

"Of course I do," cried Tom. "That's Mark Tapley."

"Mark Tapley is it?" said the gentleman. "Then Mark
Tapley had not only the great politeness to follow me to
this house, but is waiting now, to see me home again.
And for that act of attention, Sir," added Mr. Tigg, strok-
ing his moustache, "I can tell you, that Mark Tapley had
better in his infancy have been fed to suffocation by Mrs.
Tapley, than preserved to this time."

Mr. Pinch was not so dismayed by this terrible threat,
but that he had voice enough to call to Mark to come in,
and up stairs; a summons which he so speedily obeyed,
that almost as soon as Tom and Mr. Tigg had drawn in their
heads and closed the window again, he the denounced appeared before them.

"Come here, Mark!" said Mr. Pinch. "Good gracious

7—5

me! what's the matter between Mrs. Lupin and this gentleman?"

"What gentleman, Sir?" said Mark. "I don't see no gentleman here, Sir, excepting you and the new gentleman," to whom he made a rough kind of bow—"and there's nothing wrong between Mrs. Lupin and either of you, Mr. Pinch, I am sure."

"Nonsense, Mark!" cried Tom. "You see Mr.—"

"Tigg," interposed that gentleman. "Wait a bit. I shall crush him soon. All in good time!"

"Oh *him!*" rejoined Mark, with an air of careless defiance. "Yes, I see *him.* I could see him a little better, if he'd shave himself, and get his hair cut."

Mr. Tigg shook his head with a ferocious look, and smote himself once upon the breast.

"It's no use," said Mark. "If you knock ever so much in that quarter, you'll get no answer. I know better. There's nothing there but padding: and a greasy sort it is."

"Nay, Mark," urged Mr. Pinch, interposing to prevent hostilities, "tell me what I ask you. You're not out of temper, I hope?"

"Out of temper, Sir!" cried Mark, with a grin; "why no, Sir. There's a little credit—not much—in being jolly, when such fellows as him is a going about like roaring lions: if there *is* any breed of lions, at least, as is all roar and mane. What is there between him and Mrs. Lupin, Sir? Why, there's a score between him and Mrs. Lupin. And I think Mrs. Lupin lets him and his friend off very easy in not charging 'em double prices for being a disgrace to the Dragon. That's my opinion. I wouldn't have any such Peter the Wild Boy as him in my house, Sir, not if I was paid race-week prices for it. He's enough to turn the very beer in the casks sour, with his looks, he is! So he would, if it had judgment enough."

"You're not answering my question, you know, Mark," observed Mr. Pinch.

"Well, Sir," said Mark, "I don't know as there's much to answer further than that. Him and his friend goes and stops at the Moon and Stars till they've run a bill there; and then comes and stops with us and does the same. The running of bills is common enough, Mr. Pinch; it an't that as we object to; it's the ways of this chap. Nothing's good enough for him; all the women is dying for him he thinks, and is over-paid if he winks at 'em; and all the men was made to be ordered about by him. This not being aggravation enough, he says this morning to me, in his usual captivating way, 'We're going to night, my man.' 'Are you, Sir?' says I. 'Perhaps you'd like the bill got ready, Sir?' 'Oh no, my man,' he says; 'you needn't mind that. I'll give Pecksniff orders to see to that.' In reply to which the Dragon makes answer, 'Thankee, Sir, you're very kind to honour us so far, but as we don't know any particular good of you, and you don't travel with luggage, and Mr. Pecksniff an't at home (which perhaps you mayn't happen to be aware of, Sir), we should prefer something more satisfactory;' and that's where the matter stands. And I ask," said Mr. Tapley, pointing, in conclusion, to Mr. Tigg, with his hat, "any lady or gentleman, possessing ordinary strength of mind, to say, whether he's a disagreeable-looking chap or not!"

"Let me inquire," said Martin, interposing between this candid speech and the delivery of some blighting anathema by Mr. Tigg, "what the amount of this debt may be."

"In point of money, Sir, very little," answered Mark. "Only just turned of three pounds. But it an't that; it's the——"

"Yes, yes, you told us so before," said Martin. "Pinch, a word with you."

"What is it?" asked Tom, retiring with him to a corner of the room.

"Why, simply—I am ashamed to say—that this Mr. Slyme is a relation of mine, of whom I never heard anything pleasant; and that I don't want him here just now, and think he would be cheaply got rid of, perhaps, for three or four pounds. You haven't enough money to pay this bill, I suppose?"

Tom shook his head to an extent that left no doubt of his entire sincerity.

"That's unfortunate, for I am poor too; and in case you had had it, I'd have borrowed it of you. But if we told this landlady we would see her paid, I suppose that would answer the same purpose?"

"Oh dear, yes!" said Tom. "She knows me, bless you!"

"Then, let us go down at once and tell her so; for the

sooner we are rid of their company the better. As you
have conducted the conversation with this gentleman
hitherto, perhaps you'll tell him what we purpose doing;
will you?"

Mr. Pinch complying, at once imparted the intelligence
to Mr. Tigg, who shook him warmly by the hand in return,
assuring him that his faith in anything and everything was
again restored. It was not so much, he said, for the temporary relief of this assistance that he prized it, as for its
vindication of the high principle that Nature's Nobs felt
with Nature's Nobs, and true greatness of soul sympathised with true greatness of soul, all the world over. It
proved to him, he said, that like him they admired genius,
even when it was coupled with the alloy occasionally visible
in the metal of his friend Slyme; and on behalf of that
friend, he thanked them; as warmly and heartily as if the
cause were his own. Being cut short in these speeches by
a general move towards the stairs, he took possession at
the street-door of the lapel of Mr. Pinch's coat, as a security against further interruption; and entertained that gentleman with some highly improving discourse until they
reached the Dragon, whither they were closely followed by
Mark and the new pupil.

The rosy hostess scarcely needed Mr. Pinch's word as a
preliminary to the release of her two visitors, of whom she
was glad to be rid on any terms: indeed, their brief deten-
tion had originated mainly with Mr. Tapley, who entertained a constitutional dislike to gentlemen out-at-elbows
who flourished on false pretences; and had conceived a
particular aversion to Mr. Tigg and his friend, as choice
specimens of the species. The business in hand thus easily
settled, Mr. Pinch and Martin would have withdrawn immediately, but for the urgent entreaties of Mr. Tigg that
they would allow him the honour of presenting them to his
friend Slyme, which were so very difficult of resistance
that, yielding partly to these persuasions and partly to
their own curiosity, they suffered themselves to be ushered
into the presence of that distinguished gentleman.

He was brooding over the remains of yesterday's decan-
ter of brandy, and was engaged in the thoughtful occupation of making a chain of rings on the top of the table with
the wet foot of his drinking-glass. Wretched and forlorn
as he looked, Mr. Slyme had once been, in his way, the

choicest of swaggerers: putting forth his pretensions, boldly, as a man of infinite taste and most undoubted promise. The stock-in-trade requisite to set up an amateur in this department of business is very slight, and easily got together; a trick of the nose and a curl of the lip sufficient to compound a tolerable sneer, being ample provision for any exigency. But, in an evil hour, this off-shoot of the Chuzzlewit trunk, being lazy, and ill qualified for any regular pursuit, and having dissipated such means as he ever possessed, had formally established himself as a professor of Taste for a livelihood; and finding, too late, that something more than his old amount of qualifications was necessary to sustain him in this calling, had quickly fallen to his present level, where he retained nothing of his old self but his boastfulness and his bile, and seemed to have no existence separate or apart from his friend Tigg. And now so abject and so pitiful was he—at once so maudlin, insolent, beggarly, and proud—that even his friend and parasite, standing erect beside him, swelled into a Man by contrast.

"Chiv," said Mr. Tigg, clapping him on the back, "my friend Pecksniff not being at home, I have arranged our trifling piece of business with Mr. Pinch and friend. Mr. Pinch and friend, Mr. Chevy Slyme—Chiv, Mr. Pinch and friend!"

"These are agreeable circumstances in which to be introduced to strangers," said Chevy Slyme, turning his bloodshot eyes towards Tom Pinch. "I am the most miserable man in the world, I believe!"

Tom begged he wouldn't mention it; and finding him in this condition, retired, after an awkward pause, followed by Martin. But Mr. Tigg so urgently conjured them, by coughs and signs, to remain in the shadow of the door, that they stopped there.

"I swear," cried Mr. Slyme, giving the table an imbecile blow with his fist, and then feebly leaning his head upon his hand, while some drunken drops oozed from his eyes, "that I am the wretchedest creature on record. Society is in a conspiracy against me. I'm the most literary man alive. I'm full of scholarship; I'm full of genius; I'm full of information; I'm full of novel views on every subject; yet look at my condition! I'm at this moment obliged to two strangers for a tavern bill!"

8

Mr. Tigg replenished his friend's glass, pressed it into his hand, and nodded an intimation to the visitors that they would see him in a better aspect immediately.

"Obliged to two strangers for a tavern bill, eh!" repeated Mr. Slyme, after a sulky application to his glass. "Very pretty! And crowds of impostors, the while, becoming famous: men who are no more on a level with me than—Tigg, I take you to witness that I am the most persecuted hound on the face of the earth."

With a whine, not unlike the cry of the animal he named, in its lowest state of humiliation, he raised his glass to his mouth again. He found some encouragement in it; for when he set it down, he laughed scornfully. Upon that Mr. Tigg gesticulated to the visitors once more, and with great expression: implying that now the time was come when they would see Chiv in his greatness.

"Ha, ha, ha!" laughed Mr. Slyme. "Obliged to two strangers for a tavern bill! Yet I think I've a rich uncle, Tigg, who could buy up the uncles of fifty strangers? Have I, or have I not? I come of a good family, I believe? Do I, or do I not? I'm not a man of common capacity or accomplishments, I think. Am I, or am I not?"

"You are the American aloe of the human race, my dear Chiv," said Mr. Tigg, "which only blooms once in a hundred years!"

"Ha, ha, ha!" laughed Mr. Slyme, again. "Obliged to two strangers for a tavern bill! I! Obliged to two architect's apprentices—fellows who measure earth with iron chains, and build houses like bricklayers. Give me the names of those two apprentices. How dare they oblige me!"

Mr. Tigg was quite lost in admiration of this noble trait in his friend's character; as he made known to Mr. Pinch in a neat little ballet of action, spontaneously invented for the purpose.

"I'll let 'em know, and I'll let all men know," cried Chevy Slyme, "that I'm none of the mean, grovelling, tame characters they meet with commonly. I have an independent spirit. I have a heart that swells in my bosom. I have a soul that rises superior to base considerations."

"Oh, Chiv, Chiv," murmured Mr. Tigg, "you have a nobly independent nature, Chiv!"

"You go and do your duty, Sir," said Mr. Slyme, an-

grily, "and borrow money for travelling expenses; and
whoever you borrow it of, let 'em know that I possess a
haughty spirit, and a proud spirit, and have infernally
finely-touched chords in my nature, which won't brook patronage. Do you hear? Tell 'em I hate 'em, and that
that's the way I preserve my self-respect; and tell 'em
that no man ever respected himself more than I do!"

He might have added that he hated two sorts of men;
all those who did him favours, and all those who were better off than himself; as in either case their position was an
insult to a man of his stupendous merits. But he did not;
for with the apt closing words above recited, Mr. Slyme—
of too haughty a stomach to work, to beg, to borrow, or to
steal; yet mean enough to be worked or borrowed, begged
or stolen for, by any catspaw that would serve his turn;
too insolent to lick the hand that fed him in his need, yet
cur enough to bite and tear it in the dark—with these apt
closing words, Mr. Slyme fell forward with his head upon
the table, and so declined into a sodden sleep.

"Was there ever," cried Mr. Tigg, joining the young
men at the door, and shutting it carefully behind him,
"such an independent spirit as is possessed by that extraordinary creature? Was there ever such a Roman as our
friend Chiv? Was there ever a man of such a purely classical turn of thought, and of such a toga-like simplicity of
nature? Was there ever a man with such a flow of eloquence? Might he not, gents both, I ask, have sat upon a
tripod in the ancient times, and prophesied to a perfectly
unlimited extent, if previously supplied with gin-and-water
at the public cost?"

Mr. Pinch was about to contest this latter position with
his usual mildness, when, observing that his companion
had already gone down stairs, he prepared to follow him.

"You are not going, Mr. Pinch?" said Tigg.

"Thank you," answered Tom. "Yes. Don't come
down."

"Do you know that I should like one little word in private with you, Mr. Pinch?" said Tigg, following him.
"One minute of your company in the skittle-ground would
very much relieve my mind. Might I beseech that favour?"

"Oh, certainly," replied Tom, "if you really wish it."
So he accompanied Mr. Tigg to the retreat in question: on

arriving at which place that gentleman took from his hat what seemed to be the fossil remains of an antediluvian pocket-handkerchief, and wiped his eyes therewith.

"You have not beheld me this day," said Mr. Tigg, "in a favourable light."

"Don't mention that," said Tom, "I beg."

"But you have *not*," cried Tigg. "I must persist in that opinion. If you could have seen me, Mr. Pinch, at the head of my regiment on the coast of Africa, charging in the form of a hollow square with the women and children and the regimental plate-chest in the centre, you would not have known me for the same man. You would have respected me, Sir."

Tom had certain ideas of his own upon the subject of glory; and consequently he was not quite so much excited by this picture as Mr. Tigg could have desired.

"But no matter!" said that gentleman. "The schoolboy writing home to his parents and describing the milk-and-water, said 'This is indeed weakness.' I repeat that assertion in reference to myself at the present moment: and I ask your pardon. Sir, you have seen my friend Slyme?"

"No doubt," said Mr. Pinch.

"Sir, you have been impressed by my friend Slyme?"

"Not very pleasantly, I must say," answered Tom, after a little hesitation.

"I am grieved but not surprised," cried Mr. Tigg, detaining him by both lapels, "to hear that you have come to that conclusion; for it is my own. But, Mr. Pinch, though I am a rough and thoughtless man, I can honour Mind. I honour Mind in following my friend. To you of all men, Mr. Pinch, I have a right to make appeal on Mind's behalf, when it has not the art to push its fortune in the world. And so, Sir—not for myself, who have no claim upon you, but for my crushed, my sensitive and independent friend, who has—I ask the loan of three half-crowns. I ask you for the loan of three half-crowns, distinctly, and without a blush. I ask it, almost as a right. And when I add that they will be returned by post, this week, I feel that you will blame me for that sordid stipulation."

Mr. Pinch took from his pocket an old-fashioned red-leather purse with a steel clasp, which had probably once belonged to his deceased grandmother. It held one half-sovereign and no more. All Tom's worldly wealth until next quarter-day.

"Stay!" cried Mr. Tigg, who had watched this proceeding keenly. "I was just about to say, that for the convenience of posting you had better make it gold. Thank you. A general direction, I suppose, to Mr. Pinch, at Mr. Pecksniff's—will that find you?"

"That'll find me," said Tom. "You had better put Esquire to Mr. Pecksniff's name, if you please. Direct to me, you know, at Seth Pecksniff's, Esquire."

"At Seth Pecksniff's, Esquire," repeated Mr. Tigg, taking an exact note of it, with a stump of pencil. "We said this week, I believe?"

"Yes; or Monday will do," observed Tom.

"No, no, I beg your pardon. Monday will not do," said Mr. Tigg. "If we stipulated for this week, Saturday is the latest day. Did we stipulate for this week?"

"Since you are so particular about it," said Tom, "I think we did."

Mr. Tigg added this condition to his memorandum; read the entry over to himself with a severe frown; and that the transaction might be the more correct and business-like, appended his initials to the whole. That done, he assured Mr. Pinch that everything was now perfectly regular; and, after squeezing his hand with great fervour, departed.

Tom entertained enough suspicion that Martin might possibly turn this interview into a jest, to render him desirous to avoid the company of that young gentleman for the present. With this view he took a few turns up and down the skittle-ground, and did not re-enter the house until Mr. Tigg and his friend had quitted it, and the new pupil and Mark were watching their departure from one of the windows.

"I was just a saying, Sir, that if one could live by it," observed Mark, pointing after their late guests, "that would be the sort of service for me. Waiting on such individuals as them, would be better than grave-digging, Sir."

"And staying here would be better than either, Mark," replied Tom. "So take my advice, and continue to swim easily in smooth water."

"It's too late to take it now, Sir," said Mark. "I have broke it to her, Sir. I am off to-morrow morning."

"Off!" cried Mr. Pinch, "where to?"

"I shall go up to London, Sir."

"What to be?" asked Mr. Pinch.

"Well! I don't know yet, Sir. Nothing turned up that day I opened my mind to you, as was at all likely to suit me. All them trades I thought of was a deal too jolly; there was no credit at all to be got in any of 'em. I must look for a private service, I suppose, Sir. I might be brought out strong, perhaps, in a serious family, Mr. Pinch."

"Perhaps you might come out rather too strong for a serious family's taste, Mark."

"That's possible, Sir. If I could get into a wicked family, I might do myself justice: but the difficulty is to make sure of one's ground, because a young man can't very well advertise that he wants a place, and wages an't so much an object as a wicked sitivation; can he, Sir?"

"Why, no," said Mr. Pinch, "I don't think he can."

"An envious family," pursued Mark, with a thoughtful face; "or a quarrelsome family, or a malicious family, or even a good out-and-out mean family, would open a field of action as I might do something in. The man as would have suited me of all other men was that old gentleman as was took ill here, for he really was a trying customer. Howsever, I must wait and see what turns up, Sir; and hope for the worst."

"You are determined to go then?" said Mr. Pinch.

"My box is gone already, Sir, by the waggon, and I'm going to walk on to-morrow morning, and get a lift by the day coach when it overtakes me. So I wish you good by'e, Mr. Pinch—and you too, Sir,—and all good luck and happiness!"

They both returned his greeting laughingly, and walked home arm-in-arm; Mr. Pinch imparting to his new friend, as they went, such further particulars of Mark Tapley's whimsical restlessness as the reader is already acquainted with.

In the mean time Mark, having a shrewd notion that his mistress was in very low spirits, and that he could not exactly answer for the consequences of any lengthened tête-à-tête in the bar, kept himself obstinately out of her way all the afternoon and evening. In this piece of generalship he was very much assisted by the great influx of company into the tap-room; for the news of his intention having gone abroad, there was a perfect throng there all the evening, and much drinking of healths and clinking of mugs. At length the house was closed for the night; and there being now no help for it, Mark put the best face he could upon the matter, and walked doggedly to the bar-door.

"If I look at her," said Mark to himself, "I'm done. I feel that I'm a going fast."

"You have come at last," said Mrs. Lupin.

Ay, Mark said: There he was.

"And you are determined to leave us, Mark?" cried Mrs. Lupin.

"Why, yes; I am," said Mark; keeping his eyes hard upon the floor.

"I thought," pursued the landlady, with a most engaging hesitation, "that you had been—fond—of the Dragon?"

"So I am," said Mark.

"Then," pursued the hostess—and it really was not an unnatural inquiry—"why do you desert it?"

But as he gave no manner of answer to this question; not even on its being repeated; Mrs. Lupin put his money into his hand, and asked him, not unkindly, quite the contrary—what he would take.

It is proverbial that there are certain things which flesh and blood cannot bear. Such a question as this, propounded in such a manner, at such a time, and by such a person, proved (at least, as far as Mark's flesh and blood were concerned) to be one of them. He looked up in spite of himself directly; and having once looked up, there was no looking down again; for of all the tight, plump, buxom, bright-eyed, dimple-faced landladies that ever shone on earth, there stood before him then, bodily in that bar, the very pink and pine-apple.

"Why, I tell you what," said Mark, throwing off all his constraint in an instant, and seizing the hostess round the waist—at which she was not at all alarmed, for she knew what a good young man he was—"if I took what I liked most, I should take you. If I only thought of what was best for me, I should take you. If I took what nineteen young fellows in twenty would be glad to take, and would take at any price, I should take you. Yes, I should," cried Mr. Tapley, shaking his head, expressively enough, and looking (in a momentary state of forgetfulness) rather

hard at the hostess's ripe lips. "And no man wouldn't
wonder if I did!"

Mrs. Lupin said he amazed her. She was astonished
how he could say such things. She had never thought it
of him.

"Why, I never thought it of myself till now!" said
Mark, raising his eyebrows with a look of the merriest possible surprise. "I always expected we should part, and
never have no explanation; I meant to do it when I come
in here just now; but there's something about you, as
makes a man sensible. Then let us have a word or two together; letting it be understood beforehand—" he added
this in a grave tone, to prevent the possibility of any mistake—"that I'm not a going to make no love, you know."

There was for just one second a shade—though not by
any means a dark one—on the landlady's open brow. But
it passed off instantly, in a laugh that came from her very
heart.

"Oh, very good!" she said; "if there is to be no love-
making, you had better take your arm away."

"Lord, why should I!" cried Mark. "It's quite innocent."

"Of course it's innocent," returned the hostess, "or I
shouldn't allow it."

"Very well!" said Mark. "Then let it be."

There was so much reason in this, that the landlady
laughed again, suffered it to remain, and bade him say
what he had to say, and be quick about it. But he was
an impudent fellow, she added.

"Ha ha! I almost think I am!" cried Mark, "though I
never thought so before. Why, I can say anything to-
night!"

"Say what you're going to say if you please, and be
quick," returned the landlady, "for I want to get to bed."

"Why, then, my dear good soul," said Mark, "and a
kinder woman than you are, never drawed breath—let me
see the man as says she did!—what would be the likely
consequence of us two being—"

"Oh nonsense!" cried Mrs. Lupin. "Don't talk about
that any more."

"No, no, but it an't nonsense," said Mark; "and I wish
you'd attend. What would be the likely consequence of
us two being married? If I can't be content and comfort-

able in this here lively Dragon now, is it to be looked for as I should be then? By no means. Very good. Then you, even with your good humour, would be always on the fret and worrit, always uncomfortable in your own mind, always a thinking as you was getting too old for my taste, always a picturing me to yourself as being chained up to the Dragon door, and wanting to break away. I don't know that it would be so," said Mark, "but I don't know that it mightn't be. I *am* a roving sort of chap, I know. I'm fond of change. I'm always a thinking that with my good health and spirits it would be more creditable in me to be jolly where there's things a going on to make one dismal. It may be a mistake of mine, you see, but nothing short of trying how it acts, will set it right. Then an't it best that I should go: particular when your free way has helped me out to say all this, and we can part as good friends as we have ever been since first I entered this here noble Dragon, which," said Mr. Tapley in conclusion, "has my good word and my good wish, to the day of my death!"

The hostess sat quite silent for a little time, but she very soon put both her hands in Mark's and shook them heartily.

" For you are a good man," she said; looking into his face with a smile, which was rather serious for her. " And I do believe have been a better friend to me to-night than ever I have had in all my life."

"Oh! as to that, you know," said Mark, "that's nonsense. But love my heart alive!" he added, looking at her in a sort of rapture, "if you *are* that way disposed, what a lot of suitable husbands there is as you may drive distracted!"

She laughed again at this compliment; and, once more shaking him by both hands, and bidding him, if he should ever want a friend, to remember her, turned gaily from the little bar, and up the Dragon staircase.

" Humming a tune as she goes," said Mark, listening, "in case I should think she's at all put out, and should be made down-hearted. Come, here's some credit in being jolly, at last!"

With that piece of comfort, very ruefully uttered, he went, in anything but a jolly manner, to bed.

He rose early next morning, and was a-foot soon after sunrise. But it was of no use; the whole place was up to see Mark Tapley off: the boys, the dogs, the children, the old men, the busy people and the idlers: there they were, all calling out "Good by'e, Mark," after their own manner, and all sorry he was going. Somehow he had a kind of sense that his old mistress was peeping from her chamber-window, but he couldn't make up his mind to look back.

"Good by'e one, good by'e all!" cried Mark, waving his hat on the top of his walking-stick, as he strode at a quick pace up the little street. "Hearty chaps them wheelwrights—hurrah! Here's the butcher's dog a-coming out of the garden—down, old fellow! And Mr. Pinch a-going to his organ—good by'e, Sir! And the terrier-bitch from over the way—hie, then, lass! And children enough to hand down human natur to the latest posterity—good by'e, boys and girls! There's some credit in it now. I'm a-coming out strong at last. These are the circumstances as would try a ordinary mind; but I'm uncommon jolly; not quite as jolly as I could wish to be, but very near. Good by'e! good by'e!"

CHAPTER VIII.

ACCOMPANIES MR. PECKSNIFF AND HIS CHARMING DAUGHTERS TO THE CITY OF LONDON; AND RELATES WHAT FELL OUT, UPON THEIR WAY THITHER.

WHEN Mr. Pecksniff and the two young ladies got into the heavy coach at the end of the lane, they found it empty, which was a great comfort; particularly as the outside was quite full and the passengers looked very frosty For as Mr. Pecksniff justly observed—when he and his daughters had burrowed their feet deep in the straw, wrapped themselves to the chin, and pulled up both windows—it is always satisfactory to feel, in keen weather, that many other people are not as warm as you are. And this, he said, was quite natural, and a very beautiful arrangement; not confined to coaches, but extending itself into many social ramifications. "For" (he observed), "if every one were warm and well-fed, we should lose the satisfaction of admiring the fortitude with which certain con-

ditions of men bear cold and hunger. And if we were no
better off than anybody else, what would become of our
sense of gratitude; which," said Mr. Pecksniff with tears
in his eyes, as he shook his fist at a beggar who wanted to
get up behind, "is one of the holiest feelings of our common nature."

His children heard with becoming reverence these moral
precepts from the lips of their father, and signified their
acquiescence in the same, by smiles. That he might the
better feed and cherish that sacred flame of gratitude in
his breast, Mr. Pecksniff remarked that he would trouble
his eldest daughter, even in this early stage of their journey, for the brandy-bottle. And from the narrow neck of
that stone vessel, he imbibed a copious refreshment.

"What are we?" said Mr. Pecksniff, "but coaches?
Some of us are slow coaches"—

"Goodness, Pa!" cried Charity.

"Some of us, I say," resumed her parent with increased
emphasis, "are slow coaches; some of us are fast coaches. Our passions are the horses; and rampant animals
too!"—

"Really, Pa!" cried both the daughters at once. "How
very unpleasant."

"And rampant animals too!" repeated Mr. Pecksniff,
with so much determination, that he may be said to have
exhibited, at the moment, a sort of moral rampancy himself: "and Virtue is the drag. We start from The Mother's Arms, and we run to The Dust Shovel."

When he had said this, Mr. Pecksniff, being exhausted,
took some further refreshment. When he had done that,
he corked the bottle tight, with the air of a man who had
effectually corked the subject also; and went to sleep for
three stages.

The tendency of mankind when it falls asleep in coaches,
is to wake up cross; to find its legs in its way; and its
corns an aggravation. Mr. Pecksniff not being exempt
from the common lot of humanity, found himself, at the
end of his nap, so decidedly the victim of these infirmities,
that he had an irresistible inclination to visit them upon
his daughters; which he had already begun to do in the
shape of divers random kicks, and other unexpected mo-
tions of his shoes, when the coach stopped, and after a
short delay, the door was opened.

"Now mind," said a thin sharp voice in the dark. "I and my son go inside, because the roof is full, but you agree only to charge us outside prices. It's quite understood that we won't pay more. Is it?"

"All right, Sir," replied the guard.

"Is there anybody inside now?" inquired the voice

"Three passengers," returned the guard.

"Then I ask the three passengers to witness this bargain, if they will be so good," said the voice. "My boy, I think we may safely get in."

In pursuance of which opinion, two people took their seats in the vehicle, which was solemnly licensed by Act of Parliament to carry any six persons who could be got in at the door.

"That was lucky!" whispered the old man, when they moved on again. "And a great stroke of policy in you to observe it. He, he, he! We couldn't have gone outside. I should have died of the rheumatism!"

Whether it occurred to the dutiful son that he had in some degree over-reached himself by contributing to the prolongation of his father's days; or whether the cold had affected his temper; is doubtful. But he gave his father such a nudge in reply, that that good old gentleman was taken with a cough which lasted for full five minutes, without intermission, and goaded Mr. Pecksniff to that pitch of irritation, that he said at last—and very suddenly—

"There is no room! There is really no room in this coach for any gentleman with a cold in his head!"

"Mine," said the old man, after a moment's pause, "is upon my chest, Pecksniff."

The voice and manner, together, now that he spoke out; the composure of the speaker; the presence of his son; and his knowledge of Mr. Pecksniff; afforded a clue to his identity which it was impossible to mistake.

"Hem! I thought," said Mr. Pecksniff, returning to his usual mildness, "that I addressed a stranger. I find that I address a relative. Mr. Anthony Chuzzlewit and his son Mr. Jonas—for they, my dear children, are our travelling companions—will excuse me for an apparently harsh remark. It is not *my* desire to wound the feelings of any person with whom I am connected in family bonds. I may be a Hypocrite," said Mr. Pecksniff, cuttingly, "but I am not a Brute."

"Pooh, pooh!" said the old man. "What signifies that word, Pecksniff? Hypocrite! why, we are all hypocrites. We were all hypocrites t'other day. I am sure I felt that to be agreed upon among us, or I shouldn't have called you one. We should not have been there at all, if we had not been hypocrites. The only difference between you and the rest was—shall I tell you the difference between you and the rest now, Pecksniff?"

"If you please, my good Sir; if you please."

"Why, the annoying quality in *you*, is," said the old man, "that you never have a confederate or partner in *your* juggling; you would deceive everybody, even those who practise the same art; and have a way with you, as if you —he, he, he!—as if you really believed yourself. I'd lay a handsome wager now," said the old man, "if I laid wagers, which I don't and never did, that you keep up appearances by a tacit understanding, even before your own daughters here. Now I, when I have a business scheme in hand, tell Jonas what it is, and we discuss it openly. You're not offended, Pecksniff?"

"Offended, my good Sir!" cried that gentleman, as if he had received the highest compliments that language could convey.

"Are you travelling to London, Mr. Pecksniff?" asked the son.

"Yes, Mr. Jonas, we are travelling to London. We shall have the pleasure of your company all the way, I trust?"

"Oh! ecod, you had better ask father that," said Jonas. "I am not a going to commit myself."

Mr. Pecksniff was, as a matter of course, greatly entertained by this retort. His mirth having subsided, Mr. Jonas gave him to understand that himself and parent were in fact travelling to their home in the metropolis: and that, since the memorable day of the great family gathering, they had been tarrying in that part of the country, watching the sale of certain eligible investments, which they had had in their copartnership eye when they came down; for it was their custom, Mr. Jonas said, whenever such a thing was practicable, to kill two birds with one stone, and never to throw away sprats, but as bait for whales. When he had communicated, to Mr. Pecksniff, these pithy scraps of intelligence, he said "That if it was

all the same to him, he would turn him over to father, and
have a chat with the gals;" and in furtherance of this
polite scheme, he vacated his seat adjoining that gentleman, and established himself in the opposite corner, next
to the fair Miss Mercy.

The education of Mr. Jonas had been conducted from his
cradle on the strictest principles of the main chance. The
very first word he learnt to spell was "gain," and the second (when he got into two syllables), "money." But for
two results, which were not clearly foreseen perhaps by his
watchful parent in the beginning, his training may be said
to have been unexceptionable. One of these flaws was,
that having been long taught by his father to over-reach
everybody, he had imperceptibly acquired a love of over-
reaching that venerable monitor himself. The other, that
from his early habits of considering everything as a question of property, he had gradually come to look, with impatience, on his parent as a certain amount of personal
estate, which had no right whatever to be going at large,
but ought to be secured in that particular description of
iron safe which is commonly called a coffin, and banked in
the grave.

"Well, cousin!" said Mr. Jonas—"Because we *are*
cousins, you know, a few times removed—so you're going
to London?"

Miss Mercy replied in the affirmative, pinching her sister's arm at the same time, and giggling excessively.

"Lots of beaux in London, cousin!" said Mr. Jonas,
slightly advancing his elbow.

"Indeed, Sir!" cried the young lady. "They won't
hurt us, Sir, I dare say." And having given him this answer with great demureness, she was so overcome by her
own humour, that she was fain to stifle her merriment in
her sister's shawl.

"Merry," cried that more prudent damsel, "really I am
ashamed of you. How can you go on so? You wild
thing!" At which Miss Merry only laughed the more, of
course.

"I saw a wildness in her eye, t'other day," said Mr.
Jonas, addressing Charity. "But you're the one to sit
solemn! I say—you were regularly prim, cousin!"

"Oh! The old-fashioned fright!" cried Merry, in a
whisper. "Cherry, my dear, upon my word you must sit

next him. I shall die outright if he talks to me any more; I shall positively!" To prevent which fatal consequence, the buoyant creature skipped out of her seat as she spoke, and squeezed her sister into the place from which she had risen.

"Don't mind crowding me," cried Mr. Jonas. "I like to be crowded by gals. Come a little closer, cousin."

"No, thank you, Sir," said Charity.

"There's that other one a laughing again," said Mr. Jonas; "she's a laughing at my father, I shouldn't wonder. If he puts on that old flannel nightcap of his, I don't know what she'll do! Is that my father a snoring, Pecksniff?"

"Yes, Mr. Jonas."

"Tread upon his foot, will you be so good?" said the young gentleman. "The foot next you's the gouty one."

Mr. Pecksniff hesitating to perform this friendly office, Mr. Jonas did it himself; at the same time crying—

"Come, wake up, father, or you'll be having the nightmare, and screeching out, I know.—Do you ever have the nightmare, cousin?" he asked his neighbour, with characteristic gallantry, as he dropped his voice again.

"Sometimes," answered Charity. "Not often."

"The other one," said Mr. Jonas, after a pause. "Does she ever have the nightmare?"

"I don't know," replied Charity. "You had better ask her."

"She laughs so;" said Jonas; "there's no talking to her. Only hark how she's a going on now! You're the sensible one, cousin!"

"Tut, tut!" cried Charity.

"Oh! But you are! You know you are!"

"Mercy is a little giddy," said Miss Charity. "But she'll sober down in time."

"It'll be a very long time, then, if she does at all," rejoined her cousin. "Take a little more room."

"I am afraid of crowding you," said Charity. But she took it notwithstanding; and after one or two remarks on the extreme heaviness of the coach, and the number of places it stopped at, they fell into a silence which remained unbroken by any member of the party until suppertime.

Although Mr. Jonas conducted Charity to the hotel and sat himself beside her at the board, it was pretty clear that

he had an eye to "the other one" also, for he often glanced
across at Mercy, and seemed to draw comparisons between
the personal appearance of the two, which were not unfa-
vourable to the superior plumpness of the younger sister.
He allowed himself no great leisure for this kind of observation, however, being busily engaged with the supper,
which, as he whispered in his fair companion's ear, was a
contract business, and therefore the more she ate, the better the bargain was. His father and Mr. Pecksniff, probably acting on the same wise principle, demolished everything that came within their reach, and by that means
acquired a greasy expression of countenance, indicating
contentment, if not repietion, which it was very pleasant
to contemplate.

When they could eat no more, Mr. Pecksniff and Mr.
Jonas subscribed for two sixpennyworths of hot brandy-
and-water, which the latter gentleman considered a more
politic order than one shillingsworth; there being a chance
of their getting more spirit out of the innkeeper under this
arrangement than if it were all in one glass. Having
swallowed his share of the enlivening fluid, Mr. Pecksniff,
under pretence of going to see if the coach were ready,
went secretly to the bar, and had his own little bottle
filled, in order that he might refresh himself at leisure in
the dark coach without being observed.

These arrangements concluded, and the coach being
ready, they got into their old places and jogged on again.
But before he composed himself for a nap, Mr. Pecksniff
delivered a kind of grace after meat, in these words:

"The process of digestion, as I have been informed by
anatomical friends, is one of the most wonderful works of
nature. I do not know how it may be with others, but it
is a great satisfaction to me to know, when regaling on my
humble fare, that I am putting in motion the most beautiful machinery with which we have any acquaintance. I
really feel at such times as if I was doing a public service.
When I have wound myself up, if I may employ such a
term," said Mr. Pecksniff with exquisite tenderness, "and
know that I am Going, I feel that in the lesson afforded by
the works within me, I am a Benefactor to my Kind!"

As nothing could be added to this, nothing was said; and
Mr. Pecksniff, exulting, it may be presumed, in his moral
utility, went to sleep again.

The rest of the night wore away in the usual manner. Mr. Pecksniff and old Anthony kept tumbling against each other and waking up much terrified; or crushed their heads in opposite corners of the coach and strangely tattooed the surface of their faces—Heaven knows how—in their sleep. The coach stopped and went on, and went on and stopped, times out of number. Passengers got up and passengers got down, and fresh horses came and went and came again, with scarcely any interval between each team as it seemed to those who were dozing, and with a gap of a whole night between every one as it seemed to those who were broad awake. At length they began to jolt and rumble over horribly uneven stones, and Mr. Pecksniff looking out of window said it was to-morrow morning, and they were there.

Very soon afterwards the coach stopped at the office in the City; and the street in which it was situated was already in a bustle, that fully bore out Mr. Pecksniff's words about its being morning, though for any signs of day yet appearing in the sky it might have been midnight. There was a dense fog too—as if it were a city in the clouds, which they had been travelling to all night up a magic beanstalk—and a thick crust upon the pavement like oil-cake; which, one of the outsides (mad, no doubt) said to another (his keeper, of course), was snow.

Taking a confused leave of Anthony and his son, and leaving the luggage of himself and daughters at the office to be called for afterwards, Mr. Pecksniff, with one of the young ladies under each arm, dived across the street, and then across other streets, and so up the queerest courts, and down the strangest alleys and under the blindest arch-ways, in a kind of frenzy: now skipping over a kennel, now running for his life from a coach and horses; now thinking he had lost his way, now thinking he had found it; now in a state of the highest confidence, now despondent to the last degree, but always in a great perspiration and flurry; until at length they stopped in a kind of paved yard near the Monument. That is to say, Mr. Pecksniff told them so; for as to anything they could see of the Monument, or anything else but the buildings close at hand, they might as well have been playing blindman's buff at Salisbury.

Mr. Pecksniff looked about him for a moment, and then
9

knocked at the door of a very dingy edifice, even among
the choice collection of dingy edifices at hand; on the front
of which was a little oval board like a tea-tray, with this
inscription—"Commercial Boarding-House.   M. Todgers."
It seemed that M. Todgers was not up yet, for Mr. Pecksniff knocked twice and rang thrice, without making any
impression on anything but a dog over the way. At last
a chain and some bolts were withdrawn with a rusty noise,
as if the weather had made the very fastenings hoarse, and
a small boy with a large red head, and no nose to speak of,
and a very dirty Wellington boot on his left arm, appeared;
who (being surprised) rubbed the nose just mentioned with
the back of his shoe-brush, and said nothing.

"Still a-bed, my man?" asked Mr. Pecksniff.

"Still a-bed!" replied the boy. "I wish they wos still
a-bed. They're very noisy a-bed; all calling for their
boots at once. I thought you was the Paper, and wondered
why you didn't shove yourself through the grating as usual.
What do you want?"

Considering his years, which were tender, the youth may
be said to have preferred this question sternly, and in something of a defiant manner. But Mr. Pecksniff, without
taking umbrage at his bearing, put a card in his hand, and
bade him take that upstairs, and show them in the meanwhile into a room where there was a fire.

"Or if there's one in the eating parlour," said Mr. Pecksniff, "I can find it myself." So he led his daughters,
without waiting for any further introduction, into a room
on the ground-floor, where a table-cloth (rather a tight and
scanty fit in reference to the table it covered) was already
spread for breakfast: displaying a mighty dish of pink
boiled beef; an instance of that particular style of loaf
which is known to housekeepers as a slack-baked, crummy
quartern; a liberal provision of cups and saucers; and the
usual appendages.

Inside the fender were some half-dozen pairs of shoes and
boots, of various sizes, just cleaned and turned with the
soles upwards to dry; and a pair of short black gaiters, on
one of which was chalked—in sport, it would appear, by
some gentleman who had slipped down for the purpose,
pending his toilet, and gone up again—"Jinkins's Particular," while the other exhibited a sketch in profile, claiming
to be the portrait of Jinkins himself.

M. Todgers's Commercial Boarding-House was a house of that sort which is likely to be dark at any time; but that morning it was especially dark. There was an odd smell in the passage, as if the concentrated essence of all the dinners that had been cooked in the kitchen since the house was built, lingered at the top of the kitchen stairs to that hour, and, like the Black Friar in *Don Juan*, "wouldn't be driven away." In particular, there was a sensation of cabbage; as if all the greens that had ever been boiled there, were evergreens, and flourished in immortal strength. The parlour was wainscoted, and communicated to strangers a magnetic and instinctive consciousness of rats and mice. The staircase was very gloomy and very broad, with balustrades so thick and heavy that they would have served for a bridge. In a sombre corner on the first landing, stood a gruff old giant of a clock, with a preposterous coronet of three brass balls on his head; whom few had ever seen—none ever looked in the face—and who seemed to continue his heavy tick for no other reason than to warn heedless people from running into him accidentally. It had not been papered or painted, hadn't Todgers's, within the memory of man. It was very black, begrimed, and mouldy. And, at the top of the staircase, was an old, disjointed, rickety, ill-favoured skylight, patched and mended in all kinds of ways, which looked distrustfully down at everything that passed below, and covered Todgers's up as if it were a sort of human cucumber-frame, and only people of a peculiar growth were reared there.

Mr. Pecksniff and his fair daughters had not stood warming themselves at the fire ten minutes, when the sound of feet was heard upon the stairs, and the presiding deity of the establishment came hurrying in.

M. Todgers was a lady, rather a bony and hard-featured lady, with a row of curls in front of her head, shaped like little barrels of beer; and on the top of it something made of net—you couldn't call it a cap exactly—which looked like a black cobweb. She had a little basket on her arm, and in it a bunch of keys that jingled as she came. In her other hand she bore a flaming tallow candle, which, after surveying Mr. Pecksniff for one instant by its light, she put down upon the table, to the end that she might receive him with the greater cordiality.

"Mr. Pecksniff," cried Mrs. Todgers. "Welcome to

London! Who would have thought of such a visit as this,
after so—dear, dear!—so many years! How do you *do*,
Mr. Pecksniff?"

"As well as ever; and as glad to see you, as ever;" Mr.
Pecksniff made response. "Why, you are younger than
you used to be!"

"*You* are, I am sure!" said Mrs. Todgers. "You're not
a bit changed."

"What do you say to this?" cried Mr. Pecksniff, stretching out his hand towards the young ladies. "Does this
make me no older?"

"Not your daughters!" exclaimed the lady, raising her
hands and clasping them. "Oh, no, Mr. Pecksniff! Your
second, and her bridesmaid!"

Mr. Pecksniff smiled complacently; shook his head; and
said, "My daughters, Mrs. Todgers: merely my daughters."

"Ah!" sighed the good lady, "I must believe you, for
now I look at 'em I think I should have known 'em anywhere. My dear Miss Pecksniffs, how happy your Pa has
made me!"

She hugged them both; and being by this time overpow-
ered by her feelings or the inclemency of the morning,
jerked a little pocket-handkerchief out of the little basket,
and applied the same to her face.

"Now, my good madam," said Mr. Pecksniff, "I know
the rules of your establishment, and that you only receive
gentlemen boarders. But it occurred to me, when I left
home, that perhaps you would give my daughters house
room, and make an exception in their favour."

"Perhaps?" cried Mrs. Todgers ecstatically. "Perhaps?"

"I may say then, that I was sure you would," said Mr.
Pecksniff. "I know that you have a little room of your
own, and that they can be comfortable there, without appearing at the general table."

"Dear girls!" said Mrs. Todgers. "I must take that
liberty once more."

Mrs. Todgers meant by this that she must embrace them
once more, which she accordingly did, with great ardour.
But the truth was, that, the house being full with the exception of one bed, which would now be occupied by Mr.
Pecksniff, she wanted time for consideration; and so much

time too (for it was a knotty point how to dispose of them), that even when this second embrace was over, she stood for some moments gazing at the sisters, with affection beaming in one eye, and calculation shining out of the other.

"I think I know how to arrange it," said Mrs. Todgers, at length. "A sofa bedstead in the little third room which opens from my own parlour—Oh, you dear girls!"

Thereupon she embraced them once more, observing that she could not decide which was most like their poor mother (which was highly probable: seeing that she had never beheld that lady), but that she rather thought the youngest was; and then she said that as the gentlemen would be down directly, and the ladies were fatigued with travelling, would they step into her room at once?

It was on the same floor; being, in fact, the back parlour; and had, as Mrs. Todgers said, the great advantage (in London) of not being overlooked; as they would see when the fog cleared off. Nor was this a vain-glorious boast, for it commanded at a perspective of two feet, a brown wall with a black cistern on the top. The sleeping apartment designed for the young ladies was approached from this chamber by a mightily convenient little door, which would only open when fallen against by a strong person. It commanded from a similar point of sight another angle of the wall, and another side of the cistern. "Not the damp side," said Mrs. Todgers. "*That* is Mr. Jinkins's."

In the first of these sanctuaries a fire was speedily kindled by the youthful porter, who, whistling at his work in the absence of Mrs. Todgers (not to mention his sketching figures on his corduroys with burnt firewood), and being afterwards taken by that lady in the fact, was dismissed with a box on his ears. Having prepared breakfast for the young ladies with her own hands, she withdrew to preside in the other room; where the joke at Mr. Jinkins's expense, seemed to be proceeding rather noisily.

"I won't ask you yet, my dears," said Mr. Pecksniff, looking in at the door, "how you like London. Shall I?"

"We haven't seen much of it, Pa!" cried Merry.

"Nothing, I hope," said Cherry. (Both very miserably.)

"Indeed," said Mr. Pecksniff, "that's true. We have our pleasure, and our business too, before us. All in good time. All in good time!"

Whether Mr. Pecksniff's business in London was as
strictly professional as he had given his new pupil to understand, we shall see, to adopt that worthy man's phrase-
ology, "all in good time."

CHAPTER IX.

TOWN AND TODGERS'S.

SURELY there never was, in any other borough, city, or
hamlet, in the world, such a singular sort of a place as
Todgers's. And surely London, to judge from that part
of it which hemmed Todgers's round, and hustled it, and
crushed it, and stuck its brick-and-mortar elbows into it,
and kept the air from it, and stood perpetually between it
and the light, was worthy of Todgers's, and qualified to be
on terms of close relationship and alliance with hundreds
and thousands of the odd family to which Todgers's belonged.

You couldn't walk about in Todgers's neighbourhood, as
you could in any other neighbourhood. You groped your
way for an hour through lanes and bye-ways, and court-
yards and passages; and never once emerged upon anything that might be reasonably called a street. A kind of
resigned distraction came over the stranger as he trod those
devious mazes, and, giving himself up for lost, went in and
out and round about, and quietly turned back again when
he came to a dead wall or was stopped by an iron railing,
and felt that the means of escape might possibly present
themselves in their own good time, but that to anticipate
them was hopeless. Instances were known of people who,
being asked to dine at Todgers's, had travelled round and
round it for a weary time, with its very chimney-pots in
view; and finding it, at last, impossible of attainment, had
gone home again with a gentle melancholy on their spirits,
tranquil and uncomplaining. Nobody had ever found Todgers's on a verbal direction, though given within a minute's
walk of it. Cautious emigrants from Scotland or the
North of England had been known to reach it safely by im-
pressing a charity-boy, town-bred, and bringing him along
with them; or by clinging tenaciously to the postman; but

these were rare exceptions, and only went to prove the rule that Todgers's was in a labyrinth, whereof the mystery was known but to a chosen few.

Several fruit-brokers had their marts near Todgers's; and one of the first impressions wrought upon the stranger's senses was of oranges—of damaged oranges, with blue and green bruises on them, festering in boxes, or mouldering away in cellars. All day long, a stream of porters from the wharves beside the river, each bearing on his back a bursting chest of oranges, poured slowly through the narrow passages; while underneath the archway by the public-house, the knots of those who rested and regaled within, were piled from morning until night. Strange solitary pumps were found near Todgers's, hiding themselves for the most part in blind alleys, and keeping company with fire-ladders. There were churches also by dozens, with many a ghostly little churchyard, all overgrown with such straggling vegetation as springs up spontaneously from damp, and graves, and rubbish. In some of these dingy resting-places, which bore much the same analogy to green churchyards, as the pots of earth for mignonette and wall-flower in the windows overlooking them, did to rustic gardens, there were trees; tall trees; still putting forth their leaves in each succeeding year, with such a languishing remembrance of their kind (so one might fancy, looking on their sickly boughs) as birds in cages have of theirs. Here, paralysed old watchmen guarded the bodies of the dead at night, year after year, until at last they joined that solemn brotherhood; and, saving that they slept below the ground a sounder sleep than even they had ever known above it, and were shut up in another kind of box, their condition can hardly be said to have undergone any material change when they, in turn, were watched themselves.

Among the narrow thoroughfares at hand, there lingered, here and there, an ancient doorway of carved oak, from which, of old, the sounds of revelry and feasting often came; but now these mansions, only used for storehouses, were dark and dull, and, being filled with wool, and cotton, and the like—such heavy merchandise as stifles sound and stops the throat of echo—had an air of palpable deadness about them which, added to their silence and desertion, made them very grim. In like manner, there were

gloomy court-yards in these parts, into which few but be-
lated wayfarers ever strayed, and where vast bags and
packs of goods, upward or downward bound, were for ever
dangling between heaven and earth from lofty cranes.
There were more trucks near Todgers's than you would
suppose a whole city could ever need; not active trucks,
but a vagabond race, for ever lounging in the narrow lanes
before their masters' doors and stopping up the pass; so
that when a stray hackney-coach or lumbering waggon
came that way, they were the cause of such an uproar as
enlivened the whole neighbourhood, and made the very
bells in the next church-tower vibrate again. In the
throats and maws of dark no-thoroughfares near Todgers's,
individual wine-merchants and wholesale dealers in grocery-
ware had perfect little towns of their own; and, deep among
the very foundations of these buildings, the ground was un-
dermined and burrowed out into stables, where cart-horses,
troubled by rats, might be heard on a quiet Sunday rattling
their halters, as disturbed spirits in tales of haunted houses
are said to clank their chains.

To tell of half the queer old taverns that had a drowsy
and secret existence near Todgers's, would fill a goodly
book; while a second volume no less capacious might be
devoted to an account of the quaint old guests who fre-
quented their dimly-lighted parlours. These were, in general, ancient inhabitants of that region; born, and bred
there from boyhood; who had long since become wheezy
and asthmatical, and short of breath, except in the article
of story-telling: in which respect they were still marvel-
lously long-winded. These gentry were much opposed to
steam and all new-fangled ways, and held ballooning to be
sinful, and deplored the degeneracy of the times; which
that particular member of each little club who kept the
keys of the nearest church, professionally, always attributed to the prevalence of dissent and irreligion; though
the major part of the company inclined to the belief that
virtue went out with hair-powder, and that Old England's
greatness had decayed amain with barbers.

As to Todgers's itself—speaking of it only as a house in
that neighbourhood, and making no reference to its merits
as a commercial boarding establishment—it was worthy to
stand where it did. There was one staircase-window in it·
at the side of the house, on the ground-floor: which tradi·

tion said had not been opened for a hundred years at least,
and which, abutting on an always dirty lane, was so begrimed and coated with a century's mud, that no one pane
of glass could possibly fall out, though all were cracked
and broken twenty times.   But the grand mystery of Todgers's was the cellarage, approachable only by a little back
door and a rusty grating: which cellarage within the memory of man had had no connexion with the house, but had
always been the freehold property of somebody else, and
was reported to be full of wealth: though in what shape—
whether in silver, brass, or gold, or butts of wine, or casks
of gunpowder—was matter of profound uncertainty and su-
preme indifference to Todgers's, and all its inmates.

The top of the house was worthy of notice.   There was
a sort of terrace on the roof, with posts and fragments of
rotten lines, once intended to dry clothes upon; and there
were two or three tea-chests out there, full of earth, with forgotten plants in them, like old walking-sticks.   Whoever
climbed to this observatory, was stunned at first from having knocked his head against the little door in coming out;
and after that, was for the moment choked from having
looked, perforce, straight down the kitchen chimney; but
these two stages over, there were things to gaze at from the
top of Todgers's, well worth your seeing too.   For first and
foremost, if the day were bright, you observed upon the
house-tops, stretching far away, a long dark path: the
shadow of the Monument: and turning round, the tall
original was close beside you, with every hair erect upon
his golden head, as if the doings of the city frightened
him.   Then there were steeples, towers, belfries, shining
vanes, and masts of ships: a very forest.   Gables, house-
tops, garret-windows, wilderness upon wilderness.   Smoke
and noise enough for all the world at once.

After the first glance, there were slight features in the
midst of this crowd of objects, which sprang out from the
mass without any reason, as it were, and took hold of
the attention whether the spectator would or no   Thus,
the revolving chimney-pots on one great stack of buildings,
seemed to be turning gravely to each other every now and
then, and whispering the result of their separate observation of what was going on below.   Others, of a crook-
backed shape, appeared to be maliciously holding themselves askew, that they might shut the prospect out and baffle

Todgers's. The man who was mending a pen at an upper
window over the way, became of paramount importance in
the scene, and made a blank in it, ridiculously dispropor-
tionate in its extent, when he retired. The gambols of a
piece of cloth upon the dyer's pole had far more interest
for the moment than all the changing motion of the crowd.
Yet even while the looker-on felt angry with himself for
this, and wondered how it was, the tumult swelled into a
roar; the host of objects seemed to thicken and expand a
hundred-fold; and after gazing round him, quite scared, he
turned into Todgers's again, much more rapidly than he
came out; and ten to one he told M. Todgers afterwards
that if he hadn't done so, he would certainly have come into
the street by the shortest cut: that is to say, headforemost.

So said the two Miss Pecksniffs, when they retired with
Mrs. Todgers from this place of espial, leaving the youthful porter to close the door and follow them down stairs:
who being of a playful temperament, and contemplating
with a delight peculiar to his sex and time of life, any
chance of dashing himself into small fragments, lingered
behind to walk upon the parapet.

It being the second day of their stay in London, the
Miss Pecksniffs and Mrs. Todgers were by this time highly
confidential, insomuch that the last-named lady had already
communicated the particulars of three early disappointments
of a tender nature; and had furthermore possessed her young
friends with a general summary of the life, conduct, and
character of Mr. Todgers: who, it seemed, had cut his
matrimonial career rather short, by unlawfully running
away from his happiness, and establishing himself in foreign countries as a bachelor.

"Your pa was once a little particular in his attentions,
my dears," said Mrs. Todgers: "but to be your ma was too
much happiness denied me. You'd hardly know who this
was done for, perhaps?"

She called their attention to an oval miniature, like a little blister, which was tacked up over the kettle-holder, and
in which there was a dreamy shadowing forth of her own
visage

"It's a speaking likeness!" cried the two Miss Pecksniffs.

"It was considered so once," said Mrs. Todgers, warming herself in a gentlemanly manner at the fire: "but I
hardly thought you would have known it, my loves."

They would have known it anywhere. If they could have met with it in the street, or seen it in a shop window, they would have cried: "Good gracious! Mrs. Todgers!"

"Presiding over an establishment like this, makes sad havoc with the features, my dear Miss Pecksniffs," said Mrs. Todgers. "The gravy alone, is enough to add twenty years to one's age, I do assure you."

"Lor!" cried the two Miss Pecksniffs.

"The anxiety of that one item, my dears," said Mrs. Todgers, "keeps the mind continually upon the stretch. There is no such passion in human nature, as the passion for gravy among commercial gentlemen. It's nothing to say a joint won't yield—a whole animal wouldn't yield—the amount of gravy they expect each day at dinner. And what I have undergone in consequence," cried Mrs. Todgers, raising her eyes and shaking her head, "no one would believe!"

"Just like Mr. Pinch, Merry!" said Charity. "We have always noticed it in him, you remember?"

"Yes, my dear," giggled Merry, "but we have never given it him, you know."

"You, my dears, having to deal with your pa's pupils who can't help themselves, are able to take your own way," said Mrs. Todgers, "but in a commercial establishment, where any gentleman may say, any Saturday evening, 'Mrs. Todgers, this day week we part, in consequence of the cheese,' it is not so easy to preserve a pleasant understanding. Your pa was kind enough," added the good lady, "to invite me to take a ride with you to-day; and I think he mentioned that you were going to call upon Miss Pinch. Any relation to the gentleman you were speaking of just now, Miss Pecksniff?"

"For goodness sake, Mrs. Todgers," interposed the lively Merry, "don't call him a gentleman. My dear Cherry, Pinch a gentleman! The idea!"

"What a wicked girl you are!" cried Mrs. Todgers, embracing her with great affection. "You are quite a quiz I do declare! My dear Miss Pecksniff, what a happiness your sister's spirits must be to your pa and self!"

"He's the most hideous, goggle-eyed creature, Mrs. Todgers, in existence," resumed Merry: "quite an ogre. The ugliest, awkwardest, frightfullest being, you can imagine. This is his sister, so I leave you to suppose what

she is. I shall be obliged to laugh outright, I know 1
shall!" cried the charming girl, "I never shall be able to
keep my countenance. The notion of a Miss Pinch pre-
suming to exist at all is sufficient to kill one, but to see her
—oh my stars!"

Mrs. Todgers laughed immensely at the dear love's humour, and declared she was quite afraid of her, that she
was. She was so very severe.

"Who is severe?" cried a voice at the door. "There is
no such thing as severity in our family, I hope!" And
then Mr. Pecksniff peeped smilingly into the room, and
said, "May I come in, Mrs. Todgers?"

Mrs. Todgers almost screamed, for the little door of
communication between that room and the inner one being
wide open, there was a full disclosure of the sofa bedstead
in all its monstrous impropriety. But she had the presence of mind to close this portal in the twinkling of an eye;
and having done so, said, though not without confusion,
"Oh yes, Mr. Pecksniff, you can come in, if you please."

"How are we to-day," said Mr. Pecksniff, jocosely; "and
what are our plans? Are we ready to go and see Tom
Pinch's sister? Ha, ha, ha! Poor Thomas Pinch!"

"Are we ready," returned Mrs. Todgers, nodding her
head with mysterious intelligence, "to send a favourable
reply to Mr. Jinkins's round-robin? That's the first question, Mr. Pecksniff."

"Why Mr. Jinkins's robin, my dear madam?" asked
Mr. Pecksniff, putting one arm round Mercy, and the other
round Mrs. Todgers, whom he seemed, in the abstraction
of the moment, to mistake for Charity. "Why Mr. Jinkins's?"

"Because he began to get it up, and indeed always takes
the lead in the house," said Mrs. Todgers, playfully.
"That's why, Sir."

"Jinkins is a man of superior talents," observed Mr.
Pecksniff. "I have conceived a great regard for Jinkins.
I take Jinkins's desire to pay polite attention to my
daughters, as an additional proof of the friendly feeling of
Jinkins, Mrs. Todgers."

"Well now," returned that lady, "having said so much,
you must say the rest, Mr. Pecksniff: so tell the dear
young ladies all about it."

With these words, she gently eluded Mr. Pecksniff's

grasp, and took Miss Charity into her own embrace;
though whether she was impelled to this proceeding solely
by the irrepressible affection she had conceived for that
young lady, or whether it had any reference to a lowering
not to say distinctly spiteful expression which had been
visible in her face for some moments, has never been exactly ascertained. Be this as it may, Mr. Pecksniff went
on to inform his daughters of the purport and history of
the round-robin aforesaid, which was in brief, that the
commercial gentlemen who helped to make up the sum and
substance of that noun of multitude or signifying many,
called Todgers's, desired the honour of their presence at
the general table, so long as they remained in the house,
and besought that they would grace the board at dinner-
time next day, the same being Sunday. He further said,
that Mrs. Todgers being a consenting party to this
invitation, he was willing, for his part, to accept it; and
so left them that he might write his gracious answer, the
while they armed themselves with their best bonnets for
the utter defeat and overthrow of Miss Pinch.

Tom Pinch's sister was governess in a family, a lofty
family; perhaps the wealthiest brass and copper founders'
family known to mankind. They lived at Camberwell; in
a house so big and fierce that its mere outside, like the
outside of a giant's castle, struck terror into vulgar minds
and made bold persons quail. There was a great front
gate; with a great bell, whose handle was in itself a note
of admiration; and a great lodge; which being close to the
house, rather spoilt the look-out certainly, but made the
look-in tremendous. At this entry, a great porter kept
constant watch and ward; and when he gave the visitor
high leave to pass, he rang a second great bell, responsive
to whose note a great footman appeared in due time at the
great hall-door, with such great tags upon his liveried
shoulder that he was perpetually entangling and hooking
himself among the chairs and tables, and led a life of torment which could scarcely have been surpassed, if he had
been a blue-bottle in a world of cobwebs.

To this mansion, Mr. Pecksniff, accompanied by his
daughters and Mrs. Todgers, drove gallantly in a one-horse
fly. The foregoing ceremonies having been all performed,
they were ushered into the house; and so, by degrees, they
got at last into a small room with books in it, where Mr

7—6

Pinch's sister was at that moment, instructing her eldest
pupil: to wit, a premature little woman of thirteen years
old, who had already arrived at such a pitch of whalebone
and education that she had nothing girlish about her, which
was a source of great rejoicing to all her relations and
friends.

"Visitors for Miss Pinch!" said the footman. He must
have been an ingenious young man, for he said it very
cleverly: with a nice discrimination between the cold respect with which he would have announced visitors to the
family, and the warm personal interest with which he
would have announced visitors to the cook.

"Visitors for Miss Pinch!"

Miss Pinch rose hastily; with such tokens of agitation as
plainly declared tha' her list of callers was not numerous.
At the same time, the little pupil became alarmingly upright, and prepared herself to take mental notes of all that
migLt be said and done. For the lady of the establishment
was curious in the natural history and habits of the animal
called Governess, and encouraged her daughters to report
thereon whenever occasion served; which was, in reference
to all parties concerned, very laudable, improving, and
pleasant.

It is a melancholy fact; but it must be related, that Mr.
Pinch's sister was not at all ugly. On the contrary, she
had a good face; a very mild and prepossessing face; and
a pretty little figure—slight and short, but remarkable for
its neatness. There was something of her brother, much
of him indeed, in a certain gentleness of manner, and in
her look of timid trustfulness; but she was so far from
being a fright, or a dowdy, or a horror, or anything else,
predicted by the two Miss Pecksniffs, that those young
ladies naturally regarded her with great indignation, feeling that this was by no means what they had come to see.

Miss Mercy, as having the larger share of gaiety, bore
up the best against this disappointment, and carried it off,
in outward show at least, with a titter; but her sister, not
caring to hide her disdain, expressed it pretty openly in her
looks. As to Mrs. Todgers, she leaned on Mr. Pecksniff's
arm and preserved a kind of genteel grimness, suitable to
any state of mind, and involving any shade of opinion.

"Don't be alarmed, Miss Pinch," said Mr. Pecksniff,
taking her hand condescendingly in one of his, and patting

it with the other. "I have called to see you, in pursuance of a promise given to your brother, Thomas Pinch. My name—compose yourself, Miss Pinch—is Pecksniff."

The good man emphasized these words as though he would have said, "You see in me, young person, the benefactor of your race; the patron of your house; the preserver of your brother, who is fed with manna daily from my table; and in right of whom there is a considerable balance in my favour at present standing in the books beyond the sky. But I have no pride, for I can afford to do with‧out it!"

The poor girl felt it all as if it had been Gospel Truth Her brother writing in the fulness of his simple heart, had often told her so, and how much more! As Mr. Pecksniff ceased to speak, she hung her head, and dropped a tear upon his hand.

"Oh very well, Miss Pinch!" thought the sharp pupil, "crying before strangers, as if you didn't like the situation!"

"Thomas is well," said Mr. Pecksniff; "and sends his love and this letter. I cannot say, poor fellow, that he will ever be distinguished in our profession; but he has the will to do well, which is the next thing to having the power; and, therefore, we must bear with him. Eh?"

"I know he has the will, Sir," said Tom Pinch's sister, "and I know how kindly and considerately you cherish it, for which neither he nor I can ever be grateful enough, as we very often say in writing to each other. The young ladies too," she added, glancing gratefully at his two daughters, "I know how much we owe to them."

"My dears," said Mr. Pecksniff, turning to them with a smile: "Thomas's sister is saying something you will be glad to hear, I think."

"We can't take any merit to ourselves, papa!" cried Cherry, as they both apprised Tom Pinch's sister, with a curtsey, that they would feel obliged if she would keep her distance. "Mr. Pinch's being so well provided for is owing to you alone, and we can only say how glad we are to hear that he is as grateful as he ought to be."

"Oh very well, Miss Pinch!" thought the pupil again. "Got a grateful brother, living on other people's kindness!"

"It was very kind of you," said Tom Pinch's sister, with Tom's own simplicity, and Tom's own smile, "to come

nere: very kind indeed: though how great a kindness you
have done me in gratifying my wish to see you, and to
thank you with my own lips, you, who make so light of
benefits conferred, can scarcely think."

"Very grateful; very pleasant; very proper," murmured
Mr. Pecksniff.

"It makes me happy too," said Ruth Pinch, who now
that her first surprise was over, had a chatty, cheerful way
with her, and a single-hearted desire to look upon the best
side of everything, which was the very moral and image
of Tom; "very happy to think that you will be able to tell
him how more than comfortably I am situated here, and
how unnecessary it is that he should ever waste a regret on
my being cast upon my own resources. Dear me! So
long as I heard that he was happy, and he heard that
I was," said Tom's sister, "we could both bear, without one
impatient or complaining thought, a great deal more than
ever we have had to endure, I am very certain." And if
ever the plain truth were spoken on this occasionally false
earth, Tom's sister spoke it when she said that.

"Ah!" cried Mr. Pecksniff, whose eyes had in the meantime wandered to the pupil; "certainly. And how do *you*
do, my very interesting child?"

"Quite well, I thank you, Sir," replied that frosty innocent.

"A sweet face this, my dears," said Mr. Pecksniff, turning to his daughters. "A charming manner!"

Both young ladies had been in ecstacies with the scion
of a wealthy house (through whom the nearest road and
shortest cut to her parents might be supposed to lie) from
the first. Mrs. Tⁿdgers vowed that anything one quarter
so angelic she had ɪever seen. She wanted but a pair of
wings, a dear," **said** that good woman, "to be a young
syrup,"—meaning, possibly, young sylph, or seraph.

"If you will ɡive that to your distinguished parents, my
amiable litᵗle friend," said Mr. Pecksniff, producing one
of his professional cards, "and will say that I and my
daughters—"

"And Mrs. Todgers, pa," said Merry.

"And Mrs. Todgers, of London," added Mr. Pecksniff;
"that I, and my daughters, and Mrs. Todgers, of London,
did not intrude upon them, as our object simply was to take
some notice of Miss Pinch, whose brother is a young man

in my employment; but that I could not leave this very chaste mansion, without adding my humble tribute, as an Architect, to the corr;ctness and elegance of the owner's taste, and to his just appreciation of that beautiful art, to the cultivation of which I have devoted a life, and to the promotion of whose glory and advancement I have sacrificed a—a fortune—I shall be very much obliged to you."

"Missis's compliments to Miss Pinch," said the footman, suddenly appearing, and speaking in exactly the same key as before, "and begs to know wot my young lady is a learning of just now."

"Oh!" said Mr. Pecksniff, "here is the young man. *He* will take the card. With my compliments, if you please, young man. My dears, we are interrupting the studies. Let us go."

Some confusion was occasioned for an instant by Mrs. Todgers's unstrapping her little flat hand-basket, and hurriedly entrusting the "young man" with one of her own cards, which, in addition to certain detailed information relative to the terms of the commercial establishment, bore a foot-note to the effect that M. T. took that opportunity of thanking those gentlemen who had honoured her with their favours, and begged that they would have the goodness, if satisfied with the table, to recommend her to their friends. But Mr. Pecksniff, with admirable presence of mind, recovered this document, and buttoned it up in his own pocket.

Then he said to Miss Pinch—with more condescension and kindness than ever, for it was desirable the footman should expressly understand that they were not friends of hers, but patrons:

"Good morning. Good bye. God bless you! You may depend upon my continued protection of your brother Thomas. Keep your mind quite at ease, Miss Pinch!"

"Thank you," said Tom's sister heartily: "a thousand times."

"Not at all," he retorted, patting her gently on the head. "Don't mention it. You will make me angry if you do. My sweet child"—to the pupil, "farewell! That fairy creature," said Mr. Pecksniff, looking in his pensive mood hard at the footman, as if he meant him, "has shed a vision on my path, refulgent in its nature, and not easily to be obliterated. My dears, are you ready?"

10

They were not quite ready yet, for they were still caressing the pupil. But they tore themselves away at length; and sweeping past Miss Pinch with each a haughty inclination of the head and a curtsey strangled in its birth, flounced into the passage.

The "young man" had rather a long job in showing them out; for Mr. Pecksniff's delight in the tastefulness of the house was such that he could not help often stopping (particularly when they were near the parlour door) and giving it expression, in a loud voice and very learned terms. Indeed, he delivered, between the study and the hall, a familiar exposition of the whole science of architecture as applied to dwelling-houses, and was yet in the freshness of his eloquence when they reached the garden.

"If you look," said Mr. Pecksniff, backing from the steps, with his head on one side and his eyes half-shut that he might the better take in the proportions of the exterior: "If you look, my dears, at the cornice which supports the roof, and observe the airiness of its construction, especially where it sweeps the southern angle of the building, you will feel with me—How do you do, Sir? I hope you're well!"

Interrupting himself with these words, he very politely bowed to a middle-aged gentleman at an upper window, to whom he spoke, not because the gentleman could hear him (for he certainly could not), but as an appropriate accompaniment to his salutation.

"I have no doubt, my dears," said Mr. Pecksniff, feigning to point out other beauties with his hand, "that that is the proprietor. I should be glad to know him. It might lead to something. Is he looking this way, Charity?"

"He is opening the window, pa!"

"Ha, ha!" cried Mr. Pecksniff, softly. "All right! He has found I'm professional. He heard me inside just now, I have no doubt. Don't look! With regard to the fluted pillars in the portico, my dears—"

"Hallo!" cried the gentleman.

"Sir, your servant!" said Mr. Pecksniff, taking off his hat. "I am proud to make your acquaintance."

"Come off the grass, will you!" roared the gentleman.

"I beg your pardon, Sir," said Mr. Pecksniff, doubtful of his having heard aright. "Did you—?"

"Come off the grass!" repeated the gentleman, warmly.

"We are unwilling to intrude, Sir," Mr. Pecksniff smilingly began.

"But you *are* intruding," returned the other, "unwarrantably intruding—trespassing. You see a gravel walk, don't you? What do you think it's meant for? Open the gate there! Show that party out!"

With that, he clapped down the window again, and disappeared.

Mr. Pecksniff put on his hat, and walked with great deliberation and in profound silence to the fly, gazing at the clouds as he went, with great interest. After helping his daughters and Mrs. Todgers into that conveyance, he stood looking at it for some moments, as if he were not quite certain whether it was a carriage or a temple; but, having settled this point in his mind, he got into his place, spread his hands out on his knees, and smiled upon the three beholders.

But his daughters, less tranquil-minded, burst into a torrent of indignation. This came, they said, of cherishing such creatures as the Pinches. This came of lowering themselves to their level. This came of putting themselves in the humiliating position of seeming to know such bold, audacious, cunning, dreadful girls as that. They had expected this. They had predicted it to Mrs. Todgers, as she (Todgers) could depone, that very morning. To this, they added, that the owner of the house, supposing them to be Miss Pinch's friends, had acted, in their opinion, quite correctly, and had done no more than, under such circumstances, might reasonably have been expected. To that they added (with a trifling inconsistency), that he was a brute and a bear; and then they merged into a flood of tears, which swept away all wandering epithets before it.

Perhaps Miss Pinch was scarcely so much to blame in the matter as the Seraph, who, immediately on the withdrawal of the visitors, had hastened to report them at headquarters, with a full account of their having presumptuously charged her with the delivery of a message afterwards consigned to the footman; which outrage, taken in conjunction with Mr. Pecksniff's unobtrusive remarks on the establishment, might possibly have had some share in their dismissal. Poor Miss Pinch, however, had to bear the brunt of it with both parties: being so severely taken to task by the Seraph's mother for having such vulgar acquaintances, that she was fain to retire to her own room in tears, which her natural cheerfulness and submission, and the delight of having seen Mr. Pecksniff, and having received a letter from her brother, were at first insufficient to repress.

As to Mr. Pecksniff, he told them in the fly, that a good action was its own reward; and rather gave them to understand, that if he could have been kicked in such a cause, he would have liked it all the better. But this was no comfort to the young ladies, who scolded violently the whole way back, and even exhibited, more than once, a keen desire to attack the devoted Mrs. Todgers: on whose personal appearance, but particularly on whose offending card and hand-basket, they were secretly inclined to lay the blame of half their failure.

Todgers's was in a great bustle that evening, partly owing to some additional domestic preparations for the morrow, and partly to the excitement always inseparable in that house from Saturday night, when every gentleman's linen arrived at a different hour in its own little bundle, with his private account pinned on the outside. There was always a great clinking of pattens down stairs, too, until midnight or so, on Saturdays; together with a frequent gleaming of mysterious lights in the area; much working at the pump; and a constant jangling of the iron handle of the pail. Shrill altercations from time to time arose between Mrs. Todgers and unknown females in remote back kitchens; and sounds were occasionally heard, indicative of small articles of ironmongery and hardware being thrown at the boy. It was the custom of that youth on Saturdays, to roll up his shirt sleeves to his shoulders, and pervade all parts of the house in an apron of coarse green baize; moreover, he was more strongly tempted on Saturdays than on other days (it being a busy time), to make excursive bolts into the neighbouring alleys when he answered the door, and there to play at leap-frog and other sports with vagrant lads, until pursued and brought back by the hair of his head, or the lobe of his ear; so that he was quite a conspicuous feature among the peculiar incidents of the last day in the week at Todgers's.

He was especially so on this particular Saturday evening, and honoured the Miss Pecksniffs with a deal of notice; seldom passing the door of Mrs. Todgers's private room, where they sat alone before the fire, working by the light of a solitary candle, without putting in his head and greeting them with some such compliments as, "There you are agin!" "An't it nice?"—and similar humorous attentions.

"I say," he whispered, stopping in one of his journeys to and fro, "young ladies, there's soup to-morrow. She's a making it now. An't she a putting in the water? Oh! not at all neither!"

In the course of answering another knock, he thrust in his head again.

"I say—there's fowls to-morrow. Not skinny ones. Oh no!"

Presently he called through the key-hole:

"There's a fish to-morrow—just come. Don't eat none of him!" And, with this special warning, vanished again.

By-and-bye, he returned to lay the cloth for supper: it having been arranged between Mrs. Todgers and the young ladies, that they should partake of an exclusive veal-cutlet together in the privacy of that apartment. He entertained them on this occasion by thrusting the lighted candle into his mouth, and exhibiting his face in a state of transparency; after the performance of which feat, he went on with his professional duties; brightening every knife as he laid it on the table, by breathing on the blade and afterwards polishing the same on the apron already mentioned. When he had completed his preparations, he grinned at the sisters, and expressed his belief that the approaching collation would be of "rather a spicy sort."

"Will it be long before it's ready, Bailey?" asked Mercy.

"No," said Bailey, "it *is* cooked. When I come up, she was dodging among the tender pieces with a fork, and eating of 'em."

But he had scarcely achieved the utterance of these words, when he received a manual compliment on the head, which sent him staggering against the wall; and Mrs. Todgers, dish in hand, stood indignantly before him.

"Oh you little villain!" said that lady. "Oh you bad, false boy!"

"No worse than yerself," retorted Bailey, guarding his head, on a principle invented by Mr. Thomas Cribb. "Ah! Come now! Do that agin, will yer!"

"He's the most dreadful child," said Mrs. Todgers, setting down the dish, "I ever had to deal with. The gentle-

men spoil him to that extent, and teach him such things,
that I'm afraid nothing but hanging will ever do him any
good."

"Won't it?" cried Bailey. "Oh! Yes! Wot do you
go a lowerin the table-beer for then, and destroying my
constitooshun?"

"Go down stairs, you vicious boy," said Mrs. Todgers,
holding the door open. "Do you hear me? Go along!"

After two or three dexterous feints, he went, and was
seen no more that night, save once, when he brought up
some tumblers and hot water, and much disturbed the two
Miss Pecksniffs by squinting hideously behind the back of
the unconscious Mrs. Todgers. Having done this justice
to his wounded feelings, he retired underground; where, in
company with a swarm of black beetles and a kitchen candle, he employed his faculties in cleaning boots and brushing clothes until the night was far advanced.

Benjamin was supposed to be the real name of this young
retainer, but he was known by a great variety of names.
Benjamin, for instance, had been converted into Uncle Ben,
and that again had been corrupted into Uncle; which, by
an easy transition, had again passed into Barnwell, in
memory of the celebrated relative in that degree who was
shot by his nephew George, while meditating in his garden
at Camberwell. The gentlemen at Todgers's had a merry
habit, too, of bestowing upon him, for the time being, the
name of any notorious malefactor or minister; and sometimes, when current events were flat, they even sought the
pages of history for these distinctions; as Mr. Pitt, Young
Brownrigg, and the like. At the period of which we write,
he was generally known among the gentlemen as Bailey
junior; a name bestowed upon him in contradistinction,
perhaps, to Old Bailey; and possibly as involving the recollection of an unfortunate lady of the same name, who perished by her own hand early in life, and has been immor-
talised in a ballad.

The usual Sunday dinner-hour at Todgers's was two
o'clock,—a suitable time, it was considered, for all parties;
convenient to Mrs. Todgers, on account of the baker's; and
convenient to the gentlemen, with reference to their afternoon engagements. But on the Sunday which was to introduce the two Miss Pecksniffs to a full knowledge of
Todgers's and its society, the dinner was postponed until

five, in order that everything might be as genteel as the occasion demanded.

When the hour drew nigh, Bailey junior, testifying great excitement, appeared in a complete suit of cast-off clothes several sizes too large for him, and in particular, mounted a clean shirt of such extraordinary magnitude, that one of the gentlemen (remarkable for his ready wit) called him "collars" on the spot. At about a quarter before five, a deputation, consisting of Mr. Jinkins, and another gentleman whose name was Gander, knocked at the door of Mrs. Todgers's room, and, being formally introduced to the two Miss Pecksniffs by their parent, who was in waiting, besought the honour of conducting them up stairs.

The drawing-room at Todgers's was out of the common style; so much so indeed, that you would hardly have taken it to be a drawing-room, unless you were told so by somebody who was in the secret. It was floor-clothed all over; and the ceiling, including a great beam in the middle, was papered. Besides the three little windows, with seats in them, commanding the opposite archway, there was another window looking point blank, without any compromise at all about it, into Jinkins's bed-room; and high up all along one side of the wall was a strip of panes of glass, two-deep, giving light to the staircase. There were the oddest closets possible, with little casements in them like eight-day clocks, lurking in the wainscot and taking the shape of the stairs; the very door itself (which was painted black) had two great glass eyes in its forehead, with an inquisitive green pupil in the middle of each.

Here the gentlemen were all assembled. There was a general cry of "Hear, hear!" and "Bravo Jink!" when Mr. Jinkins appeared with Charity on his arm: which became quite rapturous as Mr. Gander followed, escorting Mercy, and Mr. Pecksniff brought up the rear with Mrs. Todgers.

Then the presentations took place. They included a gentleman of a sporting turn, who propounded questions on jockey subjects to the editors of Sunday papers, which were regarded by his friends as rather stiff things to answer; and they included a gentleman of a theatrical turn, who had once entertained serious thoughts of "coming out," but had been kept in by the wickedness of human nature; and they included a gentleman of a debating turn, who was strong at speech-making; and a gentleman of a literary turn, who wrote squibs upon the rest, and knew the weak side of everybody's character but his own. There was a gentleman of a vocal turn, and a gentleman of a smoking turn, and a gentleman of a convivial turn; some of the gentlemen had a turn for whist, and a large proportion of the gentlemen had a strong turn for billiards and betting. They had all, it may be presumed, a turn for business; being all commercially employed in one way or other; and had, every one in his own way, a decided turn for pleasure to boot. Mr. Jinkins was of a fashionable turn; being a regular frequenter of the Parks on Sundays, and knowing a great many carriages by sight. He spoke mysteriously, too, of splendid women, and was suspected of having once committed himself with a Countess. Mr. Gander was of a witty turn, being indeed the gentleman who had originated the sally about "collars; " which sparkling pleasantry was now retailed from mouth to mouth, under the title of Gander's Last, and was received in all parts of the room with great applause. Mr. Jinkins, it may be added, was much the oldest of the party: being a fish-salesman's bookkeeper, aged forty. He was the oldest boarder also; and in right of his double seniority, took the lead in the house, as Mrs. Todgers had already said.

There was considerable delay in the production of dinner, and poor Mrs. Todgers, being reproached in confidence by Jinkins, slipped in and out, at least twenty times to see about it; always coming back as though she had no such thing upon her mind, and hadn't been out at all. But there was no hitch in the conversation, nevertheless; for one gentleman, who travelled in the perfumery line, exhibited an interesting nick-nack, in the way of a remarkable cake of shaving soap, which he had lately met with in Germany; and the gentleman of a literary turn repeated (by desire) some sarcastic stanzas he had recently produced on the freezing of the tank at the back of the house. These amusements, with the miscellaneous conversation arising out of them, passed the time splendidly, until dinner was announced by Bailey junior in these terms:

"The wittles is up! "

On which notice they immediately descended to the banquet-hall; some of the more facetious spirits in the rear taking down gentlemen as if they were ladies, in imitation of the fortunate possessors of the two Miss Pecksniffs.

Mr. Pecksniff said grace—a short and pious grace, invoking a blessing on the appetites of those present, and committing all persons who had nothing to eat, to the care of Providence: whose business (so said the grace, in effect) it clearly was, to look after them. This done, they fell to, with less ceremony than appetite; the table groaning beneath the weight, not only of the delicacies whereof the Miss Pecksniffs had been previously forewarned, but of boiled beef, roast veal, bacon, pies, and abundance of such heavy vegetables as are favourably known to housekeepers for their satisfying qualities. Besides which, there were bottles of stout, bottles of wine, bottles of ale, and divers other strong drinks, native and foreign.

All this was highly agreeable to the two Miss Pecksniffs, who were in immense request; sitting one on either hand of Mr. Jinkins at the bottom of the table; and who were called upon to take wine with some new admirer every minute. They had hardly ever felt so pleasant, and so full of conversation, in their lives; Mercy, in particular, was uncommonly brilliant, and said so many good things in the way of lively repartee that she was looked upon as a prodigy. "In short," as that young lady observed, "they felt now, indeed, that they were in London, and for the first time too."

Their young friend Bailey sympathised in these feelings to the fullest extent, and, abating nothing of his patronage, gave them every encouragement in his power: favouring them, when the general attention was diverted from his proceedings, with many nods and winks and other tokens of recognition, and occasionally touching his nose with a corkscrew, as if to express the Bacchanalian character of the meeting. In truth, perhaps even the spirits of the two Miss Pecksniffs, and the hungry watchfulness of Mrs. Todgers, were less worthy of note than the proceedings of this remarkable boy, whom nothing disconcerted or put out of his way. If any piece of crockery—a dish or otherwise—chanced to slip through his hands (which happened once or twice), he let it go with perfect good breeding, and never added to the painful emotion of the company by exhibiting the least regret. Nor did he, by hurrying to and fro, disturb the repose of the assembly, as many well-trained servants do; on the contrary, feeling the hopelessness of waiting upon so large a party, he left the gentlemen to help themselves to what they wanted, and seldom stirred from behind Mr. Jinkins's chair, where, with his hands in his pockets, and his legs planted pretty wide apart, he led the laughter, and enjoyed the conversation.

The dessert was splendid. No waiting either. The pudding-plates had been washed in a little tub outside the door while cheese was on, and though they were moist and warm with friction, still there they were again, up to the mark, and true to time. Quarts of almonds; dozens of oranges; pounds of raisins; stacks of biffins; soup-plates full of nuts.—Oh, Todgers's could do it when it chose! Mind that.

Then more wine came on; red wines and white wines; and a large china bowl of punch, brewed by the gentleman of a convivial turn, who adjured the Miss Pecksniffs not to be despondent on account of its dimensions, as there were materials in the house for the concoction of half-a-dozen more of the same size. Good gracious, how they laughed! How they coughed when they sipped it, because it was so strong; and how they laughed again, when somebody vowed that but for its colour it might have been mistaken, in regard of its innocuous qualities, for new milk! What a shout of "No!" burst from the gentlemen when they pathetically implored Mr. Jinkins to suffer them to qualify it with hot water; and how blushingly, by little and little, did each of them drink her whole glassful, down to its very dregs!

Now comes the trying time. The sun, as Mr. Jinkins says (gentlemanly creature, Jinkins—never at a loss!), is about to leave the firmament. "Miss Pecksniff!" says Mrs. Todgers, softly, "will you—?" "Oh dear, no more, Mrs. Todgers." Mrs. Todgers rises; the two Miss Pecksniffs rise; all rise. Miss Mercy Pecksniff looks downward for her scarf. Where is it? Dear me, where *can* it be? Sweet girl, she has it on—not on her fair neck, but loose upon her flowing figure. A dozen hands assist her. She is all confusion. The youngest gentleman in company thirsts to murder Jinkins. She skips and joins her sister at the door. Her sister has her arm about the waist of Mrs. Todgers. She winds her arm around her sister. Diana, what a picture! The last things visible are a shape and a skip. "Gentlemen, let us drink the ladies!"

The enthusiasm is tremendous. The gentleman of a de-

bating turn rises in the midst, and suddenly lets loose a
tide of eloquence which bears down everything before it.
He is reminded of a toast—a toast to which they will respond. There is an individual present; he has him in his
eye; to whom they owe a debt of gratitude. He repeats
it—a debt of gratitude. Their rugged natures have been
softened and ameliorated that day by the society of lovely
woman. There is a gentleman in company whom two ac-
complished and delightful females regard with veneration,
as the fountain of their existence. Yes, when yet the two
Miss Pecksniffs lisped in language scarce intelligible, they
called that individual "Father!" There is great applause.
He gives them "Mr. Pecksniff, and God bless him!" They
all shake hands with Mr. Pecksniff, as they drink the
toast. The youngest gentleman in company does so with
a thrill; for he feels that a mysterious influence pervades
the man who claims that being in the pink scarf for his
daughter.

What saith Mr. Pecksniff in reply? Or rather let the
question be, What leaves he unsaid? Nothing. More
punch is called for, and produced, and drunk. Enthusiasm
mounts still higher. Every man comes out freely in his
own character. The gentleman of a theatrical turn recites.
The vocal gentleman regales them with a song. Gander
leaves the Gander of all former feasts whole leagues behind. _He_ rises to propose a toast. It is, The Father of
Todgers's. It is their common friend Jink—it is Old Jink,
if he may call him by that familiar and endearing appellation. The youngest gentleman in company utters a frantic
negative. He won't have it—he can't bear it—it mustn't
be. But his depth of feeling is misunderstood. He is supposed to be a little elevated; and nobody heeds him.

Mr. Jinkins thanks them from his heart. It is, by many
degrees, the proudest day in his humble career. When he
looks around him on the present occasion, he feels that he
wants words in which to express his gratitude. One thing
he will say. He hopes it has been shown that Todgers's
can be true to itself; and, an opportunity arising, that it
can come out quite as strong as its neighbours—perhaps
stronger. He reminds them, amidst thunders of encouragement, that they have heard of a somewhat similar establishment in Cannon Street; and that they have heard it
praised. He wishes to draw no invidious comparisons; he

would be the last man to do it; but when that Cannon
Street establishment shall be able to produce such a combination of wit and beauty as has graced that board that
day, and shall be able to serve up (all things considered)
such a dinner as that of which they have just partaken, he
will be happy to talk to it. Until then, gentlemen, he will
stick to Todgers's.

More punch, more enthusiasm, more speeches. Everybody's health is drunk, saving the youngest gentleman's in
company. He sits apart, with his elbow on the back of a
vacant chair, and glares disdainfully at Jinkins. Gander,
in a convulsing speech, gives them the health of Bailey
junior; hiccups are heard; and a glass is broken. Mr.
Jinkins feels that it is time to join the ladies. He pro-
poses, as a final sentiment, Mrs. Todgers. She is worthy
to be remembered separately. Hear, hear. So she is: no
doubt of it. They all find fault with her at other times;
but every man feels, now, that he could die in her defence.

They go up-stairs, where they are not expected so soon;
for Mrs. Todgers is asleep, Miss Charity is adjusting her
hair, and Mercy, who has made a sofa of one of the win-
dow-seats, is in a gracefully recumbent attitude. She is
rising hastily, when Mr. Jinkins implores her, for all their
sakes, not to stir; she looks too graceful and too lovely, he
remarks, to be disturbed. She laughs, and yields, and
fans herself, and drops her fan, and there is a rush to pick
it up. Being now installed, by one consent, as the beauty
of the party, she is cruel and capricious, and sends gentlemen on messages to other gentlemen, and forgets all about
them before they can return with the answer, and invents
a thousand tortures, rending their hearts to pieces. Bailey
brings up the tea and coffee. There is a small cluster of
admirers round Charity; but they are only those who cannot get near her sister. The youngest gentleman in company is pale, but collected, and still sits apart; for his
spirit loves to hold communion with itself, and his soul
recoils from noisy revellers. She has a consciousness of
his presence and his adoration. He sees it flashing sometimes in the corner of her eye. Have a care, Jinkins, ere
you provoke a desperate man to frenzy!

Mr. Pecksniff had followed his younger friends up-stairs,
and taken a chair at the side of Mrs. Todgers. He had

also spilt a cup of coffee over his legs without appearing to be aware of the circumstance; nor did he seem to know that there was muffin on his knee.

"And how have they used you down-stairs, Sir?" asked the hostess.

"Their conduct has been such, my dear madam," said Mr. Pecksniff, "as I can never think of without emotion, or remember without a tear. Oh, Mrs. Todgers!"

"My goodness!" exclaimed that lady. "How low you are in your spirits, Sir!"

"I am a man, my dear Madam," said Mr. Pecksniff, shedding tears, and speaking with an imperfect articulation, "but I am also a father. I am also a widower. My feelings, Mrs. Todgers, will not consent to be entirely smothered, like the young children in the Tower. They are grown up, and the more I press the bolster on them, the more they look round the corner of it."

He suddenly became conscious of the bit of 'muffin, and stared at it intently: shaking his head the while, in a forlorn and imbecile manner, as if he regarded it as his evil genius, and mildly reproached it.

"She was beautiful, Mrs. Todgers," he said, turning his glazed eye again upon her, without the least preliminary notice. "She had a small property."

"So I have heard," cried Mrs. Todgers with great sympathy.

"Those are her daughters," said Mr. Pecksniff, pointing out the young ladies, with increased emotion.

Mrs. Todgers had no doubt of it.

"Mercy and Charity," said Mr. Pecksniff, "Charity and Mercy. Not unholy names, I hope?"

"Mr. Pecksniff!" cried Mrs. Todgers, "what a ghastly smile! Are you ill, Sir?"

He pressed his hand upon her arm, and answered in a solemn manner, and a faint voice, "Chronic."

"Cholic?" cried the frightened Mrs. Todgers.

"Chron-ic," he repeated with some difficulty. "Chronic. A chronic disorder. I have been its victim from childhood. It is carrying me to my grave."

"Heaven forbid!" cried Mrs. Todgers.

"Yes it is," said Mr. Pecksniff, reckless with despair. "I am rather glad of it, upon the whole. You are like her, Mrs. Todgers."

"Don't squeeze me so tight, pray, Mr. Pecksniff. If any of the gentlemen should notice us."

"For her sake!" said Mr. Pecksniff. "Permit me—in honour of her memory. For the sake of a voice from the tomb. You are *very* like her, Mrs. Todgers! What a world this is!"

"Ah! Indeed you may say that!" cried Mrs. Todgers.

"I'm afraid it's a vain and thoughtless world," said Mr. Pecksniff, overflowing with despondency. "These young people about us. Oh! what sense have they of their responsibilities? None. Give me your other hand, Mrs. Todgers."

That lady hesitated, and said "she didn't like."

"Has a voice from the grave no influence?" said Mr. Pecksniff, with dismal tenderness. "This is irreligious! My dear creature."

"Hush!" urged Mrs. Todgers. "Really you musn't."

"It's not me," said Mr. Pecksniff. "Don't suppose it's me; it's the voice; it's her voice."

Mrs. Pecksniff deceased, must have had an unusually thick and husky voice for a lady, and rather a stuttering voice, and to say the truth somewhat of a drunken voice, if it had ever borne much resemblance to that in which Mr. Pecksniff spoke just then. But perhaps this was delusion on his part.

"It has been a day of enjoyment, Mrs. Todgers, but still it has been a day of torture. It has reminded me of my loneliness. What am I in the world?"

"An excellent gentleman, Mr. Pecksniff," said Mrs. Todgers.

"There is consolation in that too," cried Mr. Pecksniff. "Am I?"

"There is no better man living," said Mrs. Todgers, "I am sure."

Mr. Pecksniff smiled through his tears, and slightly shook his head. "You are very good," he said, "thank you. It is a great happiness to me, Mrs. Todgers, to make young people happy. The happiness of my pupils is my chief object. I dote upon 'em. They dote upon me too —sometimes."

"Always," said Mrs. Todgers.

"When they say they haven't improved, ma'am," whispered Mr. Pecksniff, looking at her with profound mystery, and motioning to her to advance her ear a little closer to his mouth. "When they say they haven't improved, ma'am, and the premium was too high, they lie! I shouldn't wish it to be mentioned; you will understand me; but I say to you as to an old friend, they lie."

"Base wretches they must be!" said Mrs. Todgers.

"Madam," said Mr. Pecksniff, "you are right. I respect you for that observation. A word in your ear. To Parents and Guardians—This is in confidence, Mrs. Todgers?"

"The strictest, of course!" cried that lady.

"To Parents and Guardians," repeated Mr. Pecksniff. "An eligible opportunity now offers, which unites the advantages of the best practical architectural education with the comforts of a home, and the constant association with some, who, however humble their sphere and limited their capacity—observe!—are not unmindful of their moral responsibilities."

Mrs. Todgers looked a little puzzled to know what this might mean, as well she might; for it was, as the reader may perchance remember, Mr. Pecksniff's usual form of advertisement when he wanted a pupil; and seemed to have no particular reference, at present, to anything. But Mr. Pecksniff held up his finger as a caution to her not to interrupt him.

"Do you know any parent or guardian, Mrs. Todgers," said Mr. Pecksniff, "who desires to avail himself of such an opportunity for a young gentleman? An orphan would be preferred. Do you know of any orphan with three or four hundred pound?"

Mrs. Todgers reflected, and shook her head.

"When you hear of an orphan with three or four hundred pound," said Mr. Pecksniff, "let that dear orphan's friends apply, by letter post-paid, to S. P., Post-office, Salisbury. I don't know who he is, exactly. Don't be alarmed, Mrs. Todgers," said Mr. Pecksniff, falling heavily against her: "Chronic—chronic! Let's have a little drop of something to drink."

"Bless my life, Miss Pecksniffs!" cried Mrs. Todgers, aloud, "your dear pa's took very poorly!"

Mr. Pecksniff straightened himself by a surprising effort, as every one turned hastily towards him; and standing on his feet, regarded the assembly with a look of ineffable wisdom. Gradually it gave place to a smile; a feeble, helpless, melancholy smile; bland, almost to sickliness. "Do not repine, my friends," said Mr. Pecksniff, tenderly. "Do not weep for me. It is chronic." And with these words, after making a futile attempt to pull off his shoes, he fell into the fire-place.

The youngest gentleman in company had him out in a second. Yes, before a hair upon his head was singed, he had him on the hearth-rug.—Her father!

She was almost beside herself. So was her sister. Jinkins consoled them both. They all consoled them. Everybody had something to say except the youngest gentleman in the company, who with a noble self-devotion did the heavy work, and held up Mr. Pecksniff's head without being taken any notice of by anybody. At last they gathered round, and agreed to carry him up-stairs to bed. The youngest gentleman in company was rebuked by Jinkins for tearing Mr. Pecksniff's coat! Ha, ha! But no matter.

They carried him up-stairs, and crushed the youngest gentleman at every step. His bedroom was at the top of the house, and it was a long way; but they got him there in course of time. He asked them frequently upon the road for a little drop of something to drink. It seemed an idiosyncrasy. The youngest gentleman in company proposed a draught of water. Mr. Pecksniff called him opprobrious names for the suggestion.

Jinkins and Gander took the rest upon themselves, and made him as comfortable as they could, on the outside of his bed; and when he seemed disposed to sleep, they left him. But before they had all gained the bottom of the staircase, a vision of Mr. Pecksniff, strangely attired, was seen to flutter on the top landing. He desired to collect their sentiments, it seemed, upon the nature of human life.

"My friends," cried Mr. Pecksniff, looking over the banisters, "let us improve our minds by mutual inquiry and discussion. Let us be moral. Let us contemplate existence. Where is Jinkins?"

"Here," cried that gentleman. "Go to bed again!"

"To bed!" said Mr. Pecksniff. "Bed! 'Tis the voice of the sluggard; I hear him complain; you have woke me too soon; I must slumber again. If any young orphan will repeat the remainder of that simple piece from Doctor Watts's collection, an eligible opportunity now offers."

Nobody volunteered.

"Do not repine, my friends," said Mr. Pecksniff, tenderly.   "Do not weep for me.   It is chronic."
—*Martin Chuzzlewit*. ch. ix., p. 160.

"This is very soothing," said Mr. Pecksniff, after a pause. "Extremely so. Cool and refreshing; particularly to the legs! The legs of the human subject, my friends, are a beautiful production. Compare them with wooden legs, and observe the difference between the anatomy of nature and the anatomy of art. Do you know," said Mr. Pecksniff, leaning over the banisters, with an odd recollection of his familiar manner among new pupils at home, "that I should very much like to see Mrs. Todgers's notion of a wooden leg, if perfectly agreeable to herself!"

As it appeared impossible to entertain any reasonable hopes of him after this speech, Mr. Jinkins and Mr. Gander went up-stairs again, and once more got him into bed. But they had not descended to the second floor before he was out again; nor, when they had repeated the process, had they descended the first flight, before he was out again. In a word, as often as he was shut up in his own room, he darted out afresh, charged with some new moral sentiment, which he continually repeated over the banisters, with extraordinary relish, and an irrepressible desire for the improvement of his fellow-creatures that nothing could subdue.

Under these circumstances, when they had got him into bed for the thirtieth time or so, Mr. Jinkins held him, while his companion went down stairs in search of Bailey junior, with whom he presently returned. That youth, having been apprised of the service required of him, was in great spirits, and brought up a stool, a candle, and his supper; to the end that he might keep watch outside the bedroom door with tolerable comfort.

When he had completed his arrangements, they locked Mr. Pecksniff in, and left the key on the outside; charging the young page to listen attentively for symptoms of an apoplectic nature, with which the patient might be troubled, and, in case of any such presenting themselves, to summon them without delay: to which Mr. Bailey modestly replied that "he hoped he knowed wot o'clock it wos in gineral, and didn't date his letters to his friends, from Todgers's, for nothing."

11

CHAPTER X.

CONTAINING STRANGE MATTER; ON WHICH MANY
EVENTS IN THIS HISTORY MAY, FOR THEIR GOOD
OR EVIL INFLUENCE, CHIEFLY DEPEND.

But Mr. Pecksniff came to town on business. Had he
forgotten that? Was he always taking his pleasure with
Todgers's jovial brood, unmindful of the serious demands,
whatever they might be, upon his calm consideration? No.
. Time and tide will wait for no man, saith the adage.
But all men have to wait for time and tide. That tide,
which, taken at the flood, would lead Seth Pecksniff on to
fortune, was marked down in the table, and about to flow.
No idle Pecksniff lingered far inland, unmindful of the
changes of the stream; but there, upon the water's edge,
over his shoes already, stood the worthy creature, prepared to wallow in the very mud, so that it slid towards
the quarter of his hope.

The trustfulness of his two fair daughters was beautiful
indeed. They had that firm reliance on their parent's
nature which taught them to feel certain that in all he did,
he had his purpose straight and full before him. And
that its noble end and object was himself, which almost
of necessity included them, they knew. The devotion of
these maids was perfect.

Their filial confidence was rendered the more touching,
by their having no knowledge of their parent's real designs,
in the present instance. All that they knew of his proceedings, was, that every morning, after the early breakfast, he repaired to the post-office and inquired for letters.
That task performed, his business for the day was over;
and he again relaxed, until the rising of another sun proclaimed the advent of another post.

This went on for four or five days. At length, one
morning, Mr. Pecksniff returned with a breathless rapidity,
strange to observe in him, at other times so calm; and,
seeking immediate speech with his daughters, shut himself
up with them in private conference, for two whole hours.
Of all that passed in this period, only the following words
of Mr. Pecksniff's utterance are known:

"How he has come to change so very much (if it should turn out as I expect, that he has), we needn't stop to inquire. My dears, I have my thoughts upon the subject, but I will not impart them. It is enough that we will not be proud, resentful, or unforgiving. If he wants our friendship, he shall have it. We know our duty, I hope!"

That same day at noon, an old gentleman alighted from a hackney-coach at the post-office, and, giving his name, inquired for a letter addressed to himself, and directed to be left till called for. It had been lying there, some days. The superscription was in Mr. Pecksniff's hand, and it was sealed with Mr. Pecksniff's seal.

It was very short, containing indeed nothing more than an address "with Mr. Pecksniff's respectful, and (notwithstanding what has passed) sincerely affectionate regards." The old gentleman tore off the direction—scattering the rest in fragments to the winds—and giving it to the coachman, bade him drive as near that place as he could. In pursuance of these instructions he was driven to the Monument; where he again alighted, dismissed the vehicle, and walked towards Todgers's.

Though the face, and form, and gait of this old man, and even his grip of the stout stick on which he leaned, were all expressive of a resolution not easily shaken, and a purpose (it matters little whether right or wrong, just now) such as in other days might have survived the rack, and had its strongest life in weakest death; still there were grains of hesitation in his mind, which made him now avoid the house he sought, and loiter to and fro in a gleam of sunlight, that brightened the little churchyard hard by. There may have been, in the presence of those idle heaps of dust among the busiest stir of life, something to increase his wavering; but there he walked, awakening the echoes as he paced up and down, until the church clock, striking the quarters for the second time since he had been there, roused him from his meditation. Shaking off his incertitude as the air parted with the sound of the bells, he walked rapidly to the house, and knocked at the door.

Mr. Pecksniff was seated in the landlady's little room, and his visitor found him reading—by an accident: he apologised for it—an excellent theological work. There were cake and wine upon a little table—by another accident, for which he also apologised. Indeed he said, he had given

his visitor up, and was about to partake of that simple refreshment with his children, when he knocked at the
door.

"Your daughters are well?" said old Martin, laying
down his hat and stick.

Mr. Pecksniff endeavoured to conceal his agitation as a
father, when he answered, Yes, they were. They were
good girls, he said, very good. He would not venture to
recommend Mr. Chuzzlewit to take the easy-chair, or to
keep out of the draught from the door. If he made any
such suggestion, he would expose himself, he feared, to
most unjust suspicion. He would, therefore, content himself with remarking that there was an easy-chair in the
room; and that the door was far from being air-tight.
This latter imperfection, he might perhaps venture to add,
was not uncommonly to be met with in old houses.

The old man sat down in the easy-chair, and after a few
moments' silence, said:

"In the first place, let me thank you for coming to London so promptly, at my almost unexplained request: I
need scarcely add, at my cost."

"At *your* cost, my good Sir!" cried Mr. Pecksniff, in a
tone of great surprise.

"It is not," said Martin, waving his hand impatiently,
"my habit to put my—well! my relatives—to any personal
expense to gratify my caprices."

"Caprices, my good Sir!" cried Mr. Pecksniff.

"That is scarcely the proper word either, in this instance," said the old man. "No. You are right."

Mr. Pecksniff was inwardly very much relieved to hear
it, though he didn't at all know why.

"You are right," repeated Martin. "It is not a caprice.
It is built up on reason, proof, and cool comparison.
Caprices never are. Moreover, I am not a capricious man.
I never was."

"Most assuredly not," said Mr. Pecksniff.

"How do you know?" returned the other quickly.
"You are to begin to know it now. You are to test and
prove it, in time to come. You and yours are to find that
I can be constant, and am not to be diverted from my end.
Do you hear?"

"Perfectly," said Mr. Pecksniff.

"I very much regret," Martin resumed, looking steadily

at him, and speaking in a slow and measured tone: "I very much regret that you and I held such a conversation together, as that which passed between us, at our last meeting. I very much regret that I laid open to you what were then my thoughts of you, so freely as I did. The intentions that I bear towards you, now, are of another kind; and, deserted by all in whom I have ever trusted, hoodwinked and beset by all who should help and sustain me; I fly to you for refuge. I confide in you to be my ally; to attach yourself to me by ties of Interest and Expectation"—he laid great stress upon these words, though Mr. Pecksniff particularly begged him not to mention it; "and to help me to visit the consequences of the very worst species of meanness, dissimulation, and subtlety, on the right heads."

"My noble Sir!" cried Mr. Pecksniff, catching at his outstretched hand. "And *you* regret the having harboured unjust thoughts of me! *you* with those gray hairs!"

"Regrets," said Martin, "are the natural property of gray hairs; and I enjoy, in common with all other men, at least my share of such inheritance. And so enough of that. I regret having been severed from you so long. If I had known you sooner, and sooner used you as you well deserve, I might have been a happier man."

Mr. Pecksniff looked up to the ceiling, and clasped his hands in rapture.

"Your daughters," said Martin, after a short silence. "I don't know them. Are they like you?"

"In the nose of my eldest and the chin of my youngest, Mr. Chuzzlewit," returned the widower, "their sainted parent—not myself, their mother—lives again."

"I don't mean in person," said the old man. "Morally —morally."

"'Tis not for me to say," retorted Mr. Pecksniff with a gentle smile. "I have done my best, Sir."

"I could wish to see them," said Martin; "are they near at hand?"

They were, very near; for they had, in fact, been listening at the door, from the beginning of this conversation until now, when they precipitately retired. Having wiped the signs of weakness from his eyes, and so given them time to get up stairs, Mr. Pecksniff opened the door, and mildly cried in the passage,

"My own darlings, where are you?"

"Here, my dear pa!" replied the distant voice of Charity.

"Come down into the back parlour, if you please, my love," said Mr. Pecksniff, "and bring your sister with you."

"Yes, my dear pa," cried Merry; and down they came directly (being all obedience), singing as they came.

Nothing could exceed the astonishment of the two Miss Pecksniffs when they found a stranger with their dear papa. Nothing could surpass their mute amazement when he said, "My children, Mr. Chuzzlewit!" But when he told them that Mr. Chuzzlewit and he were friends, and that Mr. Chuzzlewit had said such kind and tender words as pierced his very heart, the two Miss Pecksniffs cried with one accord, "Thank Heaven for this!" and fell upon the old man's neck. And when they had embraced him with such fervour of affection that no words can describe it, they grouped themselves about his chair, and hung over him: as figuring to themselves no earthly joy like that of ministering to his wants, and crowding into the remainder of his life the love they would have diffused over their whole existence, from infancy, if he—dear obdurate!—had but consented to receive the precious offering.

The old man looked attentively from one to the other, and then at Mr. Pecksniff, several times.

"What," he asked of Mr. Pecksniff, happening to catch his eye in its descent: for until now it had been piously upraised, with something of that expression which the poetry of ages has attributed to a domestic bird, when breathing its last amid the ravages of an electric storm: "What are their names?"

Mr. Pecksniff told him, and added, rather hastily—his calumniators would have said, with a view to any testamentary thoughts that might be flitting through old Martin's mind—"Perhaps, my dears, you had better write them down. Your humble autographs are of no value in themselves, but affection may prize them."

"Affection," said the old man, "will expend itself on the living originals. Do not trouble yourselves, my girls. I shall not so easily forget you, Charity and Mercy, as to need such tokens of remembrance. Cousin!"

"Sir!" said Mr. Pecksniff, with alacrity.

"Do you never sit down?"

"Why—yes—occasionally, Sir," said Mr. Pecksniff, who had been standing all this time.

"Will you do so now?"

"Can you ask me," returned Mr. Pecksniff, slipping into a chair immediately, "whether I will do anything that you desire?"

"You talk confidently," said Martin, "and you mean well; but I fear you don't know what an old man's humours are. You don't know what it is to be required to court his likings and dislikings; adapt yourself to his prejudices; do his bidding, be it what it may; bear with his distrusts and jealousies; and always still be zealous in his service. When I remember how numerous these failings are in me, and judge of their occasional enormity by the injurious thoughts I lately entertained of you, I hardly dare to claim you for my friend."

"My worthy Sir," returned his relative, "how *can* you talk in such a painful strain! What was more natural than that you should make one slight mistake, when in all other respects you were so very correct, and have had such reason —such very sad and undeniable reason—to judge of every one about you in the worst light!"

"True," replied the other. "You are very lenient with me."

"We always said—my girls and I," cried Mr. Pecksniff with increasing obsequiousness, "that while we mourned the heaviness of our misfortune in being confounded with the base and mercenary, still we could not wonder at it. My dears, you remember?"

Oh vividly! A thousand times!

"We uttered no complaint," said Mr. Pecksniff. "Occasionally we had the presumption to console ourselves with the remark that Truth would in the end prevail, and Virtue be triumphant; but not often. My loves, you recollect?"

Recollect! Could he doubt it? Dearest pa, what strange, unnecessary questions!

"And when I saw you," resumed Mr. Pecksniff, with still greater deference, "in the little, unassuming village where we take the liberty of dwelling, I said you were mistaken in me, my dear Sir: that was all, I think?"

"No—not all," said Martin, who had been sitting with his hand upon his brow for some time past, and now looked up again: "you said much more, which, added to other circumstances that have come to my knowledge, opened my eyes. You spoke to me, disinterestedly, on behalf of —I needn't name him. You know whom I mean."

Trouble was expressed in Mr. Pecksniff's visage, as he pressed his hot hands together, and replied, with humility, "Quite disinterestedly, Sir, I assure you."

"I know it," said old Martin, in his quiet way. "I am sure of it. I said so. It was disinterested too, in you, to draw that herd of harpies off from me, and be their victim yourself; most other men would have suffered them to display themselves in all their rapacity, and would have striven to rise, by contrast, in my estimation. You felt for me, and drew them off, for which I owe you many thanks. Although I left the place, I know what passed behind my back, you see!"

"You amaze me, Sir!" cried Mr. Pecksniff: which was true enough.

"My knowledge of your proceedings," said the old man, "does not stop at this. You have a new inmate in your house—"

"Yes, Sir," rejoined the architect, "I have."

"He must quit it," said Martin.

"For—for yours?" asked Mr. Pecksniff, with a quavering mildness.

"For any shelter he can find," the old man answered. "He has deceived you."

"I hope not," said Mr. Pecksniff, eagerly. "I trust not. I have been extremely well disposed towards that young man. I hope it cannot be shown that he has forfeited all claim to my protection. Deceit—deceit, my dear Mr. Chuzzlewit, would be final. I should hold myself bound, on proof of deceit, to renounce him instantly."

The old man glanced at both his fair supporters, but especially at Miss Mercy, whom, indeed, he looked full in the face, with a greater demonstration of interest than had yet appeared in his features. His gaze again encountered Mr. Pecksniff, as he said, composedly:

"Of course you know that he has made his matrimonial choice?"

"Oh dear!" cried Mr. Pecksniff, rubbing his hair up

very stiff upon his head, and staring wildly at his daughters. "This is becoming tremendous!"

"You know the fact?" repeated Martin

"Surely not without his grandfather's consent and approbation, my dear Sir!" cried Mr. Pecksniff. "Don't tell me that. For the honour of human nature, say you're not about to tell me that!"

"I thought he had suppressed it," said the old man.

The indignation felt by Mr. Pecksniff at this terrible disclosure, was only to be equalled by the kindling anger of his daughters. What! Had they taken to their hearth and home a secretly contracted serpent; a crocodile, who had made a furtive offer of his hand; an imposition on society; a bankrupt bachelor with no effects, trading with the spinster world on false pretences! And oh, to think that he should have disobeyed and practised on that sweet, that venerable gentleman, whose name he bore; that kind and tender guardian; his more than father—to say nothing at all of mother—horrible, horrible! To turn him out with ignominy would be treatment much too good. Was there nothing else that could be done to him? Had he incurred no legal pains and penalties? Could it be that the statutes of the land were so remiss as to have affixed no punishment to such delinquency? Monster; how basely had they been deceived!

"I am glad to find you second me so warmly," said the old man, holding up his hand to stay the torrent of their wrath. "I will not deny that it is a pleasure to me to find you so full of zeal. We will consider that topic as disposed of."

"No, my dear Sir," cried Mr. Pecksniff, "not as disposed of, until I have purged my house of this pollution."

"That will follow," said the old man, "in its own time. I look upon that as done."

"You are very good, Sir," answered Mr. Pecksniff, shaking his hand. "You do me honour. You *may* look upon it as done, I assure you."

"There is another topic," said Martin, "on which I hope you will assist me. You remember Mary, cousin?"

"The young lady that I mentioned to you, my dears, as having interested me so very much," remarked Mr. Pecksniff. "Excuse my interrupting you, Sir."

"I told you her history," said the old man.

"Which I also mentioned, you will recollect, my dears," cried Mr. Pecksniff. "Silly girls, Mr. Chuzzlewit—quite moved by it, they were!"

"Why, look now!" said Martin, evidently pleased: "I feared I should have had to urge her case upon you, and ask you to regard her favourably for my sake. But I find you have no jealousies! Well! You have no cause for any, to be sure. She has nothing to gain from me, my dears, and she knows it."

The two Miss Pecksniffs murmured their approval of this wise arrangement, and their cordial sympathy with its interesting object.

"If I could have anticipated what has come to pass between us four," said the old man, thoughtfully: "but it is too late to think of that. You would receive her courteously, young ladies, and be kind to her, if need were?"

Where was the orphan whom the two Miss Pecksniffs would not have cherished in their sisterly bosom! But when that orphan was commended to their care by one on whom the dammed-up love of years was gushing forth, what exhaustless stores of pure affection yearned to expend themselves upon her!

An interval ensued, during which Mr. Chuzzlewit, in an absent frame of mind, sat gazing at the ground, without uttering a word; and as it was plain that he had no desire to be interrupted in his meditations, Mr. Pecksniff and his daughters were profoundly silent also. During the whole of the foregoing dialogue, he had borne his part with a cold, passionless promptitude, as though he had learned and painfully rehearsed it all, a hundred times. Even when his expressions were warmest and his language most encouraging, he had retained the same manner, without the least abatement. But now there was a keener brightness in his eye, and more expression in his voice, as he said, awakening from his thoughtful mood:

"You know what will be said of this? Have you reflected?"

"Said of what, my dear Sir?" Mr. Pecksniff asked.

"Of this new understanding between us."

Mr. Pecksniff looked benevolently sagacious, and at the same time far above all earthly misconstruction, as he shook his head, and observed that a great many things would be said of it, no doubt.

"A great many," rejoined the old man. "Some will say that I dote in my old age; that illness has shaken me; that I have lost all strength of mind; and have grown childish. You can bear that?"

Mr. Pecksniff answered that it would be dreadfully hard to bear, but he thought he could, if he made a great effort.

"Others will say—I speak of disappointed, angry people only—that you have lied, and fawned, and wormed your self through dirty ways into my favour; by such conces sions and such crooked deeds, such meannesses and vile endurances, as nothing could repay; no, not the legacy of half the world we live in. You can bear that?"

Mr. Pecksniff made reply that this would be also very hard to bear, as reflecting, in some degree, on the discern ment of Mr. Chuzzlewit. Still he had a modest confidence that he could sustain the calumny, with the help of a good conscience, and that gentleman's friendship.

"With the great mass of slanderers," said old Martin, leaning back in his chair, "the tale, as I clearly foresee, will run thus: That to mark my contempt for the rabble whom I despised, I chose from among them the very worst, and made him do my will, and pampered and enriched him at the cost of all the rest. That, after casting about for the means of a punishment which should rankle in the bosoms of these kites the most, and strike into their gall, I devised this scheme at a time when the last link in the chain of grateful love and duty, that held me to my race, was roughly snapped asunder: roughly, for I loved him well; roughly, for I had ever put my trust in his affection; roughly, for that he broke it when I loved him most—God help me!—and he without a pang could throw me off, the while I clung about his heart! Now," said the old man, dismissing this passionate outburst, as suddenly as he had yielded to it, "is your mind made up to bear this likewise? Lay your account with having it to bear, and put no trust in being set right by me."

"My dear Mr. Chuzzlewit," cried Pecksniff in an ecstacy, "for such a man as you have shown yourself to be this day; for a man so injured, yet so very humane; for a man so—I am at a loss what precise term to use—yet at the same time so remarkably—I don't know how to express my meaning; for such a man as I have described, I hope it is no presumption to say that I, and I am sure I may add my children also (my dears, we perfectly agree in this, I think?), would bear anything whatever!"

"Enough," said Martin. "You can charge no consequences on me. When do you return home?"

"Whenever you please, my dear Sir. To-night, if you desire it."

"I desire nothing," returned the old man, "that is unreasonable. Such a request would be. Will you be ready to return at the end of this week?"

The very time of all others that Mr. Pecksniff would have suggested if it had been left to him to make his own choice. As to his daughters—the words, "Let us be at home on Saturday, dear pa," were actually upon their lips.

"Your expenses, cousin," said Martin, taking a folded slip of paper from his pocket-book, "may possibly exceed that amount. If so, let me know the balance that I owe you, when we next meet. It would be useless if I told you where I live just now: indeed, I have no fixed abode. When I have, you shall know it. You and your daughters may expect to see me before long: in the mean time I need not tell you, that we keep our own confidence. What you will do when you get home, is understood between us. Give me no account of it at any time; and never refer to it in any way. I ask that, as a favour. I am commonly a man of few words, cousin; and all that need be said just now is said, I think."

"One glass of wine—one morsel of this homely cake?" cried Mr. Pecksniff, venturing to detain him. "My dears!"

The sisters flew to wait upon him.

"Poor girls!" said Mr. Pecksniff. "You will excuse their agitation, my dear Sir. They are made up of feeling. A bad commodity to go through the world with, Mr. Chuzzlewit! My youngest daughter is almost as much of a woman as my eldest, is she not, Sir?"

"Which *is* the youngest?" asked the old man.

"Mercy, by five years," said Mr. Pecksniff. "We sometimes venture to consider her rather a fine figure, Sir Speaking as an artist, I may perhaps be permitted to suggest, that its outline is graceful and correct. I am naturally," said Mr. Pecksniff, drying his hands upon his handkerchief, and looking anxiously in his cousin's face at almost every word, "proud, if I may use the expression, to have a daughter who is constructed upon the best models."

"She seems to have a lively disposition," observed Martin.

"Dear me!" said Mr. Pecksniff, "that is quite remarkable. You have defined her character, my dear Sir, as correctly as if you had known her from her birth. She *has* a lively disposition. I assure you, my dear Sir, that in our unpretending home, her gaiety is delightful."

"No doubt," returned the old man.

"Charity, upon the other hand," said Mr. Pecksniff, "is remarkable for strong sense, and for rather a deep tone of sentiment, if the partiality of a father may be excused in saying so. A wonderful affection between them, my dear Sir! Allow me to drink your health. Bless you!"

"I little thought," retorted Martin, "but a month ago, that I should be breaking bread and pouring wine with you. I drink to you."

Not at all abashed by the extraordinary abruptness with which these latter words were spoken, Mr. Pecksniff thanked him devoutly.

"Now let me go," said Martin, putting down the wine when he had merely touched it with his lips. "My dears, good morning!"

But this distant form of farewell was by no means tender enough for the yearnings of the young ladies, who again embraced him with all their hearts—with all their arms at any rate—to which parting caresses their new-found friend submitted with a better grace than might have been expected from one who, not a moment before, had pledged their parent in such a very uncomfortable manner. These endearments terminated, he took a hasty leave of Mr. Pecksniff, and withdrew, followed to the door by both father and daughters, who stood there, kissing their hands, and beaming with affection until he disappeared: though, by the way, he never once looked back, after he had crossed the threshold.

When they returned into the house, and were again alone in Mrs. Todgers's room, the two young ladies exhibited an unusual amount of gaiety; insomuch that they clapped their hands, and laughed, and looked with roguish aspects and a bantering air upon their dear papa. This conduct was so very unaccountable, that Mr. Pecksniff (being singularly

7—7

grave himself) could scarcely choose but ask them what it meant; and took them to task, in his gentle manner, for yielding to such light emotions.

"If it was possible to divine any cause for this merriment, even the most remote," he said, "I should not reprove you. But when you can have none whatever—oh, really—really!"

This admonition had so little effect on Mercy, that she was obliged to hold her handkerchief before her rosy lips, and to throw herself back in her chair, with every demonstration of extreme amusement; which want of duty so offended Mr. Pecksniff that he reproved her in set terms, and gave her his parental advice to correct herself in solitude and contemplation. But at that juncture they were disturbed by the sound of voices in dispute; and as it proceeded from the next room, the subject matter of the altercation quickly reached their ears.

"I don't care that! Mrs. Todgers," said the young gentleman who had been the youngest gentleman in company on the day of the festival; "I don't care *that*, ma'am," said he, snapping his fingers, "for Jinkins. Don't suppose I do."

"I am quite certain you don't, Sir," replied Mrs. Todgers. You have too independent a spirit, I know, to yield to anybody. And quite right. There is no reason why you should give way to any gentleman. Everybody must be well aware of that."

"I should think no more of admitting daylight into the fellow," said the youngest gentleman, in a desperate voice, "than if he was a bull-dog."

Mrs. Todgers did not stop to inquire whether, as a matter of principle, there was any particular reason for admitting daylight even into a bull-dog, otherwise than by the natural channel of his eyes; but she seemed to wring her hands, and she moaned.

"Let him be careful," said the youngest gentleman. "I give him warning. No man shall step between me and the current of my vengeance. I know a cove—" he used that familiar epithet in his agitation, but corrected himself, by adding, "a gentleman of property, I mean, who practises with a pair of pistols (fellows too) of his own. If I am driven to borrow 'em, and to send a friend to Jinkins—a tragedy will get into the papers. That's all."

Again Mrs. Todgers moaned.

"I have borne this long enough," said the youngest gentleman, "but now my soul rebels against it, and I won't stand it any longer. I left home originally, because I had that within me which wouldn't be domineered over by a sister; and do you think I'm going to be put down by *him?* No."

"It is very wrong in Mr. Jinkins; I know it is perfectly inexcusable in Mr. Jinkins, if he intends it," observed Mrs. Todgers.

"If he intends it!" cried the youngest gentleman. "Don't he interrupt and contradict me on every occasion? Does he ever fail to interpose himself between me and anything or anybody that he sees I have set my mind upon? Does he make a point of always pretending to forget me, when he's pouring out the beer? Does he make bragging remarks about his razors, and insulting allusions to people who have no necessity to shave more than once a week? But let him look out; he'll find himself shaved, pretty close, before long, and so I tell him!"

The young gentleman was mistaken in this closing sentence, inasmuch as he never told it to Jinkins, but always to Mrs. Todgers.

"However," he said, "these are not proper subjects for ladies' ears. All I've got to say to you, Mrs. Todgers, is —a week's notice from next Saturday. The same house can't contain that miscreant and me any longer. If we get over the intermediate time without bloodshed, you may think yourself pretty fortunate. I don't myself expect we shall."

"Dear, dear!" cried Mrs. Todgers, "what would I have given to have prevented this! To lose you, Sir, would be like losing the house's right-hand. So popular as you are among the gentlemen; so generally looked up to; and so much liked! I do hope you'll think better of it; if on nobody else's account, on mine."

"There's Jinkins," said the youngest gentleman, moodily. "Your favourite. He'll console you and the gentlemen too for the loss of twenty such as me. I'm not understood in this house. I never have been."

"Don't run away with that opinion, Sir!" cried Mrs. Todgers, with a show of honest indignation. "Don't make such a charge as that against the establishment, I must

beg of you. It is not so bad as that comes to, Sir. Make
any remark you please against the gentlemen, or against
me; but don't say you're not understood in this house."

"I'm not treated as if I was," said the youngest gentleman.

"There you make a great mistake, Sir," returned Mrs.
Todgers, in the same strain. "As many of the gentlemen
and I have often said, you are too sensitive. That's where
it is. You are of too susceptible a nature; it's in your
spirit."

The young gentleman coughed.

"And as," said Mrs. Todgers, "as to Mr. Jinkins, I
must beg of you, if we *are* to part, to understand that I
don't abet Mr. Jinkins by any means. Far from it. I
could wish that Mr. Jinkins would take a lower tone in
this establishment; and would not be the means of raising
differences between me and gentlemen that I can much less
bear to part with, than I could with him. Mr. Jinkins is
not such a boarder, Sir," added Mrs. Todgers, "that all
considerations of private feeling and respect give way before him. Quite the contrary, I assure you."

The young gentleman was so much mollified by these
and similar speeches on the part of Mrs. Todgers, that he
and that lady gradually changed positions; so that she became the injured party, and he was understood to be the
injurer; but in a complimentary, not in an offensive sense;
his cruel conduct being attributable to his exalted nature,
and to that alone. So, in the end, the young gentleman
withdrew his notice, and assured Mrs. Todgers of his un-
alterable regard: and having done so, went back to business.

"Goodness me, Miss Pecksniffs!" cried that lady, as she
came into the back room, and sat wearily down, with her
basket on her knees, and her hands folded upon it, "what
a trial of temper it is to keep a house like this! You must
have heard most of what has just passed. Now did you
ever hear the like?"

"Never!" said the two Miss Pecksniffs.

"Of all the ridiculous young fellows that ever I had to
deal with," resumed Mrs. Todgers, "that is the most ridiculous and unreasonable. Mr. Jinkins is hard upon him
sometimes, but not half as hard as he deserves. To mention such a gentleman as Mr. Jinkins, in the same breath

with *him*—you know it's too much! And yet he's as jealous of him, bless you, as if he was his equal."

The young ladies were greatly entertained by Mrs. Todgers's account, no less than with certain anecdotes illustrative of the youngest gentleman's character, which she went on to tell them. But Mr. Pecksniff looked quite stern and angry: and when she had concluded, said in a solemn voice:

"Pray, Mrs. Todgers, if I may inquire, what does that young gentleman contribute towards the support of these premises?"

"Why, Sir, for what *he* has, he pays about eighteen shillings a week," said Mrs. Todgers.

"Eighteen shillings a week!" repeated Mr. Pecksniff.

"Taking one week with another; as near that as possible," said Mrs. Todgers.

Mr. Pecksniff rose from his chair, folded his arms, looked at her, and shook his head.

"And do you mean to say, ma'am—is it possible, Mrs. Todgers—that for such a miserable consideration as eighteen shillings a week, a female of your understanding can so far demean herself as to wear a double face, even for an instant?"

"I am forced to keep things on the square if I can, Sir," faltered Mrs. Todgers. "I must preserve peace among them, and keep my connection together, if possible, Mr. Pecksniff. The profit is very small."

"The profit!" cried that gentleman, laying great stress upon the word. "The profit, Mrs. Todgers! You amaze me!"

He was so severe, that Mrs. Todgers shed tears.

"The profit!" repeated Mr. Pecksniff. "The profit of dissimulation! To worship the golden calf of Baal, for eighteen shillings a week!"

"Don't in your own goodness be too hard upon me, Mr. Pecksniff," cried Mrs. Todgers, taking out her handkerchief.

"Oh Calf, Calf!" cried Mr. Pecksniff mournfully. "Oh Baal, Baal! Oh my friend Mrs. Todgers! To barter away that precious jewel, self-esteem, and cringe to any mortal creature—for eighteen shillings a week!"

He was so subdued and overcome by the reflection, that he immediately took down his hat from its peg in the pas-

12

sage, and went out for a walk, to compose his feelings.
Anybody passing him in the street might have known him
for a good man at first sight; for his whole figure teemed
with a consciousness of the moral homily he had read to
Mrs. Todgers.

Eighteen shillings a week! Just, most just, thy cen-
sure, upright Pecksniff! Had it been for the sake of a ribbon, star, or garter; sleeves of lawn, a great man's smile,
a seat in Parliament, a tap upon the shoulder from a courtly
sword; a place, a party, or a thriving lie, or eighteen thousand pounds, or even eighteen hundred;—but to worship
the golden calf for eighteen shillings a week! Oh pitiful,
pitiful!

CHAPTER XI.

WHEREIN A CERTAIN GENTLEMAN BECOMES PARTICU-
LAR IN HIS ATTENTIONS TO A CERTAIN LADY;
AND MORE COMING EVENTS THAN ONE, CAST
THEIR SHADOWS BEFORE.

THE family were within two or three days of their departure from Mrs. Todgers's, and the commercial gentlemen were to a man despondent and not to be comforted,
because of the approaching separation, when Bailey junior,
at the jocund time of noon, presented himself before Miss
Charity Pecksniff, then sitting with her sister in the banquet chamber, hemming six new pocket-handkerchiefs for
Mr. Jinkins; and having expressed a hope, preliminary
and pious, that he might be blest, gave her, in his pleasant
way, to understand that a visitor attended to pay his respects to her, and was at that moment waiting in the drawing-room. Perhaps this last announcement showed in a
more striking point of view than many lengthened speeches
could have done, the trustfulness and faith of Bailey's nature; since he had, in fact, last seen the visitor upon the
door-mat, where, after signifying to him that he would do
well to go up-stairs, he had left him to the guidance of
his own sagacity. Hence it was at least an even chance
that the visitor was then wandering on the roof of the
house, or vainly seeking to extricate himself from a maze
of bedrooms; Todgers's being precisely that kind of estab-

lishment in which an unpiloted stranger is pretty sure to
find himself in some place where he least expects and least
desires to be.

"A gentleman for me!" cried Charity, pausing in her
work; "my gracious, Bailey!"

"Ah!" said Bailey. "It *is* my gracious, a'nt it?
Wouldn't I be gracious neither, not if I wos him!"

The remark was rendered somewhat obscure in itself, by
reason (as the reader may have observed) of a redundancy
of negatives; but accompanied by action expressive of a
faithful couple walking arm-in-arm towards a parochial
church, mutually exchanging looks of love, it clearly signified this youth's conviction that the caller's purpose was of
an amorous tendency. Miss Charity affected to reprove so
great a liberty; but she could not help smiling. He was
a strange boy to be sure. There was always some ground
of probability and likelihood mingled with his absurd behaviour. That was the best of it!

"But I don't know any gentleman, Bailey," said Miss
Pecksniff. "I think you must have made a mistake."

Mr. Bailey smiled at the extreme wildness of such a
supposition, and regarded the young ladies with unimpaired affability.

"My dear Merry," said Charity, "who *can* it be? Isn't
it odd? I have a great mind not to go to him really. So
very strange you know!"

The younger sister plainly considered that this appeal
had its origin in the pride of being called upon and asked
for; and that it was intended as an assertion of superiority, and a retaliation upon her for having captured
the commercial gentlemen. Therefore, she replied, with
great affection and politeness, that it was, no doubt, very
strange indeed; and that she was totally at a loss to conceive what the ridiculous person unknown could mean by
it.

"Quite impossible to divine!" said Charity, with some
sharpness, "though still, at the same time, you needn't be
angry, my dear."

"Thank you," retorted Merry, singing at her needle.
"I am quite aware of that, my love."

"I am afraid your head is turned, you silly thing," said
Cherry.

"Do you know, my dear," said Merry, with engaging

candour, "that I have been afraid of that, myself, all
along! So much incense and nonsense, and all the rest of
it, is enough to turn a stronger head than mine. What a
relief it must be to you, my dear, to be so very comfortable
in that respect, and not to be worried by those odious men!
How *do* you do it, Cherry?"

This artless inquiry might have led to turbulent results,
but for the strong emotions of delight evinced by Bailey
junior, whose relish in the turn the conversation had lately
taken was so acute, that it impelled and forced him to the
instantaneous performance of a dancing step, extremely
difficult in its nature, and only to be achieved in a moment
of ecstacy, which is commonly called The Frog's Hornpipe.
A manifestation so lively, brought to their immediate recollection the great virtuous precept, "Keep up appearances
whatever you do," in which they had been educated.
They forbore at once, and jointly signified to Mr. Bailey
that if he should presume to practise that figure any more
in their presence, they would instantly acquaint Mrs.
Todgers with the fact, and would demand his condign punishment at the hands of that lady. The young gentleman
having expressed the bitterness of his contrition by affecting to wipe away his scalding tears with his apron, and
afterwards feigning to wring a vast amount of water from
that garment, held the door open while Miss Charity passed
out; and so that damsel went in state up-stairs to receive
her mysterious adorer.

By some strange concurrence of favourable circumstances
he had found out the drawing-room, and was sitting there
alone.

"Ah, cousin!" he said. "Here I am, you see. You
thought I was lost, I'll be bound. Well! how do you find
yourself by this time?"

Miss Charity replied that she was quite well; and gave
Mr. Jonas Chuzzlewit her hand.

"That's right," said Mr. Jonas, "and you've got over
the fatigues of the journey, have you? I say—how's the
other one?"

"My sister is very well, I believe," returned the young
lady. "I have not heard her complain of any indisposi-
tion, Sir. Perhaps you would like to see her, and ask her
yourself?"

"No, no, cousin!" said Mr. Jonas, sitting down beside

her on the window-seat. "Don't be in a hurry. There's
no occasion for that, you know. What a cruel girl you are!"
"It's impossible for *you* to know," said Cherry, "whether
I am or not."
"Well, perhaps it is," said Mr Jonas. "I say—did
you think I was lost? You haven't told me that."
"I didn't think at all about it," answered Cherry.
"Didn't you, though?" said Jonas, pondering upon this
strange reply. "Did the other one?"
"I am sure it's impossible for me to say what my sister
may, or may not have thought on such a subject," cried
Cherry. "She never said anything to me about it, one
way or other."
"Didn't she laugh about it?" inquired Jonas.
"No. She didn't even laugh about it," answered Char-
ity.
"She's a terrible one to laugh, an't she?" said Jonas,
lowering his voice.
"She is very lively," said Cherry.
"Liveliness is a pleasant thing—when it don't lead to
spending money. An't it?" asked Mr. Jonas.
"Very much so, indeed," said Cherry, with a demure-
ness of manner that gave a very disinterested character to
her assent.
"Such liveliness as yours I mean, you know," observed
Mr. Jonas, as he nudged her with his elbow. "I should
have come to see you before, but I didn't know where you
was. How quick you hurried off, that morning!"
"I was amenable to my Papa's directions," said Miss
Charity.
"I wish he had given me his direction," returned her
cousin, "and then I should have found you out before.
Why, I shouldn't have found you even now, if I hadn't
met him in the street this morning. What a sleek, sly
chap he is! Just like a tom-cat, an't he?"
"I must trouble you to have the goodness to speak more
respectfully of my Papa, Mr. Jonas," said Charity. "I
can't allow such a tone as that, even in jest."
"Ecod, you may say what you like of *my* father, then,
and so I give you leave," said Jonas. "I think it's liquid
aggravation that circulates through his veins, and not regular blood. How old should you think my father was,
cousin?"

"Old, no doubt," replied Miss Charity; "but a fine old gentleman."

"A fine old gentleman!" repeated Jonas, giving the crown of his hat an angry knock. "Ah! It's time he was thinking of being drawn out a little finer too. Why, he's eighty!"

"Is he, indeed?" said the young lady.

"And ecod," cried Jonas, "now he's gone so far without giving in, I don't see much to prevent his being ninety; no, nor even a hundred. Why, a man with any feeling ought to be ashamed of being eighty—let alone more. Where's his religion I should like to know, when he goes flying in the face of the Bible like that! Three-score-and-ten's the mark; and no man with a conscience, and a proper sense of what's expected of him, has any business to live longer."

Is any one surprised at Mr. Jonas making such a reference to such a book for such a purpose? Does any one doubt the old saw, that the Devil (being a layman) quotes Scripture for his own ends? If he will take the trouble to look about him, he may find a greater number of confirmations of the fact, in the occurrences of any single day, than the steam-gun can discharge balls in a minute.

"But there's enough of my father," said Jonas; "it's of no use to go putting one's-self out of the way by talking about *him*. I called to ask you to come and take a walk, cousin, and see some of the sights; and to come to our house afterwards, and have a bit of something. Pecksniff will most likely look in in the evening, he says, and bring you home. See, here's his writing; I made him put it down this morning, when he told me he shouldn't be back before I came here; in case you wouldn't believe me. There's nothing like proof, is there? Ha, ha! I say—you'll bring the other one, you know!"

Miss Charity cast her eyes upon her father's autograph, which merely said: "Go, my children, with your cousin. Let there be union among us when it is possible;" and after enough of hesitation to impart a proper value to her consent, withdrew, to prepare her sister and herself for the excursion. She soon returned, accompanied by Miss Mercy, who was by no means pleased to leave the brilliant triumphs of Todgers's for the society of Mr. Jonas and his respected father.

"Aha!" cried Jonas. "There you are, are you?"

"Yes, fright," said Mercy, "here I am; and I would much rather be anywhere else, I assure you."

"You don't mean that," cried Mr. Jonas. "You can't, you know. It isn't possible."

"You can have what opinion you like, fright," retorted Mercy. "I am content to keep mine; and mine is that you are a very unpleasant, odious, disagreeable person." Here she laughed heartily, and seemed to enjoy herself very much.

"Oh, you're a sharp gal!" said Mr. Jonas. "She's a regular teazer, an't she, cousin?"

Miss Charity replied in effect, that she was unable to say what the habits and propensities of a regular teazer might be; and that even if she possessed such information, it would ill become her to admit the existence of any creature with such an unceremonious name in her family; far less in the person of a beloved sister, "whatever," added Cherry with an angry glance, "whatever her real nature may be."

"Well, my dear," said Merry, "the only observation I have to make is, that if we don't go out at once, I shall certainly take my bonnet off again, and stay at home."

This threat had the desired effect of preventing any farther altercation, for Mr. Jonas immediately proposed an adjournment, and the same being carried unanimously, they departed from the house straightway. On the doorstep, Mr. Jonas gave an arm to each cousin; which act of gallantry being observed by Bailey junior, from the garret window, was by him saluted with a loud and violent fit of coughing, to which paroxysm he was still the victim when they turned the corner.

Mr. Jonas inquired in the first instance if they were good walkers, and being answered "Yes," submitted their pedestrian powers to a pretty severe test; for he showed them as many sights, in the way of bridges, churches, streets, outsides of theatres, and other free spectacles, in that one forenoon, as most people see in a twelvemonth. It was observable in this gentleman that he had an insurmountable distaste to the insides of buildings; and that he was perfectly acquainted with the merits of all shows, in respect of which there was any charge for admission, which it seemed were every one detestable, and of the very lowest grade of merit. He was so thoroughly possessed with this opinion, that when Miss Charity happened to mention the circumstance of their having been twice or thrice to the theatre with Mr. Jinkins and party, he inquired, as a matter of course, " where the orders came from? " and being told that Mr. Jinkins and party paid, was beyond description entertained, observing that " they must be nice flats, certainly;" and often in the course of the walk, bursting out again into a perfect convulsion of laughter at the surpassing silliness of those gentlemen, and (doubtless) at his own superior wisdom.

When they had been out for some hours and were thoroughly fatigued, it being by that time twilight, Mr. Jonas intimated that he would show them one of the best pieces of fun with which he was acquainted. This joke was of a practical kind, and its humour lay in taking a hackney-coach to the extreme limits of possibility for a shilling. Happily it brought them to the place where Mr. Jonas dwelt, or the young ladies might have rather missed the point and cream of the jest.

The old-established firm of Anthony Chuzzlewit and Son, Manchester Warehousemen, and so forth, had its place of business in a very narrow street somewhere behind the Post Office; where every house was in the brightest summer-morning very gloomy; and where light porters watered the pavement, each before his own employer's premises, in fantastic patterns, in the dog-days; and where spruce gentlemen with their hands in the pockets of symmetrical trousers, were always to be seen in warm weather contemplating their undeniable boots in dusty warehouse doorways, which appeared to be the hardest work they did, except now and then carrying pens behind their ears. A dim, dirty, smoky, tumble-down, rotten old house it was, as anybody would desire to see; but there the firm of Anthony Chuzzlewit and Son transacted all their business and their pleasure too, such as it was; for neither the young man nor the old had any other residence, or any care or thought beyond its narrow limits.

Business, as may be readily supposed, was the main thing in this establishment; insomuch indeed that it shouldered comfort out of doors, and jostled the domestic arrangements at every turn. Thus in the miserable bedrooms there were files of moth-eaten letters hanging up against the walls; and linen rollers, and fragments of old pattens, and odds and ends of spoiled goods, strewn upon the ground; while the meagre bedsteads, washing-stands, and scraps of carpet, were huddled away into corners as objects of secondary consideration, not to be thought of but as disagreeable necessities, furnishing no profit, and intruding on the one affair of life. The single sitting-room was on the same principle, a chaos of boxes and old papers, and had more counting-house stools in it than chairs: not to mention a great monster of a desk straddling over the middle of the floor, and an iron safe sunk into the wall above the fire-place. The solitary little table for purposes of refection and social enjoyment, bore as fair a proportion to the desk and other business furniture, as the graces and harmless relaxations of life had ever done, in the persons of the old man and his son, to their pursuit of wealth. It was meanly laid out, now, for dinner; and in a chair before the fire, sat Anthony himself, who rose to greet his son and his fair cousins as they entered.

An ancient proverb warns us that we should not expect to find old heads upon young shoulders; to which it may be added that we seldom meet with that unnatural combination, but we feel a strong desire to knock them off; merely from an inherent love we have of seeing things in their right places. It is not improbable that many men, in no wise choleric by nature, felt this impulse rising up within them, when they first made the acquaintance of Mr. Jonas; but if they had known him more intimately in his own house, and had sat with him at his own board, it would assuredly have been paramount to all other considerations.

"Well, ghost!" said Mr. Jonas, dutifully addressing his parent by that title. "Is dinner nearly ready?"

"I should think it was," rejoined the old man.

"What's the good of that?" rejoined the son. "*I* should think it was. I want to know."

"Ah! I don't know for certain," said Anthony.

"You don't know for certain," rejoined his son in a lower tone. "No. You don't know anything for certain, *you* don't. Give me your candle here. I want it for the gals."

Anthony handed him a battered old office candlestick, with which Mr. Jonas preceded the young ladies to the

nearest bedroom, where he left them to take off their
shawls and bonnets; and returning, occupied himself in
opening a bottle of wine, sharpening the carving-knife,
and muttering compliments to his father, until they and
the dinner appeared together. The repast consisted of a
hot leg of mutton with greens and potatoes; and the
dishes having been set upon the table by a slipshod old
woman, they were left to enjoy it after their own manner.

"Bachelor's Hall you know, cousin," said Mr. Jonas to
Charity, "I say—the other one will be having a laugh at
this when she gets home, won't she? Here; you sit on the
right side of me, and I'll have her upon the left. Other
one, will you come here?"

"You're such a fright," replied Mercy, "that I know I
shall have no appetite if I sit so near you; but I suppose
I must."

"An't she lively?" whispered Mr. Jonas to the elder
sister, with his favourite elbow emphasis.

"Oh I really don't know!" replied Miss Pecksniff, tartly.
"I am tired of being asked such ridiculous questions."

"What's that precious old father of mine about now?"
said Mr. Jonas, seeing that his parent was travelling up
and down the room, instead of taking his seat at table.
"What are you looking for?"

"I've lost my glasses, Jonas," said old Anthony.

"Sit down without your glasses, can't you?" returned
his son. "You don't eat or drink out of 'em, I think; and
where's that sleepy-headed old Chuffey got to! Now,
stupid. Oh! you know your name, do you?"

It would seem that he didn't, for he didn't come until
the father called. As he spoke, the door of a small glass
office, which was partitioned off from the rest of the room,
was slowly opened, and a little blear-eyed, weazen-faced,
ancient man came creeping out. He was of a remote fashion, and dusty, like the rest of the furniture; he was
dressed in a decayed suit of black; with breeches garnished
at the knees with rusty wisps of ribbon, the very paupers
of shoe-strings; on the lower portion of his spindle legs
were dingy worsted stockings of the same colour. He
looked as if he had been put away and forgotten half a century before, and somebody had just found him in a lum-
ber-closet.

Such as he was, he came slowly creeping on towards the table, until at last he crept into the vacant chair, from which, as his dim faculties became conscious of the pres-ence of strangers, and those strangers ladies, he rose again, apparently intending to make a bow. But he sat down once more, without having made it, and breathing on his shrivelled hands to warm them, remained with his poor blue nose immoveable above his plate, looking at nothing, with eyes that saw nothing, and a face that meant nothing. Take him in that state, and he was an embodiment of nothing. Nothing else.

"Our clerk," said Mr. Jonas, as host and master of the ceremonies: "Old Chuffey."

"Is he deaf?" inquired one of the young ladies.

"No, I don't know that he is. He an't deaf, is he, father?"

"I never heard him say he was," replied the old man.

"Blind?" inquired the young ladies.

"N—no. I never understood that he was at all blind," said Jonas, carelessly. "You don't consider him so, do you, father?"

"Certainly not," replied Anthony.

"What is he then?"

"Why, I'll tell you what he is," said Mr. Jonas, apart to the young ladies, "he's precious old, for one thing; and I an't best pleased with him for that, for I think my father must have caught it of him. He's a strange old chap, for another," he added in a louder voice, "and don't understand any one hardly, but *him!*" He pointed to his honoured parent with the carving-fork, in order that they might know whom he meant.

"How very strange!" cried the sisters.

"Why, you see," said Mr. Jonas, "he's been addling his old brains with figures and book-keeping all his life; and twenty year ago or so he went and took a fever. All the time he was out of his head (which was three weeks) he never left off casting up; and he got to so many million at last that I don't believe he's ever been quite right since. We don't do much business now though, and he an't a bad clerk."

"A very good one," said Anthony.

"Well! He an't a dear one at all events," observed Jonas; "and he earns his salt, which is enough for our

look-out. I was telling you that he hardly understands
any one except my father; he always understands him,
though, and wakes up quite wonderful. He's been used to
his ways so long, you see! Why, I've seen him play
whist, with my father for a partner; and a good rubber
too; when he had no more notion what sort of people he
was playing against, than you have."

"Has he no appetite?" asked Merry.

"Oh yes," said Jonas, plying his own knife and fork
very fast. "He eats—when he's helped. But he don't
care whether he waits a minute or an hour, as long as father's here; so when I'm at all sharp set, as I am to-day,
I come to him after I've taken the edge off my own hunger,
you know. Now, Chuffey, stupid, are you ready?"

Chuffey remained immoveable.

"Always a perverse old file, he was," said Mr. Jonas,
coolly helping himself to another slice. "Ask him, father."

"Are you ready for your dinner, Chuffey?" asked the
old man.

"Yes, yes," said Chuffey, lighting up into a sentient human creature at the first sound of the voice, so that it was
at once a curious and quite a moving sight to see him.
"Yes, yes. Quite ready, Mr. Chuzzlewit. Quite ready,
Sir. All ready, all ready, all ready." With that he
stopped, smilingly, and listened for some further address;
but being spoken to no more, the light forsook his face by
little and little, until he was nothing again.

"He'll be very disagreeable, mind," said Jonas, addressing his cousins as he handed the old man's portion to
his father. "He always chokes himself when it an't broth.
Look at him, now! Did you ever see a horse with such a
wall-eyed expression as he's got? If it hadn't been for
the joke of it, I wouldn't have let him come in to-day; but
I thought he'd amuse you."

The poor old subject of this humane speech, was, happily for himself, as unconscious of its purport, as of most
other remarks that were made in his presence. But the
mutton being tough, and his gums weak, he quickly verified
the statement relative to his choking propensities, and underwent so much in his attempts to dine, that Mr. Jonas
was infinitely amused: protesting that he had seldom seen
him better company in all his life, and that he was enough
to make a man split his sides with laughing. Indeed, he

went so far as to assure the sisters, that in this point of view he considered Chuffey superior to his own father; which, as he significantly added, was saying a great deal. It was strange enough that Anthony Chuzzlewit, himself so old a man, should take a pleasure in these gibings of his estimable son, at the expense of the poor shadow at their table. But he did, unquestionably: though not so much— to do him justice—with reference to their ancient clerk, as in exultation at the sharpness of Jonas. For the same reason, that young man's coarse allusions, even to himself, filled him with a stealthy glee: causing him to rub his hands and chuckle covertly, as if he said in his sleeve, "*I* taught him. *I* trained him. This is the heir of my bring-ing-up. Sly, cunning, and covetous, he'll not squander my money. I worked for this; I hoped for this; it has been the great end and aim of my life."

What a noble end and aim it was to contemplate in the attainment, truly! But there be some who manufacture idols after the fashion of themselves, and fail to worship them when they are made; charging their deformity on outraged nature. Anthony was better than these at any rate.

Chuffey boggled over his plate so long, that Mr. Jonas, losing patience, took it from him at last with his own hands, and requested his father to signify to that venerable person that he had better "peg away at his bread:" which Anthony did.

"Ay, ay!" cried the old man, brightening up as before, when this was communicated to him in the same voice; "quite right, quite right. He's your own son, Mr. Chuz-zlewit! Bless him for a sharp lad! Bless him, bless him!"

Mr. Jonas considered this so particularly childish—per-haps with some reason—that he only laughed the more, and told his cousins that he was afraid one of these fine days, Chuffey would be the death of him. The cloth was then removed, and the bottle of wine set upon the table, from which Mr. Jonas filled the young ladies' glasses, call-ing on them not to spare it, as they might be certain there was plenty more where that came from. But he added with some haste after this sally, that it was only his joke, and they wouldn't suppose him to be in earnest, he was sure.

"I shall drink," said Anthony, "to Pecksniff. Your

father, my dears. A clever man, Pecksniff. A wary man!
A hypocrite, though, eh? A hypocrite, girls, eh? Ha,
ha, ha! Well, so he is. Now, among friends—he is. I
don't think the worse of him for that, unless it is that he
overdoes it. You may overdo anything, my darlings. You
may overdo even hypocrisy. Ask Jonas!"

"You can't overdo taking care of yourself," observed
that hopeful gentleman with his mouth full.

"Do you hear that, my dears?" cried Anthony, quite
enraptured. "Wisdom, wisdom! A good exception, Jonas.
No. It's not easy to overdo that."

"Except," whispered Mr. Jonas to his favourite cousin,
"except when one lives too long. Ha, ha! Tell the other
one that—I say!"

"Good gracious me!" said Cherry, in a petulant manner. "You can tell her yourself, if you wish, can't you?"

"She seems to make such game of one," replied Mr.
Jonas

"Then why need you trouble yourself about her?" said
Charity. "I am sure she doesn't trouble herself much
about you."

"Don't she though?" asked Jonas.

"Good gracious me, need I tell you that she don't?"
returned the young lady.

Mr. Jonas made no verbal rejoinder, but he glanced at
Mercy with an odd expression in his face; and said *that*
wouldn't break his heart, she might depend upon it. Then
he looked on Charity with even greater favour than before,
and besought her, as his polite manner was, to "come a
little closer."

"There's another thing that's not easily overdone, father," remarked Jonas, after a short silence.

"What's that?" asked the father; grinning already
in anticipation.

"A bargain," said the son. "Here's the rule for bargains—'Do other men, for they would do you.' That's
the true business precept. All others are counterfeits."

The delighted father applauded this sentiment to the
echo; and was so much tickled by it, that he was at the
pains of imparting the same to his ancient clerk, who
rubbed his hands, nodded his palsied head, winked his
watery eyes, and cried in his whistling tones, "Good!
good! Your own son, Mr. Chuzzlewit!" with every feeble

demonstration of delight that he was capable of making. But this old man's enthusiasm had the redeeming quality of being felt in sympathy with the only creature to whom he was linked by ties of long association, and by his present helplessness. And if there had been anybody there, who cared to think about it, some dregs of a better nature unawakened, might perhaps have been descried through that very medium, melancholy though it was, yet lingering at the bottom of the worn-out cask, called Chuffey.

As matters stood, nobody thought or said anything upon the subject; so Chuffey fell back into a dark corner on one side of the fire-place, where he always spent his evenings, and was neither seen nor heard again that night; save once, when a cup of tea was given him, in which he was seen to soak his bread mechanically. There was no reason to suppose that he went to sleep at these seasons, or that he heard, or saw, or felt, or thought. He remained, as it were, frozen up—if any term expressive of such a vigorous process can be applied to him—until he was again thawed for the moment by a word or touch from Anthony.

Miss Charity made tea by desire of Mr. Jonas, and felt and looked so like the lady of the house, that she was in the prettiest confusion imaginable; the more so, from Mr. Jonas sitting close beside her, and whispering a variety of admiring expressions in her ear. Miss Mercy, for her part, felt the entertainment of the evening to be so distinctly and exclusively theirs, that she silently deplored the commercial gentlemen—at that moment, no doubt, wearying for her return—and yawned over yesterday's newspaper. As to Anthony, he went to sleep outright, so Jonas and Cherry had a clear stage to themselves as long as they chose to keep possession of it.

When the tea-tray was taken away, as it was at last, Mr. Jonas produced a dirty pack of cards, and entertained the sisters with divers small feats of dexterity: whereof the main purpose of every one was, that you were to decoy somebody into laying a wager with you that you couldn't do it; and were then immediately to win and pocket his money. Mr. Jonas informed them that these accomplishments were in high vogue in the most intellectual circles, and that large amounts were constantly changing hands on such hazards. And it may be remarked that he fully believed this; for there is a simplicity of cunning no less than a simplicity of innocence; and in all matters where a lively faith in knavery and meanness was required as the groundwork of belief, Mr. Jonas was one of the most credulous of men. His ignorance, which was stupendous, may be taken into account, if the reader pleases, separately.

This fine young man had all the inclination to be a profligate of the first water, and only lacked the one good trait in the common catalogue of debauched vices—openhandedness—to be a notable vagabond. But there his griping and penurious habits stepped in; and as one poison will sometimes neutralize another, when wholesome remedies would not avail, so he was restrained by a bad passion from quaffing his full measure of evil, when virtue might have sought to hold him back in vain.

By the time he had unfolded all the peddling schemes he knew upon the cards, it was growing late in the evening; and Mr. Pecksniff not making his appearance, the young ladies expressed a wish to return home. But this, Mr. Jonas, in his gallantry, would by no means allow, until they had partaken of some bread and cheese and porter; and even then he was excessively unwilling to allow them to depart; often beseeching Miss Charity to come a little closer, or to stop a little longer, and preferring many other complimentary petitions of that nature, in his own hospitable and earnest way. When all his efforts to detain them were fruitless, he put on his hat and great coat preparatory to escorting them to Todgers's; remarking that he knew they would rather walk thither than ride; and that for his part he was quite of their opinion.

"Good night," said Anthony. "Good night; remember me to—ha, ha, ha!—to Pecksniff. Take care of your cousin, my dears; beware of Jonas; he's a dangerous fellow. Don't quarrel for him, in any case!"

"Oh, the creature!" cried Mercy. "The idea of quarrelling for *him!* You may take him, Cherry, my love, all to yourself. I make you a present of my share."

"What! I'm a sour grape, am I, cousin?" said Jonas.

Miss Charity was more entertained by this repartee than one would have supposed likely, considering its advanced age and simple character. But in her sisterly affection she took Mr. Jonas to task for leaning so very hard upon a broken reed, and said that he must not be so cruel to poor Merry any more, or she (Charity) would positively be obliged to hate him. Mercy, who really had her share of good humour, only retorted with a laugh; and they walked home in consequence without any angry passages of words upon the way. Mr. Jonas being in the middle, and having a cousin on each arm, sometimes squeezed the wrong one; so tightly too, as to cause her not a little inconvenience; but as he talked to Charity in whispers the whole time, and paid her great attention, no doubt this was an accidental circumstance. When they arrived at Todgers's, and the door was opened, Mercy broke hastily from them, and ran up-stairs; but Charity and Jonas lingered on the steps talking together for more than five minutes; so, as Mrs. Todgers observed next morning, to a third party, "It was pretty clear what was going on *there*, and she was glad of it, for it really was high time Miss Pecksniff thought of settling."

And now the day was coming on, when that bright vision which had burst on Todgers's so suddenly, and made a sunshine in the shady breast of Jinkins, was to be seen no more; when it was to be packed like a brown-paper parcel, or a fish-basket, or an oyster-barrel, or a fat gentleman, or any other dull reality of life, in a stage-coach, and carried down into the country!

"Never, my dear Miss Pecksniffs," said Mrs. Todgers, when they retired to rest on the last night of their stay; "never have I seen an establishment so perfectly brokenhearted as mine is at this present moment of time. I don't believe the gentlemen will be the gentlemen they were, or anything like it—no, not for weeks to come. You have a great deal to answer for; both of you."

They modestly disclaimed any wilful agency in this disastrous state of things, and regretted it very much.

"Your pious Pa, too!" said Mrs. Todgers. "There's a loss! My dear Miss Pecksniffs, your Pa is a perfect missionary of peace and love."

Entertaining an uncertainty as to the particular kind of love supposed to be comprised in Mr. Pecksniff's mission, the young ladies received this compliment rather coldly.

"If I dared," said Mrs. Todgers, perceiving this, "to violate a confidence which has been reposed in me, and to tell you why I must beg of you to leave the little door between your room and mine open to-night, I think you would be interested. But I mustn't do it, for I promised

13

Mr. Jinkins faithfully that I would be as silent as the
tomb."

"Dear Mrs. Todgers! What can you mean?"

"Why then, my sweet Miss Pecksniffs," said the lady
of the house; "my own loves, if you will allow me the
privilege of taking that freedom on the eve of our separation, Mr. Jinkins and the gentlemen have made up a little
musical party among themselves, and *do* intend in the dead
of this night to perform a serenade upon the stairs outside
the door. I could have wished, I own," said Mrs. Todgers,
with her usual foresight, "that it had been fixed to take
place an hour or two earlier; because, when gentlemen sit
up late, they drink, and when they drink, they're not so
musical, perhaps, as when they don't. But this is the arrangement; and I know you will be gratified, my dear
Miss Pecksniffs, by such a mark of their attention."

The young ladies were at first so much excited by the
news, that they vowed they couldn't think of going to
bed, until the serenade was over. But half an hour of cool
waiting so altered their opinion that they not only went to
bed, but fell asleep; and were moreover not ecstatically
charmed to be awakened sometime afterwards by certain
dulcet strains breaking in upon the silent watches of the
night.

It was very affecting—very. Nothing more dismal could
have been desired by the most fastidious taste. The gentleman of a vocal turn was head mute, or chief mourner;
Jinkins took the bass; and the rest took anything they
could get. The youngest gentleman blew his melancholy
into a flute. He didn't blow much out of it, but that was
all the better. If the two Miss Pecksniffs and Mrs.
Todgers had perished by spontaneous combustion, and the
serenade had been in honour of their ashes, it would have
been impossible to surpass the unutterable despair expressed
in that one chorus, "Go where glory waits thee!" It was
a requiem, a dirge, a moan, a howl, a wail, a lament, an
abstract of everything that is sorrowful and hideous in
sound. The flute of the youngest gentleman was wild and
fitful. It came and went in gusts, like the wind. For a
long time together he seemed to have left off, and when it
was quite settled by Mrs. Todgers and the young ladies,
that, overcome by his feelings, he had retired in tears, he
unexpectedly turned up again at the very top of the tune,

gasping for breath. He was a tremendous performer. There was no knowing where to have him; and exactly when you thought he was doing nothing at all, then was he doing the very thing that ought to astonish you most.

There were several of these concerted pieces; perhaps two or three too many, though that, as Mrs. Todgers said, was a fault on the right side. But even then, even at that solemn moment, when the thrilling sounds may be presumed to have penetrated into the very depths of his nature, if he had any depths, Jinkins couldn't leave the youngest gentleman alone. He asked him distinctly, before the second song began—as a personal favour too, mark the villain in that—not to play. Yes; he said so; not to play. The breathing of the youngest gentleman was heard through the key-hole of the door. He *didn't* play. What vent was a flute for the passions swelling up within his breast? A trombone would have been a world too mild.

The serenade approached its close. Its crowning interest was at hand. The gentleman of a literary turn had written a song on the departure of the ladies, and adapted it to an old tune. They all joined, except the youngest gentleman in company, who, for the reasons aforesaid, maintained a fearful silence. The song (which was of a classical nature) invoked the oracle of Apollo, and demanded to know what would become of Todgers's when CHARITY and MERCY were banished from its walls. The oracle delivered no opinion particularly worth remembering, according to the not infrequent practice of oracles from the earliest ages down to the present time. In the absence of enlightenment on that subject, the strain deserted it, and went on to show that the Miss Pecksniffs were nearly related to Rule Britannia, and that if Great Britain hadn't been an island there could have been no Miss Pecksniffs. And being now on a nautical tack, it closed with this verse:

> " All hail to the vessel of Pecksniff the sire!
>   And favouring breezes to fan;
>   While Tritons flock round it, and proudly admire
>   The architect, artist, and man!"

As they presented this beautiful picture to the imagination, the gentlemen gradually withdrew to bed to give the music the effect of distance; and so it died away, and Todgers's was left to its repose.

Mr. Bailey reserved his vocal offering until the morning,
when he put his head into the room as the young ladies
were kneeling before their trunks, packing up, and treated
them to an imitation of the voice of a young dog, in trying
circumstances : when that animal is supposed by persons of
a lively fancy, to relieve his feelings by calling for pen and
ink.

"Well, young ladies," said the youth, "so you're a
going home, are you; worse luck? "

"Yes, Bailey, we're going home," returned Mercy.

"An't you a going to leave none of 'em a lock of your
hair? " inquired the youth.   "It's real, an't it? "

They laughed at this, and told him of course it was.

"Oh is it of course though? " said Bailey.   "I know better than that. Hers an't. Why, I see it hanging up once,
on that nail by the winder. Besides, I have gone behind
her at dinner-time and pulled it; and she never know'd.
I say, young ladies—I'm a going to leave. I an't a going
to stand being called names by her, no longer."

Miss Mercy inquired what his plans for the future
might be; in reply to whom, Mr. Bailey intimated that he
thought of going, either into top-boots, or into the army.

"Into the army! " cried the young ladies, with a laugh.

"Ah! " said Bailey, "why not? There's a many drum-
mers in the Tower. I'm acquainted with 'em. Don't their
country set a valley on 'em, mind you! Not at all! "

"You'll be shot, I see," observed Mercy.

"Well! " cried Mr. Bailey, "wot if I am? There's
something gamey in it, young ladies, an't there? I'd
sooner be hit with a cannon-ball than a rolling-pin, and
she's always a catching up something of that sort, and
throwing it at me, when the gentlemans appetites is good.
Wot," said Mr. Bailey, stung by the recollection of his
wrongs, "wot, if they *do* con-sume the per-vishuns. It
an't *my* fault, is it? "

"Surely no one says it is," said Mercy.

"Don't they though? " retorted the youth. "No. Yes.
Ah! Oh! No one mayn't say it is; but some one knows
it is. But I an't a going to have every rise in prices wis-
ited on me. I an't a going to be killed, because the markets is dear. I won't stop. And therefore," added Mr.
Bailey, relenting into a smile, "wotever you mean to give
me, you'd better give me all at once, becos if ever you

come back agin, I shan't be here; and as to the other boy, *he* won't deserve nothing, *I* know."

The young ladies, on behalf of Mr. Pecksniff and themselves, acted on this thoughtful advice; and in consideration of their private friendship, presented Mr. Bailey with a gratuity so liberal, that he could hardly do enough to show his gratitude; which found but an imperfect vent, during the remainder of the day, in divers secret slaps upon his pocket, and other such facetious pantomime. Nor was it confined to these ebullitions; for besides crushing a bandbox, with a bonnet in it, he seriously damaged Mr. Pecksniff's luggage, by ardently hauling it down from the top of the house; and in short evinced, by every means in his power, a lively sense of the favours he had received from that gentleman and his family.

Mr. Pecksniff and Mr. Jinkins came home to dinner, arm-in-arm; for the latter gentleman had made half-holiday, on purpose; thus gaining an immense advantage over the youngest gentleman and the rest, whose time, as it perversely chanced, was all bespoke, until the evening. The bottle of wine was Mr. Pecksniff's treat, and they were very sociable indeed; though full of lamentations on the necessity of parting. While they were in the midst of their enjoyment, old Anthony and his son were announced; much to the surprise of Mr. Pecksniff, and greatly to the discomfiture of Jinkins.

"Come to say good bye, you see," said Anthony, in a low voice, to Mr. Pecksniff, as they took their seats apart at the table, while the rest conversed among themselves. "Where's the use of a division between you and me? We are the two halves of a pair of scissors, when apart, Pecksniff; but together we are something. Eh?"

"Unanimity, my good sir," rejoined Mr. Pecksniff, "is always delightful."

"I don't know about that," said the old man, "for there are some people I would rather differ from than agree with. But you know my opinion of you."

Mr. Pecksniff, still having "hypocrite" in his mind, only replied by a motion of his head, which was something between an affirmative bow, and a negative shake.

"Complimentary," said Anthony. "Complimentary, upon my word. It was an involuntary tribute to your abilities, even at the time; and it was not a time to suggest compliments either. But we agreed in the coach, you know, that we quite understood each other."

"Oh, quite!" assented Mr. Pecksniff, in a manner which implied that he himself was misunderstood most cruelly, but would not complain.

Anthony glanced at his son as he sat beside Miss Charity, and then at Mr. Pecksniff, and then at his son again, very many times. It happened that Mr. Pecksniff's glances took a similar direction; but when he became aware of it, he first cast down his eyes, and then closed them; as if he were determined that the old man should read nothing there.

"Jonas is a shrewd lad," said the old man.

"He appears," rejoined Mr. Pecksniff in his most candid manner, "to be very shrewd."

"And careful," said the old man.

"And careful, I have no doubt," returned Mr. Pecksniff.

"Lookye!" said Anthony in his ear. "I think he is sweet upon your daughter."

"Tut, my good sir," said Mr. Pecksniff, with his eyes still closed; "young people—young people—a kind of cousins, too—no more sweetness than is in that, sir."

"Why, there is very little sweetness in that, according to our experience," returned Anthony. "Isn't there a trifle more here?"

"Impossible to say," rejoined Mr. Pecksniff. "Quite impossible! You surprise me."

"Yes, I know that," said the old man, drily. "It may last; I mean the sweetness, not the surprise; and it may die off. Supposing it should last, perhaps (you having feathered your nest pretty well, and I having done the same) we might have a mutual interest in the matter."

Mr. Pecksniff, smiling gently, was about to speak, but Anthony stopped him.

"I know what you are going to say. It's quite unnecessary. You have never thought of this for a moment; and in a point so nearly affecting the happiness of your dear child, you couldn't, as a tender father, express an opinion; and so forth. Yes, quite right. And like you! But it seems to me, my dear Pecksniff," added Anthony, laying his hand upon his sleeve, "that if you and I kept up the joke of pretending not to see this, one of us might possibly be placed in a position of disadvantge; and as I am very unwilling to be that party myself, you will excuse my taking the liberty of putting the matter beyond a doubt, thus early; and having it distinctly understood, as it is now, that we do see it, and do know it. Thank you for your attention. We are now upon an equal footing; which is agreeable to us both, I am sure."

He rose as he spoke; and giving Mr. Pecksniff a nod of intelligence, moved away from him to where the young people were sitting: leaving that good man somewhat puzzled and discomfited by such very plain dealing, and not quite free from a sense of having been foiled in the exercise of his familiar weapons.

But the night-coach had a punctual character, and it was time to join it at the office; which was so near at hand, that they had already sent their luggage, and arranged to walk. Thither the whole party repaired, therefore, after no more delay than sufficed for the equipment of the Miss Pecksniffs and Mrs. Todgers. They found the coach already at its starting-place, and the horses in; there, too, were a large majority of the commercial gentlemen, including the youngest, who was visibly agitated, and in a state of deep mental dejection.

Nothing could equal the distress of Mrs. Todgers in parting from the young ladies, except the strong emotions with which she bade adieu to Mr. Pecksniff. Never surely was a pocket-handkerchief taken in and out of a flat reticule so often as Mrs. Todgers's was, as she stood upon the pavement by the coach-door, supported on either side by a commercial gentleman; and by the light of the coach-lamps caught such brief snatches and glimpses of the good man's face, as the constant interposition of Mr. Jinkins allowed. For Jinkins, to the last the youngest gentleman's rock ahead in life, stood upon the coach-step talking to the ladies. Upon the other step was Mr. Jonas, who maintained that position in right of his cousinship; whereas the youngest gentleman, who had been first upon the ground, was deep in the booking-office among the black and red placards, and the portraits of fast coaches, where he was ignominiously harassed by porters, and had to contend and strive perpetually with heavy baggage. This false position, combined with his nervous excitement, brought about the very consummation and catastrophe of his miseries; for when, in the moment of parting, he aimed a flower—a hot-house flower, that had cost money—at the fair hand of Mercy, it reached, instead, the coachman on the box, who thanked him kindly, and stuck it in his button-hole.

They were off now; and Todgers's was alone again. The two young ladies, leaning back in their separate corners, resigned themselves to their own regretful thoughts. But Mr. Pecksniff, dismissing all ephemeral considerations of social pleasure and enjoyment, concentrated his meditations on the one great virtuous purpose before him, of casting out that ingrate and deceiver, whose presence yet troubled his domestic hearth, and was a sacrilege upon the altars of his household gods.

CHAPTER XII.

WILL BE SEEN IN THE LONG RUN, IF NOT IN THE SHORT ONE, TO CONCERN MR. PINCH AND OTHERS, NEARLY. MR. PECKSNIFF ASSERTS THE DIGNITY OF OUTRAGED VIRTUE; AND YOUNG MARTIN CHUZZLEWIT FORMS A DESPERATE RESOLUTION.

MR. PINCH and Martin, little dreaming of the stormy weather that impended, made themselves very comfortable in the Pecksniffian halls, and improved their friendship daily. Martin's facility, both of invention and execution, being remarkable, the grammar-school proceeded with great vigour; and Tom repeatedly declared, that if there were anything like certainty in human affairs, or impartiality in human judges, a design so new and full of merit could not fail to carry off the first prize when the time of competition arrived. Without being quite so sanguine himself, Martin had his hopeful anticipations too; and they served to make him brisk and eager at his task.

"If I should turn out a great architect, Tom," said the new pupil one day, as he stood at a little distance from his drawing, and eyed it with much complacency, "I'll tell you what should be one of the things I'd build."

"Ay!" cried Tom. "What?"

"Why, your fortune."

"No; " said Tom Pinch, quite as much delighted as if
the thing were done. "Would you though? How kind
of you to say so."

"I'd build it up, Tom," returned Martin, "on such a
strong foundation, that it should last your life—ay, and
your children's lives too, and their children's after them.
I'd be your patron, Tom. I'd take you under my protection. Let me see the man who should give the cold shoulder to anybody I chose to protect and patronise, if I were
at the top of the tree, Tom! "

"Now, I don't think," said Mr. Pinch, "upon my word,
that I was ever more gratified than by this. I really
don't."

"Oh! I mean what I say," retorted Martin, with a
manner as free and easy in its condescension to, not to say
in its compassion for, the other, as if he were already First
Architect in Ordinary to all the Crowned Heads in Europe.
"I'd do it—I'd provide for you."

"I am afraid," said Tom, shaking his head, "that I
should be a mighty awkward person to provide for."

"Pooh, pooh! " rejoined Martin. "Never mind that.
If I took it in my head to say, ' Pinch is a clever fellow; I
approve of Pinch;' I should like to know the man who
would venture to put himself in opposition to me. Besides,
confound it, Tom, you could be useful to me in a hundred
ways."

"If I were not useful in one or two, it shouldn't be for
want of trying," said Tom.

"For instance," pursued Martin, after a short reflection,
"you'd be a capital fellow, now, to see that my ideas were
properly carried out; and to overlook the works in their
progress before they were sufficiently advanced to be very
interesting to *me;* and to take all that sort of plain sailing.
Then you'd be a splendid fellow to show people over my
studio, and to talk about Art to 'em, when I couldn't be
bored myself, and all that kind of thing. For it would be
devilish creditable, Tom (I'm quite in earnest, I give you
my word), to have a man of your information about one,
instead of some ordinary blockhead. Oh, I'd take care of
you. You'd be useful, rely upon it! "

To say that Tom had no idea of playing first fiddle in
any social orchestra, but was always quite satisfied to be
set down for the hundred and fiftieth violin in the band,

or thereabouts, is to express his modesty in very inadequate
terms. He was much delighted, therefore, by these observations.

"I should be married to her then, Tom, of course," said
Martin.

What was that which checked Tom Pinch so suddenly,
in the high flow of his gladness: bringing the blood
into his honest cheeks, and a remorseful feeling to his
honest heart, as if he were unworthy of his friend's
regard?

"I should be married to her then," said Martin, looking
with a smile towards the light: "and we should have, I
hope, children about us. They'd be very fond of you,
Tom."

But not a word said Mr. Pinch. The words he would
have uttered, died upon his lips, and found a life more
spiritual in self-denying thoughts.

"All the children hereabouts are fond of you, Tom, and
mine would be, of course," pursued Martin. "Perhaps I
might name one of 'em after you. Tom, eh? Well, I
don't know; Tom's not a bad name. Thomas Pinch Chuzzlewit. T. P. C. on his pinafores—no objection to that, I
should say?"

Tom cleared his throat, and smiled.

"*She* would like you, Tom, I know," said Martin.

"Ay!" cried Tom Pinch, faintly.

"I can tell exactly what she would think of you," said
Martin, leaning his chin upon his hand, and looking
through the window-glass as if he read there what he said;
"I know her so well. She would smile, Tom, often at
first when you spoke to her, or when she looked at you—
merrily too—but you wouldn't mind that. A brighter
smile you never saw!"

"No, no," said Tom. "I wouldn't mind that."

"She would be as tender with you, Tom," said Martin,
"as if you were a child yourself. So you are almost, in
some things, an't you, Tom?"

Mr. Pinch nodded his entire assent.

"She would always be kind and good-humoured, and
glad to see you," said Martin; "and when she found out
exactly what sort of fellow you were (which she'd do, very
soon), she would pretend to give you little commissions to
execute, and to ask little services of you, which she knew

you were burning to render; so that when she really pleased you most, she would try to make you think you most pleased her. She would take to you uncommonly, Tom; and would understand you far more delicately than I ever shall; and would often say, I know, that you were a harmless, gentle, well-intentioned, good fellow."

How silent Tom Pinch was!

"In honour of old times," said Martin, "and of her having heard you play the organ in this damp little church down here—for nothing too—we will have one in the house. I shall build an architectural music-room on a plan of my own, and it'll look rather knowing in a recess at one end. There you shall play away, Tom, till you tire yourself; and, as you like to do so in the dark, it shall *be* dark; and many's the summer evening she and I will sit and listen to you, Tom; be sure of that!"

It may have required a stronger effort on Tom Pinch's part to leave the seat on which he sat, and shake his friend by both hands, with nothing but serenity and grateful feeling painted on his face; it may have required a stronger effort to perform this simple act with a pure heart, than to achieve many and many a deed to which the doubtful trumpet blown by Fame has lustily resounded. Doubtful, because from its long hovering over scenes of violence, the smoke and steam of death have clogged the keys of that brave instrument; and it is not always that its notes are either true or tuneful.

"It's a proof of the kindness of human nature," said Tom, characteristically putting himself quite out of sight in the matter, "that everybody who comes here, as you have done, is more considerate and affectionate to me than I should have any right to hope, if I were the most sanguine creature in the world; or should have any power to express, if I were the most eloquent. It really overpowers me. But trust me," said Tom, "that I am not ungrateful —that I never forget—and that, if I can ever prove the truth of my words to you, I will."

"That's all right," observed Martin, leaning back in his chair with a hand in each pocket, and yawning drearily. "Very fine talking, Tom; but I'm at Pecksniff's, I remember, and perhaps a mile or so out of the high-road to fortune just at this minute. So you've heard again this morning from what's his name, eh?"

"Who may that be?" asked Tom, seeming to enter a mild protest on behalf of the dignity of an absent person.

" *You* know. What is it? Northkey."

"Westlock," rejoined Tom, in rather a louder tone than usual.

".Ah! to be sure," said Martin, "Westlock. I knew it was something connected with a point of the compass and a door. Well! and what says Westlock?"

"Oh! he has come into his property," answered Tom, nodding his head, and smiling.

"He's a lucky dog," said Martin. "I wish it were mine instead. Is that all the mystery you were to tell me?"

"No," said Tom: "not all."

"What's the rest?" asked Martin.

"For the matter of that," said Tom, "it's no mystery, and you won't think much of it; but it's very pleasant to me. John always used to say when he was here, 'Mark my words, Pinch. When my father's executors cash up'—he used strange expressions now and then, but that was his way."

"Cash-up's a very good expression," observed Martin, "when other people don't apply it to you. Well?—What a slow fellow you are, Pinch!"

"Yes, I am I know," said Tom; "but you'll make me nervous if you tell me so. I'm afraid you have put me out a little now, for I forget what I was going to say."

"When John's father's executors cashed up—" said Martin impatiently.

"Oh yes, to be sure," cried Tom; "yes. 'Then,' says John, 'I'll give you a dinner, Pinch, and come down to Salisbury on purpose.' Now, when John wrote the other day—the morning Pecksniff left, you know—he said his business was on the point of being immediately settled, and as he was to receive his money directly, when could I meet him at Salisbury? I wrote and said, any day this week; and I told him besides, that there was a new pupil here, and what a fine fellow you were, and what friends we had become. Upon which John writes back this letter"—Tom produced it—"fixes to-morrow; sends his compliments to you; and begs that we three may have the pleasure of dining together—not at the house where you and I were, either; but at the very first hotel in the town. Read what he says."

"Very well," said Martin, glancing over it with his customary coolness: "much obliged to him. I'm agreeable."

Tom could have wished him to be a little more astonished, a little more pleased, or in some form or other a little more interested in such a great event. But he was perfectly self-possessed: and, falling into his favourite solace of whistling, took another turn at the grammar-school, as if nothing at all had happened.

Mr. Pecksniff's horse being regarded in the light of a sacred animal, only to be driven by him, the chief priest of that temple, or by some person distinctly nominated for the time being to that high office by himself, the two young men agreed to walk to Salisbury; and so, when the time came, they set off on foot; which was, after all, a better mode of travelling than in the gig, as the weather was very cold and very dry.

Better! A rare strong, hearty, healthy walk—four statute miles an hour—preferable to that rumbling, tumbling, jolting, shaking, scraping, creaking, villanous old gig? Why, the two things will not admit of comparison. It is an insult to the walk, to set them side by side. Where is an instance of a gig having ever circulated a man's blood, unless when, putting him in danger of his neck, it awakened in his veins and in his ears, and all along his spine, a tingling heat, much more peculiar than agreeable? When did a gig ever sharpen anybody's wits and energies, unless it was when the horse bolted, and, crashing madly down a steep hill with a stone wall at the bottom, his desperate circumstances suggested to the only gentleman left inside, some novel and unheard-of mode of dropping out behind? Better than the gig!

The air was cold, Tom; so it was, there is no denying it; but would it have been more genial in the gig? The blacksmith's fire burned very bright, and leaped up high, as though it wanted men to warm; but would it have been less tempting, looked at from the clammy cushions of a gig? The wind blew keenly, nipping the features of the hardy wight who fought his way along; blinding him with his own hair if he had enough of it, and with wintry dust if he hadn't; stopping his breath as though he had been soused in a cold bath; tearing aside his wrappings-up, and whistling in the very marrow of his bones; but it would have done all this a hundred times more fiercely to a man in a gig, wouldn't it? A fig for gigs!

Better than the gig! When were travellers by wheels and hoofs seen with such red-hot cheeks as those? when were they so good humouredly and merrily bloused? when did their laughter ring upon the air, as they turned them round, what time the stronger gusts came sweeping up; and, facing round again as they passed by, dashed on in such a glow of ruddy health as nothing could keep pace with, but the high spirits it engendered? Better than the gig! Why, here *is* a man in a gig coming the same way now. Look at him as he passes his whip into his left hand, chafes his numbed right fingers on his granite leg, and beats those marble toes of his upon the foot-board. Ha, ha, ha! Who would exchange this rapid hurry of the blood for yonder stagnant misery, though its pace were twenty miles for one?

Better than the gig! No man in a gig could have such interest in the milestones. No man in a gig could see, or feel, or think, like merry users of their legs. How, as the wind sweeps on, upon these breezy downs, it tracks its flight in darkening ripples on the grass, and smoothest shadows on the hills! Look round and round upon this bare plain, and see even here, upon a winter's day, how beautiful the shadows are! Alas! it is the nature of their kind to be so. The loveliest things in life, Tom, are but shadows; and they come and go, and change and fade away, as rapidly as these!

Another mile, and then begins a fall of snow, making the crow, who skims away so close above the ground to shirk the wind, a blot of ink upon the landscape. But though it drives and drifts against them as they walk, stiffening on their skirts, and freezing in the lashes of their eyes, they wouldn't have it fall more sparingly, no, not so much as by a single flake, although they had to go a score of miles. And, lo! the towers of the Old Cathedral rise before them, even now! and bye and bye they come into the sheltered streets, made strangely silent by their white carpet; and so to the Inn for which they are bound; where they present such flushed and burning faces to the cold waiter, and are so brimful of vigour, that he almost feels assaulted by their presence; and, having nothing to oppose to the attack (being fresh, or rather stale, from the blazing

fire in the coffee-room), is quite put out of his pale countenance.

A famous Inn! the hall a very grove of dead game, and
dangling joints of mutton; and in one corner an illustrious
larder, with glass doors, developing cold fowls and noble
joints, and tarts wherein the raspberry jam coyly withdrew
itself, as such a precious creature should, behind a lattice-
work of pastry. And behold, on the first floor, at the
court-end of the house, in a room with all the window-cur-
tains drawn, a fire piled half-way up the chimney, plates
warming before it, wax candles gleaming everywhere, and
a table spread for three, with silver and glass enough for
thirty—John Westlock: not the old John of Pecksniff's,
but a proper gentleman: looking another and a grander
person, with the consciousness of being his own master and
having money in the bank: and yet in some respects the
old John too, for he seized Tom Pinch by both his hands
the instant he appeared, and fairly hugged him, in his cordial welcome.

"And this," said John, "is Mr. Chuzzlewit. I am very
glad to see him!"—John had an off-hand manner of his
own; so they shook hands warmly, and were friends in no
time.

"Stand off a moment, Tom," cried the old pupil, laying
one hand on each of Mr. Pinch's shoulders, and holding
him out at arm's length. "Let me look at you! Just the
same! Not a bit changed!"

"Why, it's not so very long ago, you know," said Tom
Pinch, "after all."

"It seems an age to me," cried John; "and so it ought
to seem to you, you dog." And then he pushed Tom down
into the easiest chair, and clapped him on the back so
heartily, and so like his old self in their old bed-room at
old Pecksniff's, that it was a toss-up with Tom Pinch
whether he should laugh or cry. Laughter won it; and
they all three laughed together.

"I have ordered everything for dinner, that we used to
say we'd have, Tom," observed John Westlock.

"No!" said Tom Pinch. "Have you?"

"Everything. Don't laugh, if you can help it, before
the waiters. I couldn't when I was ordering it. It's like
a dream."

John was wrong there, because nobody ever dreamed

such soup as was put upon the table directly afterwards; or such fish; or such side-dishes; or such a top and bottom; or such a course of birds and sweets; or in short anything approaching the reality of that entertainment at ten-and-sixpence a head, exclusive of wines. As to *them*, the man who can dream such iced champagne, such claret, port, or sherry, had better go to bed and stop there.

But perhaps the finest feature of the banquet was, that nobody was half so much amazed by everything as John himself, who, in his high delight, was constantly bursting into fits of laughter, and then endeavouring to appear preternaturally solemn, lest the waiters should conceive he wasn't used to it. Some of the things they brought him to carve, were such outrageous practical jokes, though, that it was impossible to stand it; and when Tom Pinch insisted, in spite of the deferential advice of an attendant, not only on breaking down the outer wall of a raised pie with a tablespoon, but on trying to eat it afterwards, John lost all dignity, and sat behind the gorgeous dish-cover at the head of the table, roaring to that extent that he was audible in the kitchen. Nor had he the least objection to laugh at himself, as he demonstrated when they had all three gathered round the fire, and the dessert was on the table; at which period, the head waiter inquired with respectful solicitude whether that port, being a light and tawny wine, was suited to his taste, or whether he would wish to try a fruity port with greater body. To this John gravely answered that he was well satisfied with what he had, which he esteemed, as one might say, a pretty tidy vintage; for which the waiter thanked him and withdrew. And then John told his friends, with a broad grin, that he supposed it was all right, but he didn't know; and went off into a perfect shout.

They were very merry and full of enjoyment the whole time, but not the least pleasant part of the festival was when they all three sat about the fire, cracking nuts, drinking wine, and talking cheerfully. It happened that Tom Pinch had a word to say to his friend the organist's assistant, and so deserted his warm corner for a few minutes at this season, lest it should grow too late; leaving the other two young men together.

They drank his health in his absence, of course; and John Westlock took that opportunity of saying, that he had never had even a peevish word with Tom during the whole term of their residence in Mr. Pecksniff's house. This naturally led him to dwell upon Tom's character, and to hint that Mr. Pecksniff understood it pretty well. He only hinted this, and very distantly: knowing that it pained Tom Pinch to have that gentleman disparaged, and thinking it would be as well to leave the new pupil to his own discoveries.

"Yes," said Martin. "It's impossible to like Pinch better than I do, or to do greater justice to his good qualities. He is the most willing fellow I ever saw."

"He's rather too willing," observed John, who was quick in observation. "It's quite a fault in him."

"So it is," said Martin. "Very true. There was a fellow only a week or so ago—a Mr. Tigg—who borrowed all the money he had, on a promise to repay it in a few days. It was but half a sovereign, to be sure; but it's well it was no more, for he'll never see it again."

"Poor fellow!" said John, who had been very attentive to these few words. "Perhaps you have not had an opportunity of observing that, in his own pecuniary transactions, Tom's proud."

"You don't say so! No, I haven't. What do you mean? Won't he borrow?"

John Westlock shook his head.

"That's very odd," said Martin, setting down his empty glass. "He's a strange compound, to be sure."

"As to receiving money as a gift," resumed John Westlock; "I think he'd die first."

"He's made up of simplicity," said Martin. "Help yourself."

"You, however," pursued John, filling his own glass, and looking at his companion with some curiosity, "who are older than the majority of Mr. Pecksniff's assistants, and have evidently had much more experience, understand him, I have no doubt, and see how liable he is to be imposed upon."

"Certainly," said Martin, stretching out his legs, and holding his wine between his eye and the light. "Mr. Pecksniff knows that too. So do his daughters. Eh?"

John Westlock smiled, but made no answer.

"By the bye," said Martin, "that reminds me. What's your opinion of Pecksniff? How did he use you? What

14

do you think of him now?—Coolly, you know, when it's all over?"

"Ask Pinch," returned the old pupil. "He knows what my sentiments used to be upon the subject. They are not changed, I assure you."

"No, no," said Martin, "I'd rather have them from you."

"But Pinch says they are unjust," urged John with a smile.

"Oh! well! Then I know what course they take beforehand," said Martin; "and, therefore, you can have no delicacy in speaking plainly. Don't mind me, I beg. I don't like him, I tell you frankly. I am with him because it happens from particular circumstances to suit my convenience. I have some ability, I believe, in that way; and the obligation, if any, will most likely be on his side and not mine. At the lowest mark, the balance will be even and there'll be no obligation at all. So you may talk to *me*, as if I had no connexion with him."

"If you press me to give my opinion "—returned John Westlock.

"Yes, I do," said Martin. "You'll oblige me."

"—I should say," resumed the other, "that he is the most consummate scoundrel on the face of the earth."

"Oh!" said Martin, as coolly as ever. "That's rather strong."

"Not stronger than he deserves," said John; "and if he called upon me to express my opinion of him to his face, I would do so in the very same terms, without the least qualification. His treatment of Pinch is in itself enough to justify them; but when I look back upon the five years I passed in that house, and remember the hypocrisy, the knavery, the meannesses, the false pretences, the lip service of that fellow, and his trading in saintly semblances for the very worst realities; when I remember how often I was the witness of all this, and how often I was made a kind of party to it, by the faćt of being there, with him for my teacher; I swear to you, that I almost despise myself."

Martin drained his glass, and looked at the fire.

"I don't mean to say, that is a right feeling," pursued John Westlock, "because it was no fault of mine; and I can quite understand—you, for instance, fully appreciating him, and yet being forced by circumstances to remain there. I tell you simply what my feeling is; and even now, when, as you say, it's all over; and when I have the satisfaction of knowing that he always hated me, and we always quarrelled, and I always told him my mind; even now, I feel sorry that I didn't yield to an impulse I often had, as a boy, of running away from him and going abroad."

" Why abroad? " asked Martin, turning his eyes upon the speaker.

" In search," replied John Westlock, shrugging his shoulders, " of the livelihood I couldn't have earned at home. There would have been something spirited in that. But, come—fill your glass, and let us forget him."

" As soon as you please," said Martin. " In reference to myself and my connexion with him, I have only to repeat what I said before. I have taken my own way with him so far, and shall continue to do so, even more than ever; for the fact is—to tell you the truth—that I believe he looks to me to supply his defects, and couldn't afford to lose me. I had a notion of that in first going there. Your health! "

" Thank you," returned young Westlock. " Yours. And may the new pupil turn out as well as you can desire! "

" What new pupil? "

" The fortunate youth, born under an auspicious star," returned John Westlock, laughing; " whose parents, or guardians, are destined to be hooked by the advertisement. What! Don't you know that he has advertised again? "

" No."

" Oh, yes. I read it just before dinner in the old newspaper. I know it to be his; having some reason to remember the style. Hush! Here's Pinch. Strange, is it not, that the more he likes Pecksniff (if he can like him better than he does), the greater reason one has to like *him?* Not a word more, or we shall spoil his whole enjoyment."

Tom entered as the words were spoken, with a radiant smile upon his face; and rubbing his hands, more from a sense of delight than because he was cold (for he had been running fast), sat down in his warm corner again, and was as happy as—as only Tom Pinch could be. There was no other simile that will express his state of mind.

"And so," he said, when he had gazed at his friend for some time in silent pleasure, "so you really are a gentleman at last, John. Well, to be sure!"

"Trying to be, Tom; trying to be," he rejoined good-humouredly. "There is no saying what I may turn out, in time."

"I suppose you wouldn't carry your own box to the mail now," said Tom Pinch, smiling: "although you lost it altogether by not taking it."

"Wouldn't I?" retorted John. "That's all you know about it, Pinch. It must be a very heavy box that I wouldn't carry to get away from Pecksniff's, Tom."

"There!" cried Pinch, turning to Martin, "I told you so. The great fault in his character is his injustice to Pecksniff. You mustn't mind a word he says on that subject. His prejudice is most extraordinary."

"The absence of anything like prejudice on Tom's part, you know," said John Westlock, laughing heartily, as he laid his hand on Mr. Pinch's shoulder, "is perfectly wonderful. If one man ever had a profound knowledge of another, and saw him in a true light, and in his own proper colours, Tom has that knowledge of Mr. Pecksniff."

"Why, of course I have," cried Tom. "That's exactly what I have so often said to you. If you knew him as well as I do—John, I'd give almost any money to bring that about—you'd admire, respect, and reverence him. You couldn't help it. Oh, how you wounded his feelings when you went away!"

"If I had known whereabout his feelings lay," retorted young Westlock, "I'd have done my best, Tom, with that end in view, you may depend upon it. But as I couldn't wound him in what he has not, and in what he knows nothing of, except in his ability to probe them to the quick in other people, I am afraid I can lay no claim to your compliment."

Mr. Pinch, being unwilling to protract a discussion which might possibly corrupt Martin, forebore to say anything in reply to this speech; but John Westlock, whom nothing short of an iron gag would have silenced when Mr. Pecksniff's merits were once in question, continued notwithstanding.

"*His* feelings! Oh, he's a tender-hearted man. *His* feelings! Oh, he's a considerate, conscientious, self-examining, moral vagabond, he is! *His* feelings! Oh!—what's the matter, Tom?"

Mr. Pinch was by this time erect upon the hearth-rug, buttoning his coat with great energy.

"I can't bear it," said Tom, shaking his head. "No. I really cannot. You must excuse me, John. I have a great esteem and friendship for you. I love you very much; and have been perfectly charmed and overjoyed to-day, to find you just the same as ever; but I cannot listen to this."

"Why, it's my old way, Tom; and you say yourself that you are glad to find me unchanged."

"Not in this respect," said Tom Pinch. "You must excuse me, John. I cannot, really; I will not. It's very wrong; you should be more guarded in your expressions. It was bad enough when you and I used to be alone together, but under existing circumstances, I can't endure it, really. No. I cannot, indeed."

"You are quite right!" exclaimed the other, exchanging looks with Martin; "and I am quite wrong, Tom. I don't know how the deuce we fell on this unlucky theme. I beg your pardon with all my heart."

"You have a free and manly temper, I know," said Pinch; "and therefore, your being so ungenerous in this one solitary instance, only grieves me the more. It's not my pardon you have to ask, John. You have done *me* nothing but kindnesses."

"Well! Pecksniff's pardon, then," said young Westlock. "Anything, Tom, or anybody. Pecksniff's pardon —will that do? Here! let us drink Pecksniff's health!"

"Thank you," cried Tom, shaking hands with him eagerly, and filling a bumper. "Thank you; I'll drink it with all my heart, John. Mr. Pecksniff's health, and prosperity to him!"

John Westlock echoed the sentiment, or nearly so; for he drank Mr. Pecksniff's health, and Something to him— but what, was not quite audible. The general unanimity being then completely restored, they drew their chairs closer round the fire, and conversed in perfect harmony and enjoyment until bed-time.

No slight circumstance, perhaps, could have better illustrated the difference of character between John Westlock and Martin Chuzzlewit, than the manner in which each of the young men contemplated Tom Pinch, after the little rupture just described. There was a certain amount of jocularity in the looks of both, no doubt, but there all resemblance ceased. The old pupil could not do enough to show Tom how cordially he felt towards him, and his friendly regard seemed of a graver and more thoughtful kind than before. The new one, on the other hand, had no impulse but to laugh at the recollection of Tom's extreme absurdity; and mingled with his amusement there was something slighting and contemptuous, indicative, as it appeared, of his opinion that Mr. Pinch was much too far gone in simplicity, to be admitted as the friend, on serious and equal terms, of any rational man.

John Westlock, who did nothing by halves, if he could help it, had provided beds for his two guests in the hotel; and after a very happy evening, they retired. Mr. Pinch was sitting on the side of his bed with his cravat and shoes off, ruminating on the manifold good qualities of his old friend, when he was interrupted by a knock at his chamber door, and the voice of John himself.

"You're not asleep yet, are you, Tom?"

"Bless you, no! not I. I was thinking of you," replied Tom, opening the door. "Come in."

"I am not going to detain you," said John; "but I have forgotten all the evening a little commission I took upon myself; and I am afraid I may forget it again, if I fail to discharge it at once. You know a Mr. Tigg, Tom, I believe?"

"Tigg!" cried Tom. "Tigg! The gentleman who borrowed some money of me?"

"Exactly," said John Westlock. "He begged me to present his compliments, and to return it with many thanks. Here it is. I suppose it's a good one, but he is rather a doubtful kind of customer, Tom."

Mr. Pinch received the little piece of gold, with a face whose brightness might have shamed the metal; and said he had no fear about that. He was glad, he added, to find Mr. Tigg so prompt and honourable in his dealings; very glad.

"Why, to tell you the truth, Tom," replied his friend, "he is not always so. If you'll take my advice, you'll avoid him as much as you can, in the event of your encountering him again. And by no means, Tom—pray bear this in mind, for I am very serious—by no means lend him money any more."

"Ay, ay!" said Tom, with his eyes wide open.

"He is very far from being a reputable acquaintance," returned young Westlock; "and the more you let him know you think so, the better for you, Tom."

"I say, John," quoth Mr. Pinch, as his countenance fell, and he shook his head in a dejected manner, "I hope you are not getting into bad company."

"No, no," he replied, laughing. "Don't be uneasy on that score."

"Oh but I *am* uneasy," said Tom Pinch; "I can't help it, when I hear you talking in that way. If Mr. Tigg is what you describe him to be, you have no business to know him, John. You may laugh, but I don't consider it by any means a laughing matter, I assure you."

"No, no," returned his friend, composing his features. "Quite right. It is not, certainly."

"You know, John," said Mr. Pinch, "your very good nature and kindness of heart make you thoughtless; and you can't be too careful on such a point as this. Upon my word, if I thought you were falling among bad companions, I should be quite wretched, for I know how difficult you would find it to shake them off. I would much rather have lost this money, John, than I would have had it back again on such terms."

"I tell you, my dear good old fellow," cried his friend, shaking him to and fro with both hands, and smiling at him with a cheerful, open countenance, that would have carried conviction to a mind much more suspicious than Tom's; "I tell you there is no danger."

"Well!" cried Tom, "I am glad to hear it; I am over-joyed to hear it. I am sure there is not, when you say so in that manner. You won't take it ill, John, that I said what I did just now?"

"Ill!" said the other, giving his hand a hearty squeeze; "why what do you think I am made of? Mr. Tigg and I are not on such an intimate footing that you need be at all uneasy, I give you my solemn assurance of that, Tom. You are quite comfortable now?"

"Quite," said Tom.

"Then once more, good night!"

"Good night!" cried Tom; "and such pleasant dreams

to you, as should attend the sleep of the best fellow in the
world!"

"Except Pecksniff," said his friend, stopping at the
door for a moment, and looking gaily back.

"Except Pecksniff," answered Tom, with great gravity;
"of course."

And thus they parted for the night; John Westlock full
of light-heartedness and good humour, and poor Tom Pinch
quite satisfied; though still, as he turned over on his side
in bed, he muttered to himself, "I really do wish, for all
that, though, that he wasn't acquainted with Mr. Tigg!"

They breakfasted together very early next morning, for
the two young men desired to get back again in good
season; and John Westlock was to return to London by
the coach that day. As he had some hours to spare, he
bore them company for three or four miles on their walk,
and only parted from them at last in sheer necessity. The
parting was an unusually hearty one, not only as between
him and Tom Pinch, but on the side of Martin also, who
had found in the old pupil a very different sort of person
from the milksop he had prepared himself to expect.

Young Westlock stopped upon a rising ground, when he
had gone a little distance, and looked back. They were
walking at a brisk pace, and Tom appeared to be talking
earnestly. Martin had taken off his great-coat, the wind
being now behind them, and carried it upon his arm. As
he looked, he saw Tom relieve him of it, after a faint resistance, and, throwing it upon his own, encumber himself
with the weight of both. This trivial incident impressed
the old pupil mightily, for he stood there, gazing after
them, until they were hidden from his view; when he
shook his head, as if he were troubled by some uneasy reflection, and thoughtfully retraced his steps to Salisbury.

In the meantime, Martin and Tom pursued their way, until they halted, safe and sound, at Mr. Pecksniff's house,
where a brief epistle from that good gentleman to Mr.
Pinch, announced the family's return by that night's coach.
As it would pass the corner of the lane at about six o'clock
in the morning, Mr. Pecksniff requested that the gig might
be in waiting at the finger-post about that time, together
with a cart for the luggage. And to the end that he might
be received with the greater honour, the young men agreed
to rise early, and be upon the spot themselves.

It was the least cheerful day they had yet passed together. Martin was out of spirits and out of humour, and took every opportunity of comparing his condition and prospects with those of young Westlock: much to his own disadvantage always. This mood of his depressed Tom; and neither that morning's parting, nor yesterday's dinner, helped to mend the matter. So the hours dragged on heavily enough; and they were glad to go to bed early.

They were not quite so glad to get up again at half-past four o'clock, in all the shivering discomfort of a dark winter's morning; but they turned out punctually, and were at the finger-post full half-an-hour before the appointed time. It was not by any means a lively morning, for the sky was black and cloudy, and it rained hard; but Martin said there was some satisfaction in seeing that brute of a horse (by this, he meant Mr. Pecksniff's Arab steed) getting very wet; and that he rejoiced, on his account, that it rained so fast. From this it may be inferred, that Martin's spirits had not improved, as indeed they had not; for while he and Mr. Pinch stood waiting under a hedge, looking at the rain, the gig, the cart, and its reeking driver, he did nothing but grumble; and, but that it is indispensable to any dispute that there should be two parties to it, he would certainly have picked a quarrel with Tom.

At length the noise of wheels was faintly audible in the distance, and presently the coach came splashing through the mud and mire, with one miserable outside passenger crouching down among wet straw, under a saturated umbrella; and the coachman, guard, and horses, in a fellowship of dripping wretchedness. Immediately on its stopping, Mr. Pecksniff let down the window-glass and hailed Tom Pinch.

"Dear me, Mr. Pinch! Is it possible that you are out upon this very inclement morning?"

"Yes, Sir," cried Tom, advancing eagerly, "Mr. Chuzzlewit and I, Sir."

"Oh!" said Mr. Pecksniff, looking, not so much at Martin as at the spot on which he stood. "Oh! Indeed! Do me the favour to see to the trunks, if you please, Mr. Pinch."

Then Mr. Pecksniff descended, and helped his daughters to alight; but neither he nor the young ladies took the

slightest notice of Martin, who had advanced to offer his
assistance, but was repulsed by Mr. Pecksniff's standing
immediately before his person, with his back towards him.
In the same manner, and in profound silence, Mr. Pecksniff handed his daughters into the gig; and following himself and taking the reins, drove off home.

Lost in astonishment, Martin stood staring at the coach;
and when the coach had driven away, at Mr. Pinch and
the luggage, until the cart moved off too; when he said
to Tom:

"Now, will you have the goodness to tell me what *this*
portends?"

"What?" asked Tom.

"This fellow's behaviour—Mr. Pecksniff's, I mean.
You saw it?"

"No. Indeed I did not," cried Tom. "I was busy
with the trunks."

"It is no matter," said Martin. "Come! Let us make
haste back." And without another word he started off at
such a pace, that Tom had some difficulty in keeping up
with him.

He had no care where he went, but walked through little
heaps of mud and little pools of water with the utmost indifference; looking straight before him, and sometimes
laughing in a strange manner within himself. Tom felt
that anything he could say would only render him the more
obstinate, and therefore trusted to Mr. Pecksniff's manner
when they reached the house, to remove the mistaken impression under which he felt convinced so great a favourite
as the new pupil must unquestionably be labouring. But
he was not a little amazed himself, when they did reach
it, and entered the parlour where Mr. Pecksniff was sitting alone before the fire, drinking some hot tea, to find,
that instead of taking favourable notice of his relative, and
keeping him, Mr. Pinch, in the background, he did exactly
the reverse, and was so lavish in his attentions that Tom
was thoroughly confounded.

"Take some tea, Mr. Pinch—take some tea," said Peck-
sniff, stirring the fire. "You must be very cold and damp.
Pray take some tea, and come into a warm place, Mr.
Pinch."

Tom saw that Martin looked at Mr. Pecksniff as though
he could have easily found it in his heart to give *him* an

invitation to a very warm place; but he was quite silent, and standing opposite that gentleman at the table, regarded him attentively.

"Take a chair, Mr. Pinch," said Pecksniff. "Take a chair, if you please. How have things gone on in our absence, Mr. Pinch?"

"You—you will be very much pleased with the grammar school, Sir," said Tom. "It's nearly finished."

"If you will have the goodness, Mr. Pinch," said Pecksniff, waving his hand and smiling, "we will not discuss anything connected with that question at present. What have *you* been doing, Thomas, humph?"

Mr. Pinch looked from master to pupil, and from pupil to master, and was so perplexed and dismayed, that he wanted presence of mind to answer the question. In this awkward interval, Mr. Pecksniff (who was perfectly conscious of Martin's gaze, though he had never once glanced towards him) poked the fire very much, and when he couldn't do that any more, drank tea assiduously.

"Now, Mr. Pecksniff," said Martin at last, in a very quiet voice, "if you have sufficiently refreshed and recovered yourself, I shall be glad to hear what you mean by this treatment of me."

"And what," said Mr. Pecksniff, turning his eyes on Tom Pinch, even more placidly and gently than before, "what have *you* been doing, Thomas, humph?"

When he had repeated this inquiry, he looked round the walls of the room as if he were curious to see whether any nails had been left there by accident in former times.

Tom was almost at his wits' end what to say between the two, and had already made a gesture as if he would call Mr. Pecksniff's attention to the gentleman who had last addressed him, when Martin saved him further trouble, by doing so himself.

"Mr. Pecksniff," he said, softly rapping the table twice or thrice, and moving a step or two nearer so that he could have touched him with his hand; "you heard what I said just now. Do me the favour to reply, if you please. I ask you"—he raised his voice a little here—"what you mean by this?"

"I will talk to you, Sir," said Mr. Pecksniff in a severe voice, as he looked at him for the first time, "presently."

"You are very obliging," returned Martin; "presently
will not do. I must trouble you to talk to me at once."

Mr. Pecksniff made a feint of being deeply interested
in his pocket-book, but it shook in his hands; he trembled
so.

"Now," retorted Martin, rapping the table again.
"Now. Presently will not do. Now!"

"Do you threaten me, Sir?" cried Mr. Pecksniff.

Martin looked at him, and made no answer; but a curious observer might have detected an ominous twitching at
his mouth, and perhaps an involuntary attraction of his
right hand in the direction of Mr. Pecksniff's cravat.

"I lament to be obliged to say, Sir," resumed Mr. Pecksniff, "that it would be quite in keeping with your character if you did threaten me. You have deceived me.
You have imposed upon a nature which you knew to be
confiding and unsuspicious. You have obtained admission,
Sir," said Mr. Pecksniff, rising, "to this house, on per-
verted statements, and on false pretences."

"Go on," said Martin, with a scornful smile. "I understand you now. What more?"

"Thus much more, Sir," cried Mr. Pecksniff, trembling
from head to foot, and trying to rub his hands, as though
he were only cold. "Thus much more, if you force me to
publish your shame before a third party, which I was unwilling and indisposed to do. This lowly roof, Sir, must
not be contaminated by the presence of one, who has deceived, and cruelly deceived, an honourable, beloved, ven-
erated, and venerable gentleman; and who wisely suppressed that deceit from me when he sought my protection
and favour, knowing that, humble as I am, I am an honest
man, seeking to do my duty in this carnal universe, and
setting my face against all vice and treachery. I weep for
your depravity, Sir," said Mr. Pecksniff, "I mourn over
your corruption, I pity your voluntary withdrawal of yourself from the flowery paths of purity and peace;" here he
struck himself upon his breast, or moral garden; "but I
cannot have a leper and a serpent for an inmate. Go
forth," said Mr. Pecksniff, stretching out his hand: "go
forth, young man! Like all who know you, I renounce
you!"

With what intention Martin made a stride forward at
these words, it is impossible to say. It is enough to know

that Tom Pinch caught him in his arms, and that at the same moment Mr. Pecksniff stepped back so hastily, that he missed his footing, tumbled over a chair, and fell in a sitting posture on the ground; where he remained without an effort to get up again, with his head in a corner; perhaps considering it the safest place.

"Let me go, Pinch!" cried Martin, shaking him away. "Why do you hold me! Do you think a blow could make him a more abject creature than he is? Do you think that if I spat upon him, I could degrade him to a lower level than his own? Look at him. Look at him, Pinch!"

Mr. Pinch involuntarily did so. Mr. Pecksniff sitting, as has been already mentioned, on the carpet, with his head in an acute angle of the wainscot, and all the damage and detriment of an uncomfortable journey about him, was not exactly a model of all that is prepossessing and dignified in man, certainly. Still he *was* Pecksniff; it was impossible to deprive him of that unique and paramount appeal to Tom. And he returned Tom's glance, as if he would have said, "Ay, Mr. Pinch, look at me! Here I am! You know what the Poet says about an honest man; and an honest man is one of the few great works that can be seen for nothing! Look at me!"

"I tell you," said Martin, "that as he lies there, disgraced, bought, used; a cloth for dirty hands; a mat for dirty feet; a lying, fawning, servile hound; he is the very last and worst among the vermin of the world. And mark me, Pinch! The day will come—he knows it: see it written on his face, the while I speak!—when even you will find him out, and will know him as I do, and as he knows I do. *He* renounce *me!* Cast your eyes on the Renouncer, Pinch, and be the wiser for the recollection!"

He pointed at him as he spoke, with unutterable contempt, and flinging his hat upon his head, walked from the room and from the house. He went so rapidly that he was already clear of the village, when he heard Tom Pinch calling breathlessly after him in the distance.

"Well! what now?" he said, when Tom came up.

"Dear, dear!" cried Tom, "are you going?"

"Going!" he echoed. "Going!"

"I didn't so much mean that, as were you going now at once—in this bad weather—on foot—without your clothes —with no money?" cried Tom.

"Yes," he answered sternly, "I am."

"And where?" cried Tom. "Oh where will you go?"

"I don't know," he said.—"Yes I do. I'll go to America!"

"No, no," cried Tom, in a kind of agony. "Don't go there. Pray don't! Think better of it. Don't be so dreadfully regardless of yourself. Don't go to America!"

"My mind is made up," he said. "Your friend was right. I'll go to America. God bless you, Pinch!"

"Take this!" cried Tom, pressing a book upon him in great agitation. "I must make haste back, and can't say anything I would. Heaven be with you. Look at the leaf I have turned down. Good bye, good bye!"

The simple fellow wrung him by the hand, with tears stealing down his cheeks; and they parted hurriedly upon their separate ways.

CHAPTER XIII.

SHOWING WHAT BECAME OF MARTIN AND HIS DES-
PERATE RESOLVE AFTER HE LEFT MR. PECK-
SNIFF'S HOUSE; WHAT PERSONS HE ENCOUN-
TERED; WHAT ANXIETIES HE SUFFERED; AND
WHAT NEWS HE HEARD.

CARRYING Tom Pinch's book quite unconsciously under his arm, and not even buttoning his coat as a protection against the heavy rain, Martin went doggedly forward at the same quick pace, until he had passed the finger-post, and was on the high road to London. He slackened very little in his speed even then, but he began to think, and look about him, and to disengage his senses from the coil of angry passions which hitherto had held them prisoner.

It must be confessed that at that moment he had no very agreeable employment either for his moral or his physical perceptions. The day was dawning from a patch of watery light in the east, and sullen clouds came driving up before it, from which the rain descended in a thick, wet mist. It streamed from every twig and bramble in the hedge; made little gullies in the path; ran down a hundred channels in the road; and punched innumerable holes into the face of

every pond and gutter.   It fell with an oozy, slushy sound
among the grass; and made a muddy kennel of every fur-
row in the ploughed fields.   No living creature was anywhere to be seen.   The prospect could hardly have been
more desolate if animated nature had been dissolved in
water, and poured down upon the earth again in that form.

The range of view within the solitary traveller was quite
as cheerless as the scene without.   Friendless and penni-
less; incensed to the last degree; deeply wounded in his
pride and self-love; full of independent schemes, and perfectly destitute of any means of realizing them; his most
vindictive enemy might have been satisfied with the extent
of his troubles.   To add to his other miseries, he was by
this time sensible of being wet to the skin, and cold at his
very heart.

In this deplorable condition, he remembered Mr. Pinch's
book; more because it was rather troublesome to carry,
than from any hope of being comforted by that parting gift.
He looked at the dingy lettering on the back, and finding
it to be an odd volume of the " Bachelor of Salamanca," in
the French tongue, cursed Tom Pinch's folly, twenty times.
He was on the point of throwing it away, in his ill-humour
and vexation, when he bethought himself that Tom had
referred him to a leaf, turned down; and opening it, at
that place, that he might have additional cause of complaint against him for supposing that any cold scrap of
the Bachelor's wisdom could cheer him in such circumstances, found—

Well, well! not much, but Tom's all.   The half-sovereign.   He had wrapped it hastily in a piece of paper,
and pinned it to the leaf.   These words were scrawled in
pencil on the inside: "I don't want it, indeed, I should
not know what to do with it, if I had it."

There are some falsehoods, Tom, on which men mount,
as on bright wings, towards Heaven.   There are some
truths, cold, bitter, taunting truths, wherein your worldly
scholars are very apt and punctual, which bind men down
to earth with leaden chains.   Who would not rather have
to fan him, in his dying hour, the lightest feather of a
falsehood such as thine, than all the quills that have been
plucked from the sharp porcupine, reproachful truth, since
time began !

Martin felt keenly for himself, and he felt this good

deed of Tom's keenly. After a few minutes it had the
effect of raising his spirits, and reminding him that he was
not altogether destitute, as he had left a fair stock of
clothes behind him, and wore a gold hunting-watch in his
pocket. He found a curious gratification, too, in thinking
what a winning fellow he must be to have made such an
impression on Tom; and in reflecting how superior he was
to Tom; and how much more likely to make his way in
the world. Animated by these thoughts, and strengthened
in his design of endeavouring to push his fortune in another country, he resolved to get to London as a rallying-
point, in the best way he could; and to lose no time about
it.

He was ten good miles from the village made illustrious
by being the abiding-place of Mr. Pecksniff, when he
stopped to breakfast at a little roadside alehouse; and resting upon a high-backed settle before the fire, pulled off his
coat, and hung it before the cheerful blaze, to dry. It was
a very different place from the last tavern in which he had
regaled: boasting no greater extent of accommodation than
the brick-floored kitchen yielded: but the mind so soon ac-
commodates itself to the necessities of the body, that this
poor waggoner's house-of-call, which he would have despised yesterday, became now quite a choice hotel; while his
dish of eggs and bacon, and his mug of beer, were not by
any means the coarse fare he had supposed, but fully bore
out the inscription on the window-shutter, which proclaimed
those viands to be "Good entertainment for Travellers."

He pushed away his empty plate; and with a second
mug upon the hearth before him, looked thoughtfully at
the fire until his eyes ached. Then he looked at the
highly-coloured Scripture pieces on the walls, in little black
frames like common shaving-glasses, and saw how the Wise
Men (with a strong family likeness among them) worshipped in a pink manger; and how the Prodigal Son came
home in red rags to a purple father, and already feasted
his imagination on a sea-green calf. Then he glanced
through the window at the falling rain, coming down
aslant upon the sign-post over against the house, and overflowing the horse-trough; and then he looked at the fire
again, and seemed to descry a doubly-distant London, re-
treating among the fragments of the burning wood.

He had repeated this process in just the same order,

many times, as if it were a matter of necessity, when the sound of wheels called his attention to the window out of its regular turn; and there he beheld a kind of light van drawn by four horses, and laden, as well as he could see (for it was covered in), with corn and straw. The driver, who was alone, stopped at the door to water his team, and presently came stamping and shaking the wet off his hat and coat into the room where Martin sat.

He was a red-faced burly young fellow; smart in his way, and with a good-humoured countenance. As he advanced towards the fire, he touched his shining forehead with the forefinger of his stiff leather glove, by way of salutation; and said (rather unnecessarily) that it was an uncommon wet day.

"Very wet," said Martin.

"I don't know as ever I see a wetter."

"I never felt one," said Martin.

The driver glanced at Martin's soiled dress, and his damp shirt-sleeves, and his coat hung up to dry; and said, after a pause, as he warmed his hands:

"You have been caught in it, Sir?"

"Yes," was the short reply.

"Out riding, maybe?" said the driver.

"I should have been, if I owned a horse; but I don't," returned Martin.

"That's bad," said the driver.

"And may be worse," said Martin.

Now, the driver said "That's bad," not so much because Martin didn't own a horse, as because he said he didn't with all the reckless desperation of his mood and circumstances, and so left a great deal to be inferred. Martin put his hands in his pockets and whistled, when he had retorted on the driver: thus giving him to understand that he didn't care a pin for Fortune; that he was above pretending to be her favourite when he was not; and that he snapped his fingers at her, the driver, and everybody else.

The driver looked at him stealthily for a minute or so; and in the pauses of his warming, whistled too. At length he asked, as he pointed his thumb towards the road,

"Up or down?"

"Which *is* up?" asked Martin.

"London, of course," said the driver.

"Up then," said Martin. He tossed his head in a care-

15

less manner afterwards, as if he would have added, "Now
you know all about it;" put his hands deeper into his
pockets; changed his tune, and whistled a little louder.

"*I*'m going up," observed the driver; "Hounslow, ten
miles this side London."

"Are you?" cried Martin, stopping short and looking at
him.

The driver sprinkled the fire with his wet hat until it
hissed again, and answered, "Ay, to be sure he was."

"Why, then," said Martin, "I'll be plain with you.
You may suppose from my dress that I have money to
spare. I have not. All I can afford for coach-hire is a
crown, for I have but two. If you can take me for that,
and my waistcoat, or this silk handkerchief, do. If you
can't, leave it alone."

"Short and sweet," remarked the driver.

"You want more?" said Martin. "Then I haven't got
more, and I can't get it, so there's an end of that."
Whereupon he began to whistle again.

"I didn't say I wanted more, did I?" asked the driver,
with something like indignation.

"You didn't say my offer was enough," rejoined Martin.

"Why how could I, when you wouldn't let me? In regard to the waistcoat, I wouldn't have a man's waistcoat,
much less a gentleman's waistcoat, on my mind, for no
consideration; but the silk handkerchief's another thing;
and if you was satisfied when we got to Hounslow, I
shouldn't object to that as a gift."

"Is it a bargain, then?" said Martin.

"Yes, it is," returned the other.

"Then finish this beer," said Martin, handing him the
mug, and pulling on his coat with great alacrity; "and let
us be off as soon as you like."

In two minutes more he had paid his bill, which amounted
to a shilling; was lying at full length on a truss of straw,
high and dry at the top of the van, with the tilt a little
open in front for the convenience of talking to his new
friend; and was moving along in the right direction with
a most satisfactory and encouraging briskness.

The driver's name, as he soon informed Martin, was
William Simmons, better known as Bill; and his spruce appearance was sufficiently explained by his connexion with
a large stage-coaching establishment at Hounslow, whither

he was conveying his load from a farm belonging to the
concern in Wiltshire. He was frequently up and down the
road on such errands, he said, and to look after the sick
and rest horses, of which animals he had much to relate
that occupied a long time in the telling. He aspired to the
dignity of the regular box, and expected an appointment
on the first vacancy. He was musical besides, and had a
little key-bugle in his pocket, on which, whenever the conversation flagged, he played the first part of a great many
tunes, and regularly broke down in the second.

"Ah!" said Bill, with a sigh, as he drew the back of
his hand across his lips, and put this instrument in his
pocket, after screwing off the mouthpiece to drain it;
"Lummy Ned of the Light Salisbury, *he* was the one for
musical talents. He *was* a guard. What you may call a
Guardian Angel, was Ned."

"Is he dead?" asked Martin.

"Dead!" replied the other, with a contemptuous emphasis. "Not he. You won't catch Ned a dying easy.
No, no. He knows better than that."

"You spoke of him in the past tense," observed Martin,
"so I supposed he was no more."

"He's no more in England," said Bill, "if that's what
you mean. He went to the U-nited States."

"Did he?" asked Martin, with sudden interest.
"When?"

"Five year ago, or thenabout," said Bill. "He had set
up in the public line here, and couldn't meet his engagements, so he cut off to Liverpool one day without saying
anything about it, and went and shipped himself for the
U-nited States."

"Well?" said Martin.

"Well! as he landed there without a penny to bless
himself with, of course they wos very glad to see him in
the U-nited States."

"What do you mean?" asked Martin, with some scorn.

"What do I mean?" said Bill. "Why, *that*. All men
are alike in the U-nited States, an't they? It makes no
odds whether a man has a thousand pounds, or nothing,
there—particular in New York, I'm told, where Ned
landed. "

"New York, was it?" asked Martin, thoughtfully.

"Yes," said Bill. "New York. I know that, because

he sent word home that it brought Old York to his mind
quite wivid in consequence of being so exactly unlike it in
every respect. I don't understand wot particular business
Ned turned his mind to, when he got there; but he wrote
home that him and his friends was always a singing, Ale
Columbia, and blowing up the President, so I suppose it
was something in the public line, or free-and-easy way
again. Any how, he made his fortune."

"No!" cried Martin.

"Yes he did," said Bill. "I know that, because he lost
it all the day after, in six-and-twenty banks as broke. He
settled a lot of the notes on his father, when it was ascertained that they was really stopped, and sent 'em over with
a dutiful letter. I know that, because they was shown
down our yard for the old gentleman's benefit, that he
might treat himself with tobacco in the workus."

"He was a foolish fellow not to take care of his money
when he had it," said Martin, indignantly.

"There you're right," said Bill, "especially as it was all
in paper, and he might have took care of it so very easy,
by folding it up in a small parcel."

Martin said nothing in reply, but soon afterwards fell
asleep, and remained so for an hour or more. When he
awoke, finding it had ceased to rain, he took his seat beside the driver, and asked him several questions,—as how
long had the fortunate guard of the Light Salisbury been
in crossing the Atlantic; at what time of the year had he
sailed; what was the name of the ship in which he made
the voyage; how much had he paid for passage-money;
did he suffer greatly from sea-sickness? and so forth. But
on these points of detail, his friend was possessed of little
or no information; either answering obviously at random,
or acknowledging that he had never heard, or had forgotten; nor, although he returned to the charge very ofter,
could he obtain any useful intelligence on these essential
particulars.

They jogged on all day, and stopped so often—now to refresh, now to change their team of horses, now to exchange
or bring away a set of harness, now on one point of business, and now upon another, connected with the coaching
on that line of road—that it was midnight when they
reached Hounslow. A little short of the stables for which
the van was bound, Martin got down, paid his crown, and

forced his silk handkerchief upon his honest friend, notwithstanding the many protestations that he didn't wish to deprive him of it, with which he tried to give the lie to his longing looks. That done, they parted company; and when the van had driven into its own yard, and the gates were closed, Martin stood in the dark street, with a pretty strong sense of being shut out, alone, upon the dreary world, without the key of it.

But in this moment of despondency, and often afterwards, the recollection of Mr. Pecksniff operated as a cordial to him; awakening in his breast an indignation that was very wholesome in nerving him to obstinate endurance. Under the influence of this fiery dram, he started off for London without more ado; and arriving there in the middle of the night, and not knowing where to find a tavern open, was fain to stroll about the streets and market-places until morning.

He found himself, about an hour before dawn, in the humbler regions of the Adelphi; and addressing himself to a man in a fur cap who was taking down the shutters of an obscure public-house, informed him that he was a stranger, and inquired if he could have a bed there. It happened, by good luck, that he could. Though none of the gaudiest, it was tolerably clean, and Martin felt very glad and grateful when he crept into it, for warmth, rest, and forgetfulness.

It was quite late in the afternoon when he awoke; and by the time he had washed, and dressed, and broken his fast, it was growing dusk again. This was all the better, for it was now a matter of absolute necessity that he should part with his watch to some obliging pawnbroker; and he would have waited until after dark for this purpose, though it had been the longest day in the year, and he had begun it without a breakfast.

He passed more Golden Balls than all the jugglers in Europe have juggled with, in the course of their united performances, before he could determine in favour of any particular shop where those symbols were displayed. In the end, he came back to one of the first he had seen, and entering by a side-door in a court, where the three balls, with the legend "Money Lent," were repeated in a ghastly transparency, passed into one of a series of little closets, or private boxes, erected for the accommodation of the more bashful and uninitiated customers. He bolted himself in; pulled out his watch; and laid it on the counter.

"Upon my life and soul!" said a low voice in the next box to the shopman who was in treaty with him, "you must make it more: you must make it a trifle more, you must indeed! You must dispense with one half-quarter of an ounce in weighing out your pound of flesh, my best of friends, and make it two-and-six."

Martin drew back involuntarily, for he knew the voice at once.

"You're always full of your chaff," said the shopman, rolling up the article (which looked like a shirt) quite as a matter of course, and nibbing his pen upon the counter.

"I shall never be full of my wheat," said Mr. Tigg, "as long as I come here. Ha, ha! Not bad! Make it two-and-six, my dear friend, positively for this occasion only. Half-a-crown is a delightful coin—two-and-six! Going at two-and-six! For the last time, at two-and-six!"

"It'll never be the last time till it's quite worn out," rejoined the shopman. "It's grown yellow in the service as it is."

"Its master has grown yellow in the service, if you mean that, my friend," said Mr. Tigg; "in the patriotic service of an ungrateful country. You are making it two-and-six, I think?"

"I'm making it," returned the shopman, "what it always has been—two shillings. Same name as usual, I suppose?"

"Still the same name," said Mr. Tigg; "my claim to the dormant peerage not being yet established by the House of Lords."

"The old address?"

"Not at all," said Mr. Tigg; "I have removed my town establishment from thirty-eight, Mayfair, to number fifteen-hundred-and-forty-two, Park Lane."

"Come, I'm not going to put down that, you know," said the shopman, with a grin.

"You may put down what you please, my friend," quoth Mr. Tigg. "The fact is still the same. The apartments for the under-butler and the fifth footman being of a most confounded low and vulgar kind at thirty-eight, Mayfair, I have been compelled, in my regard for the feelings which do them so much honour, to take on lease, for seven, four-

teen, or twenty-one years, renewable at the option of the
tenant, the elegant and commodious family mansion, number fifteen-hundred-and-forty-two, Park Lane. Make it
two-and-six, and come and see me!"
  The shopman was so highly entertained by this piece of
humour, that Mr. Tigg himself could not repress some little show of exultation. It vented itself, in part, in a desire to see how the occupant of the next box received his
pleasantry; to ascertain which, he glanced round the partition, and immediately, by the gaslight, recognised Martin.
  "I wish I may die," said Mr. Tigg, stretching out his
body so far that his head was as much in Martin's little
cell as Martin's own head was, "but this is one of the most
tremendous meetings in Ancient or Modern History! How
are you? What is the news from the agricultural districts?
How are our friends the P.'s? Ha, ha! David, pay particular attention to this gentleman, immediately, as a friend
of mine, I beg."
  "Here! Please to give me the most you can for this,"
said Martin, handing the watch to the shopman, "I want
money sorely."
  "He wants money sorely!" cried Mr. Tigg with excessive sympathy. "David, you will have the goodness to do
your very utmost for my friend, who wants money sorely.
You will deal with my friend as if he were myself. A
gold hunting-watch, David, engine-turned, capped and
jewelled in four holes, escape movement, horizontal lever,
and warranted to perform correctly, upon my personal reputation, who have observed it narrowly for many years,
under the most trying circumstances—" here he winked at
Martin, that he might understand this recommendation
would have an immense effect upon the shopman: "what
do you say, David, to my friend? Be very particular to
deserve my custom and recommendation, David."
  "I can lend you three pound on this, if you like," said
the shopman to Martin, confidentially. "It's very old-
fashioned. I couldn't say more."
  "And devilish handsome, too," cried Mr. Tigg. "Two-
twelve-six for the watch, and seven-and-six for personal
regard. I am gratified: it may be weakness, but I am.
Three pound will do. We take it. The name of my friend
is Smivey: Chicken Smivey, of Holborn, twenty-six-and-
a-half B: lodger." Here he winked at Martin again, to

apprise him that all the forms and ceremonies prescribed
by law were now complied with, and nothing remained but
the receipt of the money.

In point of fact, this proved to be the case, for Martin,
who had no resource but to take what was offered him, signified his acquiescence by a nod of his head, and presently
came out with the cash in his pocket. He was joined in
the entry by Mr. Tigg, who warmly congratulated him, as
he took his arm and accompanied him into the street, on
the successful issue of the negotiation.

"As for my part in the same," said Mr. Tigg, "don't
mention it. Don't compliment me, for I can't bear it!"

"I have no such intention, I assure you," retorted Martin, releasing his arm and stopping.

"You oblige me very much," said Mr. Tigg. "Thank
you."

"Now, Sir," observed Martin, biting his lip, "this is
a large town, and we can easily find different ways in it.
If you will show me which is your way, I will take another."

Mr. Tigg was about to speak, but Martin interposed:

"I need scarcely tell you, after what you have just seen,
that I have nothing to bestow upon your friend, Mr.
Slyme. And it is quite as unnecessary for me to tell you
that I don't desire the honour of your company."

"Stop!" cried Mr. Tigg, holding out his hand. "Hold!
There is a most remarkably long-headed, flowing-bearded,
and patriarchal proverb, which observes that it is the duty
of a man to be just before he is generous. Be just now,
and you can be generous presently. Do not confuse me
with the man Slyme. Do not distinguish the man Slyme
as a friend of mine, for he is no such thing. I have been
compelled, Sir, to abandon the party whom you call Slyme.
I have no knowledge of the party whom you call Slyme. I
am, Sir," said Mr. Tigg, striking himself upon the breast,
"a premium tulip, of a very different growth and cultivation from the cabbage Slyme, Sir."

"It matters very little to me," said Martin coolly,
"whether you have set up as a vagabond on your own account, or are still trading on behalf of Mr. Slyme. I wish
to hold no correspondence with you. In the devil's name,
man," said Martin, scarcely able despite his vexation to
repress a smile, as Mr. Tigg stood leaning his back against

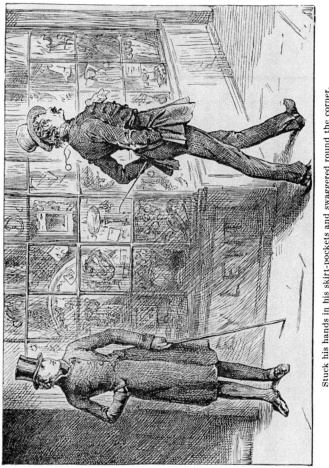

Stuck his hands in his skirt-pockets and swaggered round the corner.
— *Martin Chuzzlewit*, ch. xiii., p. 233.

the shutters of a shop window, adjusting his hair with
great composure, "will you go one way or other?"

"You will allow me to remind you, Sir," said Mr. Tigg,
with sudden dignity, "that you—not I—that you—I say emphatically, *you*—have reduced the proceedings of this evening to a cold and distant matter of business, when I was
disposed to place them on a friendly footing. It being
made a matter of business, Sir, I beg to say that I expect
a trifle (which I shall bestow in charity) as commission
upon the pecuniary advance, in which I have rendered you
my humble services. After the terms in which you have
addressed me, Sir," concluded Mr. Tigg, "you will not insult me, if you please, by offering more than half-a-crown."

Martin drew that piece of money from his pocket, and
tossed it towards him. Mr. Tigg caught it, looked at it to
assure himself of its goodness, spun it in the air after the
manner of a pieman, and buttoned it up. Finally, he raised
his hat an inch or two from his head, with a military air,
and, after pausing a moment with deep gravity, as to decide in which direction he should go, and to what Earl or
Marquis among his friends he should give the preference
in his next call, stuck his hands in his skirt-pockets and
swaggered round the corner. Martin took the directly opposite course; and so, to his great content, they parted
company.

It was with a bitter sense of humiliation that he cursed,
again and again, the mischance of having encountered this
man in the pawnbroker's shop. The only comfort he had
in the recollection was, Mr. Tigg's voluntary avowal of a
separation between himself and Slyme, that would at least
prevent his circumstances (so Martin argued) from being
known to any member of his family, the bare possibility
of which filled him with shame and wounded pride. Ab-
stractly, there was greater reason, perhaps, for supposing any declaration of Mr. Tigg's to be false, than for at-
taching the least credence to it; but remembering the terms
on which the intimacy between that gentleman and his
bosom friend had subsisted, and the strong probability of
Mr. Tigg's having established an independent business of
his own on Mr. Slyme's connexion, it had a reasonable appearance of probability: at all events, Martin hoped so;
and that went a long way.

His first step, now that he had a supply of ready money

for his present necessities, was, to retain his bed at the public-house until further notice, and to write a formal note to Tom Pinch (for he knew Pecksniff would see it) requesting to have his clothes forwarded to London by coach, with a direction to be left at the office until called for. These measures taken, he passed the interval before the box arrived—three days—in making inquiries relative to American vessels, at the offices of various shipping-agents in the City; and in lingering about the docks and wharves, with the faint hope of stumbling upon some engagement for the voyage, as clerk or supercargo, or custodian of something or somebody, which would enable him to procure a free passage. But finding soon that no such means of employment were likely to present themselves, and dreading the consequences of delay, he drew up a short advertisement, stating what he wanted, and inserted it in the leading newspapers. Pending the receipt of the twenty or thirty answers which he vaguely expected, he reduced his wardrobe to the narrowest limits consistent with decent respectability, and carried the overplus at different times to the pawnbroker's shop, for conversion into money.

And it was strange, very strange, even to himself, to find, how by quick though almost imperceptible degrees he lost his delicacy and self-respect, and gradually came to do that as a matter of course, without the least compunction, which but a few short days before had galled him to the quick. The first time he visited the pawnbroker's, he felt on his way there as if every person whom he passed suspected whither he was going; and on his way back again, as if the whole human tide he stemmed, knew well where he had come from. When did he care to think of their discernment now! In his first wanderings up and down the weary streets, he counterfeited the walk of one who had an object in his view; but soon there came upon him the sauntering, slipshod gait of listless idleness, and the lounging at street-corners, and plucking and biting of stray bits of straw, and strolling up and down the same place, and looking into the same shop-windows, with a miserable indifference, fifty times a day. At first, he came out from his lodging with an uneasy sense of being observed—even by those chance passers-by, on whom he had never looked before, and hundreds to one would never see again—issuing in the morning from a public-house; but now, in his comings-out and goings-in he did not mind to lounge about the door, or to stand sunning himself in careless thought beside the wooden stem, studded from head to heel with pegs, on which the beer-pots dangled like so many boughs upon a pewter-tree. And yet it took but five weeks to reach the lowest round of this tall ladder!

Oh, moralists, who treat of happiness and self-respect, innate in every sphere of life, and shedding light on every grain of dust in God's highway, so smooth below your carriage-wheels, so rough beneath the tread of naked feet,— bethink yourselves in looking on the swift descent of men who *have* lived in their own esteem, that there are scores of thousands breathing now, and breathing thick with painful toil, who in that high respect have never lived at all, or had a chance of life! Go ye, who rest so placidly upon the sacred Bard who had been young, and when he strung his harp was old, and had never seen the righteous forsaken, or his seed begging their bread; go, Teachers of content and honest pride, into the mine, the mill, the forge, the squalid depths of deepest ignorance, and uttermost abyss of man's neglect, and say can any hopeful plant spring up in air so foul that it extinguishes the soul's bright torch as fast as it is kindled! And, oh! ye Pharisees of the nineteen hundredth year of Christian Knowledge, who soundingly appeal to human nature, see that it be human first. Take heed it has not been transformed, during your slumber and the sleep of generations, into the nature of the Beasts!

Five weeks! Of all the twenty or thirty answers, not one had come. His money—even the additional stock he had raised from the disposal of his spare clothes (and that was not much, for clothes, though dear to buy, are cheap to pawn)—was fast diminishing. Yet what could he do? At times an agony came over him in which he darted forth again, though he was but newly home, and, returning to some place where he had been already twenty times, made some new attempt to gain his end, but always unsuccessfully. He was years and years too old for a cabin-boy, and years upon years too inexperienced to be accepted as a common seaman. His dress and manner, too, militated fatally against any such proposal as the latter; and yet he was reduced to making it; for, even if he could have contemplated the being set down in America, totally without money, he had not enough left now for a steerage passage and the poorest provisions upon the voyage.

It is an illustration of a very common tendency in the mind of man, that all this time he never once doubted, one may almost say the certainty of doing great things in the New World, if he could only get there. In proportion as he became more and more dejected by his present circumstances, and the means of gaining America receded from his grasp, the more he fretted himself with the conviction that that was the only place in which he could hope to achieve any high end, and worried his brain with the thought that men going there in the meanwhile might anticipate him in the attainment of those objects which were dearest to his heart. He often thought of John Westlock, and besides looking out for him on all occasions, actually walked about London for three days together, for the express purpose of meeting with him. But, although he failed in this; and although he would not have scrupled to borrow money of him; and although he believed that John would have lent it; yet still he could not bring his mind to write to Pinch and inquire where he was to be found. For although, as we have seen, he was fond of Tom after his own fashion, he could not endure the thought (feeling so superior to Tom) of making him the stepping-stone to his fortune, or being anything to him but a patron; and his pride so revolted from the idea, that it restrained him, even now.

It might have yielded, however; and no doubt must have yielded soon, but for a very strange and unlooked-for occurrence.

The five weeks had quite run out, and he was in a truly desperate plight, when one evening, having just returned to his lodging, and being in the act of lighting his candle at the gas jet in the bar before stalking moodily up stairs to his own room, his landlord called him by his name. Now, as he had never told it to the man, but had scrupulously kept it to himself, he was not a little startled by this; and so plainly showed his agitation, that the landlord, to reassure him, said "it was only a letter."

"A letter!" cried Martin.

"For Mr. Martin Chuzzlewit," said the landlord, reading the superscription of one he held in his hand. "Noon. Chief office. Paid."

Martin took it from him, thanked him, and walked up
stairs. It was not sealed, but pasted close; the hand-
writing was quite unknown to him. He opened it, and
found enclosed, without any name, address, or other inscription or explanation of any kind whatever, a Bank of
England note for Twenty Pounds.

To say that he was perfectly stunned with astonishment
and delight; that he looked again and again at the note
and the wrapper; that he hurried below stairs to make
quite certain that the note was a good one; and then hurried up again to satisfy himself for the fiftieth time that
he had not overlooked some scrap of writing on the wrapper; that he exhausted and bewildered himself with con-
jectures; and could make nothing of it but that there the
note was, and he was suddenly enriched; would be only
to relate so many matters of course, to no purpose. The
final upshot of the business at that time was, that he resolved to treat himself to a comfortable but frugal meal in
his own chamber; and having ordered a fire to be kindled,
went out to purchase it forthwith.

He bought some cold beef, and ham, and French bread,
and butter, and came back with his pockets pretty heavily
laden. It was somewhat of a damping circumstance to find
the room full of smoke, which was attributable to two
causes: firstly, to the flue being naturally vicious and a
smoker; and secondly, to their having forgotten, in lighting the fire, an odd sack or two and some other trifles,
which had been put up the chimney to keep the rain out.
They had already remedied this oversight, however; and
propped up the window-sash with a bundle of firewood to
keep it open; so that, except in being rather inflammatory
to the eyes and choking to the lungs, the apartment was
quite comfortable.

Martin was in no vein to quarrel with it, if it had been
in less tolerable order, especially when a gleaming pint of
porter was set upon the table, and the servant-girl withdrew, bearing with her particular instructions relative to
the production of something hot, when he should ring the
bell. The cold meat being wrapped in a play-bill, Martin
laid the cloth by spreading that document on the little
round table with the print downwards; and arranging the
collation upon it. The foot of the bed, which was very
close to the fire, answered for a sideboard; and when he

7—9

had completed these preparations, he squeezed an old arm-chair into the warmest corner, and sat down to enjoy him-self.

He had begun to eat with a great appetite, glancing round the room meanwhile with a triumphant anticipation of quitting it for ever on the morrow, when his attention was arrested by a stealthy footstep on the stairs, and presently by a knock at his chamber door, which, although it was a gentle knock enough, communicated such a start to the bundle of firewood that it instantly leaped out of window, and plunged into the street.

"More coals, I suppose," said Martin. . "Come in!"

"It an't a liberty, Sir, though it seems so," rejoined a man's voice. "Your servant, Sir. Hope you're pretty well, Sir."

Martin stared at the face that was bowing in the door-way: perfectly remembering the features and expression, but quite forgetting to whom they belonged.

"Tapley, Sir," said his visitor. "Him as formerly lived at the Dragon, Sir, and was forced to leave in consequence of a want of jollity, Sir."

"To be sure!" cried Martin. "Why, how did you come here?"

"Right through the passage and up the stairs, Sir," said Mark.

"How did you find me out, I mean?" asked Martin.

"Why, Sir," said Mark, "I've passed you once or twice in the street if I'm not mistaken; and when I was a look-ing in at the beef-and-ham shop just now, along with a hungry sweep, as was very much calculated to make a man jolly, Sir—I see you a buying that."

Martin reddened as he pointed to the table, and said, somewhat hastily:

"Well! What then?"

"Why then, Sir," said Mark, "I made bold to foller; and as I told 'em down stairs that you expected me, I was let up."

"Are you charged with any message, that you told them you were expected?" inquired Martin.

"No, Sir, I an't," said Mark. "That was what you may call a pious fraud, Sir, that was."

Martin cast an angry look at him: but there was some-thing in the fellow's merry face, and in his manner—which with all its cheerfulness was far from being obtrusive or familiar—that quite disarmed him. He had lived a solitary life too, for many weeks, and the voice was pleasant in his ear.

"Tapley," he said, "I'll deal openly with you. From all I can judge, and from all I have heard of you through Pinch, you are not a likely kind of fellow to have been brought here by impertinent curiosity or any other offensive motive. Sit down. I'm glad to see you."

"Thankee, Sir," said Mark. "I'd as lieve stand."

"If you don't sit down," retorted Martin, "I'll not talk to you."

"Very good, Sir," observed Mark. "Your will's a law, Sir. Down it is;" and he sat down accordingly, upon the bedstead.

"Help yourself," said Martin, handing him the only knife.

"Thankee, Sir," rejoined Mark. "After you've done."

"If you don't take it now, you'll not have any," said Martin.

"Very good, Sir," rejoined Mark. "That being your desire—now it is." With which reply he gravely helped himself, and went on eating. Martin having done the like for a short time in silence, said abruptly:

"What are you doing in London?"

"Nothing at all, Sir," rejoined Mark.

"How's that?" asked Martin.

"I want a place," said Mark.

"I'm sorry for you," said Martin.

"—To attend upon a single gentleman," resumed Mark. "If from the country, the more desirable. Makeshifts would be preferred. Wages no object."

He said this so pointedly, that Martin stopped in his eating, and said:

"If you mean me—"

"Yes, I do, Sir," interposed Mark.

"Then you may judge from my style of living here, of my means of keeping a man-servant. Besides, I am going to America immediately."

"Well, Sir," returned Mark, quite unmoved by this intelligence, "from all that ever I heard about it, I should say America's a very likely sort of place for me to be jolly in!"

Again Martin looked at him angrily; and again his anger melted away in spite of himself.

"Lord bless you, Sir," said Mark, "what *is* the use of us a going round and round, and hiding behind the corner, and dodging up and down, when we can come straight to the point in six words! I've had my eye upon you any time this fortnight. I see well enough there's a screw loose in your affairs. I know'd well enough the first time I see you down at the Dragon that it must be so, sooner or later. Now, Sir, here am I, without a sitiwation; without any want of wages for a year to come; for I saved up (I didn't mean to do it, but I couldn't help it) at the Dragon—here am I with a liking for what's wentersome, and a liking for you, and a wish to come out strong under circumstances as would keep other men down: and will you take me, or will you leave me?"

"How can I take you?" cried Martin.

"When I say take," rejoined Mark, "I mean will you let me go? and when I say will you let me go, I mean will you let me go along with you? for go I will, somehow or another. Now that you've said America, I see clear at once, that that's the place for me to be jolly in. Therefore, if I don't pay my own passage in the ship you go in, Sir, I'll pay my own passage in another. And mark my words, if I go alone it shall be, to carry out the principle, in the rottenest, craziest, leakingest tub of a wessel that a place can be got in for love or money. So if I'm lost upon the way, Sir, there'll be a drowned man at your door—and always a knocking double knocks at it, too, or never trust me!"

"This is mere folly," said Martin.

"Very good, Sir," returned Mark. "I'm glad to hear it, because if you don't mean to let me go, you'll be more comfortable, perhaps, on account of thinking so. Therefore I contradict no gentleman. But all I say is, that if I don't emigrate to America in that case, in the beastliest old cockleshell as goes out of port, I'm——"

"You don't mean what you say, I'm sure?" said Martin.

"Yes I do," cried Mark.

"I tell you I know better," rejoined Martin.

"Very good, Sir," said Mark, with the same air of perfect satisfaction. "Let it stand that way at present, Sir, and wait and see how it turns out. Why, love my heart alive! the only doubt I have is, whether there's any credit in going with a gentleman like you, that's as certain to make his way there as a gimlet is to go through soft deal." This was touching Martin on his weak point, and having him at a great advantage. He could not help thinking, either, what a brisk fellow this Mark was, and how great a change he had wrought in the atmosphere of the dismal little room already.

"Why, certainly, Mark," he said, "I have hopes of doing well there, or I shouldn't go. I may have the qualifications for doing well, perhaps."

"Of course you have, Sir," returned Mark Tapley. "Everybody knows that."

"You see," said Martin, leaning his chin upon his hand, and looking at the fire, "ornamental architecture applied to domestic purposes, can hardly fail to be in great request in that country; for men are constantly changing their residences there, and moving further off; and it's clear they must have houses to live in."

"I should say, Sir," observed Mark, "that that's a state of things as opens one of the jolliest look-outs for domestic architecture that ever I heerd tell on."

Martin glanced at him hastily, not feeling quite free from a suspicion that this remark implied a doubt of the successful issue of his plans. But Mr. Tapley was eating the boiled beef and bread with such entire good faith and singleness of purpose expressed in his visage, that he could not but be satisfied. Another doubt arose in his mind, however, as this one disappeared. He produced the blank cover in which the note had been enclosed, and fixing his eyes on Mark as he put it in his hands, said,

"Now tell me the truth. Do you know anything about that?"

Mark turned it over and over; held it near his eyes; held it away from him at arm's length; held it with the superscription upwards, and with the superscription downwards; and shook his head with such a genuine expression of astonishment at being asked the question, that Martin said, as he took it from him again:

"No, I see you don't. How should you? Though, indeed, your knowing about it would not be more extraordinary than its being here. Come, Tapley," he added, after a moment's thought, "I'll trust you with my history,

16

such as it is, and then you'll see, more clearly, what sort
of fortunes you would link yourself to, if you followed
me."

"I beg your pardon, Sir," said Mark; "but afore you
enter upon it, will you take me if I choose to go? Will
you turn off me—Mark Tapley—formerly of the Blue
Dragon, as can be well recommended by Mr. Pinch, and
as wants a gentleman of your strength of mind to look up
to; or will you, in climbing the ladder as you're certain to
get to the top of, take me along with you at a respectful
distance? Now, Sir," said Mark, "it's of very little importance to you, I know—there's the difficulty; but it's of
very great importance to me, and will you be so good as to
consider of it?"

If this were meant as a second appeal to Martin's weak
side, founded on his observation of the effect of the first,
Mr. Tapley was a skilful and shrewd observer. Whether
an intentional or an accidental shot, it hit the mark full;
for Martin, relenting more and more, said, with a condescension which was inexpressibly delicious to him, after
his recent humiliation:

"We'll see about it, Tapley. You shall tell me in what
disposition you find yourself to-morrow."

"Then, Sir," said Mark, rubbing his hands, "the job's
done. Go on, Sir, if you please. I'm all attention."

Throwing himself back in his arm-chair, and looking at
the fire, with now and then a glance at Mark, who at such
times nodded his head sagely, to express his profound interest and attention; Martin ran over the chief points in
his history, to the same effect as he had related them,
weeks before, to Mr. Pinch. But he adapted them, according to the best of his judgment, to Mr. Tapley's comprehension; and with that view made as light of his love
affair as he could, and referred to it in very few words.
But here he reckoned without his host; for Mark's interest
was keenest in this part of the business, and prompted
him to ask sundry questions in relation to it; for which he
apologised as one in some measure privileged to do so, from
having seen (as Martin explained to him) the young lady
at the Blue Dragon.

"And a young lady as any gentleman ought to feel more
proud of being in love with," said Mark, energetically,
"don't draw breath."

"Ay! You saw her when she was not happy," said
Martin, gazing at the fire again. "If you had seen her in
the old times, indeed—"

"Why, she certainly was a little down-hearted, Sir, and
something paler in her colour than I could have wished,"
said Mark, "but none the worse in her looks for that. I
think she seemed better, Sir, after she come to London."

Martin withdrew his eyes from the fire; stared at Mark
as if he thought he had suddenly gone mad; and asked
him what he meant.

"No offence intended, Sir," urged Mark. "I don't
mean to say she was any the happier without you; but I
thought she was a looking better, Sir."

"Do you mean to tell me she has been in London?"
asked Martin, rising hurriedly, and pushing back his chair.

"Of course I do," said Mark, rising too, in great amazement, from the bedstead.

"Do you mean to tell me she's in London now?"

"Most likely, Sir. I mean to say she was, a week ago."

"And you know where?"

"Yes!" cried Mark. "What! Don't you?"

"My good fellow!" exclaimed Martin, clutching him by
both arms, "I have never seen her since I left my grandfather's house."

"Why then!" cried Mark, giving the little table such a
blow with his clenched fist that the slices of beef and ham
danced upon it, while all his features seemed, with delight,
to be going up into his forehead, and never coming back
again any more, "if I an't your nat'ral born servant, hired
by Fate, there an't such a thing in natur' as a Blue Dragon.
What! when I was a rambling up and down a old churchyard in the City, getting myself into a jolly state, didn't I
see your grandfather a toddling to and fro for pretty nigh
a mortal hour! Didn't I watch him into Codgers's commercial boarding-house, and watch him out, and watch him
home to his hotel, and go and tell him as his was the service
for my money, and I had said so, afore I left the Dragon!
Wasn't the young lady a sitting with him then, and didn't
she fall a laughing in a manner as was beautiful to see!
Didn't your grandfather say, 'Come back again next week,'
and didn't I go next week; and didn't he say that he
couldn't make up his mind to trust nobody no more, and
therefore wouldn't engage me; but at the same time stood

something to drink as was handsome! Why," cried Mr. Tapley, with a comical mixture of delight and chagrin, "where's the credit of a man's being jolly under such circumstances! Who could help it, when things come about like this!"

For some moments, Martin stood gazing at him, as if he really doubted the evidence of his senses, and could not believe that Mark stood there, in the body, before him. At length he asked him whether, if the young lady were still in London, he thought he could contrive to deliver a letter to her secretly.

"Do I think I can!" cried Mark. "*Think* I can! Here, sit down, Sir. Write it out, Sir!"

With that he cleared the table by the summary process of tilting everything upon it into the fireplace; snatched some writing materials from the mantel-shelf; set Martin's chair before them; forced him down into it; dipped a pen into the ink; and put it in his hand.

"Cut away, Sir!" cried Mark. "Make it strong, Sir. Let it be wery pointed, Sir. Do I think so? *I* should think so. Go to work, Sir!"

Martin required no further adjuration, but went to work at a great rate; while Mr. Tapley, installing himself without any more formalities into the functions of his valet and general attendant, divested himself of his coat, and went on to clear the fireplace and arrange the room: talking to himself in a low voice the whole time.

"Jolly sort of lodgings," said Mark, rubbing his nose with the knob at the end of the fire-shovel, and looking round the poor chamber: "that's a comfort. The rain's come through the roof too. That an't bad. A lively old bedstead, I'll be bound; popilated by lots of wampires, no doubt. Come! my spirits is a getting up again. An uncommon ragged nightcap this. A very good sign. We shall do yet! Here Jane, my dear," calling down the stairs, "bring up that there hot tumbler for my master, as was a mixing when I come in. That's right, Sir," to Martin. "Go at it as if you meant it, Sir. Be very tender, Sir, if you please. You can't make it too strong, Sir!"

CHAPTER XIV.

IN WHICH MARTIN BIDS ADIEU TO THE LADY OF HIS
LOVE ; AND HONOURS AN OBSCURE INDIVIDUAL
WHOSE FORTUNE HE INTENDS TO MAKE, BY COM-
MENDING HER TO HIS PROTECTION.

THE letter being duly signed, sealed, and delivered, was
handed to Mark Tapley, for immediate conveyance if possible. And he succeeded so well in his embassy as to be
enabled to return that same night, just as the house was
closing: with the welcome intelligence that he had sent it
up stairs to the young lady, enclosed in a small manuscript
of his own, purporting to contain his further petition to
be engaged in Mr. Chuzzlewit's service; and that she had
herself come down and told him, in great haste and agitation, that she would meet the gentleman at eight o'clock
to-morrow morning in St. James's Park. It was then
agreed between the new master and the new man, that
Mark should be in waiting near the hotel in good time, to
escort the young lady to the place of appointment; and
when they had parted for the night with this understanding, Martin took up his pen again; and before he went to
bed wrote another letter, whereof more will be seen presently.

He was up before day-break, and came upon the Park
with the morning, which was clad in the least engaging of
the three hundred and sixty-five dresses in the wardrobe of
the year. It was raw, damp, dark, and dismal; the clouds
were as muddy as the ground; and the short perspective
of every street and avenue, was closed up by the mist as
by a filthy curtain.

"Fine weather indeed," Martin bitterly soliloquized, " to
be wandering up and down here in, like a thief! Fine
weather indeed, for a meeting of lovers in the open air,
and in a public walk! I need be departing, with all speed,
for another country; for I have come to a pretty pass in
this!"

He might perhaps have gone on to reflect that of all
mornings in the year, it was not the best calculated for a

young lady's coming forth on such an errand, either. But
he was stopped on the road to this reflection, if his thoughts
tended that way, by her appearance at a short distance, on
which he hurried forward to meet her. Her squire, Mr.
Tapley, at the same time fell discreetly back, and surveyed the fog above him with an appearance of attentive
interest.

"My dear Martin!" said Mary.

"My dear Mary," said Martin; and lovers are such a
singular kind of people that this is all they did say just
then, though Martin took her arm, and her hand too, and
they paced up and down a short walk that was least exposed to observation, half-a-dozen times.

"If you have changed at all, my love, since we parted,"
said Martin at length, as he looked upon her with a proud
delight, "it is only to be more beautiful than ever!"

Had she been of the common metal of love-worn young
ladies, she would have denied this in her most interesting
manner; and would have told him that she knew she had
become a perfect fright; or that she had wasted away with
weeping and anxiety; or that she was dwindling gently
into an early grave; or that her mental sufferings were
unspeakable; or would either by tears or words, or a mixture of both, have furnished him with some other information to that effect, and made him as miserable as possible.
But she had been reared up in a sterner school than the
minds of most young girls are formed in; she had had her
nature strengthened by the hands of hard endurance and
necessity; had come out from her young trials constant,
self-denying, earnest, and devoted; had acquired in her
maidenhood—whether happily in the end, for herself or
him, is foreign to our present purpose to inquire—something of that nobler quality of gentle hearts which is developed often by the sorrows and struggles of matronly
years, but often by their lessons only. Unspoiled, unpam-
pered in her joys or griefs; with frank, and full, and deep
affection for the object of her early love; she saw in him
one who for her sake was an outcast from his home and fortune, and she had no more idea of bestowing that love upon
him in other than cheerful and sustaining words, full of
high hope and grateful trustfulness, than she had of being
unworthy of it, in her lightest thought or deed, for any
base temptation that the world could offer.

"What change is there in *you*, Martin," she replied; "for that concerns me nearest? You look more anxious and more thoughtful than you used."

"Why as to that, my love," said Martin, as he drew her waist within his arm, first looking round to see that there were no observers near, and beholding Mr. Tapley more intent than ever on the fog; "it would be strange if I did not; for my life—especially of late—has been a hard one."

"I know it must have been," she answered. "When have I forgotten to think of it and you?"

"Not often, I hope," said Martin. "Not often, I am sure. Not often, I have some right to expect, Mary; for I have undergone a great deal of vexation and privation, and I naturally look for that return, you know."

"A very, very poor return," she answered with a fainter smile. "But you have it, and will have it always. You have paid a dear price for a poor heart, Martin; but it is at least your own, and a true one."

"Of course I feel quite certain of that," said Martin, "or I shouldn't have put myself in my present position. And don't say a poor heart, Mary, for I say a rich one. Now, I am about to break a design to you, dearest, which will startle you at first, but which is undertaken for your sake. I am going," he added slowly, looking far into the deep wonder of her bright dark eyes, "abroad."

"Abroad, Martin!"

"Only to America. See now—how you droop directly!"

"If I do, or, I hope I may say, if I did," she answered, raising her head after a short silence, and looking once more into his face, "it was for grief to think of what you are resolved to undergo for me. I would not venture to dissuade you, Martin; but it is a long, long distance; there is a wide ocean to be crossed; illness and want are sad calamities in any place, but in a foreign country dreadful to endure. Have you thought of all this?"

"Thought of it!" cried Martin, abating, in his fondness —and he *was* very fond of her—hardly an iota of his usual impetuosity. "What am I˙ to do? It's very well to say, Have I thought of it? my love; but you should ask me in the same breath, have I thought of starving at home; have I thought of doing porter's work for a living; have I thought of holding horses in the streets to earn my roll of bread from day to day? Come, come," he added, in a gentler tone, "do not hang down your head, my dear, for I need the encouragement that your sweet face alone can give me. Why, that's well! Now you are brave again."

"I am endeavouring to be," she answered, smiling through her tears.

"Endeavouring to be anything that's good, and being it, is, with you, all one. Don't I know that of old?" cried Martin, gaily. "So! That's famous! Now I can tell you all my plans as cheerfully as if you were my little wife already, Mary."

She hung more closely on his arm, and looking upward in his face, bade him speak on.

"You see," said Martin, playing with the little hand upon his wrist, "that my attempts to advance myself at home have been baffled and rendered abortive. I will not say by whom, Mary, for that would give pain to us both. But so it is. Have you heard him speak of late of any relative of mine or his, called Pecksniff? Only tell me what I ask you, no more."

"I have heard, to my surprise, that he is a better man than was supposed."

"I thought so," interrupted Martin.

"And that it is likely we may come to know him, if not to visit and reside with him and—I think—his daughters. He *has* daughters, has he, love?"

"A pair of them," Martin answered. "A precious pair! Gems of the first water!"

"Ah! You are jesting!"

"There is a sort of jesting which is very much in earnest, and includes some pretty serious disgust," said Martin. "I jest in reference to Mr. Pecksniff (at whose house I have been living as his assistant, and at whose hands I have received insult and injury), in that vein. Whatever betides, or however closely you may be brought into communication with his family, never forget that, Mary; and never for an instant, whatever appearances may seem to contradict me, lose sight of this assurance— Pecksniff is a scoundrel."

"Indeed!"

"In thought, and in deed, and in everything else. A scoundrel from the topmost hair of his head, to the nethermost atom of his heel. Of his daughters I will only say that. to the best of my knowledge and belief, they are duti-

ful young ladies, and take after their father closely. This
is a digression from the main point, and yet it brings me
to what I was going to say."

He stopped to look into her eyes again, and seeing, in
a hasty glance over his shoulder, that there was no one
near, and that Mark was still intent upon the fog, not
only looked at her lips too, but kissed them into the bargain.

"Now, I am going to America, with great prospects of
doing well, and of returning home myself very soon; it
may be to take you there for a few years, but, at all
events, to claim you for my wife; which, after such trials,
I should do with no fear of your still thinking it a duty to
cleave to him who will not suffer me to live (for this is
true), if he can help it, in my own land. How long I may
be absent is, of course, uncertain; but it shall not be very
long. Trust me for that."

"In the meantime, dear Martin—"

"That's the very thing I am coming to. In the meantime you shall hear, constantly, of all my goings-on.
Thus."

He paused to take from his pocket the letter he had
written overnight, and then resumed:

"In this fellow's employment, and living in this fellow's
house (by fellow, I mean Mr. Pecksniff, of course), there
is a certain person of the name of Pinch—don't forget it;
a poor, strange, simple oddity, Mary; but thoroughly honest and sincere; full of zeal; and with a cordial regard for
me; which I mean to return one of these days, by setting
him up in life in some way or other."

"Your old kind nature, Martin!"

"Oh!" said Martin, "that's not worth speaking of, my
love. He's very grateful and desirous to serve me; and I
am more than repaid. Now one night I told this Pinch
my history, and all about myself and you; in which he
was not a little interested, I can tell you, for he knows
you. Ay, you may look surprised—and the longer the
better, for it becomes you—but you have heard him play
the organ in the church of that village before now; and he
has seen you listening to his music; and has caught his
inspiration from you, too!"

"Was *he* the organist?" cried Mary "I thank him
from my heart."

"Yes he was," said Martin, "and is, and gets nothing for it either. There never was such a simple fellow! Quite an infant! But a very good sort of creature, I assure you."

"I am sure of that," she said, with great earnestness. "He must be!"

"Oh, yes, no doubt at all about it," rejoined Martin, in his usual careless way. "He is. Well! It has occurred to me—but stay, if I read you what I have written and intend sending to him by post to-night, it will explain itself. 'My dear Tom Pinch.' That's rather familiar, perhaps," said Martin, suddenly remembering that he was proud when they had last met, "but I call him my dear Tom Pinch, because he likes it, and it pleases him."

"Very right, and very kind," said Mary.

"Exactly so!" cried Martin. "It's as well to be kind whenever one can; and, as I said before, he really is an excellent fellow. 'My dear Tom Pinch,—I address this under cover to Mrs. Lupin, at the Blue Dragon, and have begged her in a short note to deliver it to you without saying anything about it elsewhere; and to do the same with all future letters she may receive from me. My reason for so doing will be at once apparent to you.' I don't know that it will be, by the bye," said Martin, breaking off, "for he's slow of comprehension, poor fellow; but he'll find it out in time. My reason simply is, that I don't want my letters to be read by other people; and particularly by the scoundrel whom he thinks an angel."

"Mr. Pecksniff again?" asked Mary.

"The same," said Martin: "'—will be at once apparent to you. I have completed my arrangements for going to America; and you will be surprised to hear that I am to be accompanied by Mark Tapley, upon whom I have stumbled strangely in London, and who insists on putting himself under my protection'—meaning, my love," said Martin, breaking off again, "our friend in the rear, of course."

She was delighted to hear this, and bestowed a kind glance upon Mark, which he brought his eyes down from the fog to encounter, and received with immense satisfaction. She said in his hearing, too, that he was a good soul and a merry creature, and would be faithful, she was certain; commendations which Mr. Tapley inwardly resolved to deserve, from such lips, if he died for it.

" ' Now, my dear Pinch,' " resumed Martin, proceeding with his letter; " ' I am going to repose great trust in you, knowing that I may do so with perfect reliance on your honour and secrecy, and having nobody else just now to trust in.' "

" I don't think I would say that, Martin."

" Wouldn't you? Well! I'll take that out. It's perfectly true, though."

" But it might seem ungracious, perhaps."

" Oh, I don't mind Pinch," said Martin. "There's no occasion to stand on any ceremony with *him*. However, I'll take it out, as you wish it, and make the full stop at ' secrecy.' Very well! ' I shall not only '—this is the letter again, you know."

" I understand."

" ' I shall not only enclose my letters to the young lady of whom I have told you, to your charge, to be forwarded as she may request; but I most earnestly commit her, the young lady herself, to your care and regard, in the event of your meeting in my absence. I have reason to think that the probabilities of your encountering each other—perhaps very frequently—are now neither remote nor few; and although in your position you can do very little to lessen the uneasiness of hers, I trust to you implicitly to do that much, and so deserve the confidence I have reposed in you.' You see, my dear Mary," said Martin, "it will be a great consolation to you to have anybody, no matter how simple, with whom you can speak about ME; and the very first time you talk to Pinch, you'll feel at once, that there is no more occasion for any embarrassment or hesitation in talking to him, than if he were an old woman."

" However that may be," she returned, smiling, "he is your friend, and that is enough."

" Oh, yes, he's my friend," said Martin, "certainly. In fact, I have told him in so many words that we'll always take notice of him, and protect him: and it's a good trait in his character that he's grateful—very grateful indeed. You'll like him of all things, my love, I know. You'll observe very much that's comical and old-fashioned about Pinch, but you needn't mind laughing at him; for he'll not care about it. He'll rather like it, indeed!"

" I don't think I shall put that to the test, Martin."

" You won't if you can help it, of course," he said, "but

I think you'll find him a little too much for your gravity.
However that's neither here nor there, and it certainly is
not the letter; which ends thus · ' Knowing that I need not
impress the nature and extent of that confidence upon you
at any greater length, as it is already sufficiently established in your mind, I will only say in bidding you farewell, and looking forward to our next meeting, that I shall
charge myself from this time, through all changes for the
better, with your advancement and happiness, as if they
were my own. You may rely upon that. And always believe me, my dear Tom Pinch, faithfully your friend, Martin Chuzzlewit. P.S. I enclose the amount which you so
kindly '—Oh," said Martin, checking himself, and folding
up the letter, " that's nothing! "

At this crisis Mark Tapley interposed, with an apology
for remarking that the clock at the Horse Guards was
striking.

" Which I shouldn't have said nothing about, Sir," added
Mark, " if the young lady hadn't begged me to be particular in mentioning it."

" I did," said Mary. " Thank you. You are quite right.
In another minute I shall be ready to return. We have
time for a very few words more, dear Martin, and although
I had much to say, it must remain unsaid until the happy
time of our next meeting. Heaven send it may come
speedily and prosperously. But I have no fear of that."

" Fear! " cried Martin. " Why, who has? What are a
few months? What is a whole year? When I come gaily
back, with a road through life hewn out before me, then
indeed, looking back upon this parting, it may seem a dismal one. But now! I swear I wouldn't have it happen
under more favourable auspices, if I could: for then I
should be less inclined to go, and less impressed with the
necessity."

" Yes, yes. I feel that too. When do you go? "

" To-night. We leave for Liverpool to-night. A vessel
sails from that port, as I hear, in three days. In a month,
or less, we shall be there. Why, what's a month! How
many months have flown by since our last parting! "

" Long to look back upon," said Mary, echoing his cheerful tone, " but nothing in their course! "

" Nothing at all! " cried Martin. " I shall have change
of scene and change of place; change of people, change of

manners, change of cares and hopes! Time will wear wings
indeed! I can bear anything, so that I have swift action,
Mary."

Was he thinking solely of her care for him, when he took
so little heed of her share in the separation; of her quiet
monotonous endurance, and her slow anxiety from day to
day? Was there nothing jarring and discordant even in
his tone of courage, with this one note "self" for ever
audible, however high the strain? Not in her ears. It
had been better otherwise, perhaps, but so it was. She
heard the same bold spirit which had flung away as dross
all gain and profit for her sake, making light of peril and
privation that she might be calm and happy; and she heard
no more. That heart where self has found no place and
raised no throne, is slow to recognise its ugly presence
when it looks upon it. As one possessed of an evil spirit
was held in old time to be alone conscious of the lurking
demon in the breasts of other men, so kindred vices know
each other in their hiding-places every day, when Virtue
is incredulous and blind.

"The quarter's gone!" cried Mr. Tapley, in a voice of
admonition.

"I shall be ready to return immediately," she said.
"One thing, dear Martin, I am bound to tell you. You
entreated me a few minutes since only to answer what you
asked me in reference to one theme, but you should and
must know—otherwise I could not be at ease—that since
that separation of which I was the unhappy occasion, he
has never once uttered your name; has never coupled it, or
any faint allusion to it, with passion or reproach; and has
never abated in his kindness to me."

"I thank him for that last act," said Martin, "and for
nothing else. Though on consideration I may thank him
for his other forbearance also, inasmuch as I neither expect
nor desire that he will mention my name again. He may
once, perhaps—to couple it with reproach—in his will.
Let him, if he please! By the time it reaches me, he will
be in his grave; a satire on his own anger, God help him!"

"Martin! If you would but sometimes, in some quiet
hour; beside the winter fire; in the summer air; when you
hear gentle music, or think of Death, or Home, or Childhood; if you would at such a season resolve to think, but
once a month, or even once a year, of him, or any one who

ever wronged you, you would forgive him in your heart, I know!"

"If I believed that to be true, Mary," he replied, "I would resolve at no such time to bear him in my mind: wishing to spare myself the shame of such a weakness. I was not born to be the toy and puppet of any man, far less his; to whose pleasure and caprice, in return for any good he did me, my whole youth was sacrificed. It became between us two a fair exchange—a barter—and no more: and there is no such balance against me that I need throw in a mawkish forgiveness to poise the scale. He has forbidden all mention of me to you, I know," he added hastily. "Come! Has he not?"

"That was long ago," she returned; "immediately after your parting; before you had left the house. He has never done so since."

"He has never done so since, because he has seen no occasion," said Martin; "but that is of little consequence, one way or other. Let all allusion to him between you and me be interdicted from this time forth. And therefore, love—" he drew her quickly to him, for the time of parting had now come—"in the first letter that you write to me through the Post-office, addressed to New York; and in all the others that you send through Pinch; remember he has no existence, but has become to us as one who is dead. Now, God bless you! This is a strange place for such a meeting and such a parting; but our next meeting shall be in a better, and our next and last parting in a worse."

"One other question, Martin, I must ask. Have you provided money for this journey?"

"Have I?" cried Martin; it might have been in his pride; it might have been in his desire to set her mind at ease: "Have I provided money? Why, there's a question for an emigrant's wife! How could I move on land or sea without it, love?"

"I mean, enough."

"Enough! More than enough. Twenty times more than enough. A pocketful. Mark and I, for all essential ends, are quite as rich as if we had the purse of Fortunatus in our baggage."

"The half-hour's a going!" cried Mr. Tapley.

"Good-bye a hundred times!" cried Mary, in a trembling voice.

But how cold the comfort in Good-bye! Mark Tapley knew it perfectly. Perhaps he knew it from his reading, perhaps from his experience, perhaps from intuition. It is impossible to say; but however he knew it, his knowledge instinctively suggested to him the wisest course of proceeding that any man could have adopted under the circumstances. He was taken with a violent fit of sneezing, and was obliged to turn his head another way. In doing which, he, in a manner, fenced and screened the lovers into a corner by themselves.

There was a short pause, but Mark had an undefined sensation that it was a satisfactory one in its way. Then Mary, with her veil lowered, passed him with a quick step, and beckoned him to follow. She stopped once more before they lost that corner; looked back; and waved her hand to Martin. He made a start towards them at the moment as if he had some other farewell words to say; but she only hurried off the faster, and Mr. Tapley followed as in duty bound.

When he rejoined Martin again in his own chamber, he found that gentleman seated moodily before the dusty grate, with his two feet on the fender, his two elbows on his knees, and his chin supported, in a not very ornamental manner, on the palms of his hands.

"Well, Mark?"

"Well, Sir," said Mark, taking a long breath, "I see the young lady safe home, and I feel pretty comfortable after it. She sent a lot of kind words, Sir, and this," handing him a ring, "for a parting keepsake."

"Diamonds!" said Martin, kissing it—let us do him justice, it was for her sake; not for theirs—and putting it on his little finger. "Splendid diamonds. My grandfather is a singular character, Mark. He must have given her this, now."

Mark Tapley knew as well that she had bought it, to the end that that unconscious speaker might carry some article of sterling value with him in his necessity; as he knew that it was day, and not night. Though he had no more acquaintance of his own knowledge with the history of the glittering trinket on Martin's outspread finger, than Martin himself had, he was as certain that in its purchase she had expended her whole stock of hoarded money, as if he had seen it paid down coin by coin. Her lover's strange obtuseness in relation to this little incident, promptly suggested to Mark's mind its real cause and root; and from that moment he had a clear and perfect insight into the one absorbing principle of Martin's character.

" She is worthy of the sacrifices I have made," said Martin, folding his arms, and looking at the ashes in the stove, as if in resumption of some former thoughts. " Well worthy of them. No riches "—here he stroked his chin, and mused—" could have compensated for the loss of such a nature. Not to mention that in gaining her affection, I have followed the bent of my own wishes, and baulked the selfish schemes of others who had no right to form them. She is quite worthy—more than worthy—of the sacrifices I have made. Yes, she is. No doubt of it."

These ruminations might or might not have reached Mark Tapley; for though they were by no means addressed to him, yet they were softly uttered. In any case, he stood there, watching Martin, with an indescribable and most involved expression on his visage, until that young man roused himself and looked towards him; when he turned away as being suddenly intent on certain preparations for the journey, and, without giving vent to any articulate sound, smiled with surpassing ghastliness, and seemed by a twist of his features and a motion of his lips, to release himself of this word:

" Jolly ! "

CHAPTER XV.

THE BURDEN WHEREOF IS HAIL, COLUMBIA!

A DARK and dreary night; people nestling in their beds or circling late about the fire; Want, colder than Charity, shivering at the street corners; church-towers humming with the faint vibration of their own tongues, but newly resting from the ghostly preachment ' One ! ' The earth covered with a sable pall as for the burial of yesterday; the clumps of dark trees, its giant plumes of funeral feathers, waving sadly to and fro: all hushed, all noiseless, and in deep repose, save the swift clouds that skim across the moon, and the cautious wind, as, creeping after them upon the ground, it stops to listen, and goes rustling on, and stops again, and follows, like a savage on the trail.

Whither go the clouds and wind, so eagerly? If like guilty spirits they repair to some dread conference with powers like themselves, in what wild region do the elements hold council, or where unbend in terrible disport? Here! Free from that cramped prison called the earth, and out upon the waste of waters. Here, roaring, raging, shrieking, howling, all night long. Hither come the sounding voices from the caverns on the coast of that small island, sleeping a thousand miles away so quietly in the midst of angry waves; and hither, to meet them, rush the blasts from unknown desert places of the world. Here, in the fury of their unchecked liberty, they storm and buffet with each other, until the sea, lashed into passion like their own, leaps up in ravings mightier than theirs, and the whole scene is whirling madness.

On, on, on, over the countless miles of angry space roll the long heaving billows. Mountains and caves are here, and yet are not; for what is now the one, is now the other; then all is but a boiling heap of rushing water. Pursuit, and flight, and mad return of wave on wave, and savage struggle, ending in a spouting-up of foam that whitens the black night; incessant change of place, and form, and hue; constancy in nothing, but eternal strife; on, on, on, they roll, and darker grows the night, and louder howls the winds, and more clamorous and fierce become the million voices in the sea, when the wild cry goes forth upon the storm, "A ship!"

Onward she comes, in gallant combat with the elements, her tall masts trembling, and her timbers starting on the strain; onward she comes, now high upon the curling billows, now low down in the hollows of the sea, as hiding for the moment from its fury; and every storm-voice in the air and water, cries more loudly yet, "A ship!"

Still she comes striving on: and at her boldness and the spreading cry, the angry waves rise up above each other's hoary heads to look; and round about the vessel, far as the mariners on her decks can pierce into the gloom, they press upon her, forcing each other down, and starting up, and rushing forward from afar, in dreadful curiosity. High over her they break; and round her surge and roar; and giving place to others, moaningly depart, and dash themselves to fragments in their baffled anger: still she comes onward bravely. And though the eager multitude crowd
17

thick and fast upon her all the night, and dawn of day discovers the untiring train yet bearing down upon the ship in an eternity of troubled water, onward she comes, with dim lights burning in her hull, and people there, asleep: as if no deadly element were peering in at every seam and chink, and no drowned seaman's grave, with but a plank to cover it, were yawning in the unfathomable depths below.

Among these sleeping voyagers were Martin and Mark Tapley, who, rocked into a heavy drowsiness by the unaccustomed motion, were as insensible to the foul air in which they lay, as to the uproar without. It was broad day, when the latter awoke with a dim idea that he was dreaming of having gone to sleep in a four-post bedstead which had turned bottom upwards in the course of the night. There was more reason in this too, than in the roasting of eggs; for the first objects Mr. Tapley recognised when he opened his eyes were his own heels—looking down at him, as he afterwards observed, from a nearly perpendicular elevation.

"Well!" said Mark, getting himself into a sitting posture, after various ineffectual struggles with the rolling of the ship. "This is the first time as I ever stood on my head all night."

"You shouldn't go to sleep upon the ground with your head to leeward, then," growled a man in one of the berths.

"With my head to *where?*" asked Mark.

The man repeated his previous sentiment.

"No, I won't another time," said Mark, "when I know whereabouts on the map that country is. In the meanwhile I can give you a better piece of advice. Don't you nor any other friend of mine never go to sleep with his head in a ship, any more."

The man gave a grunt of discontented acquiescence, turned over in his berth, and drew his blanket over his head.

"—For," said Mr. Tapley, pursuing the theme by way of soliloquy, in a low tone of voice; "the sea is as nonsensical a thing as anything going. It never knows what to do with itself. It hasn't got no employment for its mind, and is always in a state of vacancy. Like them Polar bears in the wild-beast shows as is constantly a nodding their heads from side to side, it never *can* be quiet. Which is entirely owing to its uncommon stupidity."

"Is that you, Mark?" asked a faint voice from another berth.

"It's as much of me as is left, Sir, after a fortnight of this work," Mr. Tapley replied. "What with leading the life of a fly ever since I've been aboard—for I've been perpetually holding on to something or other, in a upsidedown position—what with that, Sir, and putting a very little into myself, and taking a good deal out in various ways, there an't too much of me to swear by. How do *you* find yourself this morning, Sir?"

"Very miserable," said Martin, with a peevish groan. "Ugh! This is wretched, indeed!"

"Creditable," muttered Mark, pressing one hand upon his aching head, and looking round him with a rueful grin. "That's the great comfort. It *is* creditable to keep up one's spirits here. Virtue's its own reward. So's jollity."

Mark was so far right, that unquestionably any man who retained his cheerfulness among the steerage accommodations of that noble and fast sailing line-of-packet ship, "The Screw," was solely indebted to his own resources, and shipped his good humour, like his provisions, without any contribution or assistance from the owners. A dark, low, stifling cabin, surrounded by berths all filled to overflowing with men, women, and children, in various stages of sickness and misery, is not the liveliest place of assembly at any time; but when it is so crowded (as the steerage cabin of "The Screw" was, every passage out), that mattresses and beds are heaped upon the floor, to the extinction of everything like comfort, cleanliness, and decency, it is liable to operate not only as a pretty strong barrier against amiability of temper, but as a positive encourager of selfish and rough humours. Mark felt this, as he sat looking about him; and his spirits rose proportionately.

There were English people, Irish people, Welsh people, and Scotch people there; all with their little store of coarse food and shabby clothes; and nearly all, with their families of children. There were children of all ages; from the baby at the breast, to the slattern-girl who was as much a grown woman as her mother. Every kind of domestic suffering that is bred in poverty, illness, banishment, sorrow, and long travel in bad weather, was crammed into the little space; and yet was there infinitely

less of complaint and querulousness, and infinitely more
of mutual assistance and general kindness to be found
in that unwholesome ark, than in many brilliant ball-
rooms.

Mark looked about him wistfully, and his face brightened as he looked. Here an old grandmother was crooning
over a sick child, and rocking it to and fro, in arms hardly
more wasted than its own young limbs; here a poor woman
with an infant in her lap, mended another little creature's
clothes, and quieted another who was creeping up about
her from their scanty bed upon the floor. Here were old
men awkwardly engaged in little household offices, wherein
they would have been ridiculous but for their good-will
and kind purpose; and here were swarthy fellows—giants
in their way—doing such little acts of tenderness for those
about them, as might have belonged to gentlest-hearted
dwarfs. The very idiot in the corner who sat mowing
there, all day, had his faculty of imitation roused by what
he saw about him; and snapped his fingers, to amuse a
crying child.

"Now, then," said Mark, nodding to a woman who was
dressing her three children at no great distance from him
—and the grin upon his face had by this time spread from
ear to ear—"Hand over one of them young uns according
to custom."

"I wish you'd get breakfast, Mark, instead of worrying
with people who don't belong to you," observed Martin,
petulantly.

"All right," said Mark. "She'll do that. It's a fair
division of labour, Sir. I wash her boys, and she makes
our tea. I never *could* make tea, but any one can wash a
boy."

The woman, who was delicate and ill, felt and understood his kindness, as well she might, for she had been
covered every night with his great-coat, while he had had
for his own bed the bare boards and a rug. But Martin,
who seldom got up or looked about him, was quite incensed
by the folly of this speech, and expressed his dissatisfac-
tion, by an impatient groan.

"So it is, certainly," said Mark, brushing the child's
hair as coolly as if he had been born and bred a barber.

"What are you talking about, now?" asked Martin.

"What you said," replied Mark; "or what you meant,

when you gave that there dismal vent to your feelings. I
quite go along with it, Sir. It *is* very hard upon her."

"What is?"

"Making the voyage by herself along with these young
impediments here, and going such a way at such a time of
year to join her husband. If you don't want to be driven
mad with yellow soap in your eye, young man," said Mr.
Tapley to the second urchin, who was by this time under
his hands at the basin, "you'd better shut it."

"Where does she join her husband?" asked Martin,
yawning.

"Why, I'm very much afraid," said Mr. Tapley, in a
low voice, "that she don't know. I hope she mayn't miss
him. But she sent her last letter by hand, and it don't
seem to have been very clearly understood between 'em
without it, and if she don't see him a waving his pocket-
handkerchief on the shore, like a pictur out of a song-book,
my opinion is, she'll break her heart."

"Why, how, in Folly's name, does the woman come to
be on board ship on such a wild-goose venture!" cried
Martin.

Mr. Tapley glanced at him for a moment as he lay pros-
trate in his berth, and then said, very quietly:

"Ah! How, indeed! I can't think! He's been away
from her for two year: she's been very poor and lonely in
her own country; and has always been a looking forward
to meeting him. It's very strange she should be here.
Quite amazing! A little mad, perhaps! There can't be no
other way of accounting for it."

Martin was too far gone in the lassitude of sea-sickness
to make any reply to these words, or even to attend to
them as they were spoken. And the subject of their discourse returning at this crisis with some hot tea, effectually
put a stop to any resumption of the theme by Mr. Tapley;
who, when the meal was over and he had adjusted Martin's
bed, went up on deck to wash the breakfast service, which
consisted of two half-pint tin mugs, and a shaving-pot of
the same metal.

It is due to Mark Tapley to state, that he suffered at
least as much from sea-sickness as any man, woman, or
child, on board; and that he had a peculiar faculty of
knocking himself about on the smallest provocation, and
losing his legs at every lurch of the ship. But resolved,

in his usual phrase, to "come out strong" under disadvan-
tageous circumstances, he was the life and soul of the
steerage, and made no more of stopping in the middle of
a facetious conversation to go away and be excessively ill
by himself, and afterwards come back in the very best and
gayest of tempers to resume it, than if such a course of
proceeding had been the commonest in the world.

It cannot be said that as his illness wore off, his cheerfulness and good nature increased, because they would
hardly admit of augmentation; but his usefulness among
the weaker members of the party was much enlarged; and
at all times and seasons there he was exerting it. If a
gleam of sun shone out of the dark sky, down Mark tumbled into the cabin, and presently up he came again with a
woman in his arms, or half-a-dozen children, or a man, or
a bed, or a saucepan, or a basket, or something animate or
inanimate, that he thought would be the better for the air.
If an hour or two of fine weather in the middle of the day,
tempted those who seldom or never came on deck at other
times, to crawl into the long-boat, or lie down upon the
spare spars, and try to eat, there in the centre of the group
was Mr. Tapley, handing about salt beef and biscuit, or
dispensing tastes of grog, or cutting up the children's provisions with his pocket-knife, for their greater ease and
comfort, or reading aloud from a venerable newspaper, or
singing some roaring old song to a select party, or writing
the beginnings of letters to their friends at home for people
who couldn't write, or cracking jokes with the crew, or
nearly getting blown over the side, or emerging, half-
drowned, from a shower of spray, or lending a hand somewhere or other: but always doing something for the general entertainment. At night, when the cooking-fire was
lighted on the deck, and the driving sparks that flew among
the rigging, and the cloud of sails, seemed to menace the
ship with certain annihilation by fire, in case the elements
of air and water failed to compass her destruction; there
again was Mr. Tapley, with his coat off and his shirt-
sleeves turned up to his elbows, doing all kinds of culinary
offices; compounding the strangest dishes; recognised by
every one as an established authority; and helping all parties to achieve something, which, left to themselves, they
never could have done, and never would have dreamed of.
In short there never was a more popular character than

Mark Tapley became on board that noble and fast-sailing line-of-packet ship, the Screw; and he attained at last to such a pitch of universal admiration, that he began to have grave doubts within himself whether a man might reasonably claim any credit for being jolly under such exciting circumstances.

"If this was going to last," said Mr. Tapley, "there'd be no great difference as I can perceive, between the Screw and the Dragon. I never *am* to get any credit, I think. I begin to be afraid that the Fates is determined to make the world easy to me."

"Well, Mark," said Martin, near whose berth he had ruminated to this effect. "When will this be over?"

"Another week, they say, Sir," returned Mark, "will most likely bring us into port. The ship's going along at present, as sensible as a ship can, Sir; though I don't mean to say as that's any very high praise."

"I don't think it is, indeed," groaned Martin.

"You'd feel all the better for it, Sir, if you was to turn out," observed Mark.

"And be seen by the ladies and gentlemen on the after-deck," returned Martin, with a scornful emphasis upon the words, "mingling with the beggarly crowd that are stowed away in this vile hole. I should be greatly the better for that, no doubt!"

"I'm thankful that I can't say from my own experience what the feelings of a gentleman may be," said Mark, "but I should have thought, Sir, as a gentleman would feel a deal more uncomfortable down here, than up in the fresh air, especially when the ladies and gentlemen in the after-cabin know just as much about him, as he does about them, and are likely to trouble their heads about him in the same proportion. I should have thought that, certainly."

"I tell you, then," rejoined Martin, "you would have thought wrong, and do think wrong."

"Very likely, Sir," said Mark, with imperturbable good temper. "I often do."

"As to lying here," cried Martin, raising himself on his elbow, and looking angrily at his follower. "Do you suppose it's a pleasure to lie here?"

"All the madhouses in the world," said Mr Tapley, "couldn't produce such a maniac as the man must be who could think that."

"Then why are you for ever goading and urging me to get up?" asked Martin. "I lie here because I don't wish to be recognised, in the better days to which I aspire, by any purse-proud citizen, as the man who came over with him among the steerage passengers. I lie here, because I wish to conceal my circumstances and myself, and not to arrive in a new world badged and ticketed as an utterly poverty-stricken man. If I could have afforded a passage in the after-cabin, I should have held up my head with the rest. As I couldn't, I hide it. Do you understand that?"

"I am very sorry, Sir," said Mark. "I didn't know you took it so much to heart as this comes to."

"Of course you didn't know," returned his master. "How should you know, unless I told you? It's no trial to *you*, Mark, to make yourself comfortable and to bustle about. It's as natural for you to do so under the circumstances as it is for me not to do so. Why, you don't suppose there is a living creature in this ship who can by possibility have half so much to undergo on board of her as *I* have? Do you?" he asked, sitting upright in his berth and looking at Mark, with an expression of great earnestness not unmixed with wonder.

Mark twisted his face into a tight knot, and with his head very much on one side pondered upon this question as if he felt it an extremely difficult one to answer. He was relieved from his embarrassment by Martin himself, who said, as he stretched himself upon his back again and resumed the book he had been reading:

"But what is the use of my putting such a case to you, when the very essence of what I have been saying, is, that you cannot by possibility understand it! Make me a little brandy-and-water—cold and very weak—and give me a biscuit, and tell your friend, who is a nearer neighbour of ours than I could wish, to try and keep her children a little quieter to-night than she did last night; that's a good fellow."

Mr. Tapley set himself to obey these orders with great alacrity, and pending their execution, it may be presumed his flagging spirits revived: inasmuch as he several times observed, below his breath, that in respect of its power of imparting a credit to jollity, the Screw unquestionably had some decided advantages over the Dragon. He also remarked, that it was a high gratification to him to reflect that he would carry its main excellence ashore with him, and have it constantly beside him wherever he went; but what he meant by these consolatory thoughts he did not explain.

And now a general excitement began to prevail on board; and various predictions relative to the precise day, and even the precise hour at which they would reach New York, were freely broached. There was infinitely more crowding on deck and looking over the ship's side than there had been before; and an epidemic broke out for packing up things every morning, which required unpacking again every night. Those who had any letters to deliver, or any friends to meet, or any settled plans of going anywhere or doing anything, discussed their prospects a hundred times a day; and as this class of passengers was very small, and the number of those who had no prospects whatever was very large, there were plenty of listeners and few talkers. Those who had been ill all along got well now, and those who had been well got better. An American gentleman in the after-cabin, who had been wrapped up in fur and oilskin the whole passage, unexpectedly appeared in a very shiny, tall, black hat, and constantly overhauled a very little valise of pale leather, which contained his clothes, linen, brushes, shaving apparatus, books, trinkets, and other baggage. He likewise stuck his hands deep into his pockets, and walked the deck with his nostrils dilated, as already inhaling the air of Freedom which carries death to all tyrants, and can never (under any circumstances worth mentioning) be breathed by slaves. An English gentleman who was strongly suspected of having run away from a bank, with something in his possession belonging to its strong-box besides the key, grew eloquent upon the subject of the rights of man, and hummed the Marseillaise Hymn constantly. In a word, one great sensation pervaded the whole ship, and the soil of America lay close before them: so close at last, that, upon a certain starlight night, they took a pilot on board, and within a few hours afterwards lay to until the morning, awaiting the arrival of a steam-boat in which the passengers were to be conveyed ashore.

Off she came, soon after it was light next morning, and, lying alongside an hour or more—during which period her very firemen were objects of hardly less interest and curiosity, than if they had been so many angels, good or bad—took all her living freight aboard. Among them, Mark, who still had his friend and her three children under his close protection; and Martin, who had once more dressed himself in his usual attire, but wore a soiled, old cloak above his ordinary clothes, until such time as he should separate for ever from his late companions.

The steamer—which, with its machinery on deck, looked, as it worked its long slim legs, like some enormously magnified insect or antediluvian monster—dashed at great speed up a beautiful bay; and presently they saw some heights, and islands, and a long, flat, straggling city.

"And this," said Mr. Tapley, looking far ahead, "is the Land of Liberty, is it? Very well. I'm agreeable. Any land will do for me, after so much water!"

CHAPTER XVI.

MARTIN DISEMBARKS FROM THAT NOBLE AND FAST-SAILING LINE-OF-PACKET SHIP, THE SCREW, AT THE PORT OF NEW YORK, IN THE UNITED STATES OF AMERICA. HE MAKES SOME ACQUAINTANCES, AND DINES AT A BOARDING-HOUSE. THE PARTICULARS OF THOSE TRANSACTIONS.

SOME trifling excitement prevailed upon the very brink and margin of the Land of Liberty; for an alderman had been elected the day before; and Party Feeling naturally running rather high on such an exciting occasion, the friends of the disappointed candidate had found it necessary to assert the great principles of Purity of Election and Freedom of Opinion by breaking a few legs and arms, and furthermore pursuing one obnoxious gentleman through the streets with the design of slitting his nose. These good-humoured little outbursts of the popular fancy were not in themselves sufficiently remarkable to create any great stir, after the lapse of a whole night; but they found fresh life and notoriety in the breath of the newsboys, who not only proclaimed them with shrill yells in all the highways and byeways of the town, upon the wharves and among the shipping, but on the deck and down in the cabins of the steam-boat; which, before she touched the shore, was boarded and overrun by a legion of those young citizens.

"Here's this morning's New York Sewer!" cried one. "Here's this morning's New York Stabber! Here's the New York Family Spy! Here's the New York Private Listener! Here's the New York Peeper! Here's the New York Plunderer! Here's the New York Keyhole Reporter! Here's the New York Rowdy Journal! Here's all the New York papers! Here's full particulars of the patriotic loco-foco movement yesterday, in which the whigs was so chawed up; and the last Alabama gouging case; and the interesting Arkansas dooel with Bowie knives; and all the Political, Commercial, and Fashionable News. Here they are! Here they are! Here's the papers, here's the papers!"

"Here's the Sewer!" cried another. "Here's the New York Sewer! Here's some of the twelfth thousand of to-day's Sewer, with the best accounts of the markets, and all the shipping news, and four whole columns of country correspondence, and a full account of the Ball at Mrs. White's last night, where all the beauty and fashion of New York was assembled, with the Sewer's own particulars of the private lives of all the ladies that was there! Here's the Sewer! Here's some of the twelfth thousand of the New York Sewer! Here's the Sewer's exposure of the Wall Street Gang, and the Sewer's exposure of the Washington Gang, and the Sewer's exclusive account of a flagrant act of dishonesty committed by the Secretary of State when he was eight years old; now communicated, at a great expense, by his own nurse. Here's the Sewer! Here's the New York Sewer, in its twelfth thousand, with a whole column of New Yorkers to be shown up, and all their names printed! Here's the Sewer's article upon the Judge that tried him, day afore yesterday, for libel, and the Sewer's tribute to the independent Jury that didn't convict him, and the Sewer's account of what they might have expected if they had! Here's the Sewer, here's the Sewer! Here's the wide-awake Sewer; always on the look-out; the leading Journal of the United States, now in its twelfth thousand, and still a printing off:—here's the New York Sewer!"

"It is in such enlightened means," said a voice, almost

in Martin's ear, "that the bubbling passions of my country find a vent."

Martin turned involuntarily, and saw, standing close at his side, a sallow gentleman, with sunken cheeks, black hair, small twinkling eyes, and a singular expression hovering about that region of his face, which was not a frown, nor a leer, and yet might have been mistaken at the first glance for either. Indeed it would have been difficult, on a much closer acquaintance, to describe it in any more satisfactory terms than as a mixed expression of vulgar cunning and conceit. This gentleman wore a rather broad-brimmed hat for the greater wisdom of his appearance; and had his arms folded for the greater impressiveness of his attitude. He was somewhat shabbily dressed in a blue surtout reaching nearly to his ankles, short loose trousers of the same colour, and a faded buff waistcoat, through which a discoloured shirt-frill struggled to force itself into notice, as asserting an equality of civil rights with the other portions of his dress, and maintaining a Declaration of Independence on its own account. His feet, which were of unusually large proportions, were leisurely crossed before him as he half leaned against, half sat upon, the steamboat's side; and his thick cane, shod with a mighty ferrule at one end and armed with a great metal knob at the other, depended from a line-and-tassel on his wrist. Thus attired, and thus composed into an aspect of great profundity, the gentleman twitched up the right-hand corner of his mouth and his right eye, simultaneously, and said, once more:

"It is in such enlightened means, that the bubbling passions of my country find a vent."

As he looked at Martin, and nobody else was by, Martin inclined his head, and said:

"You allude to—"

"To the Palladium of rational Liberty at home, Sir, and the dread of Foreign oppression abroad," returned the gentleman, as he pointed with his cane to an uncommonly dirty newsboy with one eye. "To the Envy of the world, Sir, and the leaders of Human Civilization. Let me ask you, Sir," he added, bringing the ferrule of his stick heavily upon the deck with the air of a man who must not be equivocated with, "how do you like my Country?"

"I'm hardly prepared to answer that question yet," said Martin, "seeing that I have not been ashore."

"Well, I should expect you were not prepared, Sir," said the gentleman, "to behold such signs of National Prosperity as those?"

He pointed to the vessels lying at the wharves; and then gave a vague flourish with his stick, as if he would include the air and water, generally, in this remark.

"Really," said Martin, "I don't know. Yes. I think I was."

The gentleman glanced at him with a knowing look, and said he liked his policy. It was natural, he said, and it pleased him as a philosopher to observe the prejudices of human nature.

"You have brought, I see, Sir," he said, turning round towards Martin, and resting his chin on the top of his stick, "the usual amount of misery and poverty, and ignorance and crime, to be located in the bosom of the Great Republic. Well, Sir! let 'em come on in ship-loads from the old country: when vessels are about to founder, the rats are said to leave 'em. There is considerable of truth, I find, in that remark."

"The old ship will keep afloat a year or two longer yet, perhaps," said Martin with a smile, partly occasioned by what the gentleman said, and partly by his manner of saying it, which was odd enough, for he emphasized all the small words and syllables in his discourse, and left the others to take care of themselves: as if he thought the larger parts of speech could be trusted alone, but the little ones required to be constantly looked after.

"Hope is said by the poet, Sir," observed the gentleman, "to be the nurse of Young Desire."

Martin signified that he had heard of the cardinal virtue in question serving occasionally in that domestic capacity.

"She will not rear her infant in the present instance, Sir, you'll find," observed the gentleman.

"Time will show," said Martin.

The gentleman nodded his head, gravely; and said, "What is your name, Sir?"

Martin told him.

"How old are you, Sir?"

Martin told him.

"What's your profession, Sir?"

Martin told him that, also.

7—10

"What is your destination, Sir?" inquired the gentleman.

"Really," said Martin, laughing, "I can't satisfy you in
that particular, for I don't know it myself."

"Yes?" said the gentleman.

"No," said Martin.

The gentleman adjusted his cane under his left arm, and
took a more deliberate and complete survey of Martin than
he had yet had leisure to make. When he had completed
his inspection, he put out his right hand, shook Martin's
hand, and said:

"My name is Colonel Diver, Sir. I am the Editor of
the New York Rowdy Journal."

Martin received the communication with that degree of
respect which an announcement so distinguished appeared
to demand.

"The New York Rowdy Journal, Sir," resumed the
colonel, "is, as I expect you know, the organ of our aristocracy in this city."

"Oh! there *is* an aristocracy here, then?" said Martin.
"Of what is it composed?"

"Of intelligence, Sir," replied the colonel; "of intelligence and virtue. And of their necessary consequence in
this republic—dollars, Sir."

Martin was very glad to hear this, feeling well assured
that if intelligence and virtue led, as a matter of course,
to the acquisition of dollars, he would speedily become a
great capitalist. He was about to express the gratification
such news afforded him, when he was interrupted by the
captain of the ship, who came up at the moment to shake
hands with the colonel; and who, seeing a well-dressed
stranger on the deck (for Martin had thrown aside his
cloak), shook hands with him also. This was an unspeakable relief to Martin, who, in spite of the acknowledged
supremacy of Intelligence and Virtue in that happy country, would have been deeply mortified to appear before
Colonel Diver in the poor character of a steerage passenger.

"Well, cap'en!" said the colonel.

"Well, colonel!" cried the captain. "You're looking
most uncommon bright, Sir. I can hardly realise its being
you, and that's a fact."

"A good passage, cap'en?" inquired the colonel, taking
him aside.

"Well now! It was a pretty spanking run, Sir," said, or rather sung, the captain, who was a genuine New Englander: "con-siderin the weather."

"Yes?" said the colonel.

"Well! It was, Sir," said the captain. "I've just now sent a boy up to your office with the passenger-list, colonel."

"You haven't got another boy to spare, p'raps, cap'en?" said the colonel, in a tone almost amounting to severity.

"I guess there air a dozen if you want 'em, colonel," said the captain.

"One moderate big 'un could convey a dozen of champagne, perhaps," observed the colonel, musing, "to my office. You said a spanking run, I think?"

"Well, so I did," was the reply.

"It's very nigh you know," observed the colonel. "I'm glad it was a spanking run, cap'en. Don't mind about quarts if you're short of 'em. The boy can as well bring four-and-twenty pints, and travel twice as once.—A first-rate spanker, cap'en, was it? Yes?"

"A most e—tarnal spanker," said the skipper.

"I admire at your good fortune, cap'en. You might loan me a corkscrew at the same time, and half-a-dozen glasses if you liked. However bad the elements combine against my country's noble packet-ship, the Screw, Sir," said the colonel, turning to Martin, and drawing a flourish on the surface of the deck with his cane, "her passage either way, is almost certain to eventuate a spanker!"

The captain, who had the Sewer below at that moment lunching expensively in one cabin, while the amiable Stabber was drinking himself into a state of blind madness in another, took a cordial leave of his friend the colonel, and hurried away to despatch the champagne: well-knowing (as it afterwards appeared) that if he failed to conciliate the editor of the Rowdy Journal, that potentate would denounce him and his ship in large capitals before he was a day older; and would probably assault the memory of his mother also, who had not been dead more than twenty years. The colonel being again left alone with Martin, checked him as he was moving away, and offered, in consideration of his being an Englishman, to show him the town and to introduce him, if such were his desire, to a genteel boarding-house. But before they entered on these proceedings (he said), he would beseech the honour of his company at the office of the Rowdy Journal, to partake of a bottle of champagne of his own importation.

All this was so extremely kind and hospitable, that Martin, though it was quite early in the morning, readily acquiesced. So, instructing Mark, who was deeply engaged with his friend and her three children,—when he had done assisting them, and had cleared the baggage, to wait for further orders at the Rowdy Journal Office,—he accompanied his new friend on shore.

They made their way as they best could through the melancholy crowd of emigrants upon the wharf—who, grouped ..bout their beds and boxes with the bare ground below them and the bare sky above, might have fallen from another planet, for anything they knew of the country— and walked for some short distance along a busy street, bounded on one side by the quays and shipping; and on the other by a long row of staring red-brick storehouses and offices, ornamented with more black boards and white letters, and more white boards and black letters, than Martin had ever seen before, in fifty times the space. Presently they turned up a narrow street, and presently into other narrow streets, until at last they stopped before a house whereon was painted in great characters, "ROWDY JOURNAL."

The colonel, who had walked the whole way with one hand in his breast, his head occasionally wagging from side to side, and his hat thrown back upon his ears—like a man who was oppressed to inconvenience by a sense of his own greatness—led the way up a dark and dirty flight of stairs into a room of similar character, all littered and bestrewn with odds and ends of newspapers and other crumpled fragments, both in proof and manuscript. Behind a mangy old writing-table in this apartment, sat a figure with a stump of a pen in its mouth and a great pair of scissors in its right hand, clipping and slicing at a file of Rowdy Journals; and it was such a laughable figure that Martin had some difficulty in preserving his gravity, though conscious of the close observation of Colonel Diver.

The individual who sat clipping and slicing as aforesaid at the Rowdy Journals, was a small young gentleman of very juvenile appearance, and unwholesomely pale in the face; partly, perhaps, from intense thought, but partly, there is no doubt, from the excessive use of tobacco, which he was at that moment chewing vigorously. He wore his shirt-collar turned down over a black ribbon, and his lank hair—a fragile crop—was not only smoothed and parted back from his brow, that none of the Poetry of his aspect might be lost, but had here and there been grubbed up by the roots; which accounted for his loftiest developments being somewhat pimply. He had that order of nose on which the envy of mankind has bestowed the appellation "snub," and it was very much turned up at the end, as with a lofty scorn. Upon the upper lip of this young gentleman, were tokens of a sandy down—so very, very smooth and scant, that, though encouraged to the utmost, it looked more like a recent trace of gingerbread, than the fair promise of a moustache; and this conjecture, his apparently tender age went far to strengthen. He was intent upon his work; and every time he snapped the great pair of scissors, he made a corresponding motion with his jaws, which gave him a very terrible appearance.

Martin was not long in determining within himself that this must be Colonel Diver's son; the hope of the family, and future mainspring of the Rowdy Journal. Indeed he had begun to say that he presumed this was the colonel's little boy, and that it was very pleasant to see him playing at Editor in all the guilelessness of childhood; when the colonel proudly interposed, and said:

"My War Correspondent, Sir—Mr. Jefferson Brick!"

Martin could not help starting at this unexpected announcement, and the consciousness of the irretrievable mistake he had nearly made.

Mr. Brick seemed pleased with the sensation he produced upon the stranger, and shook hands with him with an air of patronage designed to reassure him, and to let him know that there was no occasion to be frightened, for he (Brick) wouldn't hurt him.

"You have heard of Jefferson Brick I see, Sir," quoth the colonel, with a smile. "England has heard of Jefferson Brick. Europe has heard of Jefferson Brick. Let me see. When did you leave England, Sir?"

"Five weeks ago," said Martin.

"Five weeks ago," repeated the colonel, thoughtfully; as he took his seat upon the table, and swung his legs. "Now let me ask you, Sir, which of Mr. Brick's articles

18

had become at that time the most obnoxious to the British Parliament and the Court of St. James's? "

"Upon my word," said Martin, "I—"

"I have reason to know, Sir," interrupted the colonel, "that the aristocratic circles of your country quail before the name of Jefferson Brick. I should like to be informed, Sir, from your lips, which of his sentiments has struck the deadliest blow—"

"—At the hundred heads of the Hydra of Corruption now grovelling in the dust beneath the lance of Reason, and spouting up to the universal arch above us, its sanguinary gore," said Mr. Brick, putting on a little blue cloth cap with a glazed front, and quoting his last article.

"The libation of freedom, Brick—" hinted the colonel.

"—Must sometimes be quaffed in blood, colonel," cried Brick. And when he said "blood," he gave the great pair of scissors a sharp snap, as if *they* said blood too, and were quite of his opinion.

This done, they both looked at Martin, pausing for a reply.

"Upon my life," said Martin, who had by this time quite recovered his usual coolness, "I can't give you any satisfactory information about it; for the truth is that I—"

"Stop!" cried the colonel, glancing sternly at his war correspondent, and giving his head one shake after every sentence. "That you never heard of Jefferson Brick, Sir. That you never read Jefferson Brick, Sir. That you never saw the Rowdy Journal, Sir. That you never knew, Sir, of its mighty influence upon the cabinets of Europe.—Yes? "

"That's what I was about to observe, certainly," said Martin.

"Keep cool, Jefferson," said the colonel gravely. Don't bust! oh you Europeans! Arter that, let's have a glass of wine!" So saying, he got down from the table, and produced, from a basket outside the door, a bottle of champagne, and three glasses.

"Mr. Jefferson Brick, Sir," said the colonel, filling Martin's glass and his own, and pushing the bottle to that gentleman, "will give us a sentiment."

"Well, Sir!" cried the war correspondent, "since you have concluded to call upon me, I will respond. I will give you, Sir, The Rowdy Journal and its brethren; the well of Truth, whose waters are black from being composed of printers' ink, but are quite clear enough for my country to behold the shadow of her Destiny reflected in."

"Hear, hear!" cried the colonel, with great complacency. "There are flowery components, Sir, in the language of my friend?"

"Very much so, indeed," said Martin.

"There is to-day's Rowdy, Sir," observed the colonel, handing him a paper. "You'll find Jefferson Brick at his usual post in the van of human civilization and moral purity."

The colonel was by this time seated on the table again. Mr. Brick also took up a position on that same piece of furniture; and they fell to drinking pretty hard. They often looked at Martin as he read the paper, and then at each other; and when he laid it down, which was not until they had finished a second bottle, the colonel asked him what he thought of it.

"Why, it's horribly personal," said Martin.

The colonel seemed much flattered by this remark; and said he hoped it was.

"We are independent here, Sir," said Mr. Jefferson Brick. "We do as we like."

"If I may judge from this specimen," returned Martin, "there must be a few thousands here, rather the reverse of independent, who do as they don't like."

"Well! They yield to the mighty mind of the Popular Instructor, Sir," said the colonel. "They rile up, sometimes; but in general we have a hold upon our citizens both in public and in private life, which is as much one of the ennobling institutions of our happy country as—"

"As nigger slavery itself," suggested Mr. Brick.

"En—tirely so," remarked the colonel.

"Pray," said Martin, after some hesitation, "may I venture to ask, with reference to a case I observe in this paper of yours, whether the Popular Instructor often deals in—I am at a loss to express it without giving you offence —in forgery? In forged letters, for instance," he pursued, for the colonel was perfectly calm and quite at his ease, "solemnly purporting to have been written at recent periods by living men?"

"Well, Sir!" replied the colonel. "It does, now and then."

"And the popular instructed—what do they do?" asked Martin.

"Buy em," said the colonel.

Mr. Jefferson Brick expectorated and laughed; the former copiously, the latter approvingly.

"Buy 'em by hundreds of thousands," resumed the colonel. "We are a smart people here, and can appreciate smartness."

"Is smartness American for forgery?" asked Martin.

"Well!" said the colonel, "I expect it's American for a good many things that you call by other names. But you can't help yourselves in Europe. We can."

"And do, sometimes," thought Martin. "You help yourselves with very little ceremony, too!"

"At all events, whatever name we choose to employ," said the colonel, stooping down to roll the third empty bottle into a corner after the other two, "I suppose the art of forgery was not invented here, Sir?"

"I suppose not," replied Martin.

"Nor any other kind of smartness, I reckon?"

"Invented! No, I presume not."

"Well!" said the colonel; "then we got it all from the old country, and the old country's to blame for it, and not the new 'un. There's an end of *that*. Now, if Mr. Jefferson Brick and you will be so good as clear, I'll come out last, and lock the door."

Rightly interpreting this as the signal for their departure, Martin walked down stairs after the war correspondent, who preceded him with great majesty. The colonel following, they left the Rowdy Journal Office and walked forth into the streets: Martin feeling doubtful whether he ought to kick the colonel for having presumed to speak to him, or whether it came within the bounds of possibility that he and his establishment could be among the boasted usages of that regenerated land.

It was clear that Colonel Diver, in the security of his strong position, and in his perfect understanding of the public sentiment, cared very little what Martin or anybody else thought about him. His high-spiced wares were made to sell, and they sold; and his thousands of readers could as rationally charge their delight in filth upon him, as a glutton can shift upon his cook the responsibility of his beastly excess. Nothing would have delighted the colonel more than to be told that no such man as he could walk in high success the streets of any other country in the world: for that would only have been a logical assurance to him of the correct adaptation of his labours to the prevailing taste, and of his being strictly and peculiarly a national feature of America.

They walked a mile or more along a handsome street which the colonel said was called Broadway, and which Mr. Jefferson Brick said "whipped the universe." Turning, at length, into one of the numerous streets which branched from this main thoroughfare, they stopped before a rather mean-looking house with jalousie blinds to every window; a flight of steps before the green street-door; a shining white ornament on the rails on either side like a petrified pine-apple, polished; a little oblong plate of the same material over the knocker, whereon the name of "Pawkins" was engraved; and four accidental pigs looking down the area.

The colonel knocked at this house with the air of a man who lived there; and an Irish girl popped her head out of one of the top windows to see who it was. Pending her journey down stairs, the pigs were joined by two or three friends from the next street, in company with whom they lay down sociably in the gutter.

"Is the major in-doors?" inquired the colonel, as he entered.

"Is it the master, Sir?" returned the girl, with a hesitation which seemed to imply that they were rather flush of majors in that establishment.

"The master!" said Colonel Diver, stopping short and looking round at his war correspondent.

"Oh! The depressing institutions of that British Empire, colonel!" said Jefferson Brick. "Master!"

"What's the matter with the word?" asked Martin.

"I should hope it was never heard in our country, Sir; that's all," said Jefferson Brick: "except when it is used by some degraded Help, as new to the blessings of our form of government, as this Help is. There are no masters here."

"All 'owners,' are they?" said Martin.

Mr. Jefferson Brick followed in the Rowdy Journal's footsteps without returning any answer. Martin took the

same course, thinking as he went, that perhaps the free
and independent citizens, who in their moral elevation,
owned the colonel for their master, might render better
homage to the goddess, Liberty, in nightly dreams upon
the oven of a Russian Serf.

The colonel led the way into a room at the back of the
house upon the ground-floor, light, and of fair dimensions,
but exquisitely uncomfortable: having nothing in it but
the four cold white walls and ceiling, a mean carpet, a
dreary waste of dining-table reaching from end to end, and
a bewildering collection of cane-bottomed chairs. In the
further region of this banqueting-hall was a stove, garnished on either side with a great brass spittoon, and shaped
in itself like three little iron barrels set up on end in a fender,
and joined together on the principle of the Siamese Twins.
Before it, swinging himself in a rocking-chair, lounged a
large gentleman with his hat on, who amused himself by
spitting alternately into the spittoon on the right hand of
the stove, and the spittoon on the left, and then working
his way back again in the same order. A negro lad in a
soiled white jacket was busily engaged in placing on the
table two long rows of knives and forks, relieved at intervals by jugs of water; and as he travelled down one side
of this festive board, he straightened with his dirty hands
the dirtier cloth, which was all askew, and had not been removed since breakfast. The atmosphere of this room was
rendered intensely hot and stifling by the stove; but being
further flavoured by a sickly gush of soup from the kitchen,
and by such remote suggestions of tobacco as lingered within
the brazen receptacles already mentioned, it became, to a
stranger's senses, almost insupportable.

The gentleman in the rocking-chair having his back
towards them, and being much engaged in his intellectual
pastime, was not aware of their approach until the colonel
walking up to the stove, contributed his mite towards the
support of the left-hand spittoon, just as the major—for
it was the major—bore down upon it. Major Pawkins
then reserved his fire, and looking upward, said, with a
peculiar air of quiet weariness, like a man who had been
up all night—an air which Martin had already observed
both in the colonel and Mr. Jefferson Brick—

"Well, colonel!"

"Here is a gentleman from England, major," the colonel

replied, "who has concluded to locate himself here if the amount of compensation suits him."

"I am glad to see you, Sir," observed the major, shaking hands with Martin, and not moving a muscle of his face. "You are pretty bright, I hope?"

"Never better," said Martin.

"You are never likely to be," returned the major. "You will see the sun shine *here*."

"I think I remember to have seen it shine at home, sometimes," said Martin, smiling.

"I think not," replied the major. He said so with a stoical indifference certainly, but still in a tone of firmness which admitted of no further dispute on that point. When he had thus settled the question, he put his hat a little on one side for the greater convenience of scratching his head, and saluted Mr. Jefferson Brick with a lazy nod.

Major Pawkins (a gentleman of Pennsylvanian origin) was distinguished by a very large skull, and a great mass of yellow forehead; in deference to which commodities, it was currently held in bar-rooms and other such places of resort, that the major was a man of huge sagacity. He was further to be known by a heavy eye and a dull slow manner; and for being a man of that kind who—mentally speaking—requires a deal of room to turn himself in. But, in trading on his stock of wisdom, he invariably proceeded on the principle of putting all the goods he had (and more) into his window; and that went a great way with his constituency of admirers. It went a great way, perhaps, with Mr. Jefferson Brick, who took occasion to whisper in Martin's ear:

"One of the most remarkable men in our country, Sir!"

It must not be supposed, however, that the perpetual exhibition in the market-place of all his stock-in-trade for sale or hire, was the major's sole claim to a very large share of sympathy and support. He was a great politician; and the one article of his creed, in reference to all public obligations involving the good faith and integrity of his country, was, "run a moist pen slick through everything, and start fresh." This made him a patriot. In commercial affairs he was a bold speculator. In plainer words he had a most distinguished genius for swindling, and could start a bank, or negotiate a loan, or form a land-jobbing company (entailing ruin, pestilence, and death, on hun-

dreds of families), with any gifted creature in the Union.
This made him an admirable man of business. He could
hang about a bar-room, discussing the affairs of the nation,
for twelve hours together; and in that time could hold forth
with more intolerable dulness, chew more tobacco, smoke
more tobacco, drink more rum-toddy, mint-julep, gin-sling,
and cock-tail, than any private gentleman of his acquaintance. This made him an orator and a man of the people.
In a word, the major was a rising character, and a popular
character, and was in a fair way to be sent by the popular
party to the State House of New York, if not in the end
to Washington itself. But as a man's private prosperity
does not always keep pace with his patriotic devotion to
public affairs; and as fraudulent transactions have their
downs as well as ups; the major was occasionally under a
cloud. Hence, just now, Mrs. Pawkins kept a boarding-
house, and Major Pawkins rather "loafed" his time away,
than otherwise.

"You have come to visit our country, Sir, at a season of
great commercial depression," said the major.

"At an alarming crisis," said the colonel.

"At a period of unprecedented stagnation," said Mr.
Jefferson Brick.

"I am sorry to hear that," returned Martin. "It's not
likely to last, I hope?"

Martin knew nothing about America, or he would have
known perfectly well that if its individual citizens, to a
man, are to be believed, it always *is* depressed, and always
is stagnated, and always *is* at an alarming crisis, and never
was otherwise; though as a body they are ready to make
oath upon the Evangelists at any hour of the day or night,
that it is the most thriving and prosperous of all countries
on the habitable globe.

"It's not likely to last, I hope?" said Martin.

"Well!" returned the major, "I expect we shall get
along somehow, and come right in the end."

"We are an elastic country," said the Rowdy Journal.

"We are a young lion," said Mr. Jefferson Brick.

"We have revivifying and vigorous principles within
ourselves," observed the major. "Shall we drink a bitter
afore dinner, colonel?"

The colonel assenting to this proposal with great alacrity,
Major Pawkins proposed an adjournment to a neighbouring

bar-room, which, as he observed, was "only in the next block." He then referred Martin to Mrs. Pawkins for all particulars connected with the rate of board and lodging, and informed him that he would have the pleasure of seeing that lady at dinner, which would soon be ready, as the dinner hour was two o'clock, and it only wanted a quarter now. This reminded him that if the bitter were to be taken at all, there was no time to lose; so he walked off without more ado, and left them to follow if they thought proper.

When the major rose from his rocking-chair before the stove and so disturbed the hot air and balmy whiff of soup which fanned their brows, the odour of stale tobacco became so decidedly prevalent as to leave no doubt of its proceeding mainly from that gentleman's attire. Indeed, as Martin walked behind him to the bar-room, he could not help thinking that the great square major, in his listlessness and languor, looked very much like a stale weed himself, such as might be hoed out of the public garden with great advantage to the decent growth of that preserve, and tossed on some congenial dunghill.

They encountered more weeds in the bar-room, some of whom (being thirsty souls as well as dirty) were pretty stale in one sense, and pretty fresh in another. Among them was a gentleman who, as Martin gathered from the conversation that took place over the bitter, started that afternoon for the Far West on a six months' business tour; and who, as his outfit and equipment for this journey, had just such another shiny hat and just such another little pale valise, as had composed the luggage of the gentleman who came from England in the Screw.

They were walking back very leisurely; Martin arm-in-arm with Mr. Jefferson Brick, and the major and the colonel side-by-side before them; when, as they came within a house or two of the major's residence, they heard a bell ringing violently. The instant this sound struck upon their ears, the colonel and the major darted off, dashed up the steps and in at the street-door (which stood ajar) like lunatics; while Mr. Jefferson Brick, detaching his arm from Martin's, made a precipitate dive in the same direction, and vanished also.

"Good Heaven!" thought Martin, "the premises are on fire! It was an alarm-bell!"

But there was no smoke to be seen, nor any flame, nor was there any smell of fire. As Martin faltered on the pavement, three more gentlemen, with horror and agitation depicted in their faces, came plunging wildly round the street corner; jostled each other on the steps; struggled for an instant; and rushed into the house, in a confused heap of arms and legs. Unable to bear it any longer, Martin followed. Even in his rapid progress, he was run down, thrust aside, and passed, by two more gentlemen, stark mad, as it appeared, with fierce excitement.

"Where is it?" cried Martin, breathlessly, to a negro whom he encountered in the passage.

"In a eatin room, sa. 'Kernel, sa, him kep a seat 'side himself, sa."

"A seat!" cried Martin.

"For a dinnar, sa."

Martin stared at him for a moment, and burst into a hearty laugh; to which the negro, out of his natural good humour and desire to please, so heartily responded, that his teeth shone like a gleam of light. "You're the pleasantest fellow I have seen yet," said Martin, clapping him on the back, "and give me a better appetite than bitters."

With this sentiment he walked into the dining-room and slipped into a chair next the colonel, which that gentleman (by this time nearly through his dinner) had turned down, in reserve for him, with its back against the table.

It was a numerous company—eighteen or twenty, perhaps. Of these some five or six were ladies, who sat wedged together in a little phalanx by themselves. All the knives and forks were working away at a rate that was quite alarming; very few words were spoken; and everybody seemed to eat his utmost in self-defence, as if a famine were expected to set in before breakfast-time to-morrow morning, and it had become high time to assert the first law of nature. The poultry, which may perhaps be considered to have formed the staple of the entertainment—for there was a turkey at the top, a pair of ducks at the bottom, and two fowls in the middle—disappeared as rapidly as if every bird had had the use of its wings, and had flown in desperation down a human throat. The oysters, stewed and pickled, leaped from their capacious reservoirs, and slid by scores into the mouths of the assembly. The sharpest pickles vanished; whole cucumbers at once, like sugar-plums; and no man winked his eye. Great heaps of indigestible matter melted away as ice before the sun. It was a solemn and an awful thing to see. Dyspeptic individuals bolted their food in wedges; feeding, not themselves, but broods of night-mares, who were continually standing at livery within them. Spare men, with lank and rigid cheeks, came out unsatisfied from the destruction of heavy dishes, and glared with watchful eyes upon the pastry. What Mrs. Pawkins felt each day at dinner-time is hidden from all human knowledge. But she had one comfort. It was very soon over.

When the colonel had finished his dinner, which event took place while Martin, who had sent his plate for some turkey, was waiting to begin, he asked him what he thought of the boarders, who were from all parts of the Union, and whether he would like to know any particulars concerning them.

"Pray," said Martin, "who is that sickly little girl opposite, with the tight round eyes? I don't see anybody here, who looks like her mother, or who seems to have charge of her."

"Do you mean the matron in blue, Sir?" asked the colonel, with emphasis. "That is Mrs. Jefferson Brick, Sir."

"No, no," said Martin, "I mean the little girl, like a doll—directly opposite."

"Well, Sir!" cried the colonel. "*That* is Mrs. Jefferson Brick."

Martin glanced at the colonel's face, but he was quite serious.

"Bless my soul! I suppose there will be a young Brick then, one of these days?" said Martin.

"There are two young Bricks already, Sir," returned the colonel.

The matron looked so uncommonly like a child herself, that Martin could not help saying as much. "Yes, Sir," returned the colonel, "but some institutions develop human natur: others retard it."

"Jefferson Brick," he observed after a short silence, in commendation of his correspondent, "is one of the most remarkable men in our country, Sir!"

This had passed almost in a whisper, for the distinguished gentleman alluded to, sat on Martin's other hand.

"Pray, Mr. Brick," said Martin turning to him, and asking a question more for conversation's sake than from any feeling of interest in its subject, "who is that—" he was going to say "young" but thought it prudent to eschew the word—"that very short gentleman yonder, with the red nose?"

"That is Pro—fessor Mullit, Sir," replied Jefferson.

"May I ask what he is professor of?" asked Martin.

"Of education, Sir," said Jefferson Brick.

"A sort of schoolmaster, possibly?" Martin ventured to observe.

"He is a man of fine moral elements, Sir, and not commonly endowed," said the war correspondent. "He felt it necessary, at the last election for President, to repudiate and denounce his father, who voted on the wrong interest. He has since written some powerful pamphlets, under the signature of 'Suturb,' or Brutus reversed. He is one of the most remarkable men in our country, Sir."

"There seem to be plenty of 'em," thought Martin, "at any rate."

Pursuing his inquiries, Martin found that there were no fewer than four majors present, two colonels, one general, and a captain, so that he could not help thinking how strongly officered the American militia must be; and wondering very much whether the officers commanded each other; or if they did not, where on earth the privates came from. There seemed to be no man there without a title: for those who had not attained to military honours were either doctors, professors, or reverends. Three very hard and disagreeable gentlemen were on missions from neighbouring States; one on monetary affairs, one on political, one on sectarian. Among the ladies, there were Mrs. Pawkins, who was very straight, bony, and silent; and a wiry-faced old damsel, who held strong sentiments touching the rights of women, and had diffused the same in lectures; but the rest were strangely devoid of individual traits of character, insomuch that any one of them might have changed minds with the other, and nobody would have found it out. These, by the way, were the only members of the party who did not appear to be among the most remarkable people in the country.

Several of the gentlemen got up, one by one, and walked off as they swallowed their last morsel; pausing generally

by the stove for a minute or so to refresh themselves at the
brass spittoons. A few sedentary characters, however, remained at table full a quarter of an hour, and did not rise
until the ladies rose, when all stood up.

"Where are they going?" asked Martin, in the ear of Mr.
Jefferson Brick.

"To their bed-rooms, Sir."

"Is there no dessert, or other interval of conversation?"
asked Martin, who was disposed to enjoy himself after his
long voyage.

"We are a busy people here, Sir, and have no time for
that," was the reply.

So the ladies passed out in single file; Mr. Jefferson
Brick and such other married gentlemen as were left, acknowledging the departure of their other halves by a nod;
and there was an end of *them*. Martin thought this an uncomfortable custom, but he kept his opinion to himself for
the present, being anxious to hear, and inform himself by,
the conversation of the busy gentlemen, who now lounged
about the stove as if a great weight had been taken off
their minds by the withdrawal of the other sex; and who
made a plentiful use of the spittoons and their tooth-
picks.

It was rather barren of interest, to say the truth; and
the greater part of it may be summed up in one word—
dollars. All their cares, hopes, joys, affections, virtues,
and associations, seemed to be melted down into dollars.
Whatever the chance contributions that fell into the slow
cauldron of their talk, they made the gruel thick and slab
with dollars. Men were weighed by their dollars, measures
gauged by their dollars; life was auctioneered, appraised,
put up, and knocked down for its dollars. The next respectable thing to dollars was any venture having their attainment for its end. The more of that worthless ballast,
honour and fair-dealing, which any man cast overboard from
the ship of his Good Name and Good Intent, the more ample
stowage-room he had for dollars. Make commerce one
huge lie and mighty theft. Deface the banner of the nation for an idle rag; pollute it star by star; and cut out
stripe by stripe as from the arm of a degraded soldier. Do
anything for dollars! What is a flag to *them!*

One who rides at all hazards of limb and life in the chase
of a fox, will prefer to ride recklessly at most times. So

it was with these gentlemen. He was the greatest patriot, in their eyes, who brawled the loudest, and who cared the least for decency. He was their champion, who in the brutal fury of his own pursuit, could cast no stigma upon them, for the hot knavery of theirs. Thus, Martin learned in the five minutes' straggling talk about the stove, that to carry pistols into legislative assemblies, and swords in sticks, and other such peaceful toys; to seize opponents by the throat, as dogs or rats might do; to bluster, bully, and overbear by personal assailment; were glowing deeds. Not thrusts and stabs at Freedom, striking far deeper into her House of Life than any sultan's scimetar could reach; but rare incense on her altars, having a grateful scent in patriotic nostrils, and curling upward to the seventh heaven of Fame.

Once or twice, when there was a pause, Martin asked such questions as naturally occurred to him, being a stranger, about the national poets, the theatre, literature, and the arts. But the information which these gentlemen were in a condition to give him on such topics, did not extend beyond the effusions of such master-spirits of the time, as Colonel Diver, Mr. Jefferson Brick, and others; renowned, as it appeared, for excellence in the achievement of a peculiar style of broadside-essay called "a screamer."

"We are a busy people, Sir," said one of the captains, who was from the West, "and have no time for reading mere notions. We don't mind 'em if they come to us in newspapers along with almighty strong stuff of another sort, but darn your books."

Here the general, who appeared to quite grow faint at the bare thought of reading anything which was neither mercantile nor political, and was not in a newspaper, inquired "if any gentleman would drink some?" Most of the company, considering this a very choice and seasonable idea, lounged out one by one to the bar-room in the next block. Thence they probably went to their stores and counting-houses; thence to the bar-room again, to talk once more of dollars, and enlarge their minds with the perusal and discussion of screamers; and thence each man to snore in the bosom of his own family.

"Which would seem," said Martin, pursuing the current of his own thoughts, "to be the principal recreation they enjoy in common." With that, he fell a-musing again on dollars, demagogues, and bar-rooms; debating within himself whether busy people of this class were really as busy as they claimed to be, or only had an inaptitude for social and domestic pleasure.

It was a difficult question to solve; and the mere fact of its being strongly presented to his mind by all that he had seen and heard, was not encouraging. He sat down at the deserted board, and becoming more and more despondent, as he thought of all the uncertainties and difficulties of his precarious situation, sighed heavily.

Now, there had been at the dinner-table a middle-aged man with a dark eye and a sunburnt face, who had attracted Martin's attention by having something very engaging and honest in the expression of his features; but of whom he could learn nothing from either of his neighbours, who seemed to consider him quite beneath their notice. He had taken no part in the conversation round the stove, nor had he gone forth with the rest; and now, when he heard Martin sigh for the third or fourth time, he interposed with some casual remark, as if he desired, without obtruding himself upon a stranger's notice, to engage him in cheerful conversation if he could. His motive was so obvious, and yet so delicately expressed, that Martin felt really grateful to him, and showed him so, in the manner of his reply.

"I will not ask you," said this gentleman with a smile, as he rose and moved towards him, "how you like my country, for I can quite anticipate your real feeling on that point. But, as I am an American, and consequently bound to begin with a question, I'll ask you how do you like the colonel?"

"You are so very frank," returned Martin, "that I have no hesitation in saying I don't like him at all. Though I must add that I am beholden to him for his civility in bringing me here—and arranging for my stay, on pretty reasonable terms, by the way," he added: remembering that the colonel had whispered him to that effect, before going out.

"Not much beholden," said the stranger drily. "The colonel occasionally boards packet-ships, I have heard, to glean the latest information for his journal; and he occasionally brings strangers to board here, I believe, with a view to the little percentage which attaches to those good offices; and which the hostess deducts from his weekly bill.

I don't offend you, I hope?" he added, seeing that Martin reddened.

"My dear Sir," returned Martin, as they shook hands, "how is that possible! to tell you the truth, I—a—"

"Yes?" said the gentleman, sitting down beside him.

"I am rather at a loss, since I must speak plainly," said Martin, getting the better of his hesitation, "to know how this colonel escapes being beaten."

"Well! He has been beaten once or twice," remarked the gentleman quietly. "He is one of a class of men, in whom our own Franklin, so long ago as ten years before the close of the last century, foresaw our danger and disgrace. Perhaps you don't know that Franklin, in very severe terms, published his opinion that those who were slandered by such fellows as this colonel, having no sufficient remedy in the administration of this country's laws or in the decent and right-minded feeling of its people, were justified in retorting on such public nuisances by means of a stout cudgel?"

"I was not aware of that," said Martin, "but I am very glad to know it, and I think it worthy of his memory; especially"—here he hesitated again.

"Go on," said the other, smiling as if he knew what stuck in Martin's throat.

"Especially," pursued Martin, "as I can already understand that it may have required great courage even in his time to write freely on any question which was not a party one in this very free country."

"Some courage, no doubt," returned his new friend. "Do you think it would require any to do so, now?"

"Indeed I think it would; and not a little," said Martin.

"You are right. So very right, that I believe no satirist could breathe this air. If another Juvenal or Swift could rise up among us to-morrow, he would be hunted down. If you have any knowledge of our literature, and can give me the name of any man, American born and bred, who has anatomised our follies as a people, and not as this or that party; and has escaped the foulest and most brutal slander, the most inveterate hatred and intolerant pursuit; it will be a strange name in my ears, believe me. In some cases I could name to you, where a native writer has ventured on the most harmless and good-humoured illustrations of our vices or defects, it has been found necessary to announce, that in a second edition the passage has been expunged, or altered, or explained away, or patched into praise."

"And how has this been brought about?" asked Martin, in dismay.

"Think of what you have seen and heard to-day, beginning with the colonel," said his friend, "and ask yourself. How *they* came about is another question. Heaven forbid that they should be samples of the intelligence and virtue of America, but they come uppermost; and in great numbers too; and too often represent it. Will you walk?"

There was a cordial candour in his manner, and an engaging confidence that it would not be abused; a manly bearing on his own part, and a simple reliance on the manly faith of a stranger; which Martin had never seen before. He linked his arm readily in that of the American gentleman, and they walked out together.

It was perhaps to men like this, his new companion, that a traveller of honoured name, who trod those shores now nearly forty years ago, and woke upon that soil, as many have done since, to blots and stains upon its high pretensions, which in the brightness of his distant dreams were lost to view; appealed in these words—

> Oh but for such, Columbia's days were done;
> Rank without ripeness, quickened without sun,
> Crude at the surface, rotten at the core,
> Her fruits would fall before her spring were o'er!

CHAPTER XVII.

MARTIN ENLARGES HIS CIRCLE OF ACQUAINTANCE; INCREASES HIS STOCK OF WISDOM; AND HAS AN EXCELLENT OPPORTUNITY OF COMPARING HIS OWN EXPERIENCES WITH THOSE OF LUMMY NED OF THE LIGHT SALISBURY, AS RELATED BY HIS FRIEND MR. WILLIAM SIMMONS.

It was characteristic of Martin, that all this while he had either forgotten Mark Tapley as completely as if there had been no such person in existence, or, if for a moment the figure of that gentleman rose before his mental vision,

19

had dismissed it as something by no means of a pressing nature, which might be attended to by-and-by, and could wait his perfect leisure. But, being now in the streets again, it occurred to him as just coming within the bare limits of possibility that Mr. Tapley might, in course of time, grow tired of waiting on the threshold of the Rowdy Journal Office; so he intimated to his new friend, that if they could conveniently walk in that direction, he would be glad to get this piece of business off his mind.

"And speaking of business," said Martin, "may I ask, in order that I may not be behind-hand with questions either, whether your occupation holds you to this city, or, like myself, you are a visitor here?"

"A visitor," replied his friend. "I was 'raised' in the State of Massachusetts, and reside there still. My home is in a quiet country town. I am not often in these busy places; and my inclination to visit them does not increase with our better acquaintance, I assure you."

"You have been abroad?" asked Martin.

"Oh yes."

"And, like most people who travel, have become more than ever attached to your home and native country," said Martin, eyeing him curiously.

"To my home—yes," rejoined his friend. "To my native country as my home—yes, also."

"You imply some reservation," said Martin.

"Well," returned his new friend, "if you ask me whether I came back here with a greater relish for my country's faults; with a greater fondness for those who claim (at the rate of so many dollars a day) to be her friends; with a cooler indifference to the growth of principles among us in respect of public matters and of private dealings between man and man, the advocacy of which, beyond the foul atmosphere of a criminal trial, would disgrace your own Old Bailey lawyers; why, then I answer plainly, No."

"Oh!" said Martin; in so exactly the same key as his friend's No, that it sounded like an echo.

"If you ask me," his companion pursued, "whether I came back here better satisfied with a state of things which broadly divides society into two classes—whereof one, the great mass, asserts a spurious independence, most miserably dependent for its mean existence on the disregard of humanizing conventionalities of manner and social custom, so that the coarser a man is, the more distinctly it shall appeal to his taste; while the other, disgusted with the low standard thus set up and made adaptable to everything, takes refuge among the graces and refinements it can bring to bear on private life, and leaves the public weal to such fortune as may betide it in the press and uproar of a general scramble—then again I answer, No."

And again Martin said "Oh!" in the same odd way as before, being anxious and disconcerted; not so much, to say the truth, on public grounds, as with reference to the fading prospects of domestic architecture.

"In a word," resumed the other, "I do not find and cannot believe, and therefore will not allow that we are a model of wisdom, and an example to the world, and the perfection of human reason; and a great deal more to the same purpose, which you may hear any hour in the day; simply because we began our political life with two inestimable advantages."

"What were they?" asked Martin.

"One, that our history commenced at so late a period as to escape the ages of bloodshed and cruelty through which other nations have passed; and so had all the light of their probation, and none of its darkness. The other, that we have a vast territory, and not—as yet—too many people on it. These facts considered, we have done little enough, I think."

"Education?" suggested Martin, faintly.

"Pretty well on that head," said the other, shrugging his shoulders, "still no mighty matter to boast of; for old countries, and despotic countries too, have done as much, if not more, and made less noise about it. We shine out brightly in comparison with England, certainly; but hers is a very extreme case. You complimented me on my frankness, you know," he added, laughing.

"Oh! I am not at all astonished at your speaking thus openly when my country is in question," returned Martin. "It is your plain-speaking in reference to your own that surprises me."

"You will not find it a scarce quality here, I assure you, saving among the Colonel Divers, and Jefferson Bricks, and Major Pawkinses—though the best of us are something like the man in Goldsmith's comedy, who wouldn't suffer anybody but himself to abuse his master. Come!"

he added, "let us talk of something else. You have come
here on some design of improving your fortune, I dare say;
and I should grieve to put you out of heart. I am some
years older than you, besides; and may, on a few trivial
points, advise you, perhaps."

There was not the least curiosity or impertinence in the
manner of this offer, which was open-hearted, unaffected,
and good-natured. As it was next to impossible that he
should not have his confidence awakened by a deportment
so prepossessing and kind, Martin plainly stated what had
brought him into those parts, and even made the very difficult avowal that he was poor. He did not say how poor,
it must be admitted, rather throwing off the declaration
with an air which might have implied that he had money
enough for six months, instead of as many weeks; but poor
he said he was, and grateful he said he would be, for any
counsel that his friend would give him.

It would not have been very difficult for any one to see;
but it was particularly easy for Martin, whose perceptions
were sharpened by his circumstances, to discern; that the
stranger's face grew infinitely longer as the domestic-archi-
tecture project was developed. Nor, although he made a
great effort to be as encouraging as possible, could he prevent his head from shaking once involuntarily, as if it said
in the vulgar tongue, upon its own account, "No go!"
But he spoke in a cheerful tone, and said, that although
there was no such opening as Martin wished in that city,
he would make it matter of immediate consideration and
enquiry where one was most likely to exist; and then he
made Martin acquainted with his name, which was Bevan;
and with his profession, which was physic, though he seldom or never practised; and with other circumstances connected with himself and family, which fully occupied the
time, until they reached the Rowdy Journal Office.

Mr. Tapley appeared to be taking his ease on the landing of the first floor; for sounds as of some gentleman
established in that region, whistling "Rule Britannia"
with all his might and main, greeted their ears before they
reached the house. On ascending to the spot from whence
this music proceeded, they found him recumbent in the
midst of a fortification of luggage, apparently performing
his national anthem for the gratification of a grey-haired
black man, who sat on one of the outworks (a portman-

teau), staring intently at Mark, while Mark, with his head reclining on his hand, returned the compliment in a thoughtful manner, and whistled all the time. He seemed to have recently dined, for his knife, a case-bottle, and certain broken meats in a handkerchief, lay near at hand. He had employed a portion of his leisure in the decoration of the Rowdy Journal door, whereon his own initials now appeared in letters nearly half a foot long, together with the day of the month in smaller type: the whole surrounded by an ornamental border, and looking very fresh and bold.

"I was a'most afraid you was lost, Sir!" cried Mark, rising, and stopping the tune at that point where Britons generally are supposed to declare (when it is whistled) that they never, never, never—

"Nothing gone wrong, I hope, Sir?"

"No, Mark. Where's your friend?"

"The mad woman, Sir?" said Mr. Tapley. "Oh! she's all right, Sir."

"Did she find her husband?"

"Yes, sir. Least ways she's found his remains," said Mark, correcting himself.

"The man's not dead, I hope?"

"Not altogether dead, Sir," returned Mark; "but he's had more fevers and agues than is quite reconcileable with being alive. When she didn't see him a waiting for her, I thought she'd have died herself, I did!"

"Was he not here, then?"

"*He* wasn't here. There was a feeble old shadow come a creeping down at last, as much like his substance when she know'd him, as your shadow when it's drawn out to its very finest and longest by the sun, is like you. But it was his remains, there's no doubt about that. She took on with joy, poor thing, as much as if it had been all of him!"

"Had he bought land?" asked Mr. Bevan.

"Ah! He'd bought land," said Mark, shaking his head, "and paid for it too. Every sort of nateral advantage was connected with it, the agents said; and there certainly was *one*, quite unlimited. No end to the water!"

"It's a thing he couldn't have done without, I suppose," observed Martin, peevishly.

"Certainly not, Sir. There it was, any way; always turned on, and no water-rate. Independent of three or four slimy old rivers close by, it varied on the farm four to

six foot deep in the dry season. He couldn't say how deep
it was in the rainy time, for he never had anything long
enough to sound it with."

"Is this true?" asked Martin of his companion.

"Extremely probable," he answered. "Some Mississippi or Missouri lot, I dare say."

"However," pursued Mark, "he came from I-don't-know-
where-and-all, down to New York here to meet his wife
and children; and they started off again in a steamboat this
blessed afternoon, as happy to be along with each other, as
if they was going to Heaven. I should think they was,
pretty straight, if I may judge fom the poor man's looks."

"And may I ask," said Martin, glancing, but not with
any displeasure, from Mark to the negro, "who this gentleman is? Another friend of yours?"

"Why, Sir," returned Mark, taking him aside, and
speaking confidentially in his ear, "he's a man of colour,
Sir."

"Do you take me for a blind man," asked Martin, somewhat impatiently, "that you think it necessary to tell me
that, when his face is the blackest that ever was seen?"

"No, no; when I say a man of colour," returned Mark,
"I mean that he's been one of them as there's picters of in
the shops. A man and a brother, you know, Sir," said
Mr. Tapley, favouring his master with a significant indica-
tion of the figure so often represented in tracts and cheap
prints.

"A slave!" cried Martin, in a whisper.

"Ah!" said Mark in the same tone. "Nothing else.
A slave. Why, when that there man was young—don't
look at him, while I'm a telling it—he was shot in the
leg; gashed in the arm; scored in his live limbs, like pork;
beaten out of shape; had his neck galled with an iron collar, and wore iron rings upon his wrists and ankles. The
marks are on him to this day. When I was having my
dinner just now, he stripped off his coat, and took away
my appetite."

"Is *this* true?" asked Martin of his friend, who stood
beside them.

"I have no reason to doubt it," he answered, looking
down, and shaking his head. "It very often is."

"Bless you," said Mark, "I know it is, from hearing
his whole story. That master died; so did his second mas·

ter from having his head cut open with a hatchet by another slave, who, when he'd done it, went and drowned
himself; then he got a better one: in years and years he
saved up a little money, and bought his freedom, which he
got pretty cheap at last, on account of his strength being
nearly gone, and he being ill. Then he come here. And
now he's a saving up to treat himself afore he dies to one
small purchase—it's nothing to speak of; only his own
daughter; that's all!" cried Mr. Tapley, becoming excited.
"Liberty for ever! Hurrah!"

"Hush!" cried Martin, clapping his hand upon his
mouth: "and don't be an idiot. What is he doing here?"

"Waiting to take our luggage off upon a truck," said
Mark. "He'd have come for it by-and-by, but I engaged
him for a very reasonable charge—out of my own pocket—
to sit along with me and make me jolly; and I *am* jolly;
and if I was rich enough to contract with him to wait upon
me once a day, to be looked at, I'd never be anything
else."

The fact may cause a solemn impeachment of Mark's
veracity, but it must be admitted nevertheless, that there
was that in his face and manner at the moment, which
militated strongly against this emphatic declaration of his
state of mind.

"Lord love you, Sir," he added, "they're so fond of
Liberty in this part of the globe, that they buy her and sell
her and carry her to market with 'em. They've such a
passion for Liberty, that they can't help taking liberties
with her. That's what it's owing to."

"Very well," said Martin, wishing to change the theme.
"Having come to that conclusion, Mark, perhaps you'll attend to me. The place to which the luggage is to go, is
printed on this card. Mrs. Pawkins's Boarding House."

"Mrs. Pawkins's boarding-house," repeated Mark
"Now, Cicero."

"Is that his name?" asked Martin.

"That's his name, Sir," rejoined Mark. And the negro
grinning assent from under a leathern portmanteau, than
which his own face was many shades deeper, hobbled down
stairs with his portion of their worldly goods: Mark Tapley having already gone before with his share.

Martin and his friend followed them to the door below,
and were about to pursue their walk, when the latter

stopped, and asked, with some hesitation, whether that young man was to be trusted.

"Mark! Oh certainly! with anything."

"You don't understand me,—I think he had better go with us. He is an honest fellow, and speaks his mind so very plainly."

"Why, the fact is," said Martin, smiling, "that being unaccustomed to a free republic, he is used to do so."

"I think he had better go with us," returned the other. "He may get into some trouble otherwise. This is not a slave State; but I am ashamed to say that the spirit of Tolerance is not so common anywhere in these latitudes as the form. We are not remarkable for behaving very temperately to each other when we differ: but to strangers! No, I really think he had better go with us."

Martin called to him immediately to be of their party; so Cicero and the truck went one way; and they three went another.

They walked about the city for two or three hours; seeing it from the best points of view, and pausing in the principal streets, and before such public buildings as Mr. Bevan pointed out. Night then coming on apace, Martin proposed that they should adjourn to Mrs. Pawkins's establishment for coffee; but in this he was overruled by his new acquaintance, who seemed to have set his heart on carrying him, though it were only for an hour, to the house of a friend of his who lived hard by. Feeling (however disinclined he was, being weary) that it would be in bad taste, and not very gracious, to object that he was unintroduced, when this open-hearted gentleman was so ready to be his sponsor, Martin—for once in his life, at all events—sacrificed his own will and pleasure to the wishes of another, and consented with a fair grace. So travelling had done him that much good, already.

Mr. Bevan knocked at the door of a very neat house of moderate size, from the parlour windows of which, lights were shining brightly into the now dark street. It was quickly opened by a man with such a thoroughly Irish face, that it seemed as if he ought, as a matter of right and principle, to be in rags, and could have no sort of business to be looking cheerfully at anybody out of a whole suit of clothes.

Commending Mark to the care of this phenomenon—for

such he may be said to have been in Martin's eyes—Mr. Bevan led the way into the room which had shed its cheerfulness upon the street, to whose occupants he introduced Mr. Chuzzlewit as a gentleman from England, whose acquaintance he had recently had the pleasure to make. They gave him welcome in all courtesy and politeness; and in less than five minutes' time he found himself sitting very much at his ease, by the fireside, and becoming vastly well acquainted with the whole family.

There were two young ladies—one eighteen; the other twenty—both very slender, but very pretty; their mother, who looked, as Martin thought, much older and more faded than she ought to have looked; and their grandmother, a little sharp-eyed, quick old woman, who seemed to have got past that stage, and to have come all right again. Besides these, there were the young ladies' father, and the young ladies' brother; the first engaged in mercantile affairs; the second, a student at college—both, in a certain cordiality of manner, like his own friend; and not unlike him in face, which was no great wonder, for it soon appeared that he was their near relation. Martin could not help tracing the family pedigree from the two young ladies, because they were foremost in his thoughts; not only from being, as aforesaid, very pretty, but by reason of their wearing miraculously small shoes, and the thinnest possible silk stockings : the which their rocking-chairs developed to a distracting extent.

There is no doubt that it was a monstrous comfortable circumstance to be sitting in a snug well-furnished room, warmed by a cheerful fire, and full of various pleasant decorations, including four small shoes, and the like amount of silk stockings, and——yes, why not?—the feet and legs therein enshrined. And there is no doubt that Martin was monstrous well-disposed to regard his position in that light, after his recent experience of the Screw, and of Mrs. Pawkins's boarding-house. The consequence was, that he made himself very agreeable indeed; and by the time the tea and coffee arrived (with sweet preserves, and cunning tea-cakes in its train), was in a highly genial state and much esteemed by the whole family.

Another delightful circumstance turned up before the first cup of tea was drunk. The whole family had been in England. There was a pleasant thing! But Martin was

not quite so glad of this, when he found that they knew
all the great dukes, lords, viscounts, marquesses, duchesses,
knights, and baronets, quite affectionately, and were beyond everything interested in the least particular concerning them.   However, when they asked after the wearer of
this or that coronet, and said "Was he quite well?" Martin
answered "Yes, oh yes.   Never better;" and when they
said "his Lordship's mother, the Duchess, was she much
changed?"   Martin said, "Oh dear no, they would know
her anywhere if they saw her to-morrow;" and so got on
pretty well.   In like manner when the young ladies ques-
tioned him touching the Gold Fish in that Grecian fountain in such and such a nobleman's conservatory, and
whether there were as many as there used to be, he gravely
reported, after mature consideration, that there must be at
least twice as many: and as to the exotics, "Oh! well! it
was of no use talking about *them*; they must be seen to be
believed;" which improved state of circumstances reminded
the family of the splendour of that brilliant festival (com-
prehending the whole British Peerage and Court Calendar)
to which they were specially invited, and which indeed had
been partly given in their honour; and recollections of
what Mr. Norris the father had said to the Marquess, and
of what Mrs. Norris the mother had said to the Marchioness, and of what the Marquess and Marchioness had both
said, when they said that upon their words and honours
they wished Mr. Norris the father and Mrs. Norris the
mother, and the Misses Norris the daughters, and Mr.
Norris Junior, the son, would only take up their permanent
residence in England, and give them the pleasure of
their everlasting friendship, occupied a very considerable
time.
    Martin thought it rather strange, and in some sort incon-
sistent, that during the whole of these narrations, and in the
very meridian of their enjoyment thereof, both Mr. Norris
the father, and Mr. Norris Junior, the son (who corre-
sponded, every post, with four members of the English
Peerage), enlarged upon the inestimable advantage of having no such arbitrary distinctions in that enlightened land,
where there were no noblemen but nature's noblemen, and
all society was based on one broad level of brotherly love
and natural equality.   Indeed Mr. Norris the father gradually expanding into an oration on this swelling theme was

becoming tedious, when Mr. Bevan diverted his thoughts, by happening to make some casual inquiry relative to the occupier of the next house; in reply to which, this same Mr. Norris the father observed, that "that person entertained religious opinions of which he couldn't approve; and therefore he hadn't the honour of knowing the gentleman." Mrs. Norris the mother added another reason of her own, the same in effect, but varying in words; to wit, that she believed the people were well enough in their way, but they were not genteel.

Another little trait came out, which impressed itself on Martin forcibly. Mr. Bevan told them about Mark and the negro, and then it appeared that all the Norrises were abolitionists. It was a great relief to hear this, and Martin was so much encouraged on finding himself in such company, that he expressed his sympathy with the oppressed and wretched blacks. Now, one of the young ladies—the prettiest and most delicate one—was mightily amused at the earnestness with which he spoke; and on his craving leave to ask her why, was quite unable for a time to speak for laughing. As soon however as she could, she told him that the negroes were such a funny people; so excessively ludicrous in their manners and appearance; that it was wholly impossible for those who knew them well, to associate any serious ideas with such a very absurd part of the creation. Mr. Norris the father, and Mrs. Norris the mother, and Miss Norris the sister, and Mr. Norris Junior the brother, and even Mrs. Norris Senior the grandmother, were all of this opinion, and laid it down as an absolute matter of fact—as if there were nothing in suffering and slavery grim enough to cast a solemn air on any human animal; though it were as ridiculous, physically, as the most grotesque of apes, or, morally, as the mildest Nimrod among tuft-hunting republicans!

"In short," said Mr. Norris the father, settling the question comfortably, "there is a natural antipathy between the races."

"Extending," said Martin's friend, in a low voice, "to the cruellest of tortures, and the bargain and sale of unborn generations."

Mr. Norris the son said nothing, but he made a wry face, and dusted his fingers as Hamlet might after getting rid of Yorick's skull: just as though he had that moment touched a negro, and some of the black had come off upon his hands.

In order that their talk might fall again into its former pleasant channel, Martin dropped the subject, with a shrewd suspicion that it would be a dangerous theme to revive under the best of circumstances: and again addressed himself to the young ladies, who were very gorgeously attired in very beautiful colours, and had every article of dress on the same extensive scale as the little shoes and the thin silk stockings. This suggested to him that they were great proficients in the French fashions, which soon turned out to be the case, for though their information appeared to be none of the newest, it was very extensive: and the eldest sister in particular, who was distinguished by a talent for metaphysics, the laws of hydraulic pressure, and the rights of human kind, had a novel way of combining these acquirements and bringing them to bear on any subject from Millinery to the Millennium, both inclusive: which was at once improving and remarkable,—so much so, in short, that it was usually observed to reduce foreigners to a state of temporary insanity in five minutes.

Martin felt his reason going; and as a means of saving himself, besought the other sister (seeing a piano in the room) to sing. With this request she willingly complied; and a bravura concert, solely sustained by the Misses Norris, presently began. They sang in all languages except their own. German, French, Italian, Spanish, Portuguese, Swiss; but nothing native; nothing so low as native. For in this respect languages are like many other travellers—ordinary and commonplace enough at home, but 'specially genteel abroad.

There is little doubt that in course of time the Misses Norris would have come to Hebrew, if they had not been interrupted by an announcement from the Irishman, who flinging open the door, cried in a loud voice:

"Jiniral Fladdock!"

"My!" cried the sisters, desisting suddenly. "The general come back!"

As they made the exclamation, the general, attired in full uniform for a ball, came darting in with such precipitancy that, hitching his boot in the carpet, and getting his sword between his legs, he came down headlong, and presented a curious little bald place on the crown of his head to the eyes of the astonished company. Nor was this the worst of it; for being rather corpulent and very tight, the general, being down, could not get up again, but lay there, writhing and doing such things with his boots, as there is no other instance of in military history.

Of course there was an immediate rush to his assistance; and the general was promptly raised. But his uniform was so fearfully and wonderfully made that he came up stiff and without a bend in him, like a dead clown, and had no command whatever of himself until he was put quite flat upon the soles of his feet, when he became animated as by a miracle, and moving edgewise that he might go in a narrower compass and be in less danger of fraying the gold lace on his epaulettes by brushing them against anything, advanced with a smiling visage to salute the lady of the house.

To be sure, it would have been impossible for the family to testify purer delight and joy than at this unlooked-for appearance of General Fladdock! The general was as warmly received as if New York had been in a state of siege and no other general was to be got, for love or money. He shook hands with the Norrises three times all round, and then reviewed them from a little distance as a brave commander might, with his ample cloak drawn forward over the right shoulder and thrown back upon the left side to reveal his manly breast.

"And do I then," cried the general, "once again behold the choicest spirits of my country!"

"Yes," said Mr. Norris the father. "Here we are, general."

Then all the Norrises pressed round the general, inquiring how and where he had been since the date of his last letter, and how he had enjoyed himself in foreign parts, and, particularly and above all, to what extent he had become acquainted with the great dukes, lords, viscounts, marquesses, duchesses, knights, and baronets, in whom the people of those benighted countries had delight.

"Well then, don't ask me," said the general, holding up his hand. "I was among 'em all the time, and have got public journals in my trunk with my name printed"—he lowered his voice and was very impressive here—"among the fashionable news. But, oh the ⁀onventionalities of that a-mazing Europe!"

"Ah!" cried Mr. Norris the father, giving his head a
melancholy shake, and looking towards Martin as though
he would say, "I can't deny it, Sir. I would if I
could."

"The limited diffusion of a moral sense in that country!"
exclaimed the general. "The absence of a moral dignity
in man!"

"Ah!" sighed all the Norrises, quite overwhelmed with
despondency.

"I couldn't have realised it," pursued the general,
"without being located on the spot. Norris, your imagination is the imagination of a strong man, but *you* couldn't
have realised it, without being located on the spot!"

"Never," said Mr. Norris.

"The ex-clusiveness, the pride, the form, the ceremony,"
exclaimed the general, emphasizing the article more vigor-
orsly at every repetition. "The artificial barriers set up
between man and man; the division of the human race into
court cards and plain cards, of every denomination, into
clubs, diamonds, spades—anything but hearts!"

"Ah!" cried the whole family. "Too true, general!"

"But stay!" cried Mr. Norris the father, taking him by
the arm. "Surely you crossed in the Screw, general?"

"Well! so I did," was the reply.

"Possible!" cried the young ladies. "Only think!"

The general seemed at a loss to understand why his having come home in the Screw should occasion such a sensation,
nor did he seem at all clearer on the subject when Mr.
Norris, introducing him to Martin, said—

"A fellow-passenger of yours, I think?"

"Of mine!" exclaimed the general; "No!"

He had never seen Martin, but Martin had seen him, and
recognised him, now that they stood face to face, as the
gentleman who had stuck his hands in his pockets towards
the end of the voyage, and walked the deck with his nostrils dilated.

Everybody looked at Martin. There was no help for it.
The truth must out.

"I came over in the same ship as the general," said Martin, "but not in the same cabin. It being necessary for me
to observe strict economy, I took my passage in the steerage."

If the general had been carried up bodily to a loaded

cannon, and required to let it off that moment, he could not have been in a state of greater consternation than when he heard these words. He, Fladdock,—Fladdock in full militia uniform, Fladdock the General, Fladdock the caressed of foreign noblemen,—expected to know a fellow who had come over in the steerage of a line-of-packet ship, at the cost of four pound ten! And meeting that fellow in the very sanctuary of New York fashion, and nestling in the bosom of the New York aristocracy! He almost laid his hand upon his sword.

A death-like stillness fell upon the Norrises. If this story should get wind, their country relation had, by his imprudence, for ever disgraced them. They were the bright particular stars of an exalted New York sphere. There were other fashionable spheres above them, and other fashionable spheres below, and none of the stars in any one of these spheres had anything to say to the stars in any other of these spheres. But, through all the spheres it would go forth, that the Norrises, deceived by gentlemanly manners and appearances, had, falling from their high estate, "received" a dollarless and unknown man. O guardian eagle of the pure Republic, had they lived for this!

"You will allow me," said Martin, after a terrible silence, "to take my leave. I feel that I am the cause of at least as much embarrassment here, as I have brought upon myself. But I am bound, before I go, to exonerate this gentleman, who, in introducing me to such society, was quite ignorant of my unworthiness, I assure you."

With that he made his bow to the Norrises, and walked out like a man of snow, very cool externally, but pretty hot within.

"Come, come," said Mr. Norris the father, looking with a pale face on the assembled circle as Martin closed the door, "the young man has this night beheld a refinement of social manner, and an easy magnificence of social decoration, to which he is a stranger in his own country. Let us hope it may awake a moral sense within him."

If that peculiarly transatlantic article, a moral sense,—for if native statesmen, orators, and pamphleteers, are to be believed, America quite monopolizes the commodity,—if that peculiarly transatlantic article be supposed to include a benevolent love of all mankind, certainly Martin's would have borne just then a deal of waking: for as he strode along the street, with Mark at his heels, his immoral sense was in active operation; prompting him to the utterance of some rather sanguinary remarks, which it was well for his own credit that nobody overheard. He had so far cooled down however, that he had begun to laugh at the recollection of these incidents, when he heard another step behind him, and turning round encountered his friend Bevan, quite out of breath.

He drew his arm through Martin's, and entreating him to walk slowly, was silent for some minutes. At length he said:

" I hope you exonerate me in another sense? "

" How do you mean? " asked Martin.

" I hope you acquit me of intending or foreseeing the termination of our visit. But I scarcely need ask you that."

" Scarcely indeed," said Martin. " I am the more beholden to you for your kindness, when I find what kind of stuff the good citizens here are made of."

" I reckon," his friend returned, " that they are made of pretty much the same stuff as other folks, if they would but own it, and not set up on false pretences."

" In good faith, that's true," said Martin.

" I dare say," resumed his friend, " you might have such a scene as that in an English comedy, and not detect any gross improbability or anomaly in the matter of it? "

" Yes indeed! "

" Doubtless it is more ridiculous here than anywhere else," said his companion; " but our professions are to blame for that. So far as I myself am concerned, I may add that I was perfectly aware from the first that you came over in the steerage, for I had seen the list of passengers, and knew it did not comprise your name."

" I feel more obliged to you than before," said Martin.

" Norris is a very good fellow in his way," observed Mr. Bevan.

" Is he? " said Martin drily.

" Oh yes! there are a hundred good points about him. If you or anybody else addressed him as another order of being, and sued to him *in formâ pauperis*, he would be all kindness and consideration."

" I needn't have travelled three thousand miles from

home to find such a character as *that*," said Martin. Neither he nor his friend said anything more on the way back; each appearing to find sufficient occupation in his own thoughts.

The tea, or the supper, or whatever else they called the evening meal, was over when they reached the Major's; but the cloth, ornamented with a few additional smears and stains, was still upon the table. At one end of the board Mrs. Jefferson Brick 'and two other ladies were drinking tea—out of the ordinary course, evidently, for they were bonneted and shawled, and seemed to have just come home. By the light of three flaring candles of different lengths, in as many candlesticks of different patterns, the room showed to almost as little advantage as in broad day.

These ladies were all three talking together in a very loud tone when Martin and his friend entered; but, seeing those gentlemen, they stopped directly, and became excessively genteel, not to say frosty. As they went on to exchange some few remarks in whispers, the very water in the tea-pot might have fallen twenty degrees in temperature beneath their chilling coldness.

"Have you been to meeting, Mrs. Brick?" asked Martin's friend, with something of a roguish twinkle in his eye.

"To lecture, Sir."

"I beg your pardon. I forgot. You don't go to meeting, I think?"

Here the lady on the right of Mrs. Brick gave a pious cough, as much as to say "*I* do!"—As, indeed, she did, nearly every night in the week.

"A good discourse, ma'am?" asked Mr. Bevan, addressing this lady.

The lady raised her eyes in a pious manner, and answered "Yes." She had been much comforted by some good, strong, peppery doctrine, which satisfactorily disposed of all her friends and acquaintances, and quite settled *their* business. Her bonnet, too, had far outshone every bonnet in the congregation: so she was tranquil on all accounts.

"What course of lectures are you attending now, ma'am?" said Martin's friend, turning again to Mrs. Brick.

"The Philosophy of the Soul—on Wednesdays."

"On Mondays?"

20

"The Philosophy of Crime."

"On Fridays?"

"The Philosophy of Vegetables."

"You have forgotten Thursdays—the Philosophy of Government, my dear," observed the third lady.

"No," said Mrs. Brick. "That's Tuesdays."

"So it is!" cried the lady. "The Philosophy of Matter on Thursdays, of course."

"You see, Mr. Chuzzlewit, our ladies are fully employed," said Bevan.

"Indeed you have reason to say so," answered Martin. "Between these very grave pursuits abroad, and family duties at home, their time must be pretty well engrossed."

Martin stopped here, for he saw that the ladies regarded him with no very great favour, though what he had done to deserve the disdainful expression which appeared in their faces he was at a loss to divine. But on their going up stairs to their bed-rooms—which they very soon did —Mr. Bevan informed him that domestic drudgery was far beneath the exalted range of these Philosophers, and that the chances were a hundred to one that neither of the three could perform the easiest woman's work for herself, or make the simplest article of dress for any of her children.

"Though whether they might not be better employed with even such blunt instruments as knitting-needles, than with these edge-tools," he said, "is another question; but I can answer for one thing—they don't often cut themselves. Devotions and lectures are our balls and concerts. They go to these places of resort, as an escape from monotony; look at each other's clothes; and come home again."

"When you say ' home,' do you mean a house like this?"

"Very often. But I see you are tired to death, and will wish you good night. We will discuss your projects in the morning. You cannot but feel already that it is useless staying here, with any hope of advancing them. You will have to go farther."

"And to fare worse?" said Martin, pursuing the old adage.

"Well, I hope not. But sufficient for the day, you know —Good night!"

They shook hands heartily, and separated. As soon as Martin was left alone, the excitement of novelty and change which had sustained him through all the fatigues of the day, departed; and he felt so thoroughly dejected and worn out, that he even lacked the energy to crawl up stairs to bed.

In twelve or fifteen hours, how great a change had fallen on his hopes and sanguine plans! New and strange as he was to the ground on which he stood, and to the air he breathed, he could not—recalling all that he had crowded into that one day—but entertain a strong misgiving that his enterprise was doomed. Rash and ill-considered as it had often looked on shipboard, but had never seemed on shore, it wore a dismal aspect now that frightened him. Whatever thoughts he called up to his aid, they came upon him in depressing and discouraging shapes, and gave him no relief. Even the diamonds on his finger sparkled with the brightness of tears, and had no ray of hope in all their brilliant lustre.

He continued to sit in gloomy rumination by the stove —unmindful of the boarders who dropped in one by one from their stores and counting-houses, or the neighbouring bar-rooms, and after taking long pulls from a great white water-jug upon the sideboard, and lingering with a kind of hideous fascination near the brass spittoons, lounged heavily to bed—until at length Mark Tapley came and shook him by the arm, supposing him asleep.

"Mark!" he cried, starting.

"All right, Sir," said that cheerful follower, snuffing with his fingers the candle he bore. "It ain't a very large bed, your'n, Sir; and a man as wasn't thirsty might drink, before breakfast, all the water you've got to wash in, and afterwards eat the towel. But you'll sleep without rocking to-night, Sir."

"I feel as if the house were on the sea," said Martin, staggering when he rose; "and am utterly wretched."

"I'm as jolly as a sandboy, myself, Sir," said Mark. "But, Lord, I have reason to be! I ought to have been born here; that's my opinion. Take care how you go"— for they were now ascending the stairs. "You recollect the gentleman aboard the Screw as had the very small trunk, Sir?"

"The valise? Yes."

"Well, Sir, there's been a delivery of clean clothes from the wash to-night, and they're put outside the bed-room doors here. If you take notice as we go up, what a very

few shirts there are, and what a many fronts, you'll pene-
trate the mystery of his packing."

But Martin was too weary and despondent to take heed
of anything, so had no interest in this discovery. Mr.
Tapley, nothing dashed by his indifference, conducted him
to the top of the house, and into the bed-chamber prepared
for his reception: which was a very little narrow room,
with half a window in it; a bedstead like a chest without a
lid; two chairs; a piece of carpet, such as shoes are commonly tried upon at a ready-made establishment in England; a little looking-glass nailed against the wall; and a
washing-table, with a jug and ewer, that might have been
mistaken for a milk-pot and slop-basin.

"I suppose they polish themselves with a dry cloth in
this country," said Mark. "They've certainly got a touch
of the 'phoby, Sir."

"I wish you would pull off my boots for me," said Martin, dropping into one of the chairs. "I am quite knocked
up—dead beat, Mark."

"You won't say that to-morrow morning, Sir," returned
Mr. Tapley; "nor even to-night, Sir, when you've made a
trial of this." With which he produced a very large tumbler, piled up to the brim with little blocks of clear transparent ice, through which one or two thin slices of lemon,
and a golden liquid of delicious appearance, appealed
from the still depths below, to the loving eye of the spectator.

"What do you call this?" said Martin.

But Mr. Tapley made no answer: merely plunging a reed
into the mixture—which caused a pleasant commotion
among the pieces of ice—and signifying by an expressive
gesture that it was to be pumped up through that agency
by the enraptured drinker.

Martin took the glass, with an astonished look; applied
his lips to the reed; and cast up his eyes once in ecstasy.
He paused no more until the goblet was drained to the last
drop.

"There, Sir!" said Mark, taking it from him with a triumphant face; "If ever you should happen to be dead beat
again, when I ain't in the way, all you've got to do is, to
ask the nearest man to go and fetch a cobbler."

"To go and fetch a cobbler!" repeated Martin.

"This wonderful invention, Sir," said Mark, tenderly

patting the empty glass, "is called a cobbler. Sherry cobbler when you name it long; cobbler, when you name it short. Now you're equal to having your boots took off, and are, in every particular worth mentioning, another man."

Having delivered himself of this solemn preface, he brought the boot-jack.

"Mind! I am not going to relapse, Mark," said Martin; "but, good Heaven, if we should be left in some wild part of this country without goods or money!"

"Well, Sir!" replied the imperturbable Tapley; "from what we've seen already, I don't know whether, under those circumstances, we shouldn't do better in the wild parts than in the tame ones."

"Oh, Tom Pinch, Tom Pinch!" said Martin, in a thoughtful tone; "what would I give to be again beside you, and able to hear your voice, though it were even in the old bed-room at Pecksniff's!"

"Oh, Dragon, Dragon!" echoed Mark, cheerfully, "if there warn't any water between you and me, and nothing faint-hearted-like in going back, I don't know that I mightn't say the same. But here am I, Dragon, in New York, America; and there are you in Wiltshire, Europe; and there's a fortune to make, Dragon, and a beautiful young lady to make it for; and whenever you go to see the Monument, Dragon, you mustn't give in on the doorsteps, or you'll never get up to the top!"

"Wisely said, Mark," cried Martin. "We must look forward."

"In all the story-books as ever I read, Sir, the people as looked backward was turned into stones," replied Mark; "and my opinion always was, that they brought it on themselves, and it served 'em right. I wish you good night, Sir, and pleasant dreams!"

"They must be of home, then," said Martin, as he lay down in bed.

"So I say, too," whispered Mark Tapley, when he was out of hearing and in his own room; "for if there don't come a time afore we're well out of this, when there'll be a little more credit in keeping up one's jollity, I'm a United Statesman!"

Leaving them to blend and mingle in their sleep the shadows of objects afar off, as they take fantastic shapes

upon the wall in the dim light of thought without control,
be it the part of this slight chronicle—a dream within a
dream—as rapidly to change the scene, and cross the ocean
to the English shore.

CHAPTER XVIII.

DOES BUSINESS WITH THE HOUSE OF ANTHONY CHUZ-ZLEWIT AND SON, FROM WHICH ONE OF THE PARTNERS RETIRES UNEXPECTEDLY.

CHANGE begets change. Nothing propagates so fast.
If a man habituated to a narrow circle of cares and pleasures,
out of which he seldom travels, step beyond it, though for
never so brief a space, his departure from the monotonous
scene on which he has been an actor of importance, would
seem to be the signal for instant confusion. As if, in the
gap he had left, the wedge of change were driven to the
head, rending what was a solid mass to fragments; things
cemented and held together by the usages of years, burst
asunder in as many weeks. The mine which Time has
slowly dug beneath familiar objects, is sprung in an instant;
and what was rock before, becomes but sand and dust.

Most men at one time or other have proved this in some
degree. The extent to which the natural laws of change
asserted their supremacy in that limited sphere of action
which Martin had deserted, shall be faithfully set down in
these pages.

"What a cold spring it is!" whimpered old Anthony,
drawing near the evening fire. "It was a warmer season,
sure, when I was young!"

"You needn't go scorching your clothes into holes,
whether it was or not," observed the amiable Jonas, raising
his eyes from yesterday's newspaper. "Broadcloth ain't so
cheap as that comes to."

"A good lad!" cried the father, breathing on his cold
hands, and feebly chafing them against each other. "A
prudent lad! He never delivered himself up to the vani-
ties of dress. No, no!"

"I don't know but I would though, mind you, if I could
do it for nothing," said his son, as he resumed the paper.

"Ah!" chuckled the old man. "*If,* indeed!—But it's very cold."

"Let the fire be!" cried Mr. Jonas, stopping his honoured parent's hand in the use of the poker. "Do you mean to come to want in your old age, that you take to wasting now?"

"There's not time for that, Jonas," said the old man.

"Not time for what?" bawled his heir.

"For me to come to want. I wish there was!"

"You always were as selfish an old blade as need be," said Jonas, in a voice too low for him to hear, and looking at him with an angry frown. "You act up to your character. You wouldn't mind coming to want, wouldn't you? I dare say you wouldn't. And your own flesh and blood might come to want too, might they, for anything you cared? Oh you precious old flint!"

After this dutiful address, he took his tea-cup in his hand—for that meal was in progress, and the father and son and Chuffey were partakers of it. Then, looking steadfastly at his father, and stopping now and then to carry a spoonful of tea to his lips, he proceeded in the same tone, thus:

"Want, indeed! You're a nice old man to be talking of want at this time of day. Beginning to talk of want, are you? Well, I declare! There isn't time? No, I should hope not. But you'd live to be a couple of hundred if you could; and after all be discontented. *I* know you!"

The old man sighed, and still sat cowering before the fire. Mr. Jonas shook his Britannia-metal teaspoon at him, and taking a loftier position went on to argue the point on high moral grounds.

"If you're in such a state of mind as that," he grumbled, but in the same subdued key, "why don't you make over your property? Buy an annuity cheap, and make your life interesting to yourself and everybody else that watches the speculation. But no, that wouldn't suit *you.* That would be natural conduct to your own son, and you like to be unnatural, and to keep him out of his rights. Why, I should be ashamed of myself if I was you, and glad to hide my head in the what you may call it."

Possibly this general phrase supplied the place of grave, or tomb, or sepulchre, or cemetery, or mausoleum, or other such word which the filial tenderness of Mr. Jonas made

him delicate of pronouncing. He pursued the theme no
further; for Chuffey, somehow discovering, from his old
corner by the fireside, that Anthony was in the attitude of
a listener, and that Jonas appeared to be speaking, suddenly cried out, like one inspired:

"He is your own son, Mr. Chuzzlewit. Your own son,
Sir!"

Old Chuffey little suspected what depth of application
these words had, or that, in the bitter satire which they
bore, they might have sunk into the old man's very soul,
could he have known what words were hanging on his own
son's lips, or what was passing in his thoughts. But the
voice diverted the current of Anthony's reflections, and
roused him.

"Yes, yes, Chuffey, Jonas is a chip of the old block.
It's a very old block now, Chuffey," said the old man, with
a strange look of discomposure.

"Precious old," assented Jonas.

"No, no, no," said Chuffey. "No, Mr. Chuzzlewit. Not
old at all, Sir."

"Oh! He's worse than ever, you know!" cried Jonas,
quite disgusted. "Upon my soul, father, he's getting too
bad. Hold your tongue, will you?"

"He says you're wrong!" cried Anthony to the old clerk.

"Tut, tut!" was Chuffey's answer. "I know better. I
say *he's* wrong. I say *he's* wrong. He's a boy. That's
what he is. So are you, Mr. Chuzzlewit—a kind of boy.
Ha! ha! ha! You're quite a boy to many I have known;
you're a boy to me; you're a boy to hundreds of us. Don't
mind him!"

With which extraordinary speech—for in the case of
Chuffey this was a burst of eloquence without a parallel—
the poor old shadow drew through his palsied arm his master's hand, and held it there, with his own folded upon it,
as if he would defend him.

"I grow deafer every day, Chuff," said Anthony, with as
much softness of manner, or, to describe it more correctly,
with as little hardness as he was capable of expressing.

"No, no," cried Chuffey. "No you don't. What if you
did? I've been deaf this twenty year."

"I grow blinder, too," said the old man, shaking his head.

"That's a good sign!" cried Chuffey. "Ha! ha! The
best sign in the world! You saw too well before."

He patted Anthony upon the hand as one might comfort a child, and drawing the old man's arm still further through his own, shook his trembling fingers towards the spot where Jonas sat, as though he would wave him off. But Anthony remaining quite still and silent, he relaxed his hold by slow degrees and lapsed into his usual niche in the corner; merely putting forth his hand at intervals and touching his old employer gently on the coat, as with the design of assuring himself that he was yet beside him.

Mr. Jonas was so very much amazed by these proceedings that he could do nothing but stare at the two old men, until Chuffey had fallen into his usual state, and Anthony had sunk into a doze; when he gave some vent to his emotions by going close up to the former personage, and making as though he would, in vulgar parlance, "punch his head."

"They've been carrying on this game," thought Jonas in a brown study, "for the last two or three weeks. I never saw my father take so much notice of him as he has in that time. What! You're legacy hunting are you, Mister Chuff? Eh?"

But Chuffey was as little conscious of the thought as of the bodily advance of Mr. Jonas's clenched fist, which hovered fondly about his ear. When he had scowled at him to his heart's content, Jonas took the candle from the table, and walking into the glass office, produced a bunch of keys from his pocket. With one of these he opened a secret drawer in the desk: peeping stealthily out, as he did so, to be certain that the two old men were still before the fire.

"All as right as ever," said Jonas, propping the lid of the desk open with his forehead, and unfolding a paper. "Here's the will, Mister Chuff. Thirty pound a year for your maintenance, old boy, and all the rest to his only son, Jonas. You needn't trouble yourself to be too affectionate. You won't get anything by it. What's that?"

It *was* startling, certainly. A face on the other side of the glass partition looking curiously in: and not at him but at the paper in his hand. For the eyes were attentively cast down upon the writing, and were swiftly raised when he cried out. Then they met his own, and were as the eyes of Mr. Pecksniff.

Suffering the lid of the desk to fall with a loud noise,

but not forgetting even then to lock it, Jonas, pale and breathless, gazed upon this phantom. It moved, opened the door, and walked in.

"What's the matter?" cried Jonas, falling back. "Who is it? Where do you come from? What do you want?"

"Matter!" cried the voice of Mr. Pecksniff, as Pecksniff in the flesh smiled amiably upon him. "The matter, Mr. Jonas!"

"What are you prying and peering about here for?" said Jonas, angrily. "What do you mean by coming up to town in this way, and taking one unawares? It's precious odd a man can't read the—the newspaper in his own office without being startled out of his wits by people coming in without notice. Why didn't you knock at the door?"

"So I did, Mr. Jonas," answered Pecksniff, "but no one heard me. I was curious," he added in his gentle way as he laid his hand upon the young man's shoulder, "to find out what part of the newspaper interested you so much; but the glass was too dim and dirty."

Jonas glanced in haste at the partition. Well. It wasn't very clean. So far he spoke the truth.

"Was it poetry now?" said Mr. Pecksniff, shaking the forefinger of his right hand with an air of cheerful banter. "Or was it politics? Or was it the price of stocks? The main chance, Mr. Jonas, the main chance, I suspect."

"You ain't far from the truth," answered Jonas, recovering himself and snuffing the candle: "but how the deuce do you come to be in London again? Ecod! it's enough to make a man stare, to see a fellow looking at him all of a sudden, who he thought was sixty or seventy miles away."

"So it is," said Mr. Pecksniff. "No doubt of it, my dear Mr. Jonas. For while the human mind is constituted as it is—"

"O bother the human mind," interrupted Jonas with impatience, "what have you come up for?"

"A little matter of business," said Mr. Pecksniff, "which has arisen quite unexpectedly."

"Oh!" cried Jonas, "is that all? Well! Here's father in the next room. Hallo father, here's Pecksniff! He gets more addle-pated every day he lives, I do believe," muttered Jonas, shaking his honoured parent roundly. "Don't I tell you Pecksniff's here, stupid head?"

The combined effects of the shaking and this loving re-

monstrance soon awoke the old man, who gave Mr. Pecksniff a chuckling welcome, which was attributable in part
to his being glad to see that gentleman, and in part to his
unfading delight in the recollection of having called him a
hypocrite. As Mr. Pecksniff had not yet taken tea (indeed he had but an hour before arrived in London) the remains of the late collation, with a rasher of bacon, were
served up for his entertainment; and as Mr. Jonas had a
business appointment in the next street, he stepped out to
keep it: promising to return before Mr. Pecksniff could
finish his repast.

"And now, my good Sir," said Mr. Pecksniff to Anthony: "now that we are alone, pray tell me what I can do
for you. I say alone, because I believe that our dear friend
Mr. Chuffey is, metaphysically speaking, a—shall I say a
dummy?" asked Mr. Pecksniff with his sweetest smile,
and his head very much on one side.

"He neither hears us," replied Anthony, "nor sees us."

"Why then," said Mr. Pecksniff, "I will be bold to say,
with the utmost sympathy for his afflictions, and the greatest admiration of those excellent qualities which do equal
honour to his head and to his heart, that he *is* what is
playfully termed a dummy. You were going to observe,
my dear Sir—"

"I was not going to make any observation that I know
of," replied the old man.

"*I* was," said Mr. Pecksniff, mildly.

"Oh! *you* were? What was it?"

"That I never," said Mr. Pecksniff, previously rising to
see that the door was shut, and arranging his chair when
he came back, so that it could not be opened in the least
without his immediately becoming aware of the circumstance: "that I never in my life was so astonished as by
the receipt of your letter yesterday. That you should do
me the honour to wish to take counsel with me on any matter, amazed me; but that you should desire to do so to the
exclusion even of Mr. Jonas, showed an amount of confidence in one to whom you had done a verbal injury—merely
a verbal injury you were anxious to repair—which gratified,
which moved, which overcame me."

He was always a glib speaker, but he delivered this
short address very glibly; having been at some pains to
compose it outside the coach.

Although he paused for a reply, and truly said that he
was there at Anthony's request, the old man sat gazing
at him in profound silence and with a perfectly blank face.
Nor did he seem to have the least desire or impulse to
pursue the -conversation, though Mr. Pecksniff looked
towards the door, and pulled out his watch, and gave him
many other hints that their time was short, and Jonas, if
he kept his word, would soon return. But the strangest
incident in all this strange behaviour was, that of a sudden
—in a moment—so swiftly that it was impossible to trace
how, or to observe any process of change—his features fell
into their old expression, and he cried, striking his hand
passionately upon the table as if no interval at all had
taken place:

"Will you hold your tongue, Sir, and let me speak?"

Mr. Pecksniff deferred to him with a submissive bow;
and said within himself, "I knew his hand was changed,
and that his writing staggered. I said so yesterday.
Ahem! Dear me!"

"Jonas is sweet upon your daughter, Pecksniff," said
the old man, in his usual tone.

"We spoke of that, if you remember, Sir, at Mrs. Todgers's," replied the courteous architect.

"You needn't speak so loud," retorted Anthony. "I'm
not so deaf as that."

Mr. Pecksniff had certainly raised his voice pretty high:
not so much because he thought Anthony was deaf, as because he felt convinced that his perceptive faculties were
waxing dim: but this quick resentment of his considerate
behaviour greatly disconcerted him, and, not knowing
what tack to shape his course upon, he made another inclination of the head, yet more submissive than the
last.

"I have said," repeated the old man, "that Jonas is
sweet upon your daughter."

"A charming girl, Sir," murmured Mr. Pecksniff, seeing
that he waited for an answer. "A dear girl, Mr. Chuzzlewit, though I say it who should not."

"You know better," cried the old man, advancing his
weazen face at least a yard, and starting forward in his
chair to do it. "You lie! What, you *will* be a hypocrite,
will you?"

"My good Sir," Mr. Pecksniff began.

"Don't call me a good Sir," retorted Anthony, "and don't claim to be one yourself. If your daughter was what you would have me believe, she wouldn't do for Jonas. Being what she is, I think she will. He might be deceived in a wife. She might run riot, contract debts, and waste his substance. Now when I am dead—"

His face altered so horribly as he said the word, that Mr. Pecksniff really was fain to look another way.

"It will be worse for me to know of such doings, than if I was alive: for to be tormented for getting that together, which even while I suffer for its acquisition is flung into the very kennels of the streets, would be insupportable torture. No," said the old man, hoarsely, "let that be saved at least, let there be something gained, and kept fast hold of, when so much is lost."

"My dear Mr. Chuzzlewit," said Pecksniff, "these are unwholesome fancies; quite unnecessary, Sir, quite uncalled for, I am sure. The truth is, my dear Sir, that you are not well!"

"Not dying though!" cried Anthony, with something like the snarl of a wild animal. "Not yet! There are years of life in me. Why, look at him," pointing to his feeble clerk. "Death has no right to leave him standing, and to mow me down."

Mr. Pecksniff was so much afraid of the old man, and so completely taken aback by the state in which he found him, that he had not even presence of mind enough to call up a scrap of morality from the great storehouse within his own breast. Therefore he stammered out that no doubt it was, in fairness and decency, Mr. Chuffey's turn to expire; and that from all he had heard of Mr. Chuffey, and the little he had the pleasure of knowing of that gentleman, personally, he felt convinced in his own mind that he would see the propriety of expiring with as little delay as possible.

"Come here!" said the old man, beckoning him to draw nearer. "Jonas will be my heir, Jonas will be rich, and a great catch for you. You know that. Jonas is sweet upon your daughter."

"I know that too," thought Mr. Pecksniff, "for you have said it often enough."

"He might get more money than with her," said the old man, "but she will help him to take care of what they have. She is not too young or heedless, and comes of a

good hard griping stock. But don't you play too fine a
game. She only holds him by a thread; and if you draw
it too tight (I know his temper) it'll snap. Bind him when
he's in the mood, Pecksniff; bind him. You're too deep.
In your way of leading him on, you'll leave him miles behind. Bah, you man of oil, have I no eyes to see how you
have angled with him from the first? "

"Now I wonder," thought Mr. Pecksniff, looking at him
with a wistful face, "whether this is all he has to say!"

Old Anthony rubbed his hands and muttered to himself;
complained again that he was cold; drew his chair before
the fire; and, sitting with his back to Mr. Pecksniff, and
his chin sunk down upon his breast, was, in another minute, quite regardless or forgetful of his presence.

Uncouth and unsatisfactory as this short interview had
been, it had furnished Mr. Pecksniff with a hint which,
supposing nothing further were imparted to him, repaid
the journey up, and home again. For the good gentleman
had never (for want of an opportunity) dived into the
depths of Mr. Jonas's nature; and any recipe for catching
such a son-in-law (much more, one written on a leaf out of
his own father's book) was worth the having. In order
that he might lose no chance of improving so fair an opportunity by allowing Anthony to fall asleep before he had
finished all he had to say, Mr. Pecksniff, in the disposal of
the refreshments on the table—a work to which he now applied himself in earnest—resorted to many ingenious con-
trivances for attracting his attention, such as coughing,
sneezing, clattering the tea-cups, sharpening the knives,
dropping the loaf, and so forth. But all in vain, for Mr.
Jonas returned, and Anthony had said no more.

"What! My father asleep again?" he cried, as he hung
up his hat, and cast a look at him. "Ah! and snoring.
Only hear!"

"He snores very deep," said Mr. Pecksniff.

"Snores deep?" repeated Jones. "Yes; let him alone
for that. He'll snore for six, at any time."

"Do you know, Mr. Jonas," said Pecksniff, "that I
think your father is—don't let me alarm you—breaking? "

"Oh, is he though?" replied Jonas, with a shake of the
head which expressed the closeness of his dutiful observation. "Ecod, you don't know how tough he is. He ain't
upon the move yet."

"It struck me that he was changed, both in his appearance and manner," said Mr. Pecksniff.

"That's all you know about it," returned Jonas, seating himself with a melancholy air. "He never was better than he is now. How are they all at home? How's Charity?"

"Blooming, Mr. Jonas, blooming."

"And the other one—how's she?"

"Volatile trifler!" said Mr. Pecksniff, fondly musing. "She is well—she is well. Roving from parlour to bedroom, Mr. Jonas, like the bee; skimming from post to pillar, like the butterfly; dipping her young beak into our currant wine, like the humming-bird! Ah! were she a little less giddy than she is; and had she but the sterling qualities of Cherry, my young friend!"

"Is she so very giddy, then?" asked Jonas.

"Well, well!" said Mr. Pecksniff, with great feeling; "let me not be hard upon my child. Beside her sister Cherry she appears so. A strange noise that, Mr. Jonas!"

"Something wrong in the clock, I suppose," said Jonas, glancing towards it. "So the other one ain't your favourite, ain't she?"

The fond father was about to reply, and had already summoned into his face a look of intensest sensibility, when the sound he had already noticed was repeated.

"Upon my word, Mr. Jonas, that is a very extraordinary clock," said Pecksniff.

It would have been, if it had made the noise which startled them: but another kind of time-piece was fast running down, and from that the sound proceeded. A scream from Chuffey, rendered a hundred times more loud and formidable by his silent habits, made the house ring from roof to cellar; and, looking round, they saw Anthony Chuzzlewit extended on the floor, with the old clerk upon his knees beside him.

He had fallen from his chair in a fit, and lay there, battling for each gasp of breath, with every shrivelled vein and sinew starting in its place, as it were bent on bearing witness to his age, and sternly pleading with Nature against his recovery. It was frightful to see how the principle of life, shut up within his withered frame, fought like a strong devil, mad to be released, and rent its ancient prison-house. A young man in the fulness of his vigour, struggling with so much strength of desperation, would have been a dismal sight; but an old, old, shrunken body, endowed with preternatural might, and giving the lie in every motion of its every limb and joint to its enfeebled aspect, was a hideous spectacle indeed.

They raised him up, and fetched a surgeon with all haste, who bled the patient and applied some remedies; but the fits held him so long, that it was past midnight when they got him—quiet now, but quite unconscious and exhausted—into bed.

"Don't go," said Jonas, putting his ashy lips to Mr. Pecksniff's ear, and whispering across the bed. "It was a mercy you were present when he was taken ill. Some one might have said it was my doing."

" *Your* doing!" cried Mr. Pecksniff.

"I don't know but they might," he replied, wiping the moisture from his white face. "People say such things. How does he look now?"

Mr. Pecksniff shook his head.

"I used to joke, you know," said Jonas; "but I—never wished him dead. Do you think he's very bad?"

"The doctor said he was. You heard," was Mr. Pecksniff's answer.

"Ah! but he might say that to charge us more, in case of his getting well," said Jonas. "You mustn't go away, Pecksniff. Now it's come to this, I wouldn't be without a witness for a thousand pound."

Chuffey said not a word, and heard not a word. He had sat himself down in a chair at the bedside, and there he remained, motionless; except that he sometimes bent his head over the pillow, and seemed to listen. He never changed in this. Though once in the dreary night Mr. Pecksniff, having dozed, awoke with a confused impression that he had heard him praying, and strangely mingling figures—not of speech, but arithmetic—with his broken prayers.

Jonas sat there, too, all night: not where his father could have seen him, had his consciousness returned, but hiding, as it were, behind him, and only reading how he looked in Mr. Pecksniff's eyes. *He*, the coarse upstart, who had ruled the house so long—that craven cur, who was afraid to move, and shook so that his very shadow fluttered on the wall!

It was broad, bright, stirring day when, leaving the old clerk to watch him, they went down to breakfast. People hurried up and down the street; windows and doors were opened; thieves and beggars took their usual posts; workmen bestirred themselves; tradesmen set forth their shops; bailiffs and constables were on the watch; all kinds of human creatures strove, in their several ways, as hard to live, as the one sick old man who combated for every grain of sand in his fast-emptying glass, as eagerly as if it were an empire.

"If anything happens, Pecksniff," said Jonas, "you must promise me to stop here till it's all over. You shall see that I do what's right."

"I know that you will do what's right, Mr. Jonas," said Pecksniff.

"Yes, yes, but I won't be doubted. No one shall have it in his power to say a syllable against me," he returned. "I know how people will talk.—Just as if he wasn't old, or I had the secret of keeping him alive!"

Mr. Pecksniff promised that he would remain, if circumstances should render it in his esteemed friend's opinion desirable; and they were finishing their meal in silence, when suddenly an apparition stood before them, so ghastly to the view, that Jonas shrieked aloud, and both recoiled in horror.

Old Anthony, dressed in his usual clothes, was in the room—beside the table. He leaned upon the shoulder of his solitary friend; and on his livid face, and on his horny hands, and in his glassy eyes, and traced by an eternal finger in the very drops of sweat upon his brow, was one word—Death.

He spoke to them—in something of his own voice too, but sharpened and made hollow, like a dead man's face. What he would have said, God knows. He seemed to utter words, but they were such as man had never heard. And this was the most fearful circumstance of all, to see him standing there, gabbling in an unearthly tongue.

"He's better now," said Chuffey. "Better now. Let him sit in his old chair, and he'll be well again. I told him not to mind. I said so, yesterday."

They put him in his easy-chair, and wheeled it near the window; then, setting open the door, exposed him to the free current of morning air. But not all the air that is,

21

nor all the winds that ever blew 'twixt Heaven and Earth,
could have brought new life to him.

Plunge him to the throat in golden pieces now, and his
heavy fingers should not close on one.

CHAPTER XIX.

THE READER IS BROUGHT INTO COMMUNICATION WITH SOME PROFESSIONAL PERSONS, AND SHEDS A TEAR OVER THE FILIAL PIETY OF GOOD MR. JONAS.

Mr. Pecksniff was in a hackney cabriolet, for Jonas
Chuzzlewit had said "Spare no expense." Mankind is evil
in its thoughts and in its base constructions, and Jonas was
resolved it should not have an inch to stretch into an ell
against him. It never should be charged upon his father's
son that he had grudged the money for his father's funeral.
Hence, until the obsequies should be concluded, Jonas had
taken for his motto "Spend, and spare not!"

Mr. Pecksniff had been to the undertaker, and was now
upon his way to another officer in the train of mourning—
a female functionary, a nurse, and watcher, and performer
of nameless offices about the persons of the dead—whom
he had recommended. Her name, as Mr. Pecksniff gathered from a scrap of writing in his hand, was Gamp; her
residence in Kingsgate Street, High Holborn. So Mr.
Pecksniff, in a hackney cab, was rattling over Holborn
stones, in quest of Mrs. Gamp.

This lady lodged at a bird-fancier's; next door but one
to the celebrated mutton-pie shop, and directly opposite to
the original cat's meat warehouse; the renown of which
establishments was duly heralded on their respective fronts.
It was a little house, and this was the more convenient;
for Mrs. Gamp being, in her highest walk of art, a monthly
nurse, or, as her sign-board boldly had it, "Midwife," and
lodging in the first-floor front, was easily assailable at
night by pebbles, walking-sticks, and fragments of tobacco-
pipe; all much more efficacious than the street-door knocker,
which was so constructed as to wake the street with ease.

and even spread alarms of fire in Holborn, without making the smallest impression on the premises to which it was addressed.

It chanced on this particular occasion that Mrs. Gamp had been up all the previous night, in attendance upon a ceremony to which the usage of gossips has given that name which expresses, in two syllables, the curse pronounced on Adam. It chanced that Mrs Gamp had not been regularly engaged, but had been called in at a crisis, in consequence of her great repute, to assist another professional lady with her advice; and thus it happened that, all points of interest in the case being over, Mrs. Gamp had come home again to the bird-fancier's, and gone to bed. So when Mr. Pecksniff drove up in the hackney cab, Mrs. Gamp's curtains were drawn close, and Mrs. Gamp was fast asleep behind them.

If the bird-fancier had been at home, as he ought to have been, there would have been no great harm in this; but he was out, and his shop was closed. The shutters were down certainly; and in every pane of glass there was at least one tiny bird in a tiny bird-cage, twittering and hopping his little ballet of despair, and knocking his head against the roof; while one unhappy goldfinch who lived outside a red villa with his name on the door, drew the water for his own drinking, and mutely appealed to some good man to drop a farthing's worth of poison in it. Still, the door was shut. Mr. Pecksniff tried the latch, and shook it, causing a cracked bell inside to ring most mournfully; but no one came. The bird-fancier was an easy shaver also, and a fashionable hair-dresser also; and perhaps he had been sent for, express, from the court end of the town, to trim a lord, or cut and curl a lady; but however that might be, there, upon his own ground, he was not; nor was there any more distinct trace of him to assist the imagination of an inquirer, than a professional print or emblem of his calling (much favoured in the trade), representing a hair-dresser of easy manners curling a lady of distinguished fashion, in the presence of a patent upright grand piano.

Noting these circumstances, Mr. Pecksniff, in the innocence of his heart, applied himself to the knocker; but at the very first double knock, every window in the street became alive with female heads; and before he could repeat the performance, whole troops of married ladies (some about to trouble Mrs. Gamp themselves, very shortly) came flocking round the steps; all crying out with one accord, and with uncommon interest, "Knock at the winder, Sir, knock at the winder. Lord bless you, don't lose no more time than you can help—knock at the winder!"

Acting upon this suggestion, and borrowing the driver's whip for the purpose, Mr. Pecksniff soon made a commotion among the first-floor flower-pots, and roused Mrs. Gamp, whose voice—to the great satisfaction of the matrons —was heard to say, "I'm coming."

"He's as pale as a muffin," said one lady, in allusion to Mr. Pecksniff.

"So he ought to be, if he's the feelings of a man," observed another.

A third lady (with her arms folded) said she wished he had chosen any other time for fetching Mrs. Gamp, but it always happened so with *her*.

It gave Mr. Pecksniff much uneasiness to find from these remarks that he was supposed to have come to Mrs. Gamp upon an errand touching—not the close of life, but the other end. Mrs. Gamp herself was under the same impression, for throwing open the window, she cried behind the curtains, as she hastily attired herself:

"Is it Mrs. Perkins?"

"No!" returned Mr. Pecksniff, sharply, "nothing of the sort."

"What, Mr. Whilks!" cried Mrs. Gamp. "Don't say it's you, Mr. Whilks, and that poor creetur Mrs. Whilks with not even a pincushion ready. Don't say it's you, Mr. Whilks!"

"It isn't Mr. Whilks," said Pecksniff. "I don't know the man. Nothing of the kind. A gentleman is dead; and some person being wanted in the house, you have been recommended by Mr. Mould, the undertaker "

As she was by this time in a condition to appear, Mrs. Gamp, who had a face for all occasions, 1 oked out of window with her mourning countenance, and said she would be down directly. But the matrons took it very ill, that Mr. Pecksniff's mission was of so unimportant a kind; and the lady with her arms folded rated him in good round terms, signifying that she would be glad to know what he meant by terrifying delicate females "with his corpses;"

and giving it as her opinion that he was quite ugly enough to know better. The other ladies were not at all behind-hand in expressing similar sentiments; and the children, of whom some scores had now collected, hooted and defied Mr. Pecksniff quite savagely. So when Mrs. Gamp appeared, the unoffending gentleman was glad to hustle her with very little ceremony into the cabriolet, and drive off overwhelmed with popular execration.

Mrs. Gamp had a large bundle with her, a pair of pattens, and a species of gig umbrella; the latter article in colour like a faded leaf, except where a circular patch of a lively blue had been dexterously let in at the top. She was much flurried by the haste she had made, and laboured under the most erroneous views of cabriolets, which she appeared to confound with mail-coaches or stage-waggons, inasmuch as she was constantly endeavouring for the first half mile to force her luggage through the little front window, and clamouring to the driver to "put it in the boot." When she was disabused of this idea, her whole being resolved itself into an absorbing anxiety about her pattens, with which she played innumerable games at quoits, on Mr. Pecksniff's legs. It was not until they were close upon the house of mourning that she had enough composure to observe:

"And so the gentleman's dead, Sir! Ah! The more's the pity "—she didn't even know his name. "But it's what we must all come to. It's as certain as being born, except that we can't make our calculations as exact. Ah! Poor dear!"

She was a fat old woman, this Mrs. Gamp, with a husky voice and a moist eye, which she had a remarkable power of turning up, and only showing the white of. Having very little neck, it cost her some trouble to look over herself, if one may say so, at those to whom she talked. She wore a very rusty black gown, rather the worse for snuff, and a shawl and bonnet to correspond. In these dilapidated articles of dress she had, on principle, arrayed herself, time out of mind, on such occasions as the present; for this at once expressed a decent amount of veneration for the deceased, and invited the next of kin to present her with a fresher suit of weeds: an appeal so frequently successful, that the very fetch and ghost of Mrs. Gamp, bonnet and all, might be seen hanging up, any hour in the day, in at least a dozen of the second-hand clothes shops about Holborn. The face of Mrs. Gamp—the nose in particular—was somewhat red and swollen, and it was difficult to enjoy her society without becoming conscious of a smell of spirits. Like most persons who have attained to great eminence in their profession, she took to hers very kindly; insomuch, that setting aside her natural predilections as a woman, she went to a lying-in or a laying-out with equal zest and relish.

"Ah!" repeated Mrs. Gamp; for it was always a safe sentiment in cases of mourning. "Ah dear! When Gamp was summoned to his long home, and I see him a lying in Guy's Hospital with a penny-piece on each eye, and his wooden leg under his left arm, I thought I should have fainted away. But I bore up."

If certain whispers current in the Kingsgate Street circles had any truth in them, she had indeed borne up surprisingly; and had exerted such uncommon fortitude, as to dispose of Mr. Gamp's remains for the benefit of science. But it should be added, in fairness, that this had happened twenty years ago; and that Mr. and Mrs. Gamp had long been separated, on the ground of incompatibility of temper in their drink.

"You have become indifferent since then, I suppose?" said Mr. Pecksniff. "Use is second nature, Mrs. Gamp."

"You may well say second nater, Sir," returned that lady. "One's first ways is to find sich things a trial to the feelings; and so is one's lasting custom. If it wasn't for the nerve a little sip of liquor gives me (I never was able to do more than taste it), I never could go through with what I sometimes have to do. 'Mrs. Harris,' I says, at the very last case as ever I acted in, which it was but a young person; 'Mrs. Harris,' I says, 'leave the bottle on the chimley-piece, and don't ask me to take none, but let me put my lips to it when I am so dispoged, and then I will do what I'm engaged to do, according to the best of my ability.' 'Mrs. Gamp,' she says, in answer, 'if ever there was a sober creetur to be got at eighteen pence a day for working people, and three and six for gentlefolks—night watching,'" said Mrs. Gamp, with emphasis, "'being a extra charge—you are that inwalable person.' 'Mrs. Harris,' I says to her, 'don't name the charge, for if I could afford to lay all my feller creeturs out for nothink, I would gladly do it; sich is the love I bear 'em.   But what I always says to them as has the management of matters, Mrs. Harris' "—here she kept her eye on Mr. Pecksniff— "'be they gents or be they ladies—is, don't ask me whether I won't take none, or whether I will, but leave the bottle on the chimley-piece, and let me put my lips to it when I am so dispoged.'"

The conclusion of this affecting narrative brought them to the house.   In the passage they encountered Mr. Mould the undertaker: a little elderly gentleman, bald, and in a suit of black; with a note-book in his hand, a massive gold watch-chain dangling from his fob, and a face in which a queer attempt at melancholy was at odds with a smirk of satisfaction; so that he looked as a man might who, in the very act of smacking his lips over choice old wine, tried to make believe it was physic.

"Well, Mrs. Gamp, and how are *you*, Mrs. Gamp?" said this gentleman, in a voice as soft as his step.

"Pretty well, I thank you, Sir," dropping a curtsey.

"You'll be very particular here, Mrs. Gamp.   This is not a common case, Mrs. Gamp.   Let everything be very nice and comfortable, Mrs. Gamp, if you please," said the undertaker, shaking his head with a solemn air.

"It shall be, Sir," she replied, curtseying again.   "You knows me of old, Sir, I hope."

"I hope so, too, Mrs. Gamp," said the undertaker; "and I think so, also."   Mrs. Gamp curtseyed again.   "This is one of the most impressive cases, Sir," he continued, addressing Mr. Pecksniff, "that I have seen in the whole course of my professional experience."

"Indeed, Mr. Mould!" cried that gentleman.

"Such affectionate regret, Sir, I never saw.   There is no limitation—there is positively no limitation,"—opening his eyes wide, and standing on tiptoe, "in point of expense.   I have orders, Sir, to put on my whole establishment of mutes; and mutes come very dear, Mr. Pecksniff; not to mention their drink.   To provide silver-plated handles of the very best description, ornamented with angels' heads from the most expensive dies.   To be perfectly profuse in feathers.   In short, Sir, to turn out something absolutely gorgeous."

"My friend Mr. Jonas is an excellent man," said Mr. Pecksniff.

"I have seen a good deal of what is filial in my time, Sir," retorted Mould, "and of what is unfilial too. It is our lot. We come into the knowledge of those secrets. But anything so filial as this; anything so honourable to human nature; so calculated to reconcile all of us to the world we live in; never yet came under my observation. It only proves, Sir, what was so forcibly observed by the lamented theatrical poet buried—at Stratford—that there is good in everything."

"It is very pleasant to hear you say so, Mr. Mould," observed Pecksniff.

"You are very kind, Sir. And what a man Mr. Chuzzlewit was, Sir! Ah! what a man he was. You may talk of your Lord Mayors," said Mould, waving his hand at the public in general, "your Sheriffs, your Common Councilmen, your trumpery; but show me a man in this city who is worthy to walk in the shoes of the departed Mr. Chuzzlewit. No, no," cried Mould, with bitter sarcasm. "Hang 'em up, hang 'em up; sole 'em and heel 'em, and have 'em ready for his son against he's old enough to wear 'em; but don't try 'em on yourselves, for they won't fit you. We knew him," said Mould, in the same biting vein, as he pocketed his note-book; "we knew him, and are not to be caught with chaff. Mr. Pecksniff, Sir, good morning."

Mr. Pecksniff returned the compliment; and Mould, sensible of having distinguished himself, was going away with a brisk smile, when he fortunately remembered the occasion. Quickly becoming depressed again, he sighed; looked into the crown of his hat, as if for comfort; put it on without finding any; and slowly departed.

Mrs. Gamp and Mr. Pecksniff then ascended the staircase; and the former, having been shown to the chamber in which all that remained of Anthony Chuzzlewit lay covered up, with but one loving heart, and that a halting one, to mourn it, left the latter free to enter the darkened room below, and rejoin Mr. Jonas, from whom he had now been absent nearly two hours.

He found that example to bereaved sons and pattern in the eyes of all performers of funerals, musing over a fragment of writing-paper on the desk, and scratching figures on it with a pen. The old man's chair, and hat, and walking-stick, were removed from their accustomed places, and put out of sight; the window-blinds, as yellow as Novem-

ber fogs, were drawn down close; Jonas himself was so subdued, that he could scarcely be heard to speak, and only
seen to walk across the room.

" Pecksniff," he said, in a whisper, " you shall have the
regulation of it all, mind. You shall be able to tell anybody who talks about it that everything was correctly and
freely done. There isn't any one you'd like to ask to the
funeral, is there? "

" No, Mr. Jonas, I think not."

" Because if there is, you know," said Jonas, " ask him.
We don't want to make a secret of it."

" No," repeated Mr. Pecksniff, after a little reflection.
" I am not the less obliged to you on that account, Mr. Jonas,
for your liberal hospitality; but there really is no one."

" Very well," said Jonas; " then you, and I, and Chuffey,
and the doctor, will be just a coachful. We'll have the
doctor, Pecksniff, because he knows what was the matter
with him, and that it couldn't be helped."

" Where *is* our dear friend, Mr. Chuffey? " asked Pecksniff, looking round the chamber, and winking both his
eyes at once—for he was overcome by his feelings.

But here he was interrupted by Mrs. Gamp, who, divested
of her bonnet and shawl, came sidling and bridling into the
room; and, with some sharpness, demanded a conference
outside the door with Mr. Pecksniff.

" You may say whatever you wish to say here, Mrs.
Gamp," said that gentleman, shaking his head with a melancholy expression.

." It is not much as I have to say, when people is a
mourning for the dead and gone," said Mrs. Gamp; " but
what I have to say is *to* the pint and purpose, and no
offence intended, must be so considered. I have been at a
many places in my time, gentlemen, and I hope I knows
what my duties is, and how the same should be performed:
in course, if I did not, it would be very strange, and very
wrong in sich a gentleman as Mr. Mould, which has undertook the highest families in this land, and given every satisfaction, so to recommend me as he does. I have seen a
deal of trouble my own self," said Mrs. Gamp, laying
greater and greater stress upon her words, " and I can feel
for them as has their feelings tried: but I am not a Roo-
shan or a Prooshan, and consequently cannot suffer spies
to be set over me."

Before it was possible that an answer could be returned, Mrs. Gamp, now growing redder in the face, went on to say:

"It is not a easy matter, gentlemen, to live when you are left a widder woman; particular when your feelings works upon you to that extent that you often find yourself a going out on terms which is a certain loss, and never can repay. But, in whatever way you earns your bread, you may have rules and regulations of your own, which cannot be broke through. Some people," said Mrs. Gamp, again entrenching herself behind her strong point, as if it were not assailable by human ingenuity, "may be Rooshans, and some may be Prooshans; they are born so, and will please themselves. Them which is of other naturs thinks different."

"If I understand this good lady," said Mr. Pecksniff, turning to Jonas, "Mr. Chuffey is troublesome to her. Shall I fetch him down?"

"Do," said Jonas. "I was going to tell you he was up there, when she came in. I'd go myself and bring him down, only—only I'd rather you went, if you don't mind it."

Mr. Pecksniff promptly departed, followed by Mrs. Gamp, who, seeing that he took a bottle and glass from the cupboard, and carried it in his hand, was much softened.

"I am sure," she said, "that if it wasn't for his own happiness, I should no more mind his being there, poor dear, than if he was a fly. But them as isn't used to these things, thinks so much of 'em afterwards that it's a kindness to 'em not to let 'em have their wish. And even," said Mrs. Gamp, probably in reference to some flowers of speech she had already strewn on Mr. Chuffey, "even if one calls 'em names, it's only done to rouse 'em."

Whatever epithets she had bestowed upon the old clerk, they had not roused *him.* He sat beside the bed, in the chair he had occupied all the previous night, with his hands folded before him, and his head bowed down; and neither looked up, on their entrance, nor gave any sign of consciousness, until Mr. Pecksniff took him by the arm, when he meekly rose.

"Three score and ten," said Chuffey, "ought and carry seven. Some men are so strong that they live to fourscore —four times ought's an ought, four times two's eight—

eighty. Oh! why—why—why—didn't he live to four
times ought's an ought, and four times two's eight—
eighty?"

"Ah! what a wale of grief!" cried Mrs. Gamp, possessing herself of the bottle and glass.

"Why did he die before his poor old, crazy servant!"
said Chuffey, clasping his hands and looking up in anguish.
"Take him from me, and what remains?"

"Mr. Jonas," returned Pecksniff, "Mr. Jonas, my good
friend."

"I loved him," cried the old man, weeping. "He was
good to me. We learnt Tare and Tret together, at school.
I took him down once, six boys, in the arithmetic class.
God forgive me! Had I the heart to take him down!"

"Come, Mr. Chuffey," said Pecksniff, "come with me.
Summon up your fortitude, Mr. Chuffey."

"Yes, I will," returned the old clerk. "Yes. I'll sum
up my forty—How many times forty—Oh, Chuzzlewit and
Son—Your own son, Mr. Chuzzlewit; your own son, Sir!"

He yielded to the hand that guided him, as he lapsed
into this familiar expression, and submitted to be led away.
Mrs. Gamp, with the bottle on one knee, and the glass in
the other, sat upon a stool, shaking her head for a long
time, until, in a moment of abstraction, she poured out a
dram of spirits, and raised it to her lips. It was succeeded
by a second, and by a third, and then her eyes—either in
the sadness of her reflections upon life and death, or in her
admiration of the liquor—were so turned up as to be quite
invisible. But she shook her head still.

Poor Chuffey was conducted to his accustomed corner,
and there he remained, silent and quiet, save at long intervals, when he would rise, and walk about the room, and
wring his hands, or raise some strange and sudden cry.
For a whole week they all three sat about the hearth and
never stirred abroad. Mr. Pecksniff would have walked
out in the evening time, but Jonas was so averse to his
being absent for a minute, that he abandoned the idea, and
so, from morning until night, they brooded together in the
dark room, without relief or occupation.

The weight of that which was stretched out stiff and
stark, in the awful chamber above-stairs, so crushed and
bore down Jonas, that he bent beneath the load. During
the whole long seven days and nights, he was always op-

pressed and haunted by a dreadful sense of its presence in
the house. Did the door move, he looked towards it with
a livid face and starting eye, as if he fully believed that
ghostly fingers clutched the handle. Did the fire flicker
in a draught of air, he glanced over his shoulder, as almost
dreading to behold some shrouded figure fanning and flapping at it with its fearful dress. The lightest noise disturbed him; and once, in the night, at the sound of a footstep over-head, he cried out that the dead man was walking—tramp, tramp, tramp—about his coffin.

He lay at night upon a mattress on the floor of the sitting-room; his own chamber having been assigned to Mrs.
Gamp; and Mr. Pecksniff was similarly accommodated.
The howling of a dog before the house, filled him with a
terror he could not disguise. He avoided the reflection in
the opposite windows of the light that burned above, as
though it had been an angry eye. He often, in every
night, rose up from his fitful sleep, and looked and longed
for dawn; all directions and arrangements, even to the ordering of their daily meals, he abandoned to Mr. Pecksniff.
That excellent gentleman, deeming that the mourner wanted
comfort, and that high feeding was likely to do him infinite
service, availed himself of these opportunities to such good
purpose that they kept quite a dainty table during this
melancholy season; with sweetbreads, stewed kidneys,
oysters, and other such light viands for supper every night;
over which, and sundry jorums of hot punch, Mr. Pecksniff
delivered such moral reflections and spiritual consolation
as might have converted a Heathen—especially if he had
had but an imperfect acquaintance with the English
tongue.

Nor did Mr. Pecksniff alone indulge in the creature comforts during this sad time. Mrs. Gamp proved to be very
choice in her eating, and repudiated hashed mutton with
scorn. In her drinking too, she was very punctual and
particular, requiring a pint of mild porter at lunch, a pint
at dinner, half-a-pint as a species of stay or holdfast between dinner and tea, and a pint of the celebrated staggering ale, or Real Old Brighton Tipper, at supper; besides
the bottle on the chimney-piece, and such casual invita-
tions to refresh herself with wine as the good breeding of
her employers might prompt them to offer. In like manner, Mr. Mould's men found it necessary to drown their

grief, like a young kitten in the morning of its existence; for which reason they generally fuddled themselves before they began to do anything, lest it should make head and get the better of them. In short, the whole of that strange week was a round of dismal joviality and grim enjoyment; and every one, except poor Chuffey, who came within the shadow of Anthony Chuzzlewit's grave, feasted like a Ghoule.

At length the day of the funeral, pious and truthful ceremony that it was, arrived. Mr. Mould, with a glass of generous port between his eye and the light, leaned against the desk in the little glass office with his gold watch in his unoccupied hand, and conversed with Mrs. Gamp; two mutes were at the house-door, looking as mournful as could be reasonably expected of men with such a thriving job in hand; the whole of Mr. Mould's establishment were on duty within the house or without; feathers waved, horses snorted, silks and velvets fluttered; in a word, as Mr. Mould emphatically said, "everything that money could do was done."

"And what can do more, Mrs. Gamp?" exclaimed the undertaker, as he emptied his glass, and smacked his lips.

"Nothing in the world, Sir."

"Nothing in the world," repeated Mr. Mould. "You are right, Mrs. Gamp. Why do people spend more money" —here he filled his glass again—"upon a death, Mrs. Gamp, than upon a birth? Come, that's in your way; you ought to know. How do you account for that now?"

"Perhaps it is because an undertaker's charges comes dearer than a nurse's charges, Sir," said Mrs. Gamp, tittering, and smoothing down her new black dress with her hands.

"Ha, ha!" laughed Mr. Mould. "You have been breakfasting at somebody's expense this morning, Mrs. Gamp." But seeing, by the aid of a little shaving-glass which hung opposite, that he looked merry, he composed his features and became sorrowful.

"Many's the time that I've not breakfasted at my own expense along of your kind recommending, Sir; and many's the time I hope to do the same in time to come," said Mrs. Gamp, with an apologetic curtsey.

"So be it," replied Mr. Mould, "please Providence. No, Mrs. Gamp; I'll tell you why it is. It's because the lay-

ing out of money with a well-conducted establishment,
where the thing is performed upon the very best scale,
binds the broken heart, and sheds balm upon the wounded
spirit.   Hearts want binding, and spirits want balming
when people die : not when people are born.   Look at this
gentleman to-day; look at him."

"An open-handed gentleman!" cried Mrs. Gamp, with
enthusiasm.

"No, no," said the undertaker; "not an open-handed
gentleman in general, by any means.   There you mistake
him : but an afflicted gentleman, an affectionate gentleman,
who knows what it is in the power of money to do, in giving him relief, and in testifying his love and veneration for
the departed.   It can give him," said Mr. Mould, waving
his watch-chain slowly round and round, so that he described one circle after every item; "it can give him four
horses to each vehicle; it can give him velvet trappings; it
can give him drivers in cloth cloaks and top-boots; it can
give him the plumage of the ostrich, dyed black; it can
give him any number of walking attendants, dressed in the
first style of funeral fashion, and carrying batons tipped
with brass; it can give him a handsome tomb; it can give
him a place in Westminster Abbey itself, if he choose to
invest it in such a purchase.   Oh! do not let us say that
gold is dross, when it can buy such things as these, Mrs.
Gamp."

"But what a blessing, Sir," said Mrs. Gamp, "that there
are such as you, to sell or let 'em out on hire!"

"Ay, Mrs. Gamp, you are right," rejoined the under·
taker.   "We should be an honoured calling.   We do good
by stealth, and blush to have it mentioned in our little bills.   How much consolation may I—even I"—cried
Mr. Mould, "have diffused among my fellow-creatures by
means of my four long-tailed prancers, never harnessed
under ten pound ten."

Mrs. Gamp had begun to make a suitable reply, when
she was interrupted by the appearance of one of Mr. Mould's
assistants—his chief mourner in fact—an obese person,
with his waistcoat in closer connection with his legs than is
quite reconcilable with the established ideas of grace; with
that cast of feature which is figuratively called bottle-nose;
and with a face covered all over with pimples.   He had
been a tender plant once upon a time, but from constant

blowing in the fat atmosphere of funerals, had run to seed.

"Well, Tacker," said Mr. Mould, "is all ready below?"

"A beautiful show, Sir," rejoined Tacker. "The horses are prouder and fresher than ever I see 'em; and toss their heads, they do, as if they knowed how much their plumes cost. One, two, three, four," said Mr. Tacker, heaping that number of black cloaks upon his left arm.

"Is Tom there, with the cake and wine?" asked Mr. Mould.

"Ready to come in at a moment's notice, Sir," said Tacker.

"Then," rejoined Mr. Mould, putting up his watch, and glancing at himself in the little shaving-glass, that he might be sure his face had the right expression on it: "then I think we may proceed to business. Give me the paper of gloves, Tacker. Ah what a man he was! Ah Tacker, Tacker, what a man he was!"

Mr. Tacker, who from his great experience in the performance of funerals, would have made an excellent pantomime actor, winked at Mrs. Gamp without at all disturbing the gravity of his countenance, and followed his master into the next room.

It was a great point with Mr. Mould, and a part of his professional tact, not to seem to know the doctor—though in reality they were near neighbours, and very often, as in the present instance, worked together. So he advanced to fit on his black kid gloves as if he had never seen him in all his life; while the doctor, on his part, looked as distant and unconscious as if he had heard and read of undertakers, and had passed their shops, but had never before been brought into communication with one.

"Gloves, eh?" said the doctor. "Mr. Pecksniff, after you."

"I couldn't think of it," returned Mr. Pecksniff.

"You are very good," said the doctor, taking a pair. "Well, Sir, as I was saying—I was called up to attend that case at about half-past one o'clock. Cake and wine, eh? Which is port? Thank you."

Mr. Pecksniff took some also.

"At about half-past one o'clock in the morning, Sir," resumed the doctor, "I was called up to attend that case. At the first pull of the night-bell I turned out, threw up

the window, and put out my head. Cloak, eh? Don't tie
it too tight. That'll do."

Mr. Pecksniff having been likewise inducted into a similar garment, the doctor resumed.

"And put out my head,—hat, eh? My good friend,
that is not mine. Mr. Pecksniff, I beg your pardon, but I
think we have unintentionally made an exchange. Thank
you. Well, Sir, I was going to tell you "—

"We are quite ready," interrupted Mould in a low voice.

"Ready, eh?" said the doctor. "Very good. Mr. Pecksniff, I'll take an opportunity of relating the rest in the
coach. It's rather curious. Ready, eh? No rain, I
hope?"

"Quite fair, Sir," returned Mould.

"I was afraid the ground would have been wet," said the
doctor, "for my glass fell yesterday. We may congratulate ourselves upon our good fortune." But seeing by this
time that Mr. Jonas and Chuffey were going out at the
door, he put a white pocket-handkerchief to his face as if
a violent burst of grief had suddenly come upon him, and
walked down side by side with Mr. Pecksniff.

Mr. Mould and his men had not exaggerated the grand-
eur of the arrangements. They were splendid. The four
hearse-horses especially, reared and pranced, and showed
their highest action, as if they knew a man was dead, and
triumphed in it. "They break us, drive us, ride us; ill-
treat, abuse, and maim us for their pleasure—But they die;
Hurrah, they die!"

So through the narrow streets and winding city ways,
went Anthony Chuzzlewit's funeral: Mr. Jonas glancing
stealthily out of the coach-window now and then, to observe
its effect upon the crowd; Mr. Mould as he walked along,
listening with a sober pride to the exclamations of the by-
standers; the doctor whispering his story to Mr. Pecksniff,
without appearing to come any nearer the end of it; and
poor old Chuffey sobbing unregarded in a corner. But he
had greatly scandalised Mr. Mould at an early stage of the
ceremony by carrying his handkerchief in his hat in a perfectly informal manner, and wiping his eyes with his
knuckles. And as Mr. Mould himself had said already,
his behaviour was indecent, and quite unworthy of such an
occasion; and he never ought to have been there.

There he was, however; and in the churchyard there he

was, also, conducting himself in a no less unbecoming manner, and leaning for support on Tacker, who plainly told him that he was fit for nothing better than a walking funeral. But Chuffey, Heaven help him! heard no sound but the echoes, lingering in his own heart, of a voice for ever silent.

"I loved him," cried the old man, sinking down upon the grave when all was done. "He was very good to me. Oh, my dear old friend and master!"

"Come, come, Mr. Chuffey," said the doctor, "this won't do; it's a clayey soil, Mr. Chuffey. You mustn't, really."

"If it had been the commonest thing we do, and Mr. Chuffey had been a Bearer, gentlemen," said Mould, casting an imploring glance upon them, as he helped to raise him, "he couldn't have gone on worse than this."

"Be a man, Mr. Chuffey," said Pecksniff.

"Be a gentleman, Mr. Chuffey," said Mould.

"Upon my word, my good friend," murmured the doctor, in a tone of stately reproof, as he stepped up to the old man's side, "this is worse than weakness. This is bad, selfish, very wrong, Mr. Chuffey. You should take example from others, my good Sir. You forget that you were not connected by ties of blood with our deceased friend; and that he had a very near and very dear relation, Mr. Chuffey."

"Ay, his own son!" cried the old man, clasping his hands with remarkable passion. "His own, own, only son!"

"He's not right in his head, you know," said Jonas, turning pale. "You're not to mind anything he says. I shouldn't wonder if he was to talk some precious nonsense. But don't you mind him, any of you. I don't. My father left him to my charge; and whatever he says or does, that's enough. I'll take care of him."

A hum of admiration rose from the mourners (including Mr. Mould and his merry men) at this new instance of magnanimity and kind-feeling on the part of Jonas. But Chuffey put it to the test no farther. He said not a word more, and being left to himself for a little while, crept back again to the coach.

It has been said that Mr. Jonas turned pale when the behaviour of the old clerk attracted general attention; his discomposure, however, was but momentary, and he soon

22

recovered. But these were not the only changes he had
exhibited that day. The curious eyes of Mr. Pecksniff had
observed that as soon as they left the house upon their
mournful errand, he began to mend; that as the ceremonies
proceeded he gradually, by little and little, recovered his
old condition, his old looks, his old bearing, his old agreeable characteristics of speech and manner, and became, in
all respects, his old pleasant self. And now that they were
seated in the coach on their return home; and more when
they got there, and found the windows open, the light and
air admitted, and all traces of the late event removed; he
felt so well convinced that Jonas was again the Jonas he
had known a week ago, and not the Jonas of the interven-
ing time, that he voluntarily gave up his recently acquired
power without one faint attempt to exercise it, and at once
fell back into his former position of mild and deferential
guest.

Mrs. Gamp went home to the bird-fancier's, and was
knocked up again that very night for a birth of twins; Mr.
Mould dined gaily in the bosom of his family, and passed
the evening facetiously at his club; the hearse, after standing for a long time at the door of a roystering public-house,
repaired to its stables with the feathers inside and twelve
red-nosed undertakers on the roof, each holding on by a
dingy peg, to which, in times of state, a waving plume was
fitted; the various trappings of sorrow were carefully laid
by in presses for the next hirer; the fiery steeds were
quenched and quiet in their stalls; the doctor got merry
with wine at a wedding-dinner, and forgot the middle of
the story which had no end to it; the pageant of a few
short hours ago was written nowhere half so legibly as in
the undertaker's books.

Not in the churchyard? Not even there. The gates
were closed; the night was dark and wet; and the rain fell
silently, among the stagnant weeds and nettles   One new
mound was there which had not been last night. Time,
burrowing like a mole below the ground, had marked his
track by throwing up another heap of earth. And that
was all.

CHAPTER XX.

IS A CHAPTER OF LOVE.

"PECKSNIFF," said Jonas, taking off his hat, to see that the black crape band was all right; and finding that it was, putting it on again, complacently; "what do you mean to give your daughters when they marry?"

"My dear Mr. Jonas," cried the affectionate parent, with an ingenuous smile, "what a very singular inquiry!"

"Now, don't you mind whether it's a singular inquiry or a plural one," retorted Jonas, eyeing Mr. Pecksniff with no great favour, "but answer it, or let it alone. One or the other."

"Hum! The question, my dear friend," said Mr. Pecksniff, laying his hand tenderly upon his kinsman's knee, "is involved with many considerations   What would I give them? Eh?"

"Ah! what would you give 'em?" repeated Jonas.

"Why, that," said Mr Pecksniff, "would naturally depend in a great measure upon the kind of husbands they might choose, my dear young friend."

Mr. Jonas was evidently disconcerted, and at a loss how to proceed. It was a good answer. It seemed a deep one, but such is the wisdom of simplicity!

"My standard for the merits I would require in a son-in-law," said Mr. Pecksniff, after a short silence, "is a high one. Forgive me, my dear Mr. Jonas," he added, greatly moved, "if I say that you have spoiled me, and made it a fanciful one; an imaginative one; a prismatically tinged one, if I may be permitted to call it so."

"What do you mean by that?" growled Jonas, looking at him with increased disfavour.

"Indeed, my dear friend," said Mr. Pecksniff, "you may well inquire. The heart is not always a royal mint, with patent machinery, to work its metal into current coin. Sometimes it throws it out in strange forms, not easily recognised as coin at all. But it is sterling gold   It has at least that merit. It is sterling gold."

"Is it?" grumbled Jonas, with a doubtful shake of the head.

"Ay!" said Mr. Pecksniff, warming with his subject, "it is. To be plain with you, Mr. Jonas, if I could find two such sons-in-law as you will one day make to some deserving man, capable of appreciating a nature such as yours, I would—forgetful of myself—bestow upon my daughters, portions reaching to the very utmost limit of my means."

This was strong language, and it was earnestly delivered. But who can wonder that such a man as Mr. Pecksniff, after all he had seen and heard of Mr. Jonas, should be strong and earnest upon such a theme; a theme that touched even the worldly lips of undertakers with the honey of eloquence!

Mr. Jonas was silent, and looked thoughtfully at the landscape. For they were seated on the outside of the coach, at the back, and were travelling down into the country. He accompanied Mr. Pecksniff home for a few days' change of air and scene after his recent trials.

"Well," he said, at last, with captivating bluntness, "suppose you got one such son-in-law as me, what then?"

Mr. Pecksniff regarded him at first with inexpressible surprise; then gradually breaking into a sort of dejected vivacity, said:

"Then well I know whose husband he would be!"

"Whose?" asked Jonas, drily

"My eldest girl's, Mr. Jonas," replied Pecksniff, with moistening eyes. "My dear Cherry's: my staff, my scrip, my treasure, Mr. Jonas. A hard struggle, but it is in the nature of things! I must one day part with her to a husband. I know it, my dear friend. I am prepared for it."

"Ecod! you've been prepared for that, a pretty long time, I should think," said Jonas.

"Many have sought to bear her from me," said Mr. Pecksniff. "All have failed. 'I never will give my hand, papa,'—those were her words, 'unless my heart is won.' She has not been quite so happy as she used to be, of late. I don't know why."

Again Mr. Jonas looked at the landscape; then at the coachman; then at the luggage on the roof; finally, at Mr. Pecksniff.

"I suppose you'll have to part with the other one, some of these days?" he observed, as he caught that gentleman's eye.

"Probably," said the parent. "Years will tame down
the wildness of my foolish bird, and then it will be caged.
But Cherry, Mr. Jonas, Cherry—"

"Oh, ah!" interrupted Jonas. "Years have made her
all right enough. Nobody doubts that. But you haven't
answered what I asked you. Of course, you're not obliged
to do it, you know, if you don't like. You're the best
judge."

There was a warning sulkiness in the manner of this
speech, which admonished Mr. Pecksniff that his dear
friend was not to be trifled with or fenced off, and that he
must either return a straightforward reply to his question,
or plainly give him to understand that he declined to enlighten him upon the subject to which it referred. Mindful in this dilemma of the caution old Anthony had given
him almost with his latest breath, he resolved to speak to
the point, and so told Mr. Jonas—enlarging upon the communication as a proof of his great attachment and confidence—that in the case he had put, to wit, in the event of
such a man as he proposing for his daughter's hand, he
would endow her with a fortune of four thousand pounds.

"I should sadly pinch and cramp myself to do so," was
his fatherly remark; "but that would be my duty, and my
conscience would reward me. For myself, my conscience
is my bank. I have a trifle invested there—a mere trifle,
Mr. Jonas—but I prize it as a store of value, I assure
you."

The good man's enemies would have divided upon this
question into two parties. One would have asserted without scruple that if Mr. Pecksniff's conscience were his
bank, and he kept a running account there, he must have
overdrawn it beyond all mortal means of computation. The
other would have contended that it was a mere fictitious
form; a perfectly blank book; or one in which entries were
only made with a peculiar kind of invisible ink to become
legible at some indefinite time; and that he never troubled
it at all.

"It would sadly pinch and cramp me, my dear friend,"
repeated Mr. Pecksniff, "but Providence—perhaps I may
be permitted to say a special Providence—has blessed my
endeavours, and I could guarantee to make the sacrifice."

A question of philosophy arises here, whether Mr. Pecksniff had or had not good reason to say, that he was spe-

cially patronised and encouraged in his undertakings. All his life long he had been walking up and down the narrow ways and bye-places, with a hook in one hand and a crook in the other, scraping all sorts of valuable odds and ends into his pouch. Now, there being a special Providence in the fall of a sparrow, it follows (so Mr. Pecksniff might have reasoned, perhaps), that there must also be a special Providence in the alighting of the stone, or stick, or other substance which is aimed at the sparrow. And Mr. Pecksniff's hook, or crook, having invariably knocked the sparrow on the head and brought him down, that gentleman may have been led to consider himself as specially licensed to bag sparrows, and as being specially seised and possessed of all the birds he had got together. That many undertakings, national as well as individual—but especially the former—are held to be specially brought to a glorious and successful issue, which never could be so regarded on any other process of reasoning, must be clear to all men. Therefore the precedents would seem to show that Mr. Pecksniff had good argument for what he said, and might be permitted to say it, and did not say it presumptuously, vainly, or arrogantly, but in a spirit of high faith and great wisdom meriting all praise.

Mr. Jonas, not being much accustomed to perplex his mind with theories of this nature, expressed no opinion on the subject. Nor did he receive his companion's announcement with one solitary syllable, good, bad, or indifferent. He preserved this taciturnity for a quarter of an hour at least, and during the whole of that time appeared to be steadily engaged in subjecting some given amount to the operation of every known rule in figures; adding to it, taking from it, multiplying it, reducing it by long and short division; working it by the rule-of-three direct and inversed; exchange or barter; practice; simple interest; compound interest; and other means of arithmetical calculation. The result of these labours appeared to be satisfactory, for when he did break silence, it was as one who had arrived at some specific result, and freed himself from a state of distressing uncertainty.

"Come, old Pecksniff!"—such was his jocose address, as he slapped that gentleman on the back, at the end of the stage—"let's have something!"

"With all my heart," said Mr. Pecksniff.

"Let's treat the driver," cried Jonas.

"If you think it won't hurt the man, or render him dis-contented with his station—certainly," faltered Mr. Peck-sniff.

Jonas only laughed at this, and getting down from the coach-top with great alacrity, cut a cumbersome kind of caper in the road. After which, he went into the public-house, and there ordered spirituous drink to such an extent that Mr. Pecksniff had some doubts of his perfect sanity, until Jonas set them quite at rest by saying, when the coach could wait no longer:

"I've been standing treat for a whole week and more, and letting you have all the delicacies of the season. *You* shall pay for this, Pecksniff." It was not a joke either, as Mr. Pecksniff at first supposed; for he went off to the coach without further ceremony, and left his respected victim to settle the bill.

But Mr. Pecksniff was a man of meek endurance, and Mr. Jonas was his friend. Moreover, his regard for that gentleman was founded, as we know, on pure esteem, and a knowledge of the excellence of his character. He came out from the tavern with a smiling face, and even went so far as to repeat the performance, on a less expensive scale, at the next alehouse. There was a certain wildness in the spirits of Mr. Jonas (not usually a part of his character) which was far from being subdued by these means, and, for the rest of the journey, he was so very buoyant—it may be said, boisterous—that Mr. Pecksniff had some difficulty in keeping pace with him.

They were not expected—oh dear, no! Mr. Pecksniff had proposed in London to give the girls a surprise, and had said he wouldn't write a word to prepare them on any account, in order that he and Mr. Jonas might take them unawares, and just see what they were doing, when they thought their dear papa was miles and miles away. As a consequence of this playful device, there was nobody to meet them at the finger-post, but that was of small conse-quence, for they had come down by the day coach, and Mr. Pecksniff had only a carpet-bag, while Mr. Jonas had only a portmanteau. They took the portmanteau between them, put the bag upon it, and walked off up the lane without delay: Mr. Pecksniff already going on tiptoe as if, without this precaution, his fond children, being then at a distance of a couple of miles or so, would have some filial sense of his approach.

It was a lovely evening, in the spring-time of the year; and in the soft stillness of the twilight, all nature was very calm and beautiful. The day had been fine and warm; but at the coming on of night, the air grew cool, and in the mellowing distance, smoke was rising gently from the cottage chimneys. There were a thousand pleasant scents diffused around, from young leaves and fresh buds; the cuckoo had been singing all day long, and was but just now hushed; the smell of earth, newly-upturned—first breath of hope to the first labourer, after his garden withered— was fragrant in the evening breeze. It was a time when most men cherish good resolves, and sorrow for the wasted past: when most men, looking on the shadows as they gather, think of that evening which must close on all, and that to-morrow which has none beyond.

"Precious dull," said Mr. Jonas, looking about. "It's enough to make a man go melancholy mad."

"We shall have lights and a fire soon," observed Mr. Pecksniff.

"We shall need 'em by the time we get there," said Jonas. "Why the devil don't you talk? What are you thinking of?"

"To tell you the truth, Mr. Jonas," said Pecksniff with great solemnity, "my mind was running at that moment on our late dear friend, your departed father."

Mr. Jonas immediately let his burden fall, and said, threatening him with his hand:

"Drop that, Pecksniff!"

Mr. Pecksniff, not exactly knowing whether allusion was made to the subject or the portmanteau, stared at his friend in unaffected surprise.

"Drop it, I say!" cried Jonas, fiercely. "Do you hear? Drop it—now and for ever. You had better, I give you notice!"

"It was quite a mistake," urged Mr. Pecksniff, very much dismayed; "though I admit it was foolish. I might have known it was a tender string."

"Don't talk to me about tender strings," said Jonas, wiping his forehead with the cuff of his coat. "I'm not going to be crowed over by you, because I don't like dead company."

Mr. Pecksniff had got out the words "Crowed over, Mr. Jonas!" when that young man, with a dark expression in his countenance, cut him short once more:

"Mind!" he said, "I won't have it. I advise you not to revive the subject, neither to me nor anybody else. You can take a hint, if you choose, as well as another man There's enough said about it. Come along!"

Taking up his part of the load again, when he had said these words, he hurried on so fast that Mr. Pecksniff, at the other end of the portmanteau, found himself dragged forward in a very inconvenient and ungraceful manner, to the great detriment of what is called by fancy gentlemen "the bark" upon his shins, which were most unmercifully bumped against the hard leather and the iron buckles. In the course of a few minutes, however, Mr. Jonas relaxed his speed, and suffered his companion to come up with him, and to bring the portmanteau into a tolerably straight position.

It was pretty clear that he regretted his late outbreak, and that he mistrusted its effect on Mr. Pecksniff; for as often as that gentleman glanced towards Mr. Jonas, he found Mr. Jonas glancing at him, which was a new source of embarrassment. It was but a short-lived one though, for Mr. Jonas soon began to whistle, whereupon Mr. Pecksniff, taking his cue from his friend, began to hum a tune melodiously.

"Pretty nearly there, ain't we?" said Jonas, when this had lasted some time.

"Close, my dear friend," said Mr. Pecksniff.

"What'll they be doing, do you suppose?" asked Jonas.

"Impossible to say," cried Mr. Pecksniff. "Giddy truants! They may be away from home, perhaps. I was going to—he! he! he!—I was going to propose," said Mr. Pecksniff, "that we should enter by the back way, and come upon them like a clap of thunder, Mr. Jonas."

It might not have been easy to decide in respect of which of their manifold properties, Jonas, Mr. Pecksniff, the carpet-bag, and the portmanteau, could be likened to a clap of thunder. But Mr. Jonas giving his assent to this proposal, they stole round into the back yard, and softly advanced towards the kitchen window, through which the mingled light of fire and candle shone upon the darkening night.

Truly Mr. Pecksniff is blessed in his children—in one of

them, at any rate. The prudent Cherry—staff, and scrip, and treasure of her doting father—there she sits, at a little table white as driven snow, before the kitchen fire, making up accounts! See the neat maiden, as with pen in hand, and calculating look addressed towards the ceiling, and bunch of keys within a little basket at her side, she checks the housekeeping expenditure! From flat-iron, dish-cover, and warming-pan; from pot and kettle, face of brass footman, and black-leaded stove; bright glances of approbation wink and glow upon her. The very onions dangling from the beam mantle and shine like cherubs' cheeks. Something of the influence of those vegetables sinks into Mr. Pecksniff's nature. He weeps.

It is but for a moment, and he hides it from the observation of his friend—very carefully—by a somewhat elaborate use of his pocket-handkerchief, in fact: for he would not have his weakness known.

"Pleasant," he murmured—"pleasant to a father's feelings! My dear girl! Shall we let her know we are here, Mr. Jonas?"

"Why, I suppose you don't mean to spend the evening in the stable or the coach-house," he returned.

"That, indeed, is not such hospitality as I would show to you, my friend," cried Mr. Pecksniff, pressing his hand. And then he took a long breath, and, tapping at the window, shouted with stentorian blandness:

"Boh!"

Cherry dropped her pen and screamed. But innocence is ever bold—or should be. As they opened the door, the valiant girl exclaimed in a firm voice, and with a presence of mind which even in that trying moment did not desert her, "Who are you? What do you want? Speak! Or I will call my Pa."

Mr. Pecksniff held out his arms. She knew him instantly, and rushed into his fond embrace.

"It was thoughtless of us, Mr. Jonas, it was very thoughtless," said Pecksniff, smoothing his daughter's hair. "My darling, do you see that I am not alone!"

Not she. She had seen nothing but her father until now. She saw Mr. Jonas now, though; and blushed, and hung her head down, as she gave him welcome.

But where was Merry? Mr. Pecksniff didn't ask the question in reproach, but in a vein of mildness touched with a gentle sorrow. She was up stairs, reading on the parlour couch. Ah! Domestic details had no charms for *her*. "But call her down," said Mr. Pecksniff, with a placid resignation. "Call her down, my love."

She was called and came, all flushed and tumbled from reposing on the sofa; but none the worse for that. No, not at all. Rather the better, if anything.

"Oh my goodness me!" cried the arch girl, turning to her cousin when she had kissed her father on both cheeks, and in her frolicsome nature had bestowed a supernumerary salute upon the tip of his nose, "*you* here, fright! Well, I'm very thankful that you won't trouble *me* much!"

"What! you're as lively as ever, are you?" said Jonas.

"Oh! You're a wicked one!"

"There, go along!" retorted Merry, pushing him away. "I'm sure I don't know what I shall ever do, if I have to see much of you. Go along, for gracious' sake!"

Mr. Pecksniff striking in here, with a request that Mr. Jonas would immediately walk up stairs, he so far complied with the young lady's adjuration as to go at once. But though he had the fair Cherry on his arm, he could not help looking back at her sister, and exchanging some further dialogue of the same bantering description, as they all four ascended to the parlour; where—for the young ladies happened, by good fortune, to be a little later than usual that night—the tea-board was at that moment being set out.

Mr. Pinch was not at home, so they had it all to themselves, and were very snug and talkative, Jonas sitting between the two sisters, and displaying his gallantry in that engaging manner which was peculiar to him. It was a hard thing, Mr. Pecksniff said, when tea was done and cleared away, to leave so pleasant a little party, but having some important papers to examine in his own apartment, he must beg them to excuse him for half an hour. With this apology he withdrew, singing a careless strain as he went. He had not been gone five minutes, when Merry, who had been sitting in the window, apart from Jonas and her sister, burst into a half-smothered laugh, and skipped towards the door.

"Hallo!" cried Jonas. "Don't go."

"Oh, I dare say!" rejoined Merry, looking back. "You're very anxious I should stay, fright, ain't you?"

"Yes, I am," said Jonas. "Upon my word I am. I

want to speak to you." But as she left the room notwithstanding, he ran out after her, and brought her back, after a short struggle in the passage which scandalized Miss Cherry very much.

"Upon my word, Merry," urged that young lady, "I wonder at you! There are bounds even to absurdity, my dear."

"Thank you, my sweet," said Merry, pursing up her rosy lips. "Much obliged to it for its advice. Oh! do leave me alone, you monster, do!" This entreaty was wrung from her by a new proceeding on the part of Mr. Jonas, who pulled her down, all breathless as she was, into a seat beside him on the sofa, having at the same time Miss Cherry upon the other side.

"Now," said Jonas, clasping the waist of each: "I have got both arms full, haven't I?"

"One of them will be black and blue to-morrow, if you don't let me go," cried the playful Merry.

"Ah! I don't mind *your* pinching," grinned Jonas, "a bit."

"Pinch him for me, Cherry, pray," said Mercy. "I never did hate anybody so much as I hate this creature, I declare!"

"No, no, don't say that," urged Jonas, "and don't pinch either, because I want to be serious. I say—Cousin Charity—"

"Well! what?" she answered sharply.

"I want to have some sober talk," said Jonas: "I want to prevent any mistakes, you know, and to put everything upon a pleasant understanding. That's desirable and proper, ain't it?"

Neither of the sisters spoke a word. Mr. Jonas paused and cleared his throat, which was very dry.

"She'll not believe what I am going to say, will she, cousin?" said Jonas, timidly squeezing Miss Charity.

"Really, Mr. Jonas, I don't know, until I hear what it is. It's quite impossible!"

"Why, you see," said Jonas, "her way always being to make game of people, I know she'll laugh, or pretend to—I know that, beforehand. But you can tell her I'm in earnest, cousin; can't you? You'll confess you know, won't you? You'll be honourable, I'm sure," he added persuasively.

No answer. His throat seemed to grow hotter and hotter, and to be more and more difficult to control.

"You see, Cousin Charity," said Jonas, "nobody but
you can tell her what pains I took to get into her company
when you were both at the boarding-house in the City, because nobody's so well aware of it, you know. Nobody
else can tell her how hard I tried to get to know you better, in order that I might get to know her without seeming
to wish it; can they? I always asked you about her, and
said where had she gone, and when would she come, and
how lively she was, and all that; didn't I, cousin? I
know you'll tell her so, if you haven't told her so already,
and—and—I dare say you have, because I'm sure you're
honourable, ain't you?"

Still not a word. The right arm of Mr. Jonas—the
elder sister sat upon his right—may have been sensible of
some tumultuous throbbing which was not within itself;
but nothing else apprised him that his words had had the
least effect.

"Even if you kept it to yourself, and haven't told her,"
resumed Jonas, "it don't much matter, because you'll bear
honest witness now; won't you? We've been very good
friends from the first; haven't we? And of course we shall
be quite friends in future, and so I don't mind speaking
before you a bit. Cousin Mercy, you've heard what I've
been saying. She'll confirm it, every word; she must.
Will you have me for your husband? Eh?"

As he released his hold of Charity, to put this question
with better effect, she started up and hurried away to her
own room, marking her progress as she went by such a train
of passionate and incoherent sound, as nothing but a
slighted woman in her anger could produce.

"Let me go away. Let me go after her," said Merry,
pushing him off, and giving him—to tell the truth—more
than one sounding slap upon his outstretched face.

"Not till you say 'Yes.' You haven't told me. Will
you have me for your husband?"

"No, I won't. I can't bear the sight of you. I have
told you so a hundred times. You are a fright. Besides,
I always thought you liked my sister best. We all thought
so."

"But that wasn't my fault," said Jonas.

"Yes, it was: you know it was."

"Any trick is fair in love," said Jonas. "She may
have thought I liked her best, but you didn't."

"I did!"

"No, you didn't. You never could have thought I liked her best, when you were by."

"There's no accounting for tastes," said Merry; "at least I didn't mean to say that. I don't know what I mean. Let me go to her."

"Say ' Yes,' and then I will."

"If I ever brought myself to say so, it should only be, that I might hate and tease you all my life."

"That's as good," cried Jonas, "as saying it right out. It's a bargain, cousin. We're a pair, if ever there was one."

This gallant speech was succeeded by a confused noise of kissing and slapping; and then the fair, but much dishevelled Merry broke away, and followed in the footsteps of her sister.

Now, whether Mr. Pecksniff had been listening—which in one of his character appears impossible: or divined almost by inspiration what the matter was—which, in a man of his sagacity is far more probable: or happened by sheer good fortune to find himself in exactly the right place, at precisely the right time—which, under the special guardianship in which he lived might very reasonably happen: it is quite certain that at the moment when the sisters came together in their own room, he appeared at the chamber door. And a marvellous contrast it was—they so heated, noisy, and vehement; he so calm, so self-possessed, so cool and full of peace, that not a hair upon his head was stirred.

"Children!" said Mr. Pecksniff, spreading out his hands in wonder, but not before he had shut the door, and set his back against it. Girls! Daughters! What is this?"

"The wretch; the apostate; the false, mean, odious villain; has before my very face proposed to Mercy!" was his elder daughter's answer.

"Who has proposed to Mercy?" said Mr. Pecksniff.

"*He* has. That thing. Jonas, down stairs."

"Jonas proposed to Mercy!" said Mr. Pecksniff. "Ay, ay! Indeed!"

"Have you nothing else to say?" cried Charity. "Am I to be driven mad, papa? He has proposed to Mercy, not to me."

"Oh, fie! For shame!" said Mr. Pecksniff, gravely. "Oh, for shame! Can the triumph of a sister move you to this terrible display, my child? Oh, really this is very

sad! I am sorry; I am surprised and hurt to see you so.
Mercy, my girl, bless you! See to her. Ah, envy, envy,
what a passion you are!"

Uttering this apostrophe in a tone full of grief and lam-
entation, Mr. Pecksniff left the room (taking care to shut
the door behind him), and walked down stairs into the
parlour. There he found his intended son-in-law, whom
he seized by both hands.

"Jonas!" cried Mr. Pecksniff, "Jonas! the dearest wish
of my heart is now fulfilled!"

"Very well; I'm glad to hear it," said Jonas. "That'll
do. I say, as it ain't the one you're so fond of, you must
come down with another thousand, Pecksniff. You must
make it up five. It's worth that to keep your treasure to
yourself, you know. You get off very cheap that way,
and haven't a sacrifice to make."

The grin with which he accompanied this, set off his
other attractions to such unspeakable advantage, that even
Mr. Pecksniff lost his presence of mind for the moment,
and looked at the young man as if he were quite stupefied
with wonder and admiration. But he quickly regained his
composure, and was in the very act of changing the subject, when a hasty step was heard without, and Tom Pinch,
in a state of great excitement, came darting into the
room.

On seeing a stranger there, apparently engaged with Mr.
Pecksniff in private conversation, Tom was very much
abashed, though he still looked as if he had something of
great importance to communicate, which would be a sufficient apology for this intrusion.

"Mr. Pinch," said Pecksniff, "this is hardly decent.
You will excuse my saying that I think your conduct
scarcely decent, Mr. Pinch."

"I beg your pardon, Sir," replied Tom, "for not knocking at the door."

"Rather beg this gentleman's pardon, Mr. Pinch," said
Pecksniff. "*I* know you; he does not.—My young man,
Mr. Jonas."

The son-in-law that was to be gave him a slight nod—
not actively disdainful or contemptuous, only passively;
for he was in a good humour.

"Could I speak a word with you, Sir, if you please?"
said Tom. "It's rather pressing."

"It should be very pressing to justify this strange behaviour, Mr. Pinch," returned his master. "Excuse me
for a moment, my dear friend. Now, Sir, what is the
reason of this rough intrusion?"

"I am very sorry, Sir, I am sure," said Tom, standing,
cap in hand, before his patron in the passage: "and I know
it must have a very rude appearance—"

"It *has* a very rude appearance, Mr. Pinch."

"Yes, I feel that, Sir; but the truth is, I was so surprised to see them, and knew you would be too, that I ran
home very fast indeed, and really hadn't enough command
over myself to know what I was doing very well. I was
in the church just now, Sir, touching the organ for my own
amusement, when I happened to look round, and saw a
gentleman and lady standing in the aisle listening. They
seemed to be strangers, Sir, as well as I could make out in
the dusk: and I thought I didn't know them: so presently
I left off, and said, would they walk up into the organ-loft,
or take a seat? No, they said, they wouldn't do that; but
they thanked me for the music they had heard—in fact,"
observed Tom, blushing—"they said, 'Delicious music!'
at least, *she* did; and I am sure that was a greater pleasure
and honour to me, than any compliment I could have had.
I—I—beg your pardon, Sir;" he was all in a tremble, and
dropped his hat for the second time; "but I—I'm rather
flurried, and I fear I've wandered from the point."

"If you will come back to it, Thomas," said Mr. Pecksniff, with an icy look, "I shall feel obliged."

"Yes, Sir," returned Tom, "certainly. They had a posting carriage at the porch, Sir, and had stopped to hear the
organ, they said, and then they said—*she* said, I mean, 'I
believe you live with Mr. Pecksniff, Sir?' I said I had
that honour, and I took the liberty, Sir," added Tom, raising his eyes to his benefactor's face, "of saying, as I always will and must, with your permission, that I was under great obligations to you, and never could express my
sense of them sufficiently."

"That," said Mr. Pecksniff, "was very, very wrong.
Take your time, Mr. Pinch."

"Thank you, Sir," cried Tom. "On that they asked
me—she asked, I mean—'Wasn't there a bridle road to
Mr. Pecksniff's house—'"

Mr. Pecksniff suddenly became full of interest.

"'Without going by the Dragon?' When I said there
was, and said how happy I should be to show it 'em, they
sent the carriage on by the road, and came with me across
the meadows. I left 'em at the turnstile to run forward
and tell you they were coming, and they'll be here, Sir, in
—in less than a minute's time, I should say," added Tom,
fetching his breath with difficulty.

"Now, who," said Mr. Pecksniff, pondering, "who may
these people be!"

"Bless my soul, Sir!" cried Tom, "I meant to mention
that at first, I thought I had. I knew them—her, I mean
—directly. The gentleman who was ill at the Dragon,
Sir, last winter; and the young lady who attended him."

Tom's teeth chattered in his head, and he positively
staggered with amazement, at witnessing the extraordinary
effect produced on Mr. Pecksniff by these simple words.
The dread of losing the old man's favour almost as soon as
they were reconciled, through the mere fact of having
Jonas in the house; the impossibility of dismissing Jonas,
or shutting him up, or tying him hand and foot and putting him in the coal-cellar, without offending him beyond
recall; the horrible discordance prevailing in the establishment, and the impossibility of reducing it to decent harmony, with Charity in loud hysterics, Mercy in the utmost
disorder, Jonas in the parlour, and Martin Chuzzlewit and
his young charge upon the very door-steps; the total hopelessness of being able to disguise or feasibly explain this
state of rampant confusion; the sudden accumulation over
his devoted head of every complicated perplexity and en-
tanglement—for his extrication from which he had trusted
to time, good fortune, chance, and his own plotting—so
filled the entrapped architect with dismay, that if Tom
could have been a Gorgon staring at Mr. Pecksniff, and
Mr. Pecksniff could have been a Gorgon staring at Tom,
they could not have horrified each other half so much as
in their own bewildered persons.

"Dear, dear!" cried Tom, "what have I done? I hoped
it would be a pleasant surprise, Sir. I thought you would
like to know."

But at that moment a loud knocking was heard at the
hall-door.

23

CHAPTER XXI.

MORE AMERICAN EXPERIENCES. MARTIN TAKES A
PARTNER, AND MAKES A PURCHASE. SOME AC-
COUNT OF EDEN, AS IT APPEARED ON PAPER.
ALSO OF THE BRITISH LION. ALSO OF THE KIND
OF SYMPATHY PROFESSED AND ENTERTAINED BY
THE WATERTOAST ASSOCIATION OF UNITED SYM-
PATHIZERS.

THE knocking at Mr. Pecksniff's door, though loud
enough, bore no resemblance whatever to the noise of an
American railway train at full speed. It may be well to
begin the present chapter with this frank admission, lest
the reader should imagine that the sounds now deafening
this history's ears have any connexion with the knocker on
Mr. Pecksniff's door, or with the great amount of agitation
pretty equally divided between that worthy man and Mr.
Pinch, of which its strong performance was the cause.

Mr. Pecksniff's house is more than a thousand leagues
away; and again this happy chronicle has Liberty and
Moral Sensibility for its high companions. Again it
breathes the blessed air of Independence; again it contem-
plates with pious awe that moral sense which renders unto
Cæsar nothing that is his; again inhales that sacred atmosphere which was the life of him—oh noble patriot, with
many followers!—who dreamed of Freedom in a slave's
embrace, and waking sold her offspring and his own in
public markets.

How the wheels clank and rattle, and the tram-road
shakes, as the train rushes on! And now the engine yells,
as it were lashed and tortured like a living labourer, and
writhed in agony. A poor fancy; for steal and iron are of
infinitely greater account, in this commonwealth, than flesh
and blood. If the cunning work of man be urged beyond
its power of endurance, it has within it the elements of its
own revenge; whereas the wretched mechanism of the Divine Hand is dangerous with no such property, but may be
tampered with, and crushed, and broken, at the driver's
pleasure. Look at that engine! It shall cost a man more
dollars in the way of penalty and fine, and satisfaction of

the outraged law, to deface in wantonness that senseless
mass of metal, than to take the lives of twenty human
creatures! Thus the stars wink upon the bloody stripes;
and Liberty pulls down her cap upon her eyes, and owns
Oppression in its vilest aspect, for her sister.
The engine-driver of the train whose noise awoke us to
the present chapter, was certainly troubled with no such
reflections as these; nor is it very probable that his mind
was disturbed by any reflections at all. He leaned with
folded arms and crossed legs against the side of the carriage, smoking; and, except when he expressed, by a grunt
as short as his pipe, his approval of some particularly dexterous aim on the part of his colleague, the fireman, who
beguiled his leisure by throwing logs of wood from the
tender at the numerous stray cattle on the line, he preserved a composure so immovable, and an indifference so
complete, that if the locomotive had been a sucking-pig, he
could not have been more perfectly indifferent to its doings.
Notwithstanding the tranquil state of this officer, and his
unbroken peace of mind, the train was proceeding with tolerable rapidity; and the rails being but poorly laid, the
jolts and bumps it met with in its progress were neither
slight nor few.
There were three great caravans or cars attached. The
ladies' car, the gentlemen's car, and the car for negroes:
the latter painted black, as an appropriate compliment to
its company. Martin and Mark Tapley were in the first,
as it was the most comfortable; and, being far from full,
received other gentlemen who, like them, were unblessed
by the society of ladies of their own. They were seated
side by side, and were engaged in earnest conversation.
"And so, Mark," said Martin, looking at him with an
anxious expression,—"and so you are glad we have left
New York far behind us, are you?"
"Yes, Sir," said Mark. "I am. Precious glad."
"Were you not ' jolly ' there?" asked Martin.
"On the contrary, Sir," returned Mark. "The jolliest
week as ever I spent in my life, was that there week at
Pawkins's."
"What do you think of our prospects?" inquired Mar-
tin, with an air that plainly said he had avoided the ques-
tion for some time.
"Uncommon bright, Sir," returned Mark. "Impossible

for a place to have a better name, Sir, than the Walley of
Eden. No man couldn't think of settling in a better place
than the Walley of Eden. And I'm told," added Mark
after a pause, "as there's lots of serpents there, so we shall
come out, quite complete and reg'lar."

So far from dwelling upon this agreeable piece of information with the least dismay, Mark's face grew radiant as
he called it to mind: so very radiant, that a stranger might
have supposed he had all his life been yearning for the society of serpents, and now hailed with delight the approaching consummation of his fondest wishes.

"Who told you that?" asked Martin, sternly.

"A military officer," said Mark.

"Confound you for a ridiculous fellow!" cried Martin,
laughing heartily in spite of himself. "What military officer? You know they spring up in every field—"

"As thick as scarecrows in England, Sir," interposed
Mark, "which is a sort of militia themselves, being entirely
coat and wescoat, with a stick inside. Ha, ha!—Don't
mind me, Sir; it's my way sometimes. I can't help being
jolly.—Why it was one of them inwading conquerors at
Pawkins's, as told me. 'Am I rightly informed,' he says
—not exactly through his nose, but as if he'd got a stoppage in it, very high up—'that you're a going to the Walley
of Eden?' 'I heard some talk on it,' I told him. 'Oh!'
says he, 'if you should ever happen to go to bed there—
you *may*, you know,' he says, 'in course of time as civilisation progresses—don't forget to take a axe with you.'
I looks at him tolerable hard. 'Fleas?' says I. 'And
more,' says he. 'Wampires?' says I. 'And more,' says
he. 'Musquitoes, perhaps?' says I. 'And more,' says
he. 'What more?' says I. 'Snakes more,' says he;
'rattlesnakes. You're right to a certain extent, stranger;
there air some catawampous chawers in the small way too,
as graze upon a human pretty strong; but don't mind *them*
—they're company. It's snakes,' he says, 'as you'll object to: and whenever you wake and see one in a upright
poster on your bed,' he says, 'like a corkscrew with the
handle off a sittin' on its bottom ring, cut him down, for
he means wenom.'"

"Why didn't you tell me this before!" cried Martin,
with an expression of face which set off the cheerfulness of
Mark's visage to great advantage.

"I never thought on it, Sir," said Mark. "It come in at one ear, and went out at the other. But Lord love us, he was one of another Company I dare say, and only made up the story that we might go to his Eden, and not the opposition one."

"There's some probability in that," observed Martin. "I can honestly say that I hope so, with all my heart."

"I've not a doubt about it, Sir," returned Mark, who, full of the inspiriting influence of the anecdote upon himself, had for the moment forgotten its probable effect upon his master: "anyhow, we must live, you know, Sir."

"Live!" cried Martin. "Yes, it's easy to say live; but if we should happen not to wake when rattlesnakes are making corkscrews of themselves upon our beds, it may be not so easy to do it."

"And that's a fact," said a voice so close in his ear that it tickled him. "That's dreadful true."

Martin looked round, and found that a gentleman, on the seat behind, had thrust his head between himself and Mark, and sat with his chin resting on the back rail of their little bench, entertaining himself with their conversation. He was as languid and listless in his looks, as most of the gentlemen they had seen; his cheeks were so hollow that he seemed to be always sucking them in; and the sun had burnt him—not a wholesome red or brown, but dirty yellow. He had bright dark eyes, which he kept half closed; only peeping out of the corners, and even then with a glance that seemed to say, "Now you won't overreach me: you want to, but you won't." His arms rested carelessly on his knees as he leant forward; in the palm of his left hand, as English rustics have their slice of cheese, he had a cake of tobacco; in his right a penknife. He struck into the dialogue with as little reserve as if he had been specially called in, days before, to hear the arguments on both sides, and favour them with his opinion; and he no more contemplated or cared for the possibility of their not desiring the honour of his acquaintance or interference in their private affairs, than if he had been a bear or a buffalo.

"That," he repeated, nodding condescendingly to Martin, as to an outer barbarian and foreigner, "is dreadful true. Darn all manner of vermin."

Martin could not help frowning for a moment, as if he were disposed to insinuate that the gentleman had uncon-

sciously "darned " himself. But remembering the wisdom
of doing at Rome as Romans do, he smiled with the pleasantest expression he could assume upon so short a notice.

Their new friend said no more just then, being busily
employed in cutting a quid or plug from his cake of tobacco,
and whistling softly to himself the while. When he had
shaped it to his liking, he took out his old plug, and de-
posited the same on the back of the seat between Mark and
Martin, while he thrust the new one into the hollow of his
cheek, where it looked like a large walnut or tolerable pip-
pin. Finding it quite satisfactory, he struck the point of
his knife into the old plug, and holding it out for their inspection, remarked with the air of a man who had not lived
in vain, that it was "used up considerable." Then he tossed
it away; put his knife into one pocket and his tobacco into
another; rested his chin upon the rail as before; and ap-
proving of the pattern on Martin's waistcoat, reached out
his hand to feel the texture of that garment.

"What do you call this now?" he asked.

"Upon my word," said Martin, "I don't know what it's
called."

"It'll cost a dollar or more a yard, I reckon?"

"I really don't know."

"In my country," said the gentleman, "we know the
cost of our own prŏdūce."

Martin not discussing the question, there was a pause.

"Well!" resumed their new friend, after staring at
them intently during the whole interval of silence: "how's
the unnat'ral old parent by this time?"

Mr. Tapley, regarding this enquiry as only another ver-
sion of the impertinent English question—"How's your
mother?"—would have resented it instantly, but for Martin's prompt interposition.

"You mean the old country?" he said.

"Ah!" was the reply. "How's she? Progressing
back'ards, I expect, as usual? Well! How's Queen Victoria?"

"In good health, I believe," said Martin.

"Queen Victoria won't shake in her royal shoes at all,
when she hears to-morrow named," observed the stranger.
"No."

"Not that I am aware of. Why should she?"

"She won't be taken with a cold chill, when she realises

what is being done in these diggings," said the stranger.
"No."

"No," said Martin. "I think I could take my oath of that."

The strange gentleman looked at him as if in pity for his ignorance or prejudice, and said:

"Well, Sir, I tell you this—there ain't a ĕn-gīne with its biler bust, in God Almighty's free U-nited States, so fixed, and nipped, and frizzled to a most e-tarnal smash, as that young critter, in her luxurious location in the Tower of London, will be, when she reads the next double-extra Watertoast Gazette."

Several other gentlemen had left their seats and gathered round during the foregoing dialogue. They were highly delighted with this speech. One very lank gentleman, in a loose limp white cravat, a long white waistcoat, and a black great-coat, who seemed to be in authority among them, felt called upon to acknowledge it.

"Hem! Mr. La Fayette Kettle," he said, taking off his hat.

There was a grave murmur of "Hush!"

"Mr. La Fayette Kettle! Sir!"

Mr. Kettle bowed.

"In the name of this company, Sir, and in the name of our common country, and in the name of that righteous cause of holy sympathy in which we are engaged, I thank you. I thank you, Sir, in the name of the Watertoast Sympathizers; and I thank you, Sir, in the name of the Watertoast Gazette; and I thank you, Sir, in the name of the star-spangled banner of the Great United States, for your eloquent and categorical exposition. And if, Sir," said the speaker, poking Martin with the handle of his umbrella to bespeak his attention, for he was listening to a whisper from Mark; "if, Sir, in such a place, and at such a time, I might venture to con-clude with a sentiment, glancing — however slantin'dicularly — at the subject in hand, I would say, Sir, May the British Lion have his talons eradicated by the noble bill of the American Eagle, and be taught to play upon the Irish Harp and the Scotch Fiddle that music which is breathed in every empty shell that lies upon the shores of green Co-lumbia!"

Here the lank gentleman sat down again, amidst a great sensation; and every one looked very grave.

"General Choke," said Mr. La Fayette Kettle, "you warm my heart; Sir, you warm my heart. But the British Lion is not unrepresented here, Sir; and I should be glad to hear his answer to those remarks."

"Upon my word," cried Martin, laughing, "since you do me the honour to consider me his representative, I have only to say that I never heard of Queen Victoria reading the What's-his-name Gazette, and that I should scarcely think it probable."

General Choke smiled upon the rest, and said, in patient and benignant explanation:

"It is sent to her, Sir. It is sent to her. Per mail."

"But if it is addressed to the Tower of London, it would hardly come to hand, I fear," returned Martin: "for she don't live there."

"The Queen of England, gentlemen," observed Mr. Tapley, affecting the greatest politeness, and regarding them with an immovable face, "usually lives in the Mint to take care of the money. She *has* lodgings, in virtue of her office, with the Lord Mayor at the Mansion-House; but don't often occupy them, in consequence of the parlour chimney smoking."

"Mark," said Martin, "I shall be very much obliged to you if you'll have the goodness not to interfere with pre-posterous statements, however jocose they may appear to you. I was merely remarking, gentlemen—though it's a point of very little import—that the Queen of England does not happen to live in the Tower of London."

"General!" cried Mr. La Fayette Kettle. "You hear?"

"General!" echoed several others. "General!"

"Hush! Pray, silence!" said General Choke, holding up his hand, and speaking with a patient and complacent benevolence that was quite touching. "I have always re-marked it as a very extraordinary circumstance, which I impute to the natur' of British Institutions and their ten-dency to suppress that popular inquiry and information which air so widely diffused even in the trackless forests of this vast Continent of the Western Ocean; that the knowledge of Britishers themselves on such points is not to be compared with that possessed by our intelligent and lo-comotive citizens. This is interesting, and confirms my observation. When you say, Sir," he continued, address-ing Martin, "that your Queen does not reside in the Tower

of London, you fall into an error, not uncommon to your
countrymen, even when their abilities and moral elements
air such as to command respect. But, Sir, you air wrong.
She *does* live there—"

"When she is at the Court of Saint James's," interposed
Kettle.

"When she is at the Court of Saint James's, of course,"
returned the General, in the same benignant way: "for if
her location was in Windsor Pavilion it couldn't be in London at the same time. Your Tower of London, Sir," pursued the General, smiling with a mild consciousness of his
knowledge, "is nat'rally your royal residence. Being located in the immediate neighbourhood of your Parks, your
Drives, your Triumphant Arches, your Opera, and your
Royal Almacks, it nat'rally suggests itself as the place for
holding a luxurious and thoughtless court. And, consequently," said the General, "consequently, the court is
held there."

"Have you been in England?" asked Martin.

"In print I have, Sir," said the General, "not otherwise. We air a reading people here, Sir. You will meet
with much information among us that will surprise you,
Sir."

"I have not the least doubt of it," returned Martin.
But here he was interrupted by Mr. La Fayette Kettle,
who whispered in his ear:

"You know General Choke?"

"No," returned Martin, in the same tone.

"You know what he is considered?"

"One of the most remarkable men in the country?" said
Martin, at a venture.

"That's a fact," rejoined Kettle. "I was sure you must
have heard of him!"

"I think," said Martin, addressing himself to the General again, "that I have the pleasure of being the bearer of
a letter of introduction to you, Sir. From Mr. Bevan, of
Massachusetts," he added, giving it to him.

The General took it and read it attentively: now and
then stopping to glance at the two strangers. When he
had finished the note, he came over to Martin, sat down by
him, and shook hands.

"Well!" he said, "and you think of settling in Eden?"

"Subject to your opinion, and the agent's advice," replied Martin. "I am told there is nothing to be done in the old towns."

"I can introduce you to the agent, Sir," said the General. "I know him. In fact, I am a member of the Eden Land Corporation myself."

This was serious news to Martin, for his friend had laid great stress upon the General's having no connexion, as he thought, with any land company, and therefore being likely to give him disinterested advice. The General explained that he had joined the Corporation only a few weeks ago, and that no communication had passed between himself and Mr. Bevan since.

"We have very little to venture," said Martin anxiously —"only a few pounds; but it is our all. Now, do you think that for one of my profession, this would be a speculation with any hope or chance in it?"

"Well!" observed the General, gravely, "if there wasn't any hope or chance in the speculation, it wouldn't have engaged my dollars, I opinionate."

"I don't mean for the sellers," said Martin. "For the buyers—for the buyers!"

"For the buyers, Sir?" observed the General, in a most impressive manner. "Well! you come from an old country: from a country, Sir, that has piled up golden calves as high as Babel, and worshipped 'em for ages. We are a new country, Sir; man is in a more primeval state here, Sir; we have not the excuse of having lapsed in the slow course of time into degenerate practices; we have no false gods; man, Sir, here, is man in all his dignity. We fought for that or nothing. Here am I, Sir," said the General, setting up his umbrella to represent himself; and a villainous-looking umbrella it was; a very bad counter to stand for the sterling coin of his benevolence: "here am I with gray hairs, Sir, and a moral sense. Would I, with my principles, invest capital in this speculation if I didn't think it full of hopes and chances for my brother man?"

Martin tried to look convinced, but he thought of New York, and found it difficult.

"What are the Great United States for, Sir," pursued the General, "if not for the regeneration of man? But it is nat'ral in you to make such an enquery, for you come from England, and you do not know my country."

"Then you think," said Martin, "that allowing for the

hardships we are prepared to undergo, there is a reasonable —Heaven knows we don't expect much—a reasonable opening in this place? "

"A reasonable opening in Eden, Sir! But see the agent, see the agent; see the maps, and plans, Sir; and conclude to go or stay, according to the natur' of the settlement. Eden hadn't need to go a begging yet, Sir," remarked the General.

"It is an awful lovely place, sure-ly. And frightful wholesome, likewise!" said Mr. Kettle, who had made himself a party to this conversation as a matter of course.

Martin felt that to dispute such testimony, for no better reason than because he had his secret misgivings on the subject, would be ungentlemanly and indecent. So he thanked the General for his promise to put him in personal communication with the agent; and "concluded" to see that officer next morning. He then begged the General to inform him who the Watertoast Sympathizers were, of whom he had spoken in addressing Mr. La Fayette Kettle, and on what grievances they bestowed their Sympathy. To which the General, looking very serious, made answer, that he might fully enlighten himself on those points to-morrow by attending a Great Meeting of the Body, which would then be held at the town to which they were travelling: "over which, Sir," said the General, "my fellow-citizens have called on me to preside."

They came to their journey's end late in the evening. Close to the railway was an immense white edifice, like an ugly hospital, on which was painted "NATIONAL HOTEL." There was a wooden gallery or verandah in front, on which it was rather startling, when the train stopped, to behold a great many pairs of boots and shoes, and the smoke of a great many cigars, but no other evidences of human habitation. By slow degrees, however, some heads and shoulders appeared, and connecting themselves with the boots and shoes, led to the discovery that certain gentlemen boarders, who had a fancy for putting their heels where the gentlemen boarders in other countries usually put their heads, were enjoying themselves after their own manner in the cool of the evening.

There was a great bar-room in this hotel, and a great public room in which the general table was being set out for supper. There were interminable whitewashed staircases, long whitewashed galleries up stairs and down stairs, scores of little whitewashed bed-rooms, and a four-sided verandah to every story in the house, which formed a large brick square with an uncomfortable courtyard in the centre: where some clothes were drying. Here and there, some yawning gentlemen lounged up and down with their hands in their pockets; but within the house and without, where-ever half a dozen people were collected together, there, in their looks, dress, morals, manners, habits, intellect, and conversation, were Mr. Jefferson Brick, Colonel Diver, Major Pawkins, General Choke, and Mr. La Fayette Kettle, over, and over, and over again. They did the same things; said the same things; judged all subjects by, and reduced all subjects to, the same standard. Observing how they lived, and how they were always in the enchanting company of each other, Martin even began to comprehend their being the social, cheerful, winning, airy men they were.

At the sounding of a dismal gong, this pleasant company went trooping down from all parts of the house to the public room; while from the neighbouring stores other guests came flocking in, in shoals; for half the town, married folks as well as single, resided at the National Hotel. Tea, coffee, dried meats, tongue, ham, pickles, cake, toast, preserves, and bread and butter, were swallowed with the usual ravishing speed; and then, as before, the company dropped off by degrees, and lounged away to the desk, the counter, or the bar-room. The ladies had a smaller ordinary of their own, to which their husbands and brothers were admitted if they chose; and in all other respects they enjoyed themselves as at Pawkins's.

"Now, Mark, my good fellow," said Martin, closing the door of his little chamber, "we must hold a solemn counsel, for our fate is decided to-morrow morning. You are determined to invest these savings of yours in the common stock, are you?"

"If I hadn't been determined to make that wentur, Sir," answered Mr. Tapley, "I shouldn't have come."

"How much is there here, did you say?" asked Martin, holding up a little bag.

"Thirty-seven pound ten and sixpence. The Savings' Bank said so, at least. I never counted it. But *they* know, bless you!" said Mark, with a shake of the head expressive of his unbounded confidence in the wisdom and arithmetic of those Institutions.

"The money we brought with us," said Martin, "is reduced to a few shillings less than eight pounds."

Mr. Tapley smiled, and looked all manner of ways, that he might not be supposed to attach any importance to this fact.

"Upon the ring—*her* ring, Mark," said Martin, looking ruefully at his empty finger—

"Ah!" sighed Mr. Tapley. "Beg your pardon, Sir."

"—We raised, in English money, fourteen pounds. So, even with that, your share of the stock is still very much the larger of the two, you see. Now, Mark," said Martin, in his old way, just as he might have spoken to Tom Pinch, "I have thought of a means of making this up to you, more than making it up to you, I hope,—and very materially elevating your prospects in life."

"Oh! don't talk of that, you know, Sir," returned Mark. "I don't want no elevating, Sir. I'm all right enough, Sir, *I* am."

"No, but hear me," said Martin, "because this is very important to you, and a great satisfaction to me. Mark, you shall be a partner in the business: an equal partner with myself. I will put in, as my additional capital, my professional knowledge and ability; and half the annual profits, as long as it is carried on, shall be yours."

Poor Martin! For ever building castles in the air. For ever, in his very selfishness, forgetful of all but his own teeming hopes and sanguine plans. Swelling, at that instant, with the consciousness of patronising and most munificently rewarding Mark!

"I don't know, Sir," Mark rejoined, much more sadly than his custom was, though from a very different cause than Martin supposed, "what I can say to this, in the way of thanking you. I'll stand by you, Sir, to the best of my ability, and to the last. That's all."

"We quite understand each other, my good fellow," said Martin, rising in self-approval and condescension. "We are no longer master and servant, but friends and partners; and are mutually gratified. If we determine on Eden, the business shall be commenced as soon as we get there. Under the name," said Martin, who never hammered upon an idea that wasn't red hot, "under the name of Chuzzlewit and Tapley."

7—13

"Lord love you, Sir," cried Mark, "don't have my namo in it. I ain't acquainted with the business, Sir. I must be Co., I must. I've often thought," he added, in a low voice, "as I should like to know a Co.; but I little thought as ever I should live to be one."

"You shall have your own way, Mark."

"Thank'ee, Sir. If any country gentleman thereabouts, in the public way, or otherwise, wanted such a thing as a skittle-ground made, I could take that part of the bis'ness, Sir."

"Against any architect in the States," said Martin. "Get a couple of sherry-cobblers, Mark, and we'll drink success to the firm."

Either he forgot already (and often afterwards), that they were no longer master and servant, or considered this kind of duty to be among the legitimate functions of the Co. But Mark obeyed with his usual alacrity; and before they parted for the night, it was agreed between them that they should go together to the agent's in the morning, but that Martin should decide the Eden question, on his own sound judgment. And Mark made no merit, even to himself in his jollity, of this concession; perfectly well knowing that the matter would come to that in the end, any way.

The General was one of the party at the public table next day, and after breakfast suggested that they should wait upon the agent without loss of time. They, desiring nothing more, agreed; so off they all four started for the office of the Eden Settlement, which was almost within rifle-shot of the National Hotel.

It was a small place—something like a turnpike. But a great deal of land may be got into a dice-box, and why may not a whole territory be bargained for in a shed? It was but a temporary office too; for the Edeners were "going" to build a superb establishment for the transaction of their business, and had already got so far as to mark out the site; which is a great way in America. The office-door was wide open, and in the door-way was the agent: no doubt a tremendous fellow to get through his work, for he seemed to have no arrears, but was swinging backwards and forwards in a rocking-chair, with one of his legs planted high up against the door-post, and the other doubled up under him, as if he were hatching his foot.

He was a gaunt man in a huge straw hat, and a coat of green stuff. The weather being hot, he had no cravat, and wore his shirt collar wide open; so that every time he spoke something was seen to twitch and jerk up in his throat, like the little hammers in a harpsichord when the notes are struck. Perhaps it was the Truth feebly endeavouring to leap to his lips. If so, it never reached them.

Two gray eyes lurked deep within this agent's head, but one of them had no sight in it, and stood stock still. With that side of his face he seemed to listen to what the other side was doing. Thus each profile had a distinct expression; and when the movable side was most in action, the rigid one was in its coldest state of watchfulness. It was like turning the man inside out, to pass to that view of his features in his liveliest mood, and see how calculating and intent they were.

Each long black hair upon his head hung down as straight as any plummet line, but rumpled tufts were on the arches of his eyes, as if the crow whose foot was deeply printed in the corners, had pecked and torn them in a savage recognition of his kindred nature as a bird of prey.

Such was the man whom they now approached, and whom the General saluted by the name of Scadder.

"Well, Gen'ral," he returned, "and how are you?"

"Ac-tive and spry, Sir, in my country's service and the sympathetic cause. Two gentlemen on business, Mr. Scadder."

He shook hands with each of them—nothing is done in America without shaking hands—then went on rocking.

"I think I know what bis'ness you have brought these strangers here upon, then, Gen'ral?"

"Well, Sir. I expect you may."

"You air a tongue-y person, Gen'ral. For you talk too much, and that's a fact," said Scadder. "You speak a-larming well in public, but you didn't ought to go ahead so fast in private. Now!"

"If I can realise your meaning, ride me on a rail!" returned the General, after pausing for consideration.

"You know we didn't wish to sell the lots off right away to any loafer as might bid," said Scadder; "but had concluded to reserve 'em for Aristocrats of Natur'. Yes!"

"And they are here, Sir!" cried the General with warmth. "They are here, Sir!"

"If they air here," returned the agent, in reproachful accents, "that's enough. But you didn't ought to have your dander ris with *me*, Gen'ral."

The General whispered Martin that Scadder was the honestest fellow in the world, and that he wouldn't have given him offence designedly, for ten thousand dollars.

"I do my duty; and I raise the dander of my feller critters, as I wish to serve," said Scadder in a low voice, looking down the road and rocking still. "They rile up rough, along of my objecting to their selling Eden off too cheap. That's human natur'! Well!"

"Mr. Scadder," said the General, assuming his oratorical deportment. "Sir! Here is my hand, and here my heart. I esteem you, Sir, and ask your pardon. These gentlemen air friends of mine, or I would not have brought 'em here, Sir, being well aware, Sir, that the lots at present go entirely too cheap. But these air friends, Sir; these air partick'ler friends."

Mr. Scadder was so satisfied by this explanation, that he shook the General warmly by the hand, and got out of the rocking-chair to do it. He then invited the Genera''s particular friends to accompany him into the office. As to the General, he observed, with his usual berevolence, that being one of the Company, he wouldn't interfere in the transaction on any account; so he appropriated the rocking-chair to himself, and looked at the prospect, like a good Samaritan waiting for a traveller.

"Heyday!" cried Martin, as his eye rested on a great plan which occupied one whole side of the office. Indeed, the office had little else in it, but some geological and botanical specimens, one or two rusty ledgers, a homely desk, and a stool. "Heyday! what's that?"

"That's Eden," said Scadder, picking his teeth with a sort of young bayonet that flew out of his knife when he touched a spring.

"Why, I had no idea it was a city."

"Hadn't you? Oh, it's a city."

A flourishing city, too! An architectural city! There were banks, churches, cathedrals, market-places, factories, hotels, stores, mansions, wharves; an exchange, a theatre; public buildings of all kinds, down to the office of the Eden Stinger, a daily journal; all faithfully depicted in the view before them.

"Dear me! It's really a most important place!" cried Martin, turning round.

"Oh! it's very important," observed the agent.

"But, I am afraid," said Martin, glancing again at the Public Buildings, "that there's nothing left for me to do."

"Well! it ain't all built," replied the agent. "Not quite."

This was a great relief.

"The market-place, now," said Martin. "Is that built?"

"That?" said the agent, sticking his toothpick into the weathercock on the top. "Let me see. No: that ain't built."

"Rather a good job to begin with,—eh, Mark?" whispered Martin, nudging him with his elbow.

Mark, who, with a very stolid countenance had been eyeing the plan and the agent by turns, merely rejoined "Uncommon!"

A dead silence ensued, Mr. Scadder in some short recesses or vacations of his toothpick, whistled a few bars of Yankee Doodle, and blew the dust off the roof of the Theatre.

"I suppose," said Martin, feigning to look more narrowly at the plan, but showing by his tremulous voice how much depended, in his mind, upon the answer; "I suppose there are—several architects there?"

"There ain't a single one," said Scadder.

"Mark," whispered Martin, pulling him by the sleeve, "do you hear that? But whose work is all this before us, then?" he asked aloud.

"The soil being very fruitful, public buildings grows spontaneous, perhaps," said Mark.

He was on the agent's dark side as he said it; but Scadder instantly changed his place, and brought his active eye to bear upon him.

"Feel of my hands, young man," he said.

"What for?" asked Mark, declining.

"Air they dirty, or air they clean, Sir?" said Scadder, holding them out.

In a physical point of view they were decidedly dirty. But it being obvious that Mr. Scadder offered them for examination in a figurative sense, as emblems of his moral character, Martin hastened to pronounce them pure as the driven snow.

24

"I entreat, Mark," he said, with some irritation, "that you will not obtrude remarks of that nature, which, however harmless and well-intentioned, are quite out of place, and cannot be expected to be very agreeable to strangers. I am quite surprised."

"The Co.'s a putting his foot in it already," thought Mark. "He must be a sleeping partner—fast asleep and snoring—Co. must: *I* see."

Mr. Scadder said nothing, but he set his back against the plan, and thrust his toothpick into the desk some twenty times: looking at Mark all the while as if he were stabbing him in effigy.

"You haven't said whose work it is," Martin ventured to observe, at length, in a tone of mild propitiation.

"Well, never mind whose work it is, or isn't," said the agent sulkily. "No matter how it did eventuate. P'raps he cleared off, handsome, with a heap of dollars; p'raps he wasn't worth a cent. P'raps he was a loafin' rowdy; p'raps a ring-tailed roarer. Now!"

"All your doing, Mark!" said Martin.

"P'raps," pursued the agent, "them a'nt plants of Eden's raising. No! P'raps that desk and stool ain't made from Eden lumber. No! P'raps no end of squatters ain't gone out there. No! P'raps there ain't no such location in the territoary of the Great U-nited States. Oh, no!"

"I hope you're satisfied with the success of your joke, Mark," said Martin.

But here, at a most opportune and happy time, the General interposed, and called out to Scadder from the doorway to give his friends the particulars of that little lot of fifty acres with the house upon it; which, having belonged to the Company formerly, had lately lapsed again into their hands.

"You air a deal too open-handed, Gen'ral," was the answer. "It is a lot as should be rose in price. It is."

He grumblingly opened his books notwithstanding, and always keeping his bright side towards Mark, no matter at what amount of inconvenience to himself, displayed a certain leaf for their perusal. Martin read it greedily, and then inquired:

"Now where upon the plan may this place be?"

"Upon the plan?" said Scadder.

"Yes."

He turned towards it, and reflected for a short time, as if, having been put upon his mettle, he was resolved to be particular to the very minutest hair's breadth of a shade. At length, after wheeling his toothpick slowly round and round in the air, as if it were a carrier pigeon just thrown up, he suddenly made a dart at the drawing, and pierced the very centre of the main wharf, through and through.

"There!" he said, leaving his knife quivering in the wall; "that's where it is!"

Martin glanced with sparkling eyes upon his Co., and his Co. saw that the thing was done.

The bargain was not concluded as easily as might have been expected though, for Scadder was caustic and ill-humoured, and cast much unnecessary opposition in the way: at one time requesting them to think of it, and call again in a week or a fortnight; at another, predicting that they wouldn't like it; at another, offering to retract and let them off, and muttering strong imprecations upon the folly of the General. But the whole of the astoundingly small sum-total of purchase-money—it was only one hundred and fifty dollars, or something more than thirty pounds of the capital brought by Co. into the architectural concern—was ultimately paid down; and Martin's head was two inches nearer the roof of the little wooden office, with the consciousness of being a landed proprietor in the thriving city of Eden.

"If it shouldn't happen to fit," said Scadder, as he gave Martin the necessary credentials on receipt of his money, "don't blame me."

"No, no," he replied merrily. "We'll not blame you. General, are you going?"

"I am at your service, Sir; and I wish you," said the General, giving him his hand with grave cordiality, "joy of your po-ssession. You air now, Sir, a denizen of the most powerful and highly-civilised do-minion that has ever graced the world; a do-minion, Sir, where man is bound to man in one vast bond of equal love and truth. May you, Sir, be worthy of your a-dopted country!"

Martin thanked him, and took leave of Mr. Scadder; who had resumed his post in the rocking-chair, immediately on the General's rising from it, and was once more swinging away as if he had never been disturbed. Mark looked

back several times as they went down the road towards the
National Hotel, but now his blighted profile was towards
them, and nothing but attentive thoughtfulness was written
on it. Strangely different to the other side! He was not
a man much given to laughing, and never laughed outright;
but every line in the print of the crow's foot, and every
little wiry vein in that division of his head, was wrinkled
up into a grin! The compound figure of Death and the
Lady at the top of the old ballad was not divided with a
greater nicety, and hadn't halves more monstrously unlike
each other, than the two profiles of Zephaniah Scadder.

The General posted along at a great rate, for the clock
was on the stroke of twelve; and at that hour precisely,
the Great Meeting of the Watertoast Sympathisers was to
be holden in the public room of the National Hotel. Being
very curious to witness the demonstration, and know what
it was all about, Martin kept close to the General: and,
keeping closer than ever when they entered the Hall, got
by that means upon a little platform of tables at the upper
end: where an arm-chair was set for the General, and
Mr. La Fayette Kettle, as secretary, was making a great
display of some foolscap documents—Screamers, no doubt.

"Well, Sir!" he said, as he shook hands with Martin,
"here is a spectacle calc'lated to make the British Lion
put his tail between his legs, and howl with anguish, I expect!"

Martin certainly thought it possible that the British Lion
might have been rather out of his element in that Ark; but
he kept the idea to himself. The General was then voted
to the chair, on the motion of a pallid lad of the Jefferson
Brick school: who forthwith set in for a high-spiced
speech, with a good deal about hearths and homes in it,
and unriveting the chains of Tyranny.

Oh but it was a clincher for the British Lion, it was!
The indignation of the glowing young Columbian knew no
bounds. If he could only have been one of his own fore-
fathers, he said, wouldn't he have peppered that same Lion,
and been to him as another Brute Tamer with a wire whip,
teaching him lessons not easily forgotten. "Lion! (cried
that young Columbian) where is he? Who is he? What
is he? Show him to me. Let me have him here. Here!"
said the young Columbian, in a wrestling attitude, "upon
this sacred altar. Here!" cried the young Columbian,

idealising the dining-table, "upon ancestral ashes, cemented
with the glorious blood poured out like water on our native
plains of Chickabiddy Lick! Bring forth that Lion!" said
the young Columbian. "Alone, I dare him! I taunt that
Lion. I tell that Lion, that Freedom's hand once twisted
in his mane, he rolls a corse before me, and the Eagles of
the Great Republic laugh ha, ha!"

When it was found that the Lion didn't come, but kept
out of the way; that the young Columbian stood there,
with folded arms, alone in his glory; and consequently that
the Eagles were no doubt laughing wildly on the mountain
tops,—such cheers arose as might have shaken the hands
upon the Horse-Guards' clock, and changed the very mean
time of the day in England's capital.

"Who is this?" Martin telegraphed to La Fayette.

The Secretary wrote something, very gravely, on a piece
of paper, twisted it up, and had it passed to him from hand
to hand. It was an improvement on the old sentiment:
"Perhaps as remarkable a man as any in our country."

This young Columbian was succeeded by another, to the
full as eloquent as he, who drew down storms of cheers.
But both remarkable youths, in their great excitement (for
your true poetry can never stoop to details), forgot to say
with whom or what the Watertoasters sympathised, and
likewise why or wherefore they were sympathetic. Thus,
Martin remained for a long time as completely in the dark
as ever; until at length a ray of light broke in upon him
through the medium of the Secretary, who, by reading the
minutes of their past proceedings, made the matter somewhat clearer. He then learned that the Watertoast Association sympathised with a certain Public Man in Ireland,
who held a contest upon certain points with England: and
that they did so, because they didn't love England at all—
not by any means because they loved Ireland much: being
indeed horribly jealous and distrustful of its people always,
and only tolerating them because of their working hard,
which made them very useful; labour being held in greater
indignity in the simple republic than in any other country
upon earth. This rendered Martin curious to see what
grounds of sympathy the Watertoast Association put forth;
nor was he long in suspense, for the General rose to read a
letter to the Public Man, which with his own hands he had
written.

"Thus," said the General, "thus, my friends and fellow-citizens, it runs:

"'SIR,

"'I address you on behalf of the Watertoast Association of United Sympathisers. It is founded, Sir, in the great republic of America! and now holds its breath, and swells the blue veins in its forehead nigh to bursting, as it watches, Sir, with feverish intensity and sympathetic ardour, your noble efforts in the cause of Freedom.'"

At the name of Freedom, and at every repetition of that name, all the Sympathisers roared aloud; cheering with nine times nine, and nine times over.

"'In Freedom's name, Sir—holy Freedom—I address you. In Freedom's name, I send herewith a contribution to the funds of your Society. In Freedom's name, Sir, I advert with indignation and disgust to that accursed animal, with gore-stained whiskers, whose rampant cruelty and fiery lust have ever been a scourge, a torment to the world. The naked visitors to Crusoe's Island, Sir; the flying wives of Peter Wilkins; the fruit-smeared children of the tangled bush; nay, even the men of large stature, anciently bred in the mining districts of Cornwall; alike bear witness to its savage nature. Where, Sir, are the Cormorans, the Blunderbores, the Great Feefofums, named in History? All, all, exterminated by its destroying hand.

"'I allude, Sir, to the British Lion.

"'Devoted, mind and body, heart and soul, to Freedom, Sir—to Freedom, blessed solace to the snail upon the cellar-door, the oyster in his pearly bed, the still mite in his home of cheese, the very winkle of your country in his shelly lair—in her unsullied name, we offer you our sympathy. Oh, Sir, in this our cherished and our happy land, her fires burn bright and clear and smokeless: once lighted up in yours, the lion shall be roasted whole.

"'I am, Sir, in Freedom's name,

"'Your affectionate friend and faithful Sympathiser,

"'CYRUS CHOKE, General, U.S.M.'"

It happened that just as the General began to read this letter, the railroad train arrived, bringing a new mail from England; and a packet had been handed in to the Secre-

tary, which during its perusal and the frequent cheerings
in homage to freedom, he had opened.   Now, its contents
disturbed him very much, and the moment the General sat
down, he hurried to his side, and placed in his hand a letter
and several printed extracts from English newspapers; to
which, in a state of infinite excitement, he called his immediate attention.

The General, being greatly heated by his own composition, was in a fit state to receive any inflammable influence;
but he had no sooner possessed himself of the contents of
these documents, than a change came over his face, involving such a huge amount of choler and passion, that the
noisy concourse were silent in a moment, in very wonder at
the sight of him.

"My friends!" cried the General, rising; "my friends
and fellow-citizens, we have been mistaken in this man."

"In what man?" was the cry.

"In this," panted the General, holding up the letter he
had read aloud a few minutes before.   "I find that he has
been, and is, the advocate—consistent in it always too—of
Nigger emancipation!"

If anything beneath the sky be real, those Sons of Freedom would have pistolled, stabbed—in some way slain—
that man by coward hands and murderous violence, if he
had stood among them at that time.   The most confiding
of their own countrymen, would not have wagered then;
no, nor would they ever peril; one dunghill straw, upon
the life of any man in such a strait.   They tore the letter,
cast the fragments in the air, trod down the pieces as they
fell; and yelled, and groaned, and hissed, till they could
cry no longer.

"I shall move," said the General, when he could make
himself heard, "that the Watertoast Association of United
Sympathisers be immediately dissolved!"

Down with it! Away with it! Don't hear of it! Burn
its records! Pull the room down! Blot it out of human
memory!

"But, my fellow countrymen!" said the General, "the
contributions.   We have funds.   What is to be done with
the funds?"

It was hastily resolved that a piece of plate should be
presented to a certain constitutional Judge, who had laid
down from the Bench the noble principle, that it was law-

ful for any white mob to murder any black man; and that another piece of plate, of similar value, should be presented to a certain Patriot, who had declared from his high place in the Legislature, that he and his friends would hang, without trial, any Abolitionist who might pay them a visit. For the surplus, it was agreed that it should be devoted to aiding the enforcement of those free and equal laws, which render it incalculably more criminal and dangerous to teach a negro to read and write, than to roast him alive in a public city. These points adjusted, the meeting broke up in great disorder: and there was an end of the Watertoast Sympathy.

As Martin ascended to his bedroom, his eye was attracted by the Republican banner, which had been hoisted from the house-top in honour of the occasion, and was fluttering before a window which he passed.

"Tut!" said Martin. "You're a gay flag in the distance. But let a man be near enough to get the light upon the other side, and see through you; and you are but sorry fustian!"

CHAPTER XXII.

FROM WHICH IT WILL BE SEEN THAT MARTIN BECAME A LION ON HIS OWN ACCOUNT. TOGETHER WITH THE REASON WHY.

As soon as it was generally known in the National Hotel, that the young Englishman, Mr. Chuzzlewit, had purchased a "location" in the Valley of Eden, and intended to betake himself to that earthly paradise by the next steamboat; he became a popular character. Why this should be, or how it had come to pass, Martin no more knew than Mrs. Gamp, of Kingsgate Street, High Holborn, did; but that he was for the time being, the lion, by popular election, of the Watertoast community, and that his society was in rather inconvenient request, there could be no kind of doubt. The first notification he received of this change in his position, was the following epistle, written in a thin running hand, —with here and there a fat letter or two, to make the general effect more striking,—on a sheet of paper, ruled with blue lines.

"Dear Sir,   *"National Hotel, Monday Morning.*

"When I had the privillidge of being your fellow-traveller in the cars, the day before yesterday, you offered some remarks upon the subject of the Tower of London, which (in common with my fellow-citizens generally) I could wish to hear repeated to a public audience.

"As secretary to the Young Men's Watertoast Association of this town, I am requested to inform you that the Society will be proud to hear you deliver a lecture upon the Tower of London, at their Hall to-morrow evening, at seven o'clock; and as a large issue of quarter-dollar tickets may be expected, your answer and consent by bearer will be considered obliging.

"Dear Sir, yours truly,
"LA FAYETTE KETTLE.
"The Honorable M. Chuzzlewit.

"P.S.—The Society would not be particular in limiting you to the Tower of London. Permit me to suggest that any remarks upon the Elements of Geology, or (if more convenient) upon the Writings of your talented and witty countryman, the Honorable Mr. Miller, would be well received."

Very much aghast at this invitation, Martin wrote back, civilly declining it; and had scarcely done so, when he received another letter.

"(Private.)

"Sir,   *"No. 47, Bunker Hill Street, Monday Morning.*

"I was raised in those interminable solitudes where our mighty Mississippi (or Father of Waters) rolls his turbid flood.

"I am young, and ardent. For there is a poetry in wildness, and every alligator basking in the slime is in himself an Epic, self-contained. I aspire for fame. It is my yearning and my thirst.

"Are you, Sir, aware of any member of Congress in England, who would undertake to pay my expenses to that country, and for six months after my arrival?

"There is something within me which gives me the assurance that this enlightened patronage would not be thrown away. In literature or art; the bar, the pulpit, or the stage; in one or other, if not all, I feel that I am certain to succeed.

"If too much engaged to write to any such yourself, please let me have a list of three or four of those most likely to respond, and I will address them through the Post Office. May I also ask you to favour me with any critical observations that have ever presented themselves to your reflective faculties, on 'Cain: a Mystery,' by the Right Honorable Lord Byron? I am, Sir,

"Yours (forgive me if I add, soaringly),

"PUTNAM SMIF.

"P.S.—Address your answer to America Junior, Messrs. Hancock & Floby, Dry Goods Store, as above."

Both of which letters, together with Martin's reply to each, were, according to a laudable custom, much tending to the promotion of gentlemanly feeling and social confidence, published in the next number of the Watertoast Gazette.

He had scarcely got through this correspondence, when Captain Kedgick, the landlord, kindly came up stairs to see how he was getting on. The captain sat down upon the bed before he spoke; and finding it rather hard, moved to the pillow.

"Well, Sir!" said the Captain, putting his hat a little more on one side, for it was rather tight in the crown: "You're quite a public man, I calc'late."

"So it seems," retorted Martin, who was very tired.

"Our citizens, Sir," pursued the Captain, "intend to pay their respects to you. You will have to hold a sort of lĕ-vĕe, Sir, while you're here."

"Powers above!" cried Martin, "I couldn't do that, my good fellow!"

"I reckon you *must* then," said the Captain.

"Must is not a pleasant word, Captain," urged Martin.

"Well! I didn't fix the mother language, and I can't unfix it," said the Captain, coolly: "else I'd make it pleasant. You must re-ceive. That's all."

"But why should I receive people who care as much for me as I care for them?" asked Martin.

"Well! because I have had a muniment put up in the bar," returned the Captain.

"A what?" cried Martin.

"A muniment," rejoined the Captain.

Martin looked despairingly at Mark, who informed him that the Captain meant a written notice that Mr. Chuzzlewit would receive the Watertoasters that day, at and after two o'clock: which was, in effect, then hanging in the bar, as Mark from ocular inspection of the same could testify.

"You wouldn't be unpop'lar, *I* know," said the Captain, paring his nails. "Our citizens an't long of riling up, I tell you; and our Gazette could flay you like a wild cat."

Martin was going to be very wroth, but he thought better of it, and said:

"In Heaven's name let them come, then."

"Oh, *they*'ll come," returned the Captain. "I have seen the big room fixed a'purpose, with my eyes."

"But will you," said Martin, seeing that the Captain was about to go; "will you at least tell me this? What do they want to see me for? what have I done? and how do they happen to have such a sudden interest in me?"

Captain Kedgick put a thumb and three fingers to each side of the brim of his hat; lifted it a little way off his head; put it on again carefully; passed one hand all down his face, beginning at the forehead and ending at the chin; looked at Martin; then at Mark; then at Martin again; winked; and walked out.

"Upon my life, now!" said Martin, bringing his hand heavily upon the table; "such a perfectly unaccountable fellow as that, I never saw. Mark, what do you say to this?"

"Why, Sir," returned his partner, "my opinion is that we must have got to the MOST remarkable man in the country, at last. So I hope there's an end of the breed, Sir."

Although this made Martin laugh, it couldn't keep off two o'clock. Punctually, as the hour struck, Captain Kedgick returned to hand him to the room of state; and he had no sooner got him safe there, than he bawled down the staircase to his fellow-citizens below, that Mr. Chuzzlewit was "receiving."

Up they came with a rush. Up they came until the room was full, and, through the open door, a dismal perspective of more to come was shown upon the stairs. One after an-

other, one after another, dozen after dozen, score after
score, more, more, more, up they came: all shaking hands
with Martin. Such varieties of hands, the thick, the thin,
the short, the long, the fat, the lean, the coarse, the fine;
such differences of temperature, the hot, the cold, the dry,
the moist, the flabby; such diversities of grasp, the tight,
the loose, the short-lived, and the lingering! Still up, up,
up, more, more, more: and ever and anon the Captain's
voice was heard above the crowd—"There's more below;
there's more below. Now, gentlemen, you that have been
introduced to Mr. Chuzzlewit, will you clear, gentlemen?
Will you clear? Will you be so good as clear, gentlemen,
and make a little room for more? "

Regardless of the Captain's cries, they didn't clear at
all, but stood there, bolt upright and staring. Two gentlemen connected with the Watertoast Gazette had come
express to get the matter for an article on Martin. They
had agreed to divide the labour. One of them took him
below the waistcoat; one above. Each stood directly in
front of his subject with his head a little on one side, intent on his department. If Martin put one boot before the
other, the lower gentleman was down upon him; he rubbed
a pimple on his nose, and the upper gentleman booked it.
He opened his mouth to speak, and the same gentleman
was on one knee before him, looking in at his teeth, with
the nice scrutiny of a dentist. Amateurs in the physiog-
nomical and phrenological sciences roved about him with
watchful eyes and itching fingers, and sometimes one, more
daring than the rest, made a mad grasp at the back of his
head, and vanished in the crowd. They had him in all
points of view: in front, in profile, three-quarter face, and
behind. Those who were not professional or scientific,
audibly exchanged opinions on his looks. New lights shone
in upon him, in respect of his nose. Contradictory rumours
were abroad on the subject of his hair. And still the Captain's voice was heard—so stifled by the concourse, that he
seemed to speak from underneath a feather-bed—exclaim-
ing, "Gentlemen, you that have been introduced to Mr.
Chuzzlewit, *will* you clear? "

Even when they began to clear, it was no better; for
then a stream of gentlemen, every one with a lady on each
arm (exactly like the chorus to the National Anthem when
Royalty goes in state to the play), came gliding in—every

new group fresher than the last, and bent on staying to the latest moment. If they spoke to him, which was not often, they invariably asked the same questions, in the same tone; with no more remorse, or delicacy, or consideration, than if he had been a figure of stone, purchased, and paid for, and set up there, for their delight. Even when, in the slow course of time, these died off, it was as bad as ever, if not worse; for then the boys grew bold, and came in as a class of themselves, and did everything that the grown-up people had done. Uncouth stragglers too appeared; men of a ghostly kind, who being in, didn't know how to get out again: insomuch that one silent gentleman with glazed and fishy eyes, and only one button on his waistcoat (which was a very large metal one, and shone prodigiously), got behind the door, and stood there, like a clock, long after everybody else was gone.

Martin felt, from pure fatigue, and heat, and worry, as if he could have fallen on the ground and willingly remained there, if they would but have had the mercy to leave him alone. But as letters and messages threatening his public denouncement if he didn't see the senders, poured in like hail; and as more visitors came while he took his coffee by himself; and as Mark, with all his vigilance, was unable to keep them from the door; he resolved to go to bed—not that he felt at all sure of bed being any protection, but that he might not leave a forlorn hope untried.

He had communicated this design to Mark, and was on the eve of escaping, when the door was thrown open in a great hurry, and an elderly gentleman entered: bringing with him a lady who certainly could not be considered young—that was matter of fact; and probably could not be considered handsome—but that was matter of opinion. She was very straight, very tall, and not at all flexible in face or figure. On her head she wore a great straw bonnet, with trimmings of the same, in which she looked as if she had been thatched by an unskilful labourer; and in her hand she held a most enormous fan.

"Mr. Chuzzlewit, I believe?" said the gentleman.

"That is my name."

"Sir," said the gentleman, "I am pressed for time."

"Thank God!" thought Martin.

"I go back Toe my home, Sir," pursued the gentleman,

"by the return train, which starts immediate. Start is not a word you use in your country, Sir."

"Oh yes, it is," said Martin.

"You air mistaken, Sir," returned the gentleman, with great decision: "but we will not pursue the subject, lest it should awake your prĕjŭ-dĭce. Sir, Mrs. Hominy."

Martin bowed.

"Mrs. Hominy, Sir, is the lady of Major Hominy, one of our choicest spirits; and belongs Toe one of our most aristocratic families. You air, p'raps, acquainted, Sir, with Mrs. Hominy's writings?"

Martin couldn't say he was.

"You have much Toe learn, and Toe enjoy, Sir," said the gentleman. "Mrs. Hominy is going Toe stay until the end of the Fall, Sir, with her married daughter at the settlement of New Thermopylæ, three days this side of Eden. Any attention, Sir, that you can show Toe Mrs. Hominy upon the journey, will be very grateful Toe the Major and our fellow-citizens. Mrs. Hominy, I wish you good night, ma'am, and a pleasant pro-gress on your rout!"

Martin could scarcely believe it; but he had gone, and Mrs. Hominy was drinking the milk.

"A'most used-up I am, I do declare!" she observed. "The jolting in the cars is pretty nigh as bad as if the rail was full of snags and sawyers."

"Snags and sawyers, ma'am?" said Martin.

"Well, then, I do suppose you'll hardly realise my meaning, Sir," said Mrs. Hominy. "My! Only think! *Do* tell!"

It did not appear that these expressions, although they seemed to conclude with an urgent entreaty, stood in need of any answer; for Mrs. Hominy, untying her bonnet-strings, observed that she would withdraw to lay that article of dress aside, and would return immediately.

"Mark!" said Martin. "Touch me, will you. Am I awake?"

"Hominy is, Sir," returned his partner—"Broad awake! Just the sort of woman, Sir, as would be discovered with her eyes wide open, and her mind a-working for her country's good, at any hour of the day or night."

They had no opportunity of saying more, for Mrs. Hominy stalked in again—very erect, in proof of her aristocratic blood and holding in her clasped hands a red cotton pocket-handkerchief, perhaps a parting gift from that choice spirit, the Major. She had laid aside her bonnet, and now appeared in a highly aristocratic and classical cap, meeting beneath her chin; a style of head-dress so admirably adapted to her countenance, that if the late Mr. Grimaldi had appeared in the lappets of Mrs. Siddons, a more complete effect could not have been produced.

Martin handed her to a chair. Her first words arrested him before he could get back to his own seat.

"Pray, Sir!" said Mrs. Hominy, "where do you hail from?"

"I am afraid I am dull of comprehension," answered Martin, "being extremely tired; but, upon my word, I don't understand you."

Mrs. Hominy shook her head with a melancholy smile that said, not inexpressively, "They corrupt even the language in that old country!" and added then, as coming down a step or two to meet his low capacity, "Where was you rose?"

"Oh!" said Martin, "I was born in Kent."

"And how do you like our country, Sir?" asked Mrs. Hominy.

"Very much indeed," said Martin, half asleep. "At least—that is—pretty well, ma'am."

"Most strangers—and partick'larly Britishers—are much surprised by what they see in the U-nited States," remarked Mrs. Hominy.

"They have excellent reason to be so, ma'am," said Martin. "I never was so much surprised in all my life."

"Our institutions make our people smart much, Sir," Mrs. Hominy remarked.

"The most short-sighted man could see that at a glance, with his naked eye," said Martin.

Mrs. Hominy was a philosopher and an authoress, and consequently had a pretty strong digestion; but this coarse, this indecorous phrase, was almost too much for her. For a gentleman sitting alone with a lady—although the door *was* open—to talk about a naked eye!

A long interval elapsed before even she—a woman of masculine and towering intellect though she was—could call up fortitude enough to resume the conversation. But Mrs. Hominy was a traveller. Mrs. Hominy was a writer of reviews and analytical disquisitions. Mrs. Hominy had

had her letters from abroad, beginning "My ever dearest
blank," and signed "The Mother of the Modern Gracchi"
(meaning the married Miss Hominy), regularly printed in
a public journal, with all the indignation in capitals, and
all the sarcasm in italics. Mrs. Hominy had looked on
foreign countries with the eye of a perfect republican hot
from the model oven; and Mrs. Hominy could talk (or
write) about them by the hour together. So Mrs. Hominy
at last came down on Martin heavily, and as he was fast
asleep, she had it all her own way and bruised him to her
heart's content.

It is no great matter what Mrs. Hominy said, save that
she had learnt it from the cant of a class, and a large class,
of her fellow-countrymen, who, in their every word, avow
themselves to be as senseless to the high principles on
which America sprang, a nation, into life, as any Orson in
her legislative halls. Who are no more capable of feeling,
or of caring if they did feel, that by reducing their own
country to the ebb of honest men's contempt, they put in
hazard the rights of nations yet unborn, and very progress
of the human race, than are the swine who wallow in their
streets. Who think that crying out to other nations, old
in their iniquity, "We are no worse than you!" (No worse!)
is high defence and 'vantage-ground enough for that Republic, but yesterday let loose upon her noble course, and
but to-day so maimed and lame, so full of sores and ulcers,
foul to the eye and almost hopeless to the sense, that her
best friends turn from the loathsome creature with disgust.
Who, having by their ancestors declared and won their Independence, because they would not bend the knee to certain Public vices and corruptions and would not abrogate
the truth, run riot in the Bad, and turn their backs upon
the Good; and lying down contented with the wretched
boast that other Temples also are of glass, and stones which
batter theirs may be flung back; show themselves, in that
alone, as immeasurably behind the import of the trust they
hold, and as unworthy to possess it, as if the sordid huck-
sterings of all their little governments—each one a kingdom
in its small depravity—were brought into a heap for evidence against them.

Martin by degrees became so far awake, that he had a
sense of a terrible oppression on his mind; an imperfect
dream that he had murdered a particular friend, and

couldn't get rid of the body. When his eyes opened it was staring him full in the face. There was the horrible Hominy, talking deep truths in a melodious snuffle, and pouring forth her mental endowments to such an extent that the Major's bitterest enemy, hearing her, would have forgiven him from the bottom of his heart. Martin might have done something desperate if the gong had not sounded for supper; but sound it did most opportunely; and having stationed Mrs. Hominy at the upper end of the table, he took refuge at the lower end himself; whence, after a hasty meal, he stole away, while the lady was yet busied with dried beef and a whole saucer-full of pickled fixings.

It would be difficult to give an adequate idea of Mrs. Hominy's freshness next day, or of the avidity with which she went headlong into moral philosophy at breakfast. Some little additional degree of asperity, perhaps, was visible in her features, but not more than the pickles would have naturally produced. All that day, she clung to Martin. She sat beside him while he received his friends—for there was another Reception, yet more numerous than the former—propounded theories, and answered imaginary objections; so that Martin really began to think he must be dreaming, and speaking for two; quoted interminable passages from certain essays on government, written by herself; used the Major's pocket-handkerchief as if the snuffle were a temporary malady, of which she was determined to rid herself by some means or other; and, in short, was such a remarkable companion, that Martin quite settled it between himself and his conscience, that in any new settlement it would be absolutely necessary to have such a person knocked on the head for the general peace of society.

In the meantime Mark was busy, from early in the morning until late at night, in getting on board the steamboat such provisions, tools, and other necessaries, as they had been forewarned it would be wise to take. The purchase of these things, and the settlement of their bill at the National, reduced their finances to so low an ebb, that if the captain had delayed his departure any longer, they would have been in almost as bad a plight as the unfortunate poorer emigrants, who (seduced on board by solemn advertisement) had been living on the lower deck a whole week, and exhausting their miserable stock of provisions

25

before the voyage commenced. There they were, all huddled together, with the engine and the fires. Farmers who
had never seen a plough; woodmen who had never used an
axe; builders who couldn't make a box; cast out of their
own land, with not a hand to aid them: newly come into
an unknown world, children in helplessness, but men in
wants—with younger children at their backs, to live or die
as it might happen!

The morning came, and they would start at noon. Noon
came, and they would start at night. But nothing is
eternal in this world: not even the procrastination of an
American skipper: and at night all was ready.

Dispirited and weary to the last degree, but a greater
lion than ever (he had done nothing all the afternoon but
answer letters from strangers: half of them about nothing:
half about borrowing money: and all requiring an instantaneous reply), Martin walked down to the wharf, through
a concourse of people, with Mrs. Hominy upon his arm;
and went on board. But Mark was bent on solving the
riddle of this lionship, if he could; and so, not without the
risk of being left behind, ran back to the hotel.

Captain Kedgick was sitting in the colonnade, with a
julep on his knee, and a cigar in his mouth. He caught
Mark's eye, and said:

"Why, what the 'Tarnal brings you here?"

"I'll tell you plainly what it is, Captain," said Mark.
"I want to ask you a question."

"A man may *ask* a question, so he may," returned
Kedgick: strongly implying that another man might not
answer a question, so he mightn't.

"What have they been making so much of him for,
now?" said Mark, slyly. "Come!"

"Our people like ex-citement," answered Kedgick, sucking his cigar.

"But how has he excited 'em?" asked Mark.

The captain looked at him as if he were half inclined to
unburden his mind of a capital joke.

"You air a going?" he said.

"Going!" cried Mark. "Ain't every moment precious?"

"Our people like ex-citement," said the Captain, whispering. "He ain't like emigrants in gin'ral; and he excited 'em along of this;" he winked and burst into a
smothered laugh; "along of this. Scadder is a smart

man, and—and—nobody as goes to Eden ever comes back
a-live!"

The wharf was close at hand, and at that instant Mark
could hear them shouting out his name—could even hear
Martin calling to him to make haste, or they would be separated. It was too late to mend the matter, or put any
face upon it but the best. He gave the Captain a parting
benediction, and ran off like a race-horse.

"Mark! Mark!" cried Martin.

"Here am I, Sir!" shouted Mark, suddenly replying from
the edge of the quay, and leaping at a bound on board.
"Never was half so jolly, Sir. All right! Haul in! Go
a-head!"

The sparks from the wood fire streamed upward from the
two chimneys, as if the vessel were a great firework just
lighted; and they roared away upon the dark water.

CHAPTER XXIII.

MARTIN AND HIS PARTNER TAKE POSSESSION OF
THEIR ESTATE. THE JOYFUL OCCASION INVOLVES
SOME FURTHER ACCOUNT OF EDEN.

THERE happened to be on board the steamboat several
gentlemen passengers, of the same stamp as Martin's New
York friend Mr. Bevan; and in their society he was cheerful and happy. They released him as well as they could
from the intellectual entanglements of Mrs. Hominy; and
exhibited, in all they said and did, so much good sense
and high feeling, that he could not like them too well.

"If this were a republic of Intellect and Worth," he said,
"instead of vapouring and jobbing, they would not want
the levers to keep it in motion."

"Having good tools, and using bad ones," returned Mr.
Tapley, "would look as if they was rather a poor sort of
carpenters, Sir, wouldn't it?"

Martin nodded. "As if their work were infinitely above
their powers and purpose, Mark; and they botched it in
consequence."

"The best on it is," said Mark, "that when they do hap-

pen to make a decent stroke; such as better workmen, with
no such opportunities, make every day of their lives and
think nothing of; they begin to sing out so surprising loud.
Take notice of my words, Sir. If ever the defaulting part
of this here country pays its debts—along of finding that
not paying 'em won't do in a commercial point of view, you
see, and is inconvenient in its consequences—they'll take
such a shine out of it, and make such bragging speeches,
that a man might suppose no borrowed money had ever
been paid afore, since the world was first begun. That's
the way they gammon each other, Sir. Bless you, *I* know
'em. Take notice of my words, now!"

"You seem to be growing profoundly sagacious!" cried
Martin, laughing.

"Whether that is," thought Mark, "because I'm a day's
journey nearer Eden, and am brightening up, afore I die,
I can't say. P'raps by the time I get there, I shall have
growed into a prophet."

He gave no utterance to these sentiments; but the excessive joviality they inspired within him, and the merriment they brought upon his shining face, were quite
enough for Martin. Although he might sometimes profess
to make light of his partner's inexhaustible cheerfulness,
and might sometimes, as in the case of Zephaniah Scadder,
find him too jocose a commentator, he was always sensible
of the effect of his example in rousing him to hopefulness
and courage. Whether he were in the humour to profit by
it, mattered not a jot. It was contagious, and he could
not choose but be affected.

At first they parted with some of their passengers once
or twice a day, and took in others to replace them. But
by degrees, the towns upon their route became more thinly
scattered; and for many hours together they would see no
other habitations than the huts of the wood-cutters, where
the vessel stopped for fuel. Sky, wood, and water, all the
livelong day; and heat that blistered everything it touched.

On they toiled through great solitudes, where the trees
upon the banks grew thick and close; and floated in the
stream; and held up shrivelled arms from out the river's
depths; and slid down from the margin of the land: half
growing, half decaying, in the miry water. On through
the weary day and melancholy night: beneath the burning
sun, and in the mist and vapour of the evening: on, until

return appeared impossible, and restoration to their home a miserable dream.

They had now but few people on board, and these few were as flat, as dull, and stagnant, as the vegetation that oppressed their eyes. No sound of cheerfulness or hope was heard; no pleasant talk beguiled the tardy time; no little group made common cause against the dull depression of the scene. But that, at certain periods, they swallowed food together from a common trough, it might have been old Charon's boat, conveying melancholy shades to judgment.

At length they drew near New Thermopylæ; where, that same evening, Mrs. Hominy would disembark. A gleam of comfort sunk into Martin's bosom when she told him this. Mark needed none; but he was not displeased.

It was almost night when they came alongside the landing-place—a steep bank with an hotel, like a barn, on the top of it; a wooden store or two; and a few scattered sheds.

"You sleep here to-night, and go on in the morning, I suppose, ma'am?" said Martin.

"Where should I go on to?" cried the mother of the modern Gracchi.

"To New Thermopylæ."

"My! ain't I there?" said Mrs. Hominy.

Martin looked for it all round the darkening panorama; but he couldn't see it, and was obliged to say so.

"Why, that's it!" cried Mrs. Hominy, pointing to the sheds just mentioned.

"*That!*" exclaimed Martin.

"Ah! that; and work it which way you will, it whips Eden," said Mrs. Hominy, nodding her head with great expression.

The married Miss Hominy, who had come on board with her husband, gave to this statement her most unqualified support, as did that gentleman also. Martin gratefully declined their invitation to regale himself at their house during the half hour of the vessel's stay; and having escorted Mrs. Hominy and the red pocket-handkerchief (which was still on active service) safely across the gangway, returned in a thoughtful mood to watch the emigrants as they removed their goods ashore.

Mark, as he stood beside him, glanced in his face from

time to time; anxious to discover what effect this dialogue had had upon him, and not unwilling that his hopes should be dashed before they reached their destination, so that the blow he feared, might be broken in its fall. But saving that he sometimes looked up quickly at the poor erections on the hill, he gave him no clue to what was passing in his mind, until they were again upon their way.

"Mark," he said then, "are there really none but our-selves on board this boat who are bound for Eden?"

"None at all, Sir. Most of 'em, as you know, have stopped short; and the few that are left are going further on. What matters that! More room there for us, Sir."

"Oh, to be sure!" said Martin. "But I was thinking" —and there he paused.

"Yes, Sir," observed Mark.

"How odd it was that the people should have arranged to try their fortune at a wretched hole like that, for in-stance, when there is such a much better, and such a very different kind of place, near at hand, as one may say."

He spoke in a tone so very different from his usual confi-dence, and with such an obvious dread of Mark's reply, that the good-natured fellow was full of pity.

"Why, you know, Sir," said Mark, as gently as he could by any means insinuate the observation, "we must guard against being too sanguine. There's no occasion for it, either, because we're determined to make the best of every-thing, after we know the worst of it. Ain't we, Sir?"

Martin looked at him, but answered not a word.

"Even Eden, you know, ain't all built," said Mark.

"In the name of Heaven, man," cried Martin angrily, "don't talk of Eden in the same breath with that place. Are you mad? There—God forgive me!—don't think harshly of me for my temper!"

After that, he turned away, and walked to and fro upon the deck full two hours. Nor did he speak again, except to say "Good-night," until next day; nor even then upon this subject, but on other topics quite foreign to the pur-pose.

As they proceeded further on their track, and came more and more towards their journey's end, the monotonous desolation of the scene increased to that degree, that for any redeeming feature it presented to their eyes, they might have entered, in the body, on the grim domains of Giant

Despair. A flat morass, bestrewn with fallen timber; a marsh on which the good growth of the earth seemed to have been wrecked and cast away, that from its decomposing ashes vile and ugly things might rise; where the very trees took the aspect of huge weeds, begotten of the slime from which they sprang, by the hot sun that burnt them up; where fatal maladies, seeking whom they might infect, came forth at night, in misty shapes, and creeping out upon the water, haunted them like spectres until day; where even the blessed sun, shining down on festering elements of corruption and disease, became a horror; this was the realm of Hope through which they moved.

At last they stopped. At Eden too. The waters of the Deluge might have left it but a week before: so choked with slime and matted growth was the hideous swamp which bore that name.

There being no depth of water close in shore, they landed from the vessel's boat, with all their goods beside them. There were a few log-houses visible among the dark trees; the best, a cow-shed or a rude stable; but for the wharves, the market-place, the public buildings—

"Here comes an Edener," said Mark. "He'll get us help to carry these things up. Keep a good heart, Sir. Hallo there!"

The man advanced toward them through the thickening gloom, very slowly: leaning on a stick. As he drew nearer, they observed that he was pale and worn, and that his anxious eyes were deeply sunken in his head. His dress of homespun blue hung about him in rags; his feet and head were bare. He sat down on a stump half-way, and beckoned them to come to him. When they complied, he put his hand upon his side as if in pain, and while he fetched his breath stared at them, wondering.

"Strangers!" he exclaimed, as soon as he could speak.

"The very same," said Mark. "How are you, Sir?"

"I've had the fever very bad," he answered faintly. "I haven't stood upright these many weeks. Those are your notions I see," pointing to their property.

"Yes, Sir," said Mark, "they are. You couldn't recommend us some one as would lend a hand to help carry 'em up to the—to the town, could you, Sir?"

"My eldest son would do it if he could," replied the man; "but to-day he has his chill upon him, and is lying

wrapped up in the blankets. My youngest died last
week."

"I'm sorry for it, governor, with all my heart," said
Mark, shaking him by the hand. "Don't mind us. Come
along with me, and I'll give you an arm back. The goods
is safe enough, Sir,"—to Martin,—"there ain't many people about, to make away with 'em. What a comfort that
is!"

"No," cried the man. "You must look for such folk
here," knocking his stick upon the ground, "or yonder in
the bush, towards the north. We've buried most of 'em.
The rest have gone away. Them that we have here, don't
come out at night."

"The night air ain't quite wholesome, I suppose?" said
Mark.

"It's deadly poison," was the settler's answer.

Mark showed no more uneasiness than if it had been
commended to him as ambrosia; but he gave the man his
arm, and as they went along explained to him the nature
of their purchase, and inquired where it lay. Close to his
own log-house, he said: so close that he had used their
dwelling as a store-house for some corn: they must excuse
it that night, but he would endeavour to get it taken out
upon the morrow. He then gave them to understand, as
an additional scrap of local chit-chat, that he had buried
the last proprietor with his own hands; a piece of information which Mark also received without the least abatement
of his equanimity.

In a word, he conducted them to a miserable cabin,
rudely constructed of the trunks of trees; the door of
which had either fallen down or been carried away long
ago; and which was consequently open to the wild landscape and the dark night. Saving for the little store he
had mentioned, it was perfectly bare of all furniture; but
they had left a chest upon the landing-place, and he gave
them a rude torch in lieu of candle. This latter acquisition Mark planted in the hearth, and then declaring that
the mansion "looked quite comfortable," hurried Martin
off again to help bring up the chest. And all the way to
the landing-place and back, Mark talked incessantly: as if
he would infuse into his partner's breast some faint belief
that they had arrived under the most auspicious and cheerful of all imaginable circumstances.

But many a man who would have stood within a home dismantled, strong in his passion and design of vengeance, has had the firmness of his nature conquered by the razing of an air-built castle. When the log-hut received them for the second time, Martin lay down upon the ground, and wept loud.

"Lord love you, Sir!" cried Mr. Tapley, in great terror; "don't do that! Don't do that, Sir! Anything but that! It never helped man, woman, or child, over the lowest fence yet, Sir, and it never will. Besides its being of no use to you, it's worse than of no use to me, for the least sound of it will knock me flat down. I can't stand up agin it, Sir. Anything but that!"

There is no doubt he spoke the truth, for the extraordinary alarm with which he looked at Martin as he paused upon his knees before the chest, in the act of unlocking it, to say these words, sufficiently confirmed him.

"I ask your forgiveness a thousand times, my dear fellow," said Martin. "I couldn't have helped it, if death had been the penalty."

"Ask my forgiveness!" said Mark, with his accustomed cheerfulness; as he proceeded to unpack the chest. "The head partner a asking forgiveness of Co., eh? There must be something wrong in the firm when that happens. I must have the books inspected, and the accounts gone over immediate. Here we are. Everything in its proper place. Here's the salt pork. Here's the biscuit. Here's the whiskey—uncommon good it smells too. Here's the tin pot. This tin pot's a small fortun' in itself! Here's the blankets. Here's the axe. Who says we ain't got a first-rate fit out? I feel as if I was a cadet gone out to Indy, and my noble father was chairman of the Board of Directors. Now, when I've got some water from the stream afore the door and mixed the grog," cried Mark, running out to suit the action to the word, "there's a supper ready, comprising every delicacy of the season. Here we are, Sir, all complete. For what we are going to receive, et cetrer. Lord bless you, Sir, it's very like a gipsy party!"

It was impossible not to take heart, in the company of such a man as this. Martin sat upon the ground beside the box; took out his knife; and ate and drank sturdily.

"Now you see," said Mark, when they had made a hearty meal; "with your knife and mine, I sticks this

blanket right afore the door, or where, in a state of high
civilisation, the door would be. And very neat it looks.
Then I stops the aperture below, by putting the chest agin
it. And very neat *that* looks. Then there's your blanket,
Sir. Then here's mine. And what's to hinder our passing a good night?"

For all his light-hearted speaking, it was long before he
slept himself. He wrapped his blanket round him, put
the axe ready to his hand, and lay across the threshold of
the door: too anxious and too watchful to close his eyes.
The novelty of their dreary situation, the dread of some
rapacious animal or human enemy, the terrible uncertainty
of their means of subsistence, the apprehension of death,
the immense distance and the hosts of obstacles between
themselves and England, were fruitful sources of disquiet
in the deep silence of the night. Though Martin would
have had him think otherwise, Mark felt that he was waking also, and a prey to the same reflections. This was almost worse than all, for if he began to brood over their
miseries instead of trying to make head against them, there
could be little doubt that such a state of mind would pow-
erfully assist the influence of the pestilent climate. Never
had the light of day been half so welcome to his eyes, as
when awaking from a fitful doze, Mark saw it shining
through the blanket in the doorway.

He stole out gently, for his companion was sleeping now;
and having refreshed himself by washing in the river,
where it flowed before the door, took a rough survey of the
settlement. There were not above a score of cabins in the
whole; half of these appeared untenanted; all were rotten
and decayed. The most tottering, abject, and forlorn
among them, was called, with great propriety, the Bank,
and National Credit Office. It had some feeble props about
it, but was settling deep down in the mud, past all recovery.

Here and there, an effort had been made to clear the
land; and something like a field had been marked out,
where, among the stumps and ashes of burnt trees, a scanty
crop of Indian corn was growing. In some quarters, a
snake or zigzag fence had been begun, but in no instance
had it been completed; and the fallen logs, half hidden in
the soil, lay mouldering away. Three or four meagre dogs,
wasted and vexed with hunger; some long-legged pigs,

wandering away into the woods in search of food; some children, nearly naked, gazing at him from the huts; were all the living things he saw. A fetid vapour, hot and sickening as the breath of an oven, rose up from the earth, and hung on everything around; and as his foot-prints sank into the marshy ground, a black ooze started forth to blot them out.

Their own land was mere forest. The trees had grown so thick and close that they shouldered one another out of their places, and the weakest, forced into shapes of strange distortion, languished like cripples. The best were stunted, from the pressure and the want of room; and high about the stems of all, grew long rank grass, dank weeds, and frowsy underwood; not divisible into their separate kinds, but tangled all together in a heap; a jungle deep and dark, with neither earth nor water at its roots, but putrid matter, formed of the pulpy offal of the two, and of their own corruption.

He went down to the landing-place where they had left their goods last night; and there he found some half-dozen men—wan, and forlorn to look at, but ready enough to assist—who helped him to carry them to the log-house. They shook their heads in speaking of the settlement, and had no comfort to give him. Those who had the means of going away, had all deserted it. They who were left, had lost their wives, their children, friends, or brothers there, and suffered much themselves. Most of them were ill then; none were the men they had been once. They frankly offered their assistance and advice, and, leaving him for that time, went sadly off upon their several tasks.

Martin was by this time stirring; but he had greatly changed, even in one night. He was very pale and languid; he spoke of pains and weakness in his limbs, and complained that his sight was dim, and his voice feeble. Increasing in his own briskness as the prospect grew more and more dismal, Mark brought away a door from one of the deserted houses, and fitted it to their own habitation; then went back again for a rude bench he had observed, with which he presently returned in triumph; and having put this piece of furniture outside the house, arranged the notable tin-pot and other such movables upon it, that it might represent a dresser or a sideboard. Greatly satisfied with this arrangement, he next rolled their cask of flour

into the house, and set it up on end in one corner, where
it served for a side-table. No better dining-table could be
required than the chest, which he solemnly devoted to that
useful service thenceforth. Their blankets, clothes, and
the like, he hung on pegs and nails. And lastly, he
brought forth a great placard (which Martin in the exultation of his heart had prepared with his own hands at the
National Hotel), bearing the inscription, CHUZZLEWIT &
Co., ARCHITECTS AND SURVEYORS, which he displayed
upon the most conspicuous part of the prémises, with as
much gravity as if the thriving city of Eden had had a real
existence, and they expected to be overwhelmed with business.

"These here tools," said Mark, bringing forward Martin's case of instruments, and sticking the compasses upright in a stump before the door, "shall be set out in the
open air to show that we come provided. And now, if any
gentleman wants a house built, he'd better give his orders,
afore we're other ways bespoke."

Considering the intense heat of the weather, this was not
a bad morning's work; but without pausing for a moment,
though he was streaming at every pore, Mark vanished into
the house again, and presently reappeared with a hatchet:
intent on performing some impossibilities with that imple-
ment.

"Here's a ugly old tree in the way, Sir," he observed,
"which'll be all the better down. We can build the oven
in the afternoon. There never was such a handy spot for
clay as Eden is. That's convenient, anyhow."

But Martin gave him no answer. He had sat the whole
time with his head upon his hands, gazing at the current
as it rolled swiftly by; thinking, perhaps, how fast it
moved towards the open sea, the high road to the home he
never would behold again.

Not even the vigorous strokes which Mark dealt at the
tree, awoke him from his mournful meditation. Finding
all his endeavours to rouse him of no use, Mark stopped in
his work and came towards him.

"Don't give in, Sir," said Mr. Tapley.

"Oh, Mark," returned his friend, "what have I done in
all my life that has deserved this heavy fate?"

"Why, Sir," returned Mark, "for the matter of that,
ev'rybody as is here might say the same thing; many of

'em with better reason p'raps than you or me. Hold up,
Sir. Do something. Couldn't you ease your mind, now,
don't you think, by making some personal obserwations in
a letter to Scadder?"

"No," said Martin, shaking his head sorrowfully: "I
am past that."

"But if you're past that already," returned Mark, "you
must be ill, and ought to be attended to."

"Don't mind me," said Martin. "Do the best you can
for yourself. You'll soon have only yourself to consider.
And then God speed you home, and forgive me for bringing you here! I am destined to die in this place. I felt
it the instant I set foot upon the shore. Sleeping or waking, Mark, I dreamed it all last night."

"I said you must be ill," returned Mark, tenderly, "and
now I'm sure of it. A touch of fever and ague caught on
these rivers, I daresay; but bless you, *that's* nothing. It's
only a seasoning; and we must all be seasoned, one way or
another. That's religion, that is, you know," said Mark.

He only sighed and shook his head.

"Wait half a minute," said Mark cheerily, "till I run
up to one of our neighbours and ask what's best to be took,
and borrow a little of it to give you; and to-morrow you'll
find yourself as strong as ever again. I won't be gone a
minute. Don't give in, while I'm away, whatever you
do!"

Throwing down his hatchet, he sped away immediately,
but stopped when he had gone a little distance, and looked
back; then hurried on again.

"Now, Mr. Tapley," said Mark, giving himself a tremendous blow in the chest by way of reviver, "just you
attend to what I've got to say. Things is looking about as
bad as they *can* look, young man. You'll not have such
another opportunity for showing your jolly disposition, my
fine fellow, as long as you live. And therefore, Tapley,
Now's your time to come out strong; or Never!"

CHAPTER XXIV.

REPORTS PROGRESS IN CERTAIN HOMELY MATTERS
OF LOVE, HATRED, JEALOUSY, AND REVENGE.

"HALLO, Pecksniff!" cried Mr. Jonas from the parlour.
"Isn't somebody a going to open that precious old door
of yours?"

"Immediately, Mr. Jonas. Immediately."

"Ecod," muttered the orphan, "not before it's time neither. Whoever it is, has knocked three times, and each
one loud enough to wake the—" he had such a repugnance
to the idea of waking the Dead, that he stopped even then
with the words upon his tongue, and said, instead, "the
Seven Sleepers."

"Immediately, Mr. Jonas; immediately," repeated Pecksniff. "Thomas Pinch"—he couldn't make up his mind,
in his great agitation, whether to call Tom his dear friend
or a villain, so he shook his fist at him *pro tem.*—"go up
to my daughters' room, and tell them who is here. Say,
Silence. Silence! Do you hear me, Sir?"

"Directly, Sir!" cried Tom, departing, in a state of
much amazement, on his errand.

"You'll—ha ha ha!—you'll excuse me, Mr. Jonas, if I
close this door a moment, will you?" said Pecksniff.
"This may be a professional call. Indeed I am pretty sure
it is. Thank you." Then Mr. Pecksniff, gently warbling
a rustic stave, put on his garden hat, seized a spade, and
opened the street door: calmly appearing on the threshold,
as if he thought he had, from his vineyard, heard a modest rap, but was not quite certain.

Seeing a gentleman and lady before him, he started back
in as much confusion as a good man with a crystal conscience might betray in mere surprise. Recognition came
upon him the next moment, and he cried:

"Mr. Chuzzlewit! Can I believe my eyes! My dear
Sir; my good Sir! A joyful hour; a happy hour indeed.
Pray, my dear Sir, walk in. You find me in my garden-
dress. You will excuse it, I know. It is an ancient pursuit, gardening. Primitive, my dear Sir; for, if I am not

mistaken, Adam was the first of our calling. *My* Eve, I grieve to say, is no more, Sir; but"—here he pointed to his spade, and shook his head, as if he were not cheerful without an effort—"but I do a little bit of Adam still."

He had by this time got them into the best parlour, where the portrait by Spiller, and the bust by Spoker, were.

"My daughters," said Mr. Pecksniff, "will be overjoyed. If I could feel weary upon such a theme, I should have been worn out long ago, my dear Sir, by their constant anticipation of this happiness, and their repeated allusions to our meeting at Mrs. Todgers's. Their fair young friend, too," said Mr. Pecksniff, "whom they so desire to know and love—indeed to know her, *is* to love—I hope I see her well. I hope in saying, 'Welcome to my humble roof!' I find some echo in her own sentiments. If features are an index to the heart, I have no fears of that. An extremely engaging expression of countenance, Mr. Chuzzlewit, my dear Sir—very much so!"

"Mary," said the old man, "Mr. Pecksniff flatters you. But flattery from him is worth the having. He is not a dealer in it, and it comes from his heart. We thought Mr.——"

"Pinch," said Mary.

"Mr. Pinch would have arrived before us, Pecksniff."

"He did arrive before you, my dear Sir," retorted Pecksniff, raising his voice for the edification of Tom upon the stairs, "and was about, I dare say, to tell me of your coming, when I begged him first to knock at my daughters' chamber, and inquire after Charity, my dear child, who is not so well as I could wish. No," said Mr. Pecksniff, answering their looks, "I am sorry to say, she is not. It is merely an hysterical affection; nothing more. I am not uneasy. Mr. Pinch! Thomas!" exclaimed Pecksniff, in his kindest accents. "Pray come in. I shall make no stranger of you. Thomas is a friend of mine of rather long standing, Mr. Chuzzlewit, you must know."

"Thank you, Sir," said Tom. "You introduce me very kindly, and speak of me in terms of which I am very proud."

"Old Thomas!" cried his master, pleasantly, "God bless you!"

Tom reported that the young ladies would appear di-

rectly, and that the best refreshments which the house
afforded were even then in preparation, under their joint
superintendence. While he was speaking, the old man
looked at him intently, though with less harshness than
was common to him; nor did the mutual embarrassment of
Tom and the young lady, to whatever cause he attributed
it, seem to escape his observation.

"Pecksniff," he said after a pause, rising and taking him
aside towards the window, "I was much shocked on hearing of my brother's death. We had been strangers for
many years. My only comfort is, that he must have lived
the happier and better man for having associated no hopes
or schemes with me. Peace to his memory! We were
playfellows once; and it would have been better for us both
if we had died then."

Finding him in this gentle mood, Mr. Pecksniff began to
see another way out of his difficulties, besides the casting
overboard of Jonas.

"That any man, my dear Sir, could possibly be the happier for not knowing you," he returned, "you will excuse
my doubting. But that Mr. Anthony, in the evening of
his life, was happy in the affection of his excellent son—a
pattern, my dear Sir, a pattern to all sons—and in the care
of a distant relation, who, however lowly in his means of
serving him, had no bounds to his inclination; I can inform you."

"How's this?" said the old man. "You are not a
legatee?"

"You don't," said Mr. Pecksniff, with a melancholy
pressure of his hand, "quite understand my nature yet, I
find. No, Sir, I am not a legatee. I am proud to say I
am not a legatee. I am proud to say that neither of my
children is a legatee. And yet, Sir, I was with him at his
own request. *He* understood me somewhat better, Sir.
He wrote and said, 'I am sick. I am sinking. Come to
me!' I went to him. I sat beside his bed, Sir, and I
stood beside his grave. Yes, at the risk of offending even
you, I did it, Sir. Though the avowal should lead to our
instant separation, and to the severing of those tender ties
between us which have recently been formed, I make it.
But I am not a legatee," said Mr. Pecksniff, smiling dis-
passionately; "and I never expected to be a legatee. I
knew better!"

"His son a pattern!" cried old Martin. "How can you tell me that? My brother had in his wealth the usual doom of wealth, and root of misery. He carried his corrupting influence with him, go where he would; and shed it round him, even on his hearth. It made of his own child a greedy expectant, who measured every day and hour the lessening distance between his father and the grave, and cursed his tardy progress on that dismal road."

"No!" cried Mr. Pecksniff, boldly. "Not at all, Sir!"

"But I saw that shadow in his house," said Martin Chuzzlewit, "the last time we met, and warned him of its presence. I know it when I see it, do I not? I, who have lived within it all these years!"

"I deny it," Mr. Pecksniff answered, warmly. "I deny it altogether. That bereaved young man is now in this house, Sir, seeking in change of scene the peace of mind he has lost. Shall I be backward in doing justice to that young man, when even undertakers and coffin-makers have been moved by the conduct he has exhibited; when even mutes have spoken in his praise, and the medical man hasn't known what to do with himself in the excitement of his feelings! There is a person of the name of Gamp, Sir —Mrs. Gamp—ask her. She saw Mr. Jonas in a trying time. Ask *her*, Sir. She is respectable, but not sentimental, and will state the fact. A line addressed to Mrs. Gamp, at the Bird-shop, Kingsgate Street, High Holborn, London, will meet with every attention, I have no doubt. Let her be examined, my good Sir. Strike, but hear! Leap, Mr. Chuzzlewit, but look! Forgive me, my dear Sir," said Mr. Pecksniff taking both his hands, "if I am warm; but I am honest, and must state the truth."

In proof of the character he gave himself, Mr. Pecksniff suffered tears of honesty to ooze out of his eyes.

The old man gazed at him for a moment with a look of wonder, repeating to himself, "Here now! In this house!" But he mastered his surprise, and said, after a pause:

"Let me see him."

"In a friendly spirit, I hope?" said Mr. Pecksniff. "Forgive me, Sir, but he is in the receipt of my humble hospitality."

"I said," replied the old man, "let me see him. If I were disposed to regard him in any other than a friendly spirit, I should have said, keep us apart."

26

"Certainly, my dear Sir. So you would. You are frankness itself, I know. I will break this happiness to him," said Mr. Pecksniff as he left the room, "if you will excuse me for a minute—gently."

He paved the way to the disclosure so very gently, that a quarter of an hour elapsed before he returned with Mr. Jonas. In the meantime the young ladies had made their appearance, and the table had been set out for the refreshment of the travellers.

Now, however well Mr. Pecksniff, in his morality, had taught Jonas the lesson of dutiful behaviour to his uncle, and however perfectly Jonas, in the cunning of his nature, had learnt it, that young man's bearing, when presented to his father's brother, was anything but manly or engaging. Perhaps, indeed, so singular a mixture of defiance and obequiousness, of fear and hardihood, of dogged sullenness and an attempt at cringing and propitiation, never was expressed in any one human figure as in that of Jonas, when, having raised his downcast eyes to Martin's face, he let them fall again, and uneasily closing and unclosing his hands without a moment's intermission, stood swinging himself from side to side, waiting to be addressed.

"Nephew," said the old man. "You have been a dutiful son, I hear."

"As dutiful as sons in general, I suppose," returned Jonas, looking up and down once more. "I don't brag to have been any better than other sons; but I haven't been any worse, I dare say."

"A pattern to all sons, I am told," said the old man, glancing towards Mr. Pecksniff.

"Ecod!" said Jonas, looking up again for a moment, and shaking his head, "I've been as good a son as ever you were a brother. It's the pot and the kettle, if you come to that."

"You speak bitterly, in the violence of your regret," said Martin, after a pause. "Give me your hand."

Jonas did so, and was almost at his ease. "Pecksniff," he whispered, as they drew their chairs about the table; "I gave him as good as he brought, eh? He had better look at home, before he looks out of window, I think?"

Mr. Pecksniff only answered by a nudge of the elbow, which might either be construed into an indignant remonstrance or a cordial assent; but which, in any case, was an emphatic admonition to his chosen son-in-law to be silent. He then proceeded to do the honours of the house with his accustomed ease and amiability.

But not even Mr Pecksniff's guileless merriment could set such a party at their ease, or reconcile materials so utterly discordant and conflicting as those with which he had to deal. The unspeakable jealousy and hatred which that night's explanation had sown in Charity's breast, was not to be so easily kept down; and more than once it showed itself in such intensity, as seemed to render a full disclosure of all the circumstances then and there, impossible to be avoided. The beauteous Merry, too, with all the glory of her conquest fresh upon her, so probed and lanced the rankling disappointment of her sister by her capricious airs and thousand little trials of Mr. Jonas's obedience, that she almost goaded her into a fit of madness, and obliged her to retire from table in a burst of passion, hardly less vehement than that to which she had abandoned herself in the first tumult of her wrath. The constraint imposed upon the family by the presence among them for the first time of Mary Graham (for by that name old Martin Chuzzlewit had introduced her) did not at all improve this state of things : gentle and quiet though her manner was. Mr. Pecksniff's situation was peculiarly trying : for, what with having constantly to keep the peace between his daughters; to maintain a reasonable show of affection and unity in his household; to curb the growing ease and gaiety of Jonas, which vented itself in sundry insolences towards Mr. Pinch, and an indefinable coarseness of manner in reference to Mary (they being the two dependants); to make no mention at all of his having perpetually to conciliate his rich old relative, and to smooth down, or explain away, some of the ten thousand bad appearances and combinations of bad appearances, by which they were surrounded on that unlucky evening—what with having to do this, and it would be difficult to sum up how much more, without the least relief or assistance from anybody, it may be easily imagined that Mr. Pecksniff had in his enjoyment something more than that usual portion of alloy which is mixed up with the best of men's delights. Perhaps he had never in his life felt such relief as when old Martin, looking at his watch, announced that it was time to go.

"We have rooms," he said, " at the Dragon, for the present. I have a fancy for the evening walk. The nights are dark just now: perhaps Mr. Pinch would not object to light us home?"

"My dear Sir!" cried Pecksniff, "*I* shall be delighted. Merry, my child, the lantern."

"The lantern, if you please, my dear," said Martin; "but I couldn't think of taking your father out of doors to-night; and, to be brief, I won't."

Mr. Pecksniff already had his hat in his hand, but it was so emphatically said that he paused.

"I take Mr. Pinch, or go alone," said Martin. "Which shall it be?"

"It shall be Thomas, Sir," cried Pecksniff, "since you are so resolute upon it. Thomas, my friend, be very careful, if you please."

Tom was in some need of this injunction, for he felt so nervous, and trembled to such a degree, that he found it difficult to hold the lantern. How much more difficult when, at the old man's bidding, he drew her hand through his—Tom Pinch's—arm!

"And so, Mr. Pinch," said Martin, on the way, "you are very comfortably situated here; are you?"

Tom answered, with even more than his usual enthusiasm, that he was under obligations to Mr. Pecksniff which the devotion of a lifetime would but imperfectly repay.

"How long have you known my nephew?" asked Martin.

"Your nephew, Sir!" faltered Tom.

"Mr. Jonas Chuzzlewit," said Mary.

"Oh dear, yes," cried Tom, greatly relieved, for his mind was running upon Martin. "Certainly. I never spoke to him before to-night, Sir."

"Perhaps half a lifetime will suffice for the acknowledgment of *his* kindness," observed the old man.

Tom felt that this was a rebuff for him, and could not but understand it as a left-handed hit at his employer. So he was silent. Mary felt that Mr. Pinch was not remarkable for presence of mind, and that he could not say too little under existing circumstances. So *she* was silent. The old man, disgusted by what in his suspicious nature he considered a shameless and fulsome puff of Mr. Pecksniff, which was a part of Tom's hired service and in which he was determined to persevere, set him down at once for a

deceitful, servile, miserable fawner. So *he* was silent. And
though they were all sufficiently uncomfortable, it is fair to
say that Martin was perhaps the most so; for he had felt
kindly towards Tom at first, and had been interested by
his seeming simplicity.

"You're like the rest," he thought, glancing at the face
of the unconscious Tom. "You had nearly imposed upon
me, but you have lost your labour. You are too zealous
a toad-eater, and betray yourself, Mr. Pinch."

During the whole remainder of the walk, not another
word was spoken. First among the meetings to which Tom
had long looked forward with a beating heart, it was memorable for nothing but embarrassment and confusion. They
parted at the Dragon door; and sighing as he extinguished
the candle in the lantern, Tom turned back again over the
gloomy fields.

As he approached the first stile, which was in a lonely
part, made very dark by a plantation of young firs, a man
slipped past him and went on before. Coming to the stile
he stopped, and took his seat upon it. Tom was rather
startled, and for a moment stood still; but he stepped forward again immediately, and went close up to him.

It was Jonas; swinging his legs to and fro, sucking the
head of a stick, and looking with a sneer at Tom.

"Good gracious me!" cried Tom, "who would have
thought of its being you! You followed us, then?"

"What's that to you?" said Jonas. "Go to the devil!"

"You are not very civil, I think," remarked Tom.

"Civil enough for *you*," retorted Jonas. "Who are
you?"

"One who has as good a right to common consideration
as another," said Tom, mildly.

"You're a liar," said Jonas. "You haven't a right to
any consideration. You haven't a right to anything.
You're a pretty sort of fellow to talk about your rights,
upon my soul! Ha, ha!—rights, too!"

"If you proceed in this way," returned Tom, reddening,
"you will oblige me to talk about my wrongs. But I hope
your joke is over."

"It's the way with you curs," said Mr. Jonas, "that
when you know a man's in real earnest, you pretend to
think he's joking, so that you may turn it off. But that
won't do with me. It's too stale. Now just attend to me

for a bit, Mr. Pitch, or Witch, or Stitch, or whatever your
name is."

"My name is Pinch," observed Tom. "Have the goodness to call me by it."

"What! You mustn't even be called out of your name,
mustn't you!" cried Jonas. "Pauper 'prentices are looking up, I think. Ecod, we manage 'em a little better in
the City!"

"Never mind what you do in the City," said Tom.
"What have you got to say to me?"

"Just this, Mister Pinch," retorted Jonas, thrusting his
face so close to Tom's that Tom was obliged to retreat a
step. "I advise you to keep your own counsel, and to
avoid tittle-tattle, and not to cut in where you're not
wanted. I've heard something of you, my friend, and your
meek ways; and I recommend you to forget 'em till I am
married to one of Pecksniff's gals, and not to curry favour
among my relations, but to leave the course clear. You
know, when curs won't leave the course clear, they're
whipped off: so this is kind advice. Do you understand?
Eh? Damme, who are you," cried Jonas, with increased
contempt, "that you should walk home with *them*, unless
it was behind 'em, like any other servant out of livery?"

"Come!" cried Tom, "I see that you had better get off
the stile, and let me pursue my way home. Make room for
me, if you please."

"Don't think it!" said Jonas, spreading out his legs.
"Not till I choose. And I don't choose now. What!
You're afraid of my making you split upon some of your
babbling just now, are you, Sneak?"

"I am not afraid of many things, I hope," said Tom;
"and certainly not of anything that you will do. I am not
a tale-bearer, and I despise all meanness. You quite mistake me. Ah!" cried Tom, indignantly. "Is this manly
from one in your position to one in mine? Please to make
room for me to pass. The less I say, the better."

"The less you say!" retorted Jonas, dangling his legs
the more, and taking no heed of this request. "You say
very little, don't you? Ecod, I should like to know what
goes on between you and a vagabond member of my family.
There's very little in that too, I daresay!"

"I know no vagabond member of your family," cried
Tom, stoutly.

"You do!" said Jonas.

"I don't," said Tom. "Your uncle's namesake, if you mean him, is no vagabond. Any comparison between you and him"—Tom snapped his fingers at him, for he was rising fast in wrath—"is immeasurably to your disadvantage."

"Oh indeed!" sneered Jonas. "And what do you think of his deary—his beggarly leavings, eh, Mister Pinch?"

"I don't mean to say another word, or stay here another instant," replied Tom.

"As I told you before, you're a liar," said Jonas, coolly. "You'll stay here till I give you leave to go. Now, keep where you are, will you?"

He flourished his stick over Tom's head; but in a moment it was spinning harmlessly in the air, and Jonas himself lay sprawling in the ditch. In the momentary struggle for the stick, Tom had brought it into violent contact with his opponent's forehead; and the blood welled out profusely from a deep cut on the temple. Tom was first apprised of this by seeing that he pressed his handkerchief to the wounded part, and staggered as he rose: being stunned.

"Are you hurt?" said Tom. "I am very sorry. Lean on me for a moment. You can do that without forgiving me, if you still bear me malice. But I don't know why; for I never offended you before we met on this spot."

He made him no answer: not appearing at first to understand him, or even to know that he was hurt, though he several times took his handkerchief from the cut to look vacantly at the blood upon it. After one of these examinations, he looked at Tom, and then there was an expression in his features, which showed that he understood what had taken place, and would remember it.

Nothing more passed between them as they went home. Jonas kept a little in advance, and Tom Pinch sadly followed: thinking of the grief which the knowledge of this quarrel must occasion his excellent benefactor. When Jonas knocked at the door, Tom's heart beat high; higher when Miss Mercy answered it, and seeing her wounded lover, shrieked aloud; higher when he followed them into the family parlour; higher than at any other time when Jonas spoke.

"Don't make a noise about it," he said. "It's nothing

worth mentioning. I didn't know the road; the night's very dark; and just as I came up with Mr. Pinch"—he turned his face towards Tom, but not his eyes—"I ran against a tree. It's only skin deep."

"Cold water, Merry, my child!" cried Mr. Pecksniff. "Brown paper! Scissors! A piece of old linen! Charity, my dear, make a bandage. Bless me, Mr. Jonas!"

"Oh, bother *your* nonsense," returned the gracious son-in-law elect. "Be of some use if you can. If you can't, get out!"

Miss Charity, though called upon to lend her aid, sat upright in one corner, with a smile upon her face, and didn't move a finger. Though Mercy laved the wound herself; and Mr. Pecksniff held the patient's head between his two hands, as if without that assistance it must inevitably come in half; and Tom Pinch, in his guilty agitation, shook a bottle of Dutch Drops until they were nothing but English Froth, and in his other hand sustained a formidable carving-knife, really intended to reduce the swelling, but apparently designed for the ruthless infliction of another wound as soon as that was dressed; Charity rendered not the least assistance, nor uttered a word. But when Mr. Jonas's head was bound up, and he had gone to bed, and everybody else had retired, and the house was quiet, Mr. Pinch, as he sat mournfully on his bedstead, ruminating, heard a gentle tap at his door; and opening it, saw her, to his great astonishment, standing before him with her finger on her lip.

"Mr. Pinch," she whispered. "Dear Mr. Pinch! tell me the truth! You did that? There was some quarrel between you, and you struck him? I am sure of it!"

It was the first time she had ever spoken kindly to Tom, in all the many years they had passed together. He was stupefied with amazement.

"Was it so, or not?" she eagerly demanded.

"I was very much provoked," said Tom.

"Then it was?" cried Charity, with sparkling eyes.

"Ye-yes. We had a struggle for the path," said Tom. "But I didn't mean to hurt him so much."

"Not so much!" she repeated, clenching her hand and stamping her foot, to Tom's great wonder. "Don't say that. It was brave of you. I honour you for it. If you should ever quarrel again, don't spare him for the world,

but beat him down and set your shoe upon him. Not a
word of this to anybody. Dear Mr. Pinch, I am your
friend from to-night. I am always your friend from this
time."

She turned her flushed face upon Tom to confirm her
words by its kindling expression; and seizing his right
hand, pressed it to her breast, and kissed it. And there
was nothing personal in this to render it at all embarrass-
ing, for even Tom, whose power of observation was by no
means remarkable, knew from the energy with which she
did it that she would have fondled any hand, no matter
how bedaubed or dyed, that had broken the head of Jonas
Chuzzlewit.

Tom went into his room, and went to bed, full of uncomfortable thoughts. That there should be any such tremendous division in the family as he knew must have taken
place to convert Charity Pecksniff into his friend, for any
reason, but, above all, for that which was clearly the real
one; that Jonas, who had assailed him with such exceeding coarseness, should have been sufficiently magnanimous
to keep the secret of their quarrel; and that any train of
circumstances should have led to the commission of an assault and battery by Thomas Pinch upon any man calling
himself the friend of Seth Pecksniff; were matters of such
deep and painful cogitation, that he could not close his
eyes. His own violence, in particular, so preyed upon the
generous mind of Tom, that coupling it with the many
former occasions on which he had given Mr. Pecksniff pain
and anxiety (occasions of which that gentleman often reminded him), he really began to regard himself as destined
by a mysterious fate to be the evil genius and bad angel of
his patron. But he fell asleep at last, and dreamed—new
source of waking uneasiness—that he had betrayed his
trust, and run away with Mary Graham.

It must be acknowledged that, asleep or awake, Tom's
position in reference to this young lady was full of uneasiness. The more he saw of her, the more he admired her
beauty, her intelligence, the amiable qualities that even
won on the divided house of Pecksniff, and in a few days
restored at all events the semblance of harmony and kindness between the angry sisters. When she spoke, Tom
held his breath, so eagerly he listened; when she sang, he
sat like one entranced. She touched his organ, and from

that bright epoch even it, the old companion of his happiest hours, incapable as he had thought of elevation, began
a new and deified existence.

God's love upon thy patience, Tom! Who that had beheld thee, for three summer weeks, poring through half the
deadlong night over the jingling anatomy of that inscruta-
ble old harpsichord in the back parlour, could have missed
the entrance to thy secret heart: albeit it was dimly known
to thee! Who that had seen the glow upon thy cheek when
leaning down to listen, after hours of labour, for the sound
of one incorrigible note, thou foundest that it had a voice
at last, and wheezed out a flat something distantly akin to
what it ought to be,—would not have known that it was
destined for no common touch, but one that smote, though
gently as an angel's hand, upon the deepest chord within
thee! And if a friendly glance—ay, even though it were
as guileless as thine own, dear Tom—could but have
pierced the twilight of that evening, when, in a voice well
tempered to the time, sad, sweet, and low, yet hopeful,
she first sang to the altered instrument, and wondered at
the change; and thou, sitting apart at the open window,
kept a glad silence and a swelling heart—must not that
glance have read perforce the dawning of a story, Tom,
that it were well for thee had never been begun!

Tom Pinch's situation was not made the less dangerous
or difficult, by the fact of no one word passing between
them in reference to Martin. Honourably mindful of his
promise, Tom gave her opportunities of all kinds. Early
and late he was in the church; in her favourite walks; in
the village, in the garden, in the meadows; and in any or
all of these places he might have spoken freely. But no:
at all such times she carefully avoided him, or never came
in his way unaccompanied. It could not be that she disliked or distrusted him, for by a thousand little delicate
means, too slight for any notice but his own, she singled
him out when others were present, and showed herself the
very soul of kindness. Could it be that she had broken
with Martin, or had never returned his affection, save in
his own bold and heightened fancy? Tom's cheek grew
red with self-reproach, as he dismissed the thought.

All this time old Martin came and went in his own
strange manner, or sat among the rest absorbed within himself, and holding little intercourse with any one. Although

he was unsocial, he was not wilful in other things, or troublesome, or morose: being never better pleased than when
they left him quite unnoticed at his book, and pursued their
own amusements in his presence, unreserved. It was impossible to discern in whom he took an interest, or whether
he had an interest in any of them. Unless they spoke to
him directly, he never showed that he had ears or eyes for
anything that passed.

One day the lively Merry, sitting with downcast eyes
under a shady tree in the churchyard, whither she had retired after fatiguing herself by the imposition of sundry
trials on the temper of Mr. Jonas, felt that a new shadow
came between her and the sun. Raising her eyes in the
expectation of seeing her betrothed, she was not a little
surprised to see old Martin instead. Her surprise was not
diminished when he took his seat upon the turf beside her,
and opened a conversation thus:

" When are you to be married? "

" Oh! dear Mr. Chuzzlewit, my goodness me! I'm sure
I don't know. Not yet awhile, I hope."

" You hope? " said the old man.

It was very gravely said, but she took it for banter, and
giggled excessively.

" Come! " said the old man, with unusual kindness, " you
are young, good-looking, and I think good-natured! Frivolous you are, and love to be, undoubtedly; but you must
have some heart."

" I have not given it all away, I can tell you," said
Merry, nodding her head shrewdly, and plucking up the
grass.

" Have you parted with any of it? "

She threw the grass about, and looked another way, but
said nothing.

Martin repeated his question.

" Lor, my dear Mr. Chuzzlewit! really you must excuse
me! How very odd you are."

" If it be odd in me to desire to know whether you love
the young man whom I understand you are to marry, I *am*
very odd," said Martin. " For that is certainly my wish."

" He's such a monster, you know," said Merry, pouting.

" Then you don't love him? " returned the old man. " Is
that your meaning? "

" Why, my dear Mr. Chuzzlewit, I'm sure I tell him a

hundred times a day that I hate him. You must have heard me tell him that."

"Often," said Martin.

"And so I do," cried Merry. "I do positively."

"Being at the same time engaged to marry him," observed the old man.

"Oh yes," said Merry. "But I told the wretch—my dear Mr. Chuzzlewit, I told him when he asked me—that if I ever did marry him, it should only be that I might hate and tease him all my life."

She had a suspicion that the old man regarded Jonas with anything but favour, and intended these remarks to be extremely captivating. He did not appear, however, to regard them in that light by any means; for when he spoke again, it was in a tone of severity.

"Look about you," he said, pointing to the graves; "and remember that from your bridal hour to the day which sees you brought as low as these, and laid in such a bed, there will be no appeal against him. Think, and speak, and act, for once, like an accountable creature. Is any control put upon your inclinations? Are you forced into this match? Are you insidiously advised or tempted to contract it, by any one? I will not ask by whom: by any one?"

"No," said Merry, shrugging her shoulders. "I don't know that I am."

"Don't know that you are! Are you?"

"No," replied Merry. "Nobody ever said anything to me about it. If any one tried to make me have him, I wouldn't have had him at all."

"I am told that he was at first supposed to be your sister's admirer," said Martin.

"Oh, good gracious! My dear Mr. Chuzzlewit, it would be very hard to make him, though he *is* a monster, accountable for other people's vanity," said Merry. "And poor dear Cherry is the vainest darling!"

"It was her mistake then?"

"I hope it was," cried Merry; "but, all along, the dear child has been so dreadfully jealous and *so* cross, that, upon my word and honour, it's impossible to please her, and it's of no use trying."

"Not forced, persuaded, or controlled," said Martin, thoughtfully. "And that's true, I see. There is one chance yet. You may have lapsed into this engagement in very giddiness. It may have been the wanton act of a light head. Is that so?"

"My dear Mr. Chuzzlewit," simpered Merry, "as to light-headiness, there never was such a feather of a head as mine. It's a perfect balloon, I declare! You never *did*, you know!"

He waited quietly till she had finished, and then said, steadily and slowly, and in a softened voice, as if he would still invite her confidence:

"Have you any wish—or is there anything within your breast that whispers you may form the wish, if you have time to think—to be released from this engagement?"

Again Miss Merry pouted, and looked down, and plucked the grass, and shrugged her shoulders. No. She didn't know that she had. She was pretty sure she hadn't. Quite sure, she might say. She "didn't mind it."

"Has it ever occurred to you," said Martin, "that your married life may perhaps be miserable, full of bitterness, and most unhappy?"

Merry looked down again; and now she tore the grass up by the roots.

"My dear Mr. Chuzzlewit, what shocking words! Of course, I shall quarrel with him: I should quarrel with any husband. Married people always quarrel, I believe. But as to being miserable, and bitter, and all those dreadful things, you know, why I couldn't be absolutely that, unless he always had the best of it; and I mean to have the best of it myself. I always do now," cried Merry, nodding her head, and giggling very much; "for I make a perfect slave of the creature."

"Let it go on," said Martin, rising. "Let it go on! I sought to know your mind, my dear, and you have shown it me. I wish you joy. Joy!" he repeated, looking full upon her, and pointing to the wicket-gate, where Jonas entered at the moment. And then, without waiting for his nephew, he passed out at another gate, and went away.

"Oh you terrible old man!" cried the facetious Merry to herself. "What a perfectly hideous monster to be wandering about churchyards in the broad daylight, frightening people out of their wits! Don't come here, Griffin, or I'll go away directly."

Mr. Jonas was the Griffin. He sat down upon the grass at her side, in spite of this warning, and sulkily inquired:

"What's my uncle been a talking about?"

"About you," rejoined Merry. "He says you're not half good enough for me."

"Oh yes, I dare say! We all know that. He means to give you some present worth having, I hope. Did he say anything that looked like it?"

"*That* he didn't!" cried Merry, most decisively.

"A stingy old dog he is," said Jonas. "Well?"

"Griffin!" cried Miss Mercy, in counterfeit amazement; "what are you doing, Griffin?"

"Only giving you a squeeze," said the discomfited Jonas. "There's no harm in that, I suppose?"

"But there is a great deal of harm in it, if I don't consider it agreeable," returned his cousin. "Do go along, will you? You make me so hot!"

Mr. Jonas withdrew his arm; and for a moment looked at her more like a murderer than a lover. But he cleared his brow by degrees, and broke silence with:

"I say, Mel!"

"What do you say, you vulgar thing—you low savage?" cried his fair betrothed.

"When is it to be? I can't afford to go on dawdling about here half my life, I needn't tell you, and Pecksniff says that father's being so lately dead makes very little odds; for we can be married as quiet as we please down here, and my being lonely is a good reason to the neighbours for taking a wife home so soon, especially one that he knew. As to crossbones (my uncle, I mean), he's sure not to put a spoke in the wheel, whatever we settle on, for he told Pecksniff only this morning, that if *you* liked it, he'd nothing at all to say. So, Mel," said Jonas, venturing on another squeeze; "when shall it be?"

"Upon my word," cried Merry.

"Upon my soul, if you like," said Jonas. "What do you say to next week, now?"

"To next week! If you had said next quarter, I should have wondered at your impudence."

"But I didn't say next quarter," retorted Jonas. "I said next week."

"Then, Griffin," cried Miss Merry, pushing him off and rising. "I say no! not next week. It shan't be till I choose—and I may not choose it to be for months. There!"

He glanced up at her from the ground, almost as darkly as he had looked at Tom Pinch; but held his peace.

"No fright of a Griffin with a patch over his eye, shall dictate to me, or have a voice in the matter," said Merry. "There!"

Still Mr. Jonas held his peace.

"If it's next month, that shall be the very earliest; but I won't say when it shall be till to-morrow; and if you don't like that, it shall never be at all," said Merry; "and if you follow me about and won't leave me alone, it shall never be at all. There! And if you don't do everything I order you to do, it shall never be at all. So don't follow me. There, Griffin!"

And with that, she skipped away, among the trees.

"Ecod, my lady!" said Jonas, looking after her, and biting a piece of straw, almost to powder; "you'll catch it for this, when you *are* married! It's all very well now— it keeps one on, somehow, and you know it—but I'll pay you off scot and lot by and bye. This is a plaguey dull sort of place for a man to be sitting by himself in. I never could abide a mouldy old churchyard."

As he turned into the avenue himself, Miss Merry, who was far ahead, happened to look back.

"Ah!" said Jonas, with a sullen smile, and a nod that was not addressed to her; "make the most of it while it lasts. Get in your hay while the sun shines. Take your own way as long as it's in your power, my lady!"

CHAPTER XXV.

IS IN PART PROFESSIONAL; AND FURNISHES THE READER WITH SOME VALUABLE HINTS IN RELA- TION TO THE MANAGEMENT OF A SICK CHAM- BER.

Mr. Mould was surrounded by his household gods. He was enjoying the sweets of domestic repose, and gazing on them with a calm delight. The day being sultry, and the window open, the legs of Mr. Mould were on the window- seat, and his back reclined against the shutter. Over his

shining head a handkerchief was drawn, to guard his baldness from the flies. The room was fragrant with the smell
of punch, a tumbler of which grateful compound stood upon a small round table, convenient to the hand of Mr.
Mould; so deftly mixed, that as his eye looked down into
the cool transparent drink, another eye, peering brightly
from behind the crisp lemon-peel, looked up at him, and
twinkled like a star.

Deep in the City, and within the ward of Cheap, stood
Mr. Mould's establishment. His Harem, or, in other
words, the common sitting-room of Mrs. Mould and family,
was at the back, over the little counting-house behind the
shop: abutting on a churchyard, small and shady. In this
domestic chamber Mr. Mould now sat; gazing, a placid
man, upon his punch and home. If, for a moment at a
time, he sought a wider prospect, whence he might return
with freshened zest to these enjoyments, his moist glance
wandered like a sunbeam through a rural screen of scarlet
runners, trained on strings before the window; and he
looked down with an artist's eye upon the graves.

The partner of his life, and daughters twain, were Mr.
Mould's companions. Plump as any partridge was each
Miss Mould, and Mrs. M. was plumper than the two together. So round and chubby were their fair proportions,
that they might have been the bodies once belonging to the
angels' faces in the shop below, grown up, with other heads
attached to make them mortal. Even their peachy cheeks
were puffed out and distended, as though they ought of
right to be performing on celestial trumpets. The bodiless
cherubs in the shop, who were depicted as constantly blowing those instruments for ever and ever without any lungs,
played, it is to be presumed, entirely by ear.

Mr. Mould looked lovingly at Mrs. Mould, who sat hard
by, and was a helpmate to him in his punch as in all other
things. Each seraph daughter, too, enjoyed her share of
his regards, and smiled upon him in return. So bountiful
were Mr. Mould's possessions, and so large his stock in
trade, that even there, within his household sanctuary,
stood a cumbrous press, whose mahogany maw was filled
with shrouds, and winding-sheets, and other furniture of
funerals. But, though the Misses Mould had been brought
up, as one may say, beneath his eye, it had cast no shadow
on their timid infancy or blooming youth. Sporting be-

hind the scenes of death and burial from cradlehood, the Misses Mould knew better. Hatbands, to them, were but so many yards of silk or crape; the final robe but such a quantity of linen. The Misses Mould could idealize a player's habit, or a court-lady's petticoat, or even an Act of Parliament. But they were not to be taken in by palls. They made them sometimes.

The premises of Mr. Mould were hard of hearing to the boisterous noises in the great main streets, and nestled in a quiet corner, where the City strife became a drowsy hum, that sometimes rose and sometimes fell and sometimes altogether ceased: suggesting to a thoughtful mind a stoppage in Cheapside. The light came sparkling in among the scarlet runners, as if the churchyard winked at Mr. Mould, and said, "We understand each other;" and from the distant shop a pleasant sound arose of coffin-making with a low melodious hammer, rat, tat, tat, tat, alike promoting slumber and digestion.

"Quite the buzz of insects," said Mr. Mould, closing his eyes in a perfect luxury. "It puts one in mind of the sound of animated nature in the agricultural districts. It's exactly like the woodpecker tapping."

"The woodpecker tapping the hollow *elm* tree," observed Mrs. Mould, adapting the words of the popular melody to the description of wood commonly used in the trade.

"Ha, ha!" laughed Mr. Mould. "Not at all bad, my dear. We shall be glad to hear from you again, Mrs. M. Hollow elm tree, eh? Ha, ha! Very good indeed. I've seen worse than that in the Sunday papers, my love."

Mrs. Mould, thus encouraged, took a little more of the punch, and handed it to her daughters, who dutifully followed the example of their mother.

"Hollow *elm* tree, eh?" said Mr. Mould, making a slight motion with his legs in his enjoyment of the joke. "It's beech in the song. Elm, eh? Yes, to be sure. Ha, ha, ha! Upon my soul, that's one of the best things I know!" He was so excessively tickled by the jest that he couldn't forget it, but repeated twenty times, "Elm, eh? Yes, to be sure. Elm, of course. Ha, ha, ha! Upon my life, you know, that ought to be sent to somebody who could make use of it. It's one of the smartest things that ever was said. Hollow *elm* tree, eh? Of course. Very hollow. Ha, ha, ha!"

27

Here a knock was heard at the room door.

"That's Tacker, *I* know," said Mrs. Mould, "by the wheezing he makes. Who that hears him now, would suppose he'd ever had wind enough to carry the feathers on his head! Come in, Tacker."

"Beg your pardon, ma'am," said Tacker, looking in a little way. "I thought our Governor was here."

"Well! so he is," cried Mould.

"Oh! I didn't see you, I'm sure," said Tacker, looking in a little farther. "You wouldn't be inclined to take a walking one of two, with the plain wood and a tin plate, I suppose?"

"Certainly not," replied Mr. Mould, "much too common. Nothing to say to it."

"I told 'em it was precious low," observed Mr. Tacker.

"Tell 'em to go somewhere else. We don't do that style of business here," said Mr. Mould. "Like their impudence to propose it. Who is it?"

"Why," returned Tacker, pausing, "that's where it is, you see. It's the beadle's son-in-law."

"The beadle's son-in-law, eh?" said Mould. "Well! I'll do it if the beadle follows in his cocked hat; not else. We may carry it off that way, by looking official, but it'll be low enough then. His cocked hat, mind!"

"I'll take care, Sir," rejoined Tacker. "Oh! Mrs. Gamp's below, and wants to speak to you."

"Tell Mrs. Gamp to come up stairs," said Mould. "Now, Mrs. Gamp, what's *your* news?"

The lady in question was by this time in the doorway, curtseying to Mrs. Mould. At the same moment a peculiar fragrance was borne upon the breeze, as if a passing fairy had hiccoughed, and had previously been to a wine-vaults.

Mrs. Gamp made no response to Mr. Mould, but curtseyed to Mrs. Mould again, and held up her hands and eyes, as in a devout thanksgiving that she looked so well. She was neatly, but not gaudily attired, in the weeds she had worn when Mr. Pecksniff had the pleasure of making her acquaintance; and was perhaps the turning of a scale more snuffy.

"There are some happy creeturs," Mrs. Gamp observed, "as time runs back'ards with, and you are one, Mrs. Mould; not that he need do nothing except use you in his most owldacious way for years to come, I'm sure; for young you are and will be. I says to Mrs. Harris," Mrs. Gamp continued, "only t'other day; the last Monday evening fortnight as ever dawned upon this Piljian's Projiss of a mortal wale; I says to Mrs. Harris when she says to me, 'Years and our trials, Mrs. Gamp, sets marks upon us all.' —'Say not the words, Mrs. Harris, if you and me is to be continual friends, for sech is not the case. Mrs. Mould,' I says, making so free, I will confess, as use the name," (she curtseyed here), "'is one of them that goes agen the obserwation straight; and never, Mrs. Harris, whilst I've a drop of breath to draw, will I set by, and not stand up, don't think it.'—'I ast your pardon, ma'am,' says Mrs. Harris, 'and I humbly grant your grace; for if ever a woman lived as would see her feller creeturs into fits to serve her friends, well do I know that woman's name is Sairey Gamp.'"

At this point she was fain to stop for breath; and advantage may be taken of the circumstance, to state that a fearful mystery surrounded this lady of the name of Harris, whom no one in the circle of Mrs. Gamp's acquaintance had ever seen; neither did any human being know her place of residence, though Mrs. Gamp appeared on her own showing to be in constant communication with her. There were conflicting rumours on the subject; but the prevalent opinion was that she was a phantom of Mrs. Gamp's brain —as Messrs. Doe and Roe are fictions of the law—created for the express purpose of holding visionary dialogues with her on all manner of subjects, and invariably winding up with a compliment to the excellence of her nature.

"And likeways what a pleasure," said Mrs. Gamp, turning with a tearful smile towards the daughters, "to see them two young ladies as I know'd afore a tooth in their pretty heads was cut, and have many a day seen—ah, the sweet creeturs!—playing at berryins down in the shop, and follerin' the order-book to its long home in the iron safe! But that's all past and over, Mr. Mould;" as she thus got in a carefully regulated routine to that gentleman, she shook her head waggishly; "That's all past and over now, Sir, an't it?"

"Changes, Mrs. Gamp, changes!" returned the undertaker.

"More changes too, to come, afore we've done with changes, Sir," said Mrs. Gamp, nodding yet more waggishly than before. "Young ladies with such faces thinks of something else besides berryins, don't they, Sir?"

"I am sure I don't know, Mrs. Gamp," said Mould, with a chuckle.—"Not bad in Mrs. Gamp, my dear?"

"Oh yes, you do know, Sir!" said Mrs. Gamp, "and so does Mrs. Mould, your ansome pardner too, Sir; and so do I, although the blessing of a daughter was deniged me; which, if we had had one, Gamp would certainly have drunk its little shoes right off its feet, as with our precious boy he did, and arterwards send the child a errand to sell his wooden leg for any money it would fetch as matches in the rough, and bring it home in liquor: which was truly done beyond his years, for ev'ry individgle penny that child lost at toss or buy for kidney ones; and come home arterwards quite bold, to break the news, and offering to drown himself if that would be a satisfaction to his parents. —Oh yes, you do know, Sir," said Mrs. Gamp, wiping her eye with her shawl, and resuming the thread of her discourse. "There's something besides births and berryins in the newspapers, an't there, Mr. Mould?"

Mr. Mould winked at Mrs. Mould, whom he had by this time taken on his knee, and said: "No doubt. A good deal more, Mrs. Gamp. Upon my life, Mrs. Gamp is very far from bad, my dear!"

"There's marryings, an't there, Sir?" said Mrs. Gamp, while both the daughters blushed and tittered. "Bless their precious hearts, and well they knows it! Well you know'd it too, and well did Mrs. Mould, when you was at their time of life! But my opinion is, you're all of one age now. For as to you and Mrs. Mould, Sir, ever having grandchildren—"

"Oh! Fie, fie! Nonsense, Mrs. Gamp," replied the undertaker. "Devilish smart, though. Ca-pi-tal!"—This was in a whisper. "My dear—" aloud again—"Mrs. Gamp can drink a glass of rum, I dare say. Sit down, Mrs. Gamp, sit down."

Mrs. Gamp took the chair that was nearest the door, and casting up her eyes towards the ceiling, feigned to be wholly insensible to the fact of a glass of rum being in preparation, until it was placed in her hand by one of the young ladies, when she exhibited the greatest surprise.

"A thing," she said, "as hardly ever, Mrs. Mould, occurs with me unless it is when I am indispoged, and find my half a pint of porter settling heavy on the chest. Mrs. Harris often and often says to me, 'Sairey Gamp,' she says, 'you raly do amaze me!' 'Mrs. Harris,' I says to her, 'why so? Give it a name, I beg.' 'Telling the truth then, ma'am,' says Mrs. Harris, 'and shaming him as shall be nameless betwixt you and me, never did I think till I know'd you, as any woman could sick-nurse and monthly likeways, on the little that you takes to drink.' 'Mrs. Harris,' I says to her, 'none on us knows what we can do till we tries; and wunst, when me and Gamp kept ouse, I thought so too. But now,' I says, 'my half a pint of porter fully satisfies; perwisin', Mrs. Harris, that it is brought reg'lar, and draw'd mild. Whether I sicks or monthlies, ma'am, I hope I does my duty, but I am but a poor woman, and I earns my living hard; therefore I *do* require it, which I makes confession, to be brought reg'lar and draw'd mild.'"

The precise connexion between these observations and the glass of rum, did not appear; for Mrs. Gamp proposing as a toast "The best of lucks to all!" took off the dram in quite a scientific manner, without any further remarks.

"And what's your news, Mrs. Gamp?" asked Mould again, as that lady wiped her lips upon her shawl, and nibbled a corner off a soft biscuit, which she appeared to carry in her pocket as a provision against contingent drams. "How's Mr. Chuffey?"

"Mr. Chuffey, Sir," she replied, "is jest as usual; he an't no better and he an't no worse. I take it very kind in the gentleman to have wrote up to you and said, 'let Mrs. Gamp take care of him till I come home;' but ev'ry think he does is kind. There an't a many like him. If there was, we shouldn't want no churches."

"What do you want to speak to me about, Mrs. Gamp?" said Mould, coming to the point.

"Jest this, Sir," Mrs. Gamp returned, "with thanks to you for asking. There *is* a gent, Sir, at the Bull in Holborn, as has been took ill there, and is bad abed. They have a day-nurse as was recommended from Bartholomew's; and well I knows her, Mr. Mould, her name bein' Mrs. Prig, the best of creeturs. But she is otherways engaged at night, and they are in wants of night-watching; consequent she says to them, having reposed the greatest friendliness in me for twenty year, 'The soberest person going,

and the best of blessings in a sick room, is Mrs. Gamp.
Send a boy to Kingsgate Street,' she says, 'and snap her
up at any price, for Mrs. Gamp is worth her weight and
more in goldian guineas.' My landlord brings the message
down to me, and says, 'bein' in a light place where you
are, and this job promising so well, why not unite the
two?' 'No, Sir,' I says, 'not unbeknown to Mr. Mould,
and therefore do not think it. But I will go to Mr. Mould,'
I says, 'and ast him, if you like.'" Here she looked sideways at the undertaker, and came to a stop.

"Night-watching, eh?" said Mould, rubbing his chin.

"From eight o'clock till eight, Sir: I will not deceive
you," Mrs. Gamp rejoined.

"And then go back, eh?" said Mould.

"Quite free then, Sir, to attend to Mr. Chuffey. His
ways bein' quiet, and his hours early, he'd be abed, Sir,
nearly all the time. I will not deny," said Mrs. Gamp
with meekness, "that I am but a poor woman, and that the
money is a object; but do not let that act upon you, Mr.
Mould. Rich folks may ride on camels, but it ain't so easy
for 'em to see out of a needle's eye. That is my comfort,
and I hope I knows it."

"Well, Mrs. Gamp," observed Mould, "I don't see any
particular objection to your earning an honest penny under
such circumstances. I should keep it quiet. I think, Mrs.
Gamp, I wouldn't mention it to Mr. Chuzzlewit on his
return, for instance, unless it were necessary, or he asked
you point-blank."

"The very words was on my lips, Sir," Mrs. Gamp rejoined. "Suppoging that the gent should die, I hope I
might take the liberty of saying as I know'd some one in
the undertaking line, and yet give no offence to you, Sir?"

"Certainly, Mrs. Gamp," said Mould, with much condescension. "You may casually remark, in such a case,
that we do the thing pleasantly and in a great variety of
styles, and are generally considered to make it as agreeable
as possible to the feelings of the survivors. But don't
obtrude it—don't obtrude it. Easy, easy! My dear, you
may as well give Mrs. Gamp a card or two, if you
please."

Mrs. Gamp received them, and scenting no more rum in
the wind (for the bottle was locked up again) rose to take
her departure.

"Wishing ev'ry happiness to this happy family," said
Mrs. Gamp, "with all my heart. Good arternoon, Mrs.
Mould! If I was Mr. Mould, I should be jealous of you,
ma'am; and I'm sure, if I was you, I should be jealous of
Mr. Mould."

"Tut, tut! Bah, bah! Go along, Mrs. Gamp!" cried
the delighted undertaker.

"As to the young ladies," said Mrs. Gamp, dropping a
curtsey, "bless their sweet looks—how they can ever rec-
onsize it with their duties to be so grown up with such
young parents, it an't for sech as me to give a guess at."

"Nonsense, nonsense. Be off, Mrs. Gamp!" cried
Mould. But in the height of his gratification, he actually
pinched Mrs. Mould, as he said it.

"I'll tell you what, my dear," he observed, when Mrs.
Gamp had at last withdrawn, and shut the door, "that's
a ve-ry shrewd woman. That's a woman whose intellect is
immensely superior to her station in life. That's a woman
who observes and reflects in an uncommon manner. She's
the sort of woman now," said Mould, drawing his silk
handkerchief over his head again, and composing himself
for a nap, "one would almost feel disposed to bury for
nothing: and do it neatly, too!"

Mrs. Mould and her daughters fully concurred in these
remarks; the subject of which had by this time reached the
street, where she experienced so much inconvenience from
the air, that she was obliged to stand under an archway
for a short time, to recover herself. Even after this precaution, she walked so unsteadily as to attract the compassionate regards of divers kind-hearted boys, who took the
liveliest interest in her disorder; and in their simple language, bade her be of good cheer, for she was "only a little
screwed."

Whatever she was, or whatever name the vocabulary of
medical science would have bestowed upon her malady,
Mrs. Gamp was perfectly acquainted with the way home
again; and arriving at the house of Anthony Chuzzlewit &
Son, lay down to rest. Remaining there until seven o'clock
in the evening, and then persuading poor old Chuffey to
betake himself to bed, she sallied forth upon her new engagement. First, she went to her private lodgings in
Kingsgate Street, for a bundle of robes and wrappings comfortable in the night season; and then repaired to the Bull

in Holborn, which she reached as the clocks were striking eight.

As she turned into the yard, she stopped; for the land-lord, landlady, and head chambermaid, were all on the threshold together, talking earnestly with a young gentle-man who seemed to have just come or to be just going away. The first words that struck upon Mrs. Gamp's ear obviously bore reference to the patient; and it being ex-pedient that all good attendants should know as much as possible about the case on which their skill is brought to bear, Mrs. Gamp listened as a matter of duty.

"No better, then?" observed the gentleman.

"Worse!" said the landlord.

"Much worse," added the landlady.

"Oh! a deal badder," cried the chambermaid from the background, opening her eyes very wide, and shaking her head.

"Poor fellow!" said the gentleman, "I am sorry to hear it. The worst of it is, that I have no idea what friends or relations he has, or where they live, except that it cer-tainly is not in London."

The landlord looked at the landlady; the landlady looked at the landlord; and the chambermaid remarked, hysteri-cally, "that of all the many wague directions she had ever seen or heerd of (and they wasn't few in an hotel), *that* was the waguest."

"The fact is, you see," pursued the gentleman, "as I told you yesterday when you sent to me, I really know very little about him. We were schoolfellows together; but since that time I have only met him twice. On both occa-sions I was in London for a boy's holiday (having come up for a week or so from Wiltshire), and lost sight of him again directly. The letter bearing my name and address which you found upon his table, and which led to your applying to me, is in answer, you will observe, to one he wrote from this house the very day he was taken ill, making an appointment with him at his own request. Here is his letter, if you wish to see it."

The landlord read it: the landlady looked over him. The chambermaid, in the background, made out as much of it as she could, and invented the rest; believing it all from that time forth as a positive piece of evidence.

"He has very little luggage, you say?" observed the

gentleman, who was no other than our old friend, John Westlock.

"Nothing but a portmanteau," said the landlord; "and very little in it."

"A few pounds in his purse, though?"

"Yes. It's sealed up, and in the cash-box. I made a memorandum of the amount, which you're welcome to see."

"Well!" said John, "as the medical gentleman says the fever must take its course, and nothing can be done just now beyond giving him his drinks regularly and having him carefully attended to, nothing more can be said that I know of, until he is in a condition to give us some information. Can you suggest anything else?"

"N-no," replied the landlord, "except—"

"Except, who's to pay, I suppose?" said John.

"Why," hesitated the landlord, "it would be as well."

"Quite as well," said the landlady.

"Not forgetting to remember the servants," said the chambermaid in a bland whisper.

"It is but reasonable, I fully admit," said John Westlock. "At all events, you have the stock in hand to go upon for the present; and I will readily undertake to pay the doctor and the nurses."

"Ah!" cried Mrs. Gamp. "A rayal gentleman!"

She groaned her admiration so audibly, that they all turned round. Mrs. Gamp felt the necessity of advancing, bundle in hand, and introducing herself.

"The night-nurse," she observed, "from Kingsgate Street, well beknown to Mrs. Prig the day-nurse, and the best of creeturs. How is the poor dear gentleman, tonight? If he an't no better yet, still that is what must be expected and prepared for. It an't the fust time by a many score, ma'am," dropping a curtsey to the landlady, "that Mrs. Prig and me has nussed together, turn and turn about, one off, one on. We knows each other's ways, and often gives relief when others failed. Our charges 's but low, Sir"—Mrs. Gamp addressed herself to John on this head —"considerin' the nater of our painful dooty. If they wos made accordin' to our wishes, they would be easy paid."

Regarding herself as having now delivered her inauguration address, Mrs. Gamp curtseyed all round, and signified her wish to be conducted to the scene of her official duties. The chambermaid led her, through a variety of intricate passages, to the top of the house; and pointing at length to a solitary door at the end of a gallery, informed her that yonder was the chamber where the patient lay. That done, she hurried off with all the speed she could make.

Mrs. Gamp traversed the gallery in a great heat from having carried her large bundle up so many stairs, and tapped at the door, which was immediately opened by Mrs. Prig, bonneted and shawled and all impatience to be gone. Mrs. Prig was of the Gamp build, but not so fat; and her voice was deeper and more like a man's. She had also a beard.

"I began to think you warn't a coming!" Mrs. Prig observed, in some displeasure.

"It shall be made good to-morrow night," said Mrs. Gamp, "honourable. I had to go and fetch my things." She had begun to make signs of enquiry in reference to the position of the patient and his overhearing them—for there was a screen before the door—when Mrs. Prig settled that point easily.

"Oh!" she said aloud, "he's quiet, but his wits is gone. It an't no matter wot you say."

"Anythin' to tell afore you goes, my dear?" asked Mrs. Gamp, setting her bundle down inside the door, and looking affectionately at her partner.

"The pickled salmon," Mrs. Prig replied, "is quite delicious. I can partick'ler recommend it. Don't have nothink to say to the cold meat, for it tastes of the stable. The drinks is all good."

Mrs. Gamp expressed herself much gratified.

"The physic an them things is on the drawers and mankle-shelf," said Mrs. Prig, cursorily. "He took his last slime draught at seven. The easy-chair an't soft enougn. You'll want his piller."

Mrs. Gamp thanked her for these hints, and giving her a friendly good night, held the door open until she had disappeared at the other end of the gallery. Having thus performed the hospitable duty of seeing her safely off, she shut it, locked it on the inside, took up her bundle, walked round the screen, and entered on her occupation of the sick chamber.

"A little dull, but not so bad as might be," Mrs.
Gamp remarked.   "I'm glad to see a parapidge, in
case of fire, and lots of roofs and chimley-pots to walk
upon."
It will be seen from these remarks that Mrs. Gamp was
looking out of window. When she had exhausted the prospect, she tried the easy-chair, which she indignantly declared was "harder than a brickbadge." Next she pursued
her researches among the physic-bottles, glasses, jugs, and
tea-cups; and when she had entirely satisfied her curiosity
on all these subjects of investigation, she untied her bonnet-strings and strolled up to the bedside to take a look at
the patient.

A young man—dark and not ill-looking—with long black
hair, that seemed the blacker for the whiteness of the bed-
clothes. His eyes were partly open, and he never ceased
to roll his head from side to side upon the pillow, keeping
his body almost quiet. He did not utter words; but every
now and then gave vent to an expression of impatience or
fatigue, sometimes of surprise; and still his restless head
—oh, weary, weary hour!—went to and fro without a moment's intermission.

Mrs. Gamp solaced herself with a pinch of snuff, and
stood looking at him with her head inclined a little sideways,
as a connoisseur might gaze upon a doubtful work of art.
By degrees, a horrible remembrance of one branch of her
calling took possession of the woman; and stooping down,
she pinned his wandering arms against his sides, to see how
he would look if laid out as a dead man. Hideous as it
may appear, her fingers itched to compose his limbs in that
last marble attitude.

"Ah!" said Mrs. Gamp, walking away from the bed,
"he'd make a lovely corpse!"

She now proceeded to unpack her bundle; lighted a candle with the aid of a fire-box on the drawers; filled a small
kettle, as a preliminary to refreshing herself with a cup of
tea in the course of the night; laid what she called "a little bit of fire," for the same philanthropic purpose; and
also set forth a small teaboard, that nothing might be
wanting for her comfortable enjoyment. These preparations occupied so long, that when they were brought to a
conclusion it was high time to think about supper; so she
rang the bell and ordered it.

"I think, young woman," said Mrs. Gamp to the assistant chambermaid, in a tone expressive of weakness, "that I could pick a little bit of pickled salmon, with a nice little sprig of fennel, and a sprinkling of white pepper. I takes new bread, my dear, with jest a little pat of fresh butter, and a mossel of cheese. In case there should be such a thing as a cowcumber in the 'ouse, will you be so kind as bring it, for I'm rather partial to 'em, and they does a world of good in a sick room. If they draws the Brighton Tipper here, I takes *that* ale at night, my love; it bein' considered wakeful by the doctors. And whatever you do, young woman, don't bring more than a shilling's-worth of gin and water warm when I rings the bell a second time: for that is always my allowance, and I never takes a drop beyond!"

Having preferred these moderate requests, Mrs. Gamp observed that she would stand at the door until the order was executed, to the end that the patient might not be disturbed by her opening it a second time; and therefore she would thank the young woman to "look sharp."

A tray was brought with everything upon it, even to the cucumber; and Mrs. Gamp accordingly sat down to eat and drink in high good humour. The extent to which she availed herself of the vinegar, and supped up that refreshing fluid with the blade of her knife, can scarcely be expressed in narrative.

"Ah!" sighed Mrs. Gamp, as she meditated over the warm shilling's-worth, "what a blessed thing it is—living in a wale—to be contented! What a blessed thing it is to make sick people happy in their beds, and never mind one's self as long as one can do a service! I don't believe a finer cowcumber was ever grow'd. I'm sure I never see one!"

She moralised in the same vein until her glass was empty, and then administered the patient's medicine, by the simple process of clutching his windpipe to make him gasp, and immediately pouring it down his throat.

"I a'most forgot the piller, I declare!" said Mrs. Gamp, drawing it away. "There! Now he's as comfortable as he can be, I'm sure! I must try to make myself as much so as I can."

With this view, she went about the construction of an extemporaneous bed in the easy chair, with the addition of the next easy one for her feet. Having formed the best couch that the circumstances admitted of, she took out of her bundle a yellow nightcap, of prodigious size, in shape resembling a cabbage; which article of dress she fixed and tied on with the utmost care, previously divesting herself of a row of bald old curls that could scarcely be called false, they were so very innocent of anything approaching to deception. From the same repository she brought forth a night-jacket, in which she also attired herself. Finally, she produced a watchman's coat, which she tied round her neck by the sleeves, so that she became two people; and looked, behind, as if she were in the act of being embraced by one of the old patrol.

All these arrangements made, she lighted the rushlight, coiled herself up on her couch, and went to sleep. Ghostly and dark the room became, and full of lowering shadows. The distant noises in the streets were gradually hushed; the house was quiet as a sepulchre; the dead of night was coffined in the silent city.

Oh, weary, weary hour! Oh, haggard mind, groping darkly through the past; incapable of detaching itself from the miserable present; dragging its heavy chain of care through imaginary feasts and revels, and scenes of awful pomp; seeking but a moment's rest among the long-forgotten haunts of childhood, and the resorts of yesterday; and dimly finding fear and horror everywhere! Oh, weary, weary hour! What were the wanderings of Cain, to these!

Still, without a moment's interval, the burning head tossed to and fro. Still, from time to time, fatigue, impatience, suffering, and surprise, found utterance upon that rack, and plainly too, though never once in words. At length, in the solemn hour of midnight, he began to talk; waiting awfully for answers sometimes; as though invisible companions were about his bed; and so replying to their speech and questioning again.

Mrs. Gamp awoke, and sat up in her bed: presenting on the wall the shadow of a gigantic night constable, struggling with a prisoner.

"Come! Hold your tongue!" she cried, in sharp reproof. "Don't make none of that noise here."

There was no alteration in the face, or in the incessant motion of the head, but he talked on wildly.

7—15

"Ah!" said Mrs. Gamp, coming out of the chair with
an impatient shiver; "I thought I was a sleepin' too pleasant to last! The devil's in the night, I think, it's turned
so chilly."

"Don't drink so much!" cried the sick man. "You'll
ruin us all. Don't you see how the fountain sinks?
Look at the mark where the sparkling water was just
now!"

"Sparkling water, indeed!" said Mrs. Gamp. "I'll
have a sparkling cup o' tea, I think. I wish you'd hold
your noise!"

He burst into a laugh, which, being prolonged, fell off
into a dismal wail. Checking himself, with fierce incon-
stancy he began to count, fast. "One—two—three—four
—five—six."

"'One, two, buckle my shoe,'" said Mrs. Gamp, who
was now on her knees, lighting the fire, "'three, four, shut
the door'—I wish you'd shut your mouth, young man—
'five, six, picking up sticks.' If I'd got a few handy, I
should have the kettle biling all the sooner."

Awaiting this desirable consummation, she sat down so
close to the fender (which was a high one) that her nose
rested upon it; and for some time she drowsily amused
herself by sliding that feature backwards and forwards
along the brass top, as far as she could, without changing
her position to do it. She maintained, all the while, a
running commentary upon the wanderings of the man in
bed.

"That makes five hundred and twenty-one men, all
dressed alike, and with the same distortion on their faces,
that have passed in at the window, and out at the door," he
cried, anxiously. "Look there! Five hundred and twenty-
two—twenty-three—twenty-four. Do you see them?"

"Ah! *I* see em," said Mrs. Gamp; "all the whole kit of
'em numbered like hackney-coaches—ain't they?"

"Touch me! Let me be sure of this. Touch me!"

"You'll take your next draught when I've made the kettle bile," retorted Mrs. Gamp, composedly, "and you'll be
touched then. You'll be touched up, too, if you don't
take it quiet."

"Five hundred and twenty-eight, five hundred and
twenty-nine, five hundred and thirty—look here!"

"What's the matter now?" said Mrs. Gamp.

"They're coming four abreast, each man with his arm entwined in the next man's, and his hand upon his shoulder. What's that upon the arm of every man and on the flag?"

"Spiders, p'raps," said Mrs. Gamp.

"Crape! Black crape! Good God! why do they wear it outside?"

"Would you have 'em carry black crape in their insides?" Mrs. Gamp retorted. "Hold your noise, hold your noise."

The fire beginning by this time to impart a grateful warmth, Mrs. Gamp became silent; gradually rubbed her nose more and more slowly along the top of the fender; and fell into a heavy doze. She was awakened by the room ringing (as she fancied) with a name she knew:

"Chuzzlewit!"

The sound was so distinct and real, and so full of agonised entreaty, that Mrs. Gamp jumped up in terror, and ran to the door. She expected to find the passage filled with people, come to tell her that the house in the City had taken fire. But the place was empty: not a soul was there. She opened the window, and looked out. Dark, dull, dingy, and desolate house-tops. As she passed to her seat again, she glanced at the patient. Just the same; but silent. Mrs. Gamp was so warm now, that she threw off the watchman's coat, and fanned herself.

"It seemed to make the wery bottles ring," she said. "What could I have been a-dreaming of? That dratted Chuffey, I'll be bound."

The supposition was probable enough. At any rate, a pinch of snuff, and the song of the steaming kettle, quite restored the tone of Mrs. Gamp's nerves, which were none of the weakest. She brewed her tea; made some buttered toast; and sat down at the tea-board, with her face to the fire.

When once again, in a tone more terrible than that which had vibrated in her slumbering ear, these words were shrieked out:

"Chuzzlewit! Jonas! No!"

Mrs. Gamp dropped the cup she was in the act of raising to her lips, and turned round with a start that made the little tea-board leap. The cry had come from the bed.

It was bright morning the next time Mrs. Gamp looked

out of window, and the sun was rising cheerfully. Lighter and lighter grew the sky, and noisier the streets; and high into the summer air uprose the smoke of newly kindled fires, until the busy day was broad awake.

Mrs. Prig relieved punctually, having passed a good night at her other patient's. Mr. Westlock came at the same time, but he was not admitted, the disorder being infectious. The doctor came too. The doctor shook his head. It was all he could do, under the circumstances, and he did it well.

"What sort of a night, nurse?"

"Restless, Sir," said Mrs. Gamp.

"Talk much?"

"Middling, Sir," said Mrs. Gamp.

"Nothing to the purpose, I suppose?"

"Oh bless you no, Sir. Only jargon."

"Well!" said the doctor, "we must keep him quiet; keep the room cool; give him his draughts regularly; and see that he's carefully looked to. That's all!"

"And as long as Mrs. Prig and me waits upon him, Sir, no fear of that," said Mrs. Gamp.

"I suppose," observed Mrs. Prig, when they had curtseyed the doctor out: "there's nothin' new?"

"Nothin' at all, my dear," said Mrs. Gamp. "He's rather wearin' in his talk from making up a lot of names; elseways you needn't mind him."

"Oh, I shan't mind him," Mrs. Prig returned. "I have somethin' else to think of."

"I pays my debts to-night, you know, my dear, and comes afore my time," said Mrs. Gamp. "But, Betsey Prig"—speaking with great feeling, and laying her hand upon her arm—"try the cowcumbers, God bless you!"

If you enjoyed reading this book and are interested in reading other works by Charles Dickens, we encourage you to check out **COSIMO CLASSICS'** catalog of titles. The complete works of Charles Dickens (in 30 volumes, illustrated, in paperback and hardcover) are available from **COSIMO CLASSICS.**

The following and other **COSIMO CLASSICS** are available at online bookstores and through our website.

THE COMPLETE WORKS OF CHARLES DICKENS
(IN 30 VOLUMES, ILLUSTRATED)

NOVELS

- The Pickwick Papers, Vol. I (1837)
- The Pickwick Papers, Vol. II (1837)
- Oliver Twist (1838)
- Nicholas Nickleby, Vol. I (1839)
- Nicholas Nickleby, Vol. II (1839)
- The Old Curiosity Shop, Vol. I (1840)
- The Old Curiosity Shop, Vol. II (1840)
- Barnaby Rudge, Vol. I (1841)
- Barnaby Rudge, Vol. II (1841)
- A Christmas Carol and Other Christmas Books (1843 - 1848)
- Martin Chuzzlewit, Vol. I (1844)
- Martin Chuzzlewit, Vol. II (1844)
- Dombey and Son, Vol. I (1848)
- Dombey and Son, Vol. II (1848)
- David Copperfield, Vol. I (1850)
- David Copperfield, Vol. II (1850)
- Bleak House, Vol. I (1853)
- Bleak House, Vol. II (1853)

continued

The Complete Works of Charles Dickens
(in 30 volumes, illustrated), continued

- Little Dorrit, Vol. I (1857)
- Little Dorrit, Vol. II (1857)
- A Tale of Two Cities (1859)
- Great Expectations (1861)
- Our Mutual Friend, Vol. I (1865)
- Our Mutual Friend, Vol. II (1865)
- Edwin Drood and Miscellaneous (1870—*Edwin Drood*; 1840-41—*Master Humphrey's Clock*; Years unknown for the 3 other miscellaneous short stories included in this book)

SHORT STORY COLLECTIONS, NON-FICTION ETC.

- Sketches by Boz (1836)
- Christmas Stories (1851–1865)
- The Uncommercial Traveller (1860–1869)
- Pictures from Italy and American Notes (1846 and 1842)
- A Child's History of England (1852–1854)

Visit cosimobooks.com for updated information
about our classics and ordering information.

BE INSPIRED, BE INFORMED

COSIMO is a specialty publisher of books and publications that inspire, inform, and engage readers. Our mission is to offer unique books to niche audiences around the world.

COSIMO BOOKS publishes books and publications for innovative authors, nonprofit organizations, and businesses. **COSIMO BOOKS** specializes in bringing books back into print, publishing new books quickly and effectively, and making these publications available to readers around the world.

COSIMO CLASSICS offers a collection of distinctive titles by the great authors and thinkers throughout the ages. At **COSIMO CLASSICS** timeless works find new life as affordable books, covering a variety of subjects including: Business, Economics, History, Personal Development, Philosophy, Religion & Spirituality, and much more!

COSIMO REPORTS publishes public reports that affect your world, from global trends to the economy, and from health to geopolitics.

FOR MORE INFORMATION CONTACT US AT
INFO@COSIMOBOOKS.COM

➢ if you are a book lover interested in our current catalog of books

➢ if you represent a bookstore, book club, or anyone else interested in special discounts for bulk purchases

➢ if you are an author who wants to get published

➢ if you represent an organization or business seeking to publish books and other publications for your members, donors, or customers.

**COSIMO BOOKS ARE ALWAYS
AVAILABLE AT ONLINE BOOKSTORES**

VISIT COSIMOBOOKS.COM
BE INSPIRED, BE INFORMED

CPSIA information can be obtained at www.ICGtesting.com
Printed in the USA
BVOW011646211112

306077BV00002B/18/P